"*Be Mature in Understanding* is a welcome contribution to the much-needed discipleship material for new Jewish believers in Jesus. It provides a solid theological foundation. It also includes a survey of the Scriptures, the history of redemption, and principles of interpretation. The theological section is clear and straightforward, sensitive to Jewish culture, reformational in perspective, and though baptistic, is irenic toward other positions, such as mine. I heartily recommend this fine resource!"

—**Fred Klett** (USA)
Director, CHAIM Ministry

"This is one of the few books I am familiar with that is relatively short and yet in precise manner teaches biblical theology from its original Jewish-roots perspective. This is a must-read book for every Jewish believer in Messiah, and a great tool for those non-Jewish people working and discipling new Jewish believers. The authors have done a marvelous work in revealing the big idea of the Scriptures, and the redemptive plan of God."

—**David Zadok** (Israel)
Director, HaGefen Publishing

"The authors have created something special. There is very little like this work, instructive and doctrinally sensitive (and to Jewish emphases—I am Jewish); and in line with biblical evangelical doctrine and exegesis. It successfully combines thoroughness, scholarship, and intellectual clarity. Differences of viewpoint are not a hindrance to fluidity but an academic tool for the informed and the less so. This is written with modesty and care, but expertly."

—**Christopher Barder** (UK)
Sometime Foundation Scholar, Pembroke College, Cambridge

"This book is uniquely positioned as a discipleship book for Jewish believers in Jesus that is within the Reformed Christian tradition. The first and shorter part features the contributions of two Messianic Jews, while the main section consists of Morris's clearly written expositions of Christian theology that incorporate Jewish thought and topics of interest to Jewish believers. Study questions and suggestions for further reading enliven the proceedings. Highly recommended!"

—**Rich Robinson** (USA)
Senior researcher, Jews for Jesus

"As the good news of the Messiah continues to draw men and women of Jewish background, like myself, to salvation, there is a pressing need for a new generation of Jewish believers to be grounded in their faith. I am grateful to Paul and his team for their thoughtful and thorough treatment of Scripture. This significant work will inspire confidence in the clear plan of God to unite Jew and Gentile in one body through the mission of our Messiah."

—**Peter Kaldor** (Australia)
Managing director, City Bible Forum

Be Mature in Understanding

Be Mature in Understanding

A Handbook of Theology for Jewish Believers in Messiah

BEN MIDGLEY,
MARTIN PAKULA
and PAUL F. MORRIS

FOREWORD BY JOSEPH STEINBERG

WIPF & STOCK · Eugene, Oregon

BE MATURE IN UNDERSTANDING
A Handbook of Theology for Jewish Believers in Messiah

Copyright © 2021 Paul F. Morris, Ben Midgley, and Martin Pakula. All rights reserved. Except for brief quotations in critical publications or reviews, no part of this book may be reproduced in any manner without prior written permission from the publisher. Write: Permissions, Wipf and Stock Publishers, 199 W. 8th Ave., Suite 3, Eugene, OR 97401.

Wipf & Stock
An Imprint of Wipf and Stock Publishers
199 W. 8th Ave., Suite 3
Eugene, OR 97401

www.wipfandstock.com

PAPERBACK ISBN: 978-1-5326-9797-5
HARDCOVER ISBN: 978-1-5326-9798-2
EBOOK ISBN: 978-1-5326-9799-9

06/04/21

Scripture taken from the New King James Version. Copyright © 1982 by Thomas Nelson, Inc. Used by permission. All rights reserved.

Editor's Dedication

To my wife, Judy, who has immeasurably helped me to grow in grace, kept my focus on what is most important, supported me faithfully in all my ministry whilst struggling with chronic illness, and without whom this volume would never have seen the light of day.

Paul Morris

וּבְכָל־קִנְיָנְךָ קְנֵה בִינָה

Mishlei 4:7

Contents

Foreword by Joseph Steinberg | xiii
Editor's Preface | xv
About Authors | xvii
Editor's Introduction | xix
How to Use This Book | xxiii
Abbreviations | xxv
Names and Terms | xxvii
Helpful Reference Books | xxxi

BOOK ONE: GOD'S UNFOLDING REVELATION

א
Part 1: The Plan of Redemption—an Overview | 3
—Ben Midgley

1. The Plan to Send Messiah | 5
2. Disclosing the Plan to Send Messiah—Prophecy | 9
3. The Person of Messiah Progressively Revealed | 13
4. The Messiah Who Saves | 17

ב
Part 2: The Bible and Redemption's Story | 21
—Martin Pakula

5. The Shape of the Bible | 23
   (A) The Tanakh and the Brit Chadashah | 23
   (B) Three "Eras" | 23

6 The Torah | 26
  (A) Bereshit (Genesis) 1–11: Creation, Fall, the Flood, Babel | 26
  (B) Bereshit (Genesis) 12–50: The Patriarchs Avraham, Yitzhak, Yakov, and Yosef | 29
  (C) The Exodus (Shemot 1–18) | 33
  (D) Meeting with God at Sinai (Shemot 19–24, 32–34) | 35
  (E) The Tabernacle and Sacrifices (Shemot 25–31; 35–40; Vayyikra/Leviticus) | 37
  (F) In the Wilderness (Bemidbar/Numbers) | 38
  (G) Moshe's Final Speeches (Devarim/Deuteronomy) | 39

7 The Prophets (Nevi'im) | 41
  (A) The Conquest of the Promised Land (Yehoshua/Joshua) | 41
  (B) The Period of the Judges (Shoftim/Judges) | 42
  (C) The Books of Shmuel (1 and 2 Samuel): Kingship in Israel | 43
  (D) The Books of Melakhim (1 and 2 Kings): From Solomon until the Exile | 45
  (E) The Latter Prophets | 50
  (F) After the Exile: The Return to the Promised Land | 52

8 The Writings (Ketuvim) | 54

9 The Brit Chadashah (New Testament) | 56
  (A) The Gospels | 56
  (B) The Book of Acts | 59
  (C) The Epistles | 59
  (D) The Book of Revelation | 60

BOOK TWO: DOCTRINES OF GOD'S REVELATION
—Paul Morris

ג

Part 3: God | 65

10 God's Existence | 67

11 God's Revelation of Himself | 70
  (A) General Revelation | 70
  (B) Special Revelation | 71

12 The Knowledge of God (Knowability) | 97

13 God's Names and Nature | 100
  (A) God's Names | 100
  (B) God's Nature | 104
  (C) God's Unity and Triunity | 112

ד
Part 4: God's Creation | 119

14 God the Planner | 121
15 God the Creator | 123
16 God the Provider and Ruler | 127
17 Miracles | 132
18 Prayer | 135
19 Humankind: Creation and Fall | 138
    (A) The Creation of Humankind | 138
    (B) The Fall of Humankind | 150

ה
Part 5: God's Salvation | 163

God's Messiah | 167

20 Yeshua the Promised Messiah | 169
    (A) Prophet, Priest, and King | 169
    (B) The Fulfiller of Patterns | 171
    (C) The One Who Makes Israel a Blessing to the World | 171
    (D) Messiah More than a Man | 172

21 Yeshua—His Humanity | 174

22 Yeshua—His Deity | 179
    (A) Yeshua—YHWH's Only Begotten Son | 179
    (B) Yeshua—the Word of YHWH | 181
    (C) Yeshua's Self-Consciousness of His Deity | 182
    (D) Yeshua's Resurrection and Exaltation | 182
    (E) Direct New Testament Statements of Deity | 183
    (F) Doxologies, Greetings, and Benedictions | 183

23 Yeshua—His Two Natures and One Person | 184

24 Yeshua—His Work of Salvation | 188
    (A) Salvation by Atonement in the Tanakh | 188
    (B) Yeshua as Priest | 190
    (C) The Sacrificial Death of Yeshua | 191
    (D) Yeshua as Mediator | 194
    (E) The Nature and Extent of Yeshua's Atonement | 194

God's Spirit | 199

25 The Person of the Holy Spirit | 200
    (A) The Holy Spirit Is a Person | 200
    (B) The Holy Spirit Is a Divine Being | 201
    (C) The Holy Spirit—God's Executor | 202

26 The Spirit and Messiah | 203
    (A) The Work of the Spirit in Messiah's Life and Ministry | 203
    (B) Messiah's Spirit | 204

27 The Work of the Holy Spirit in Our Salvation | 206
    (A) From Death to Life | 206
    (B) Life in the Spirit | 223
    (C) The Spirit and the Life to Come | 237

ו

PART 6: GOD'S PEOPLE | 241

28 God's One People | 243

29 Israel under the Mosaic Covenant | 245
    (A) National Life | 245
    (B) Individual Life | 246
    (C) The Function of the Law | 247
    (D) Weakness and Preparation | 249

30 Messiah's People of the New Covenant | 251
    (A) Development in the New Testament | 251
    (B) New Testament Terms for God's People | 252
    (C) New Testament Images of the Church | 252
    (D) The Nature of the Church | 256
    (E) The Basic Marks of a New Testament Church | 256
    (F) Characteristics of the Church | 258
    (G) The Individual and the Church | 264
    (H) The Church and Civil Government | 264
    (I) The Purpose and Life of the Church | 271
    (J) Is It Jewish? Continuity and Change | 295
    [K] The Church's Future | 297

31 The New Testament Church in History | 299

32 Israel in the New Covenant Period | 304
    (A) God's People | 304
    (B) Israel's Privileges | 305
    (C) Remnant | 305

      (D) Cut Off | 306
      (E) Fullness or All Israel Saved | 309
      (F) Blessings and Judgments | 310
      (G) Return to the Land | 313

33 Jewish Believers in the Church and Israel (the People) | 316
      (A) The Israel of God | 316
      (B) One New Man from the Two | 318
      (C) Culturally Jewish | 320
      (D) Provoking to Jealousy | 321
      (E) Warnings from Hebrews | 322

Part 7: God's New Creation | 329

34 Messiah's Return | 331
      (A) Scripture's Terminology | 331
      (B) A Scripture Teaching | 332
      (C) The Nature of Yeshua's Return | 332
      (D) The Purpose of Yeshua's Return | 333
      (E) The Time of Yeshua's Return | 336
      (F) The Place of Yeshua's Return | 340
      (G) Further Considerations: Antichrist, Israel, Millennium | 340
      (H) Historical Survey | 352
      (I) Rabbinic Views on the Messianic Age and the World to Come | 355

35 Human Destiny | 360
      (A) Death | 360
      (B) The Intermediate State | 361
      (C) Resurrection | 363
      (D) Judgment | 364

36 Final Human Destinies | 366
      (A) Hell | 366
      (B) New Heavens and a New Earth | 367

Bibliography | 371

Foreword

NEGOTIATING THE MANY CHALLENGES that come to you when you are a new Jewish believer can be difficult. It certainly was for me. I came to faith in my teens and as a result of the understandable opposition from my parents, I was not allowed to attend church or any other Christian activities. I had to get my teaching from Christian friends and reading books I could sneak in – none of which took my perspectives as a Jewish believer into account.

This was all before the internet existed. But now, how does a new Jewish believer know where to go and whom to trust when it comes to learning about their new faith in Yeshua?

I wish there would have been a book like *Be Mature in Understanding*, written by three very capable men, Ben Midgley and Martin Pakula, who are Jewish believers engaged in pastoral and teaching ministries, and Paul Morris, who has given his life to understanding Jewish people and engaging in deep thought around the issues we Jewish people face in coming to faith and seeking to be good disciples.

In fact, Paul Morris has been a major influence in my life. More than thirty years ago he helped me to engage more deeply with Reformed theology, gave me good books to read, had helpful discussions with me, and even helped me write my first sermon! My time with Paul in those early years of my development helped form my spirituality, my theological understanding, and my missiology. And with this book, he can help you form yours too.

As you read *Be Mature in Understanding* by these three authors, you will find there is a lot to learn and plenty to think about as you seek to grow in understanding your faith. I can think of few resources like this that will give the Jewish believer in Jesus so much material to work through, with many set questions to ponder – and hopefully develop answers to, and so much food for discussion with other Christians.

I hope you enjoy and are helped by this book as much as I was. Take your time. Read, mark, and learn. And may God bless you as you seek to grow mature in your understanding of him.

Joseph Steinberg
CEO of the International Mission to Jewish People,
formerly Christian Witness to Israel

Editor's Preface

IN MY EARLY DAYS as a believer in Jesus I was greatly helped by the book *In Understanding Be Men* by T. C. Hammond, a handbook of Christian doctrine which helped to build up a framework of biblical thinking in my heart and mind. Having worked in ministry to Jewish people for many years I have been struck by the lack of a book like Hammond's that is sensitive to the context of Jewish believers. This book is an attempt, by myself and two friends of mine who are Jewish believers, to fill that gap. I want to acknowledge my indebtedness to two books in particular, which I have used as a point of reference: *In Understanding Be Men* by T. C. Hammond, and *Know the Truth* by Bruce Milne.

I am deeply grateful to all who have helped with the production and checking: to Helen Tsoromokos, who entered into the vision of the book and typed out the manuscript from my dictation with great devotion and suggested all sorts of corrections as she went; to Robert Weissman for checking the grammar, spelling, and punctuation, along with encouraging comments; to Richard Payn who read the manuscript word by word and made valuable comments on its biblical and theological accuracy; to David Bond who checked Parts 1 and 2 of Book 1 and Christopher Barder who checked Part 6 of Book 2, "God's People"; to John Woods who did a skim read and gave very helpful bird's-eye comments; to Trisha Dale who got it all up to scratch for the publishers; and finally to those who gave their time to assessing the value of the book and making those commendations which are on the back cover.

I am deeply concerned to see Jewish believers in Yeshua playing their part in the worldwide church of Messiah, in whatever ways God leads them in his service, through their knowledge of God's word, their Jewishness, their natural and spiritual gifts, and a humble, thankful heart. If this book helps them build biblical thinking in their heart and mind I, and my fellow authors, will be more than satisfied.

Paul Morris

About Authors
(in order of their contributions)

Ben Midgley was raised in a Jewish household in northwest London and came to faith in Jesus as the Messiah after reading the New Testament in his early twenties. Ben studied for the ministry in his thirties at the London Theological Seminary (now London Seminary) where he encountered reformed theology, and is presently Lead Pastor at Ebenezer Baptist Church (FIEC) in Mold, North East Wales, UK. He has held a long concern to make Christ known to the Jewish people and to relate the Jewish context of the New Testament to the church. Ben was for some time the chairman of Christian Witness to Israel, the first Jewish man to occupy that role in its 175-year history. Ben is married to Sian with whom he has four children. He has a lifelong interest in art in which he secured his first degree, and travel, the industry he worked in, specializing in Israel and the Near East.

Ben has written Part 1 of BOOK ONE.

Martin Pakula is a Jewish believer residing in Melbourne, Australia. He came to faith at university after growing up attending shul every Shabbat and at festivals, where he sang in the choir and occasionally davened shacharit. He is married to Jennie and has two adult children, Asher and Rachel. He was ordained as a minister in the Anglican Church in the late 1990s. He later completed a research Master's in theology and teaches Hebrew and Old Testament at Bible Colleges in Melbourne. He has been involved in parish ministry, university student outreach, Jewish mission, and lecturing.

Martin has written Part 2 of BOOK ONE.

Paul Morris was born in the UK and has a non-Jewish, nominal Christian background, coming to faith in 1970. He worked as a civil engineer before entering the ministry. He is married to Judy and they have a son and a daughter and six grandchildren. He studied theology with the Evangelical

Movement of Wales and was ordained by Park Hill Free Church, Brighton, in 1979. He began work as a missionary to the Jewish people with Christian Witness to Israel (CWI) in 1979, engaging in many forms of outreach, and while based in London led the Shalom Ministries team and initiated the CWI Summer School. In the 1990s he travelled widely, witnessing and seeking to open new fields of witness in Russia, Belarus, Romania, Bulgaria, Morocco, and Turkey. Paul and Judy moved to Sydney, Australia, from 2001 to 2011 where Paul led the ministry of CWI. Paul is the author of two books: *Telling Jews about Jesus* and *Jewish Themes in the New Testament*. He is now the Chairman of CWI's Council of Management and engages in a writing and teaching ministry.

Paul has written all of BOOK TWO.

All three authors have been closely associated with Christian Witness to Israel, a UK-based mission to the Jewish people established 175 years ago (www.cwi.org.uk). Christian Witness to Israel is in the process of changing its name and will be known as the International Mission to Jewish People (www.imjp.org).

Editor's Introduction

ABRAHAM WAS CALLED BY God to leave home, friends, and family, called to embark on a spiritual journey as well as a literal one. It was a journey on which he was to learn more and more of the one true God, and grow in a life of faith and loving obedience. What a privilege! And God calls all Abraham's children to follow in his footsteps of faith. I assume you are someone who has begun to do that. As a child of Abraham by birth and by faith in Yeshua (Jesus) you have obeyed God's call. Your journey has begun.

As far as we know Abraham had nothing written down to guide him but God spoke to him. By contrast you have many written words from God, recorded and preserved by Israel in the Holy Scriptures. You have a map for the journey but it is not the easiest of maps to read. In some places it is clear as day, in others it seems obscure. One thing is certain, it tells a story. It reveals the Aleph to Taw of human history and, as the story unfolds, we are taught more and more about the one true God of history; it is his story.

This book has two main divisions: in the first one the story is traced, enabling us to see the progress of revelation as God confirms truths already given and adds further revelation: this is known as biblical theology. In the second, the bulk of the book, the truths revealed are considered in more detail, with their interrelationships: this is known as systematic theology. Reading books like this enables us to make a more careful and detailed study of the truth than is usually possible in a sermon or our own daily Bible reading, and in this way greater maturity of understanding develops, which should enable us to teach others.

A book like this takes account of our fallenness, our sinful nature, with its darkness of mind and heart. When anyone comes to faith in the one, true God through Yeshua they come with some form of theological baggage. Everyone already has views about God, even if they are atheists. Many have some form of religious upbringing, and most Jewish people are influenced by the Judaism of the synagogue. They may have some knowledge of the

Scriptures but it will be mixed with human traditions and ideas, and speculations not based on Scripture. Coming to faith is the first step to getting our thinking in line with God's; reading a book like this helps with the process of renewing of our minds, so as to love God with *all* of our mind.

Furthermore, we also need to develop an ability to discern error. The Scriptures are full of warnings about false prophets and deceptive teachers, who for selfish motives lead others astray. Yeshua said, "Beware of false prophets, who come to you in sheep's clothing, but inwardly they are ravenous wolves" (Matt 7:15). Error sets no one free, but truth does, as Yeshua said, "If you abide in My word, you are My disciples indeed. And you shall know the truth, and the truth shall make you free" (John 8:31–32).

Jewish believers in Jesus come under more pressure than most in the early days of their faith. Not all churches teach the biblical gospel, and within Judaism there is the weight of teaching that opposes the gospel at many points, an opposition which is thought-out, scholarly, and centuries old. Furthermore, there is a mass of conflicting teachings especially aimed at Jewish believers. For example: some telling them that they should keep the law of Moses, others that they should ignore it, or something in between. How are they to judge such conflicting ideas? A framework of thinking from Scripture is vital. Jewish believers do indeed have a unique and challenging testimony to both church and synagogue but it will only challenge if it springs from a strong biblical foundation. This is Paul's desire for us all: "that we should no longer be children, tossed to and fro and carried about with every wind of doctrine, by the trickery of men, in the cunning craftiness of deceitful plotting, but, speaking the truth in love, may grow up in all things into Him who is the head—Christ (Eph 4:14–15).

This book aims to cover all the main biblical doctrines. Many of them are foundational, that is, believing them is essential to a true and saving faith, e.g. Yeshua rose from the dead. But there are others over which true believers differ, e.g. the mode of baptism, and with such doctrines my aim is to fairly express the differing views whilst explaining why I believe what I believe. Issues of particular interest to Jewish believers will be examined, like the relevance of the Mosaic law for today and the place of Jewish culture in a Jewish believer's life. I will also interact with other expressions of Christianity and the theologies within Judaism where it will be helpful.

Let Jeremiah (Yirmeyahu) have the last word in this introduction:

> But let him who glories glory in this,
> That he understands and knows Me,

That I am the LORD, exercising lovingkindness, judgment,
and righteousness in the earth.
For in these things I delight, says the LORD
(Jer 9:24)

Paul Morris

How to Use This Book

As the book proceeds, readers will encounter points where they are encouraged to stop and consider some questions which help to focus on what has just been read, along with some Scripture references and suggestions for further reading.

Life today seems to be more time-poor and pressured than any time before us due to the demands of the "information age." For the studies in the book to be useful it is advisable that a regular time every week should be allocated—and jealously protected. The sections between questions are designed to be read in one session; but more time may be needed to look up the Scriptures and answer the questions. It's also a good idea to write out your answers in order to clarify your thinking. You may find it valuable to ask a mature believer to act as a mentor.

Before starting each study session it is good to remind yourself, in the words of the Lord to Moses, "Take your sandals off your feet, for the place where you stand is holy ground." The Scriptures require mental effort and disciplined study, but this is no impersonal, academic exercise. We are learning about the Most High, his ways and his salvation; we are drawing near to him. Yeshayahu (Isaiah) tells us the characteristic of those with whom YHWH desires to dwell are: "poor and of a contrite spirit, And who trembles at my word" (Isa 66:2). It is therefore a good practice to pray before starting, and to close by reading a Scripture text of praise. One has been put at the close of each section.

Abbreviations

THE ENGLISH BIBLE VERSION used in this book is the New King James Version, which is effectively the fourth revision of the 1611 translation, commonly known as the Authorized Version or the King James Version. We have preferred it for a number of reasons, one of which is, according to a review of English translations written by Rabbi Louis Jacobs, the Authorized Version best preserves the cadences of the Hebrew language. Where we have quoted other versions, we mention this using the abbreviations included below.

b. Bab. B.	Babylonian Talmud, Tractate Baba Batra
b. Sabb.	Babylonian Talmud, Tractate Shabbat
b. Sanh.	Babylonian Talmud, Tractate Sanhedrin
ESV	English Standard Version
Gk.	Greek
Heb.	Hebrew
IVF	Inter Varsity Fellowship
IVP	Inter-Varsity Press
JPS	The Holy Scriptures, Jewish Publication Society in America, 1917
KJV/AV	King James Version
LXX	Septuagint (OT in Greek, third century BC)
Mid. Gen. R.	Midrash, Genesis Rabbah
NIV	New International Version
NT	New Testament
OT	Old Testament

Pes. R.	Pesikta Rabbati
Tar.	Targum
TNK	Tanakh (Old Testament)

Names and Terms

YOU WILL NOTICE THAT this book uses different names for the same person or thing. The authors are aiming to be helpful to Jewish believers who now have to relate to two worlds—that of Christianity and that of Jewishness and Judaism—and for whom Christianity is unfamiliar, and perhaps even a shock because they expected Christianity to be more "Jewish." For example the use of "Christ" has negative connotations for many Jewish people and so we will use "Messiah" more often. There is plenty that is familiar from Jewish background which is of value, e.g., the word "Tanakh" for what Christianity terms the "Old Testament." We will also use terms which come from Jewish style. We will use these terms interchangeably with terms familiar to Christianity. Our hope is to help new Jewish believers to integrate their background with their new faith and at the same time underline the Jewish roots of their faith.

There are, however, terms within Judaism which have unhelpful connotations, reflecting teaching which diverges from Scripture. For example, while the use of "Hashem" for God is not unscriptural, it can be unhelpful because of the distant feel it creates between the believer and the divine, so that its frequent use is inconsistent with the One who has become incarnate among us—Immanuel, Jesus. Our aim is that the Jewish terms used will have no unhelpful connotations.

Why is this mixing of terminology necessary? Why is Christianity's terminology so unfamiliar to Jewish thinking? First we need to remember that although the good news of Messiah Jesus was to the Jew first it was also to the Gentile, and as the Jewish apostles spread the message beyond the borders of Israel they used Greek as the main language of communication. God in his providence had created a situation whereby, when the time came for the gospel to spread in the ancient world, large numbers of people from different nations and peoples spoke Greek as well as their own language. It was a situation tailor-made for the rapid spread of the gospel, and the early

Jewish preachers took full advantage of it. One obvious outcome was that their writings—which were eventually collected into what we call the New Testament—were in Greek. Inevitably, the religious terminology which developed drew on Greek word forms much more than Hebrew (whereas Judaism's terminology draws almost exclusively on Hebrew). Other influences came in, such as Latin during the medieval period. This does not mean that Christianity ignored Hebrew and the Old Testament but it has added terms from other sources, and these are often unfamiliar to new Jewish believers. An important observation at this point is that the apostles (all Jewish) did not see it as vital to use Hebrew, as if it was the only language suitable for God's revelation. The key thing was to be understood, so at that time the obvious choice was Greek; today it would probably be English.

Another reason Christianity's terminology is unfamiliar is the need to add concepts. Messiah Yeshua has inaugurated the new covenant and further revelation was given about God and his way of salvation through Messiah, so new terms were needed for expressing new truths, for example, the terms "Trinity" and "Second Coming" expressing truths which are not clearly taught in the Tanakh.

A further reason, which is a cause for shame among Gentile Christians, is the indifference many have felt towards the Old Testament roots of their faith. They have been perfectly happy with terminology familiar to them and felt no desire to draw on Old Testament terminology to make their faith more obviously true to its Jewish origins. There were times when that indifference became hostility to all things Jewish. Such hostility arose from the conflict between the synagogue and Jewish believers in Yeshua, and the story can be seen in the Acts of the Apostles and the days after the apostles. Neither indifference or hostility are excusable; Yeshua and his apostles never played down the Jewish roots of the faith, as he said, "salvation is of the Jews" (John 4:22). The situation has improved but it is not back where it should be. This sorry history should not lead Jewish believers to dismiss as lightweight the theological reflection which Gentile believers have pursued and written upon over the centuries. All believers, Gentile and Jewish, are called to reflect in humility and trembling before God's word, and to seek the spiritual understanding the Spirit gives.

We have discussed this issue at length because Jewish believers, especially new ones, need to grasp that although the roots of Christianity are Jewish, there had to be change. As Messiah Jesus taught, you don't put new wine in old wine skins. It is not possible for God's new people, made up of Jews and Gentiles, to use exclusively Jewish terminology simply because all they believe originated in the Jewish nation. To use Paul's metaphor of a tree in Romans 11, the tree has grown out from its roots; hence new non-Jewish terms will need to be devised. But—and this is an important "but"—valid and useful Jewish terms ought to be valued, not only among believers who are Jewish.

A BRIEF WORD ABOUT NAMES

Bearing in mind all the above, the question arises, how to write the names of Bible characters, Bible books and God himself. For the Hebrew names in the Tanakh the choice is either a straightforward transliteration from the Hebrew (e.g., Moshe) or the usage familiar in a vernacular translation (e.g., Moses, in English) or both. When a name first appears we will use the transliteration from the Hebrew, with the English Bible rendering in brackets. After that the name used will vary. With more familiar Hebrew names we will use the Hebrew transliteration more often, with the unfamiliar we will stick with the familiar English rendering. This rule may be varied a little, especially when a sentence could be cluttered with too many names. The Hebrew names of Jewish people mentioned in the New Testament were not always transliterated precisely into Greek but adapted to suit the Greek language, and have been adapted from the Greek into other vernaculars, e.g. Yehudah becomes Ioudas (Greek NT and LXX) then Judas (English). As we do not have their original Hebrew names in the text of the New Testament we will use the English vernacular version, except that Jesus and Yeshua will both be used. The divine name is a unique case due to our ignorance of its pronunciation. "Lord" is the usage familiar to Christians, as is "Jehovah"; "Adonai" is used in the synagogue. The consonants of the divine name are YHWH. In this book we will use Lord or Adonai or YHWH.[1]

Our aim will be to vary the usage of the differing versions of Scripture names for all the reasons in the above paragraphs, and also because there is a wide variety of usage among Jewish people. Believers in Yeshua come from differing Jewish backgrounds: Hasidic, Orthodox, Reform, Liberal and secular, whether in the diaspora or Israel, and all have different versions of names. We want all to feel reasonably at home as they read this book.

---

1. The transliteration of Hebrew names we will use are those in popular use but we have also used some which can be found in *The Jerusalem Bible* (Jerusalem: Koren, 1998).

Helpful Reference Books

THE BIBLIOGRAPHY AT THE close of the book lists works referred to in the text but the following are useful works of reference, some of which would be good to have to hand when working through this book.

ONE-VOLUME SYSTEMATIC THEOLOGY

Boice, James Montgomery. *Foundations of the Christian Faith*. Leicester: InterVarsity, 1986.
Calvin, John. *Institutes of the Christian Religion*. Peabody, MA: Hendrickson, 2007.
Grudem, Wayne. *Bible Doctrine*. Leicester: InterVarsity, 1999.
Hammond, T. C. *In Understanding Be Men*. Leicester: InterVarsity, 2009.
Milne, Bruce. *Know the Truth*. Leicester: InterVarsity, 2009.
Packer, James. *Concise Theology*. Carol Stream, IL: Tyndale, 1993.

DOCTRINAL WRITINGS

Packer, James. *God's Words*. Leicester: InterVarsity, 1981.
Robinson, Donald. *Selected Works*, vol. 1, part 1. Sydney: Moore College, 2008.
Warfield, Benjamin B. *Biblical and Theological Studies*. Phillipsburg: Presbyterian and Reformed, 1968.

REFERENCE

Alexander, T. D., and B. S. Rosner, eds. *New Dictionary of Biblical Theology*. Leicester: InterVarsity, 2000.

Packer, James, and David F. Wright, eds. *New Dictionary of Theology.* Leicester: InterVarsity, 1988.

Wiseman, Donald, ed. *New Bible Dictionary.* 3rd ed. Leicester: InterVarsity, 1996.

HISTORICAL

Berkof, Louis. *A History of Christian Doctrines.* Edinburgh: Banner of Truth, 1969.

Kelly, J. N. D. *Early Christian Creeds.* Abingdon: Routledge, 1982.

———. *Early Christian Doctrines.* London: Continuum, 2000.

JUDAISM

Brawer, Naftali. *Judaism: Theology, History and Practice.* London: Robinson, 2008.

Epstein, Isidore. *Judaism.* Gretna: Pelican, 1979.

Jacobs, Louis. *A Jewish Theology.* Springfield, MO: Behrman House, 1973.

MESSIANIC JEWISH THEOLOGY

Fruchtenbaum, Arnold. *Hebrew Christianity: Its Theology, History, and Philosophy.* Rev. ed. San Antonio: Ariel Ministries, 1995.

BOOK ONE

God's Unfolding Revelation

PART 1

The Plan of Redemption —an Overview

Ben Midgley

IN THIS OVERVIEW OF the plan of redemption we will be doing four surveys of Scripture. Each time we will pass through the Bible and review the text with a different objective in mind. These four surveys are designed to complement one another, to help form an understanding of what the Bible has to say about God's plan to send Messiah. This is a vast subject and this exercise aims at providing a starting point from which wider study can continue. We'll be looking into the New Testament and the great treasure of the Tanakh, to inform and move our hearts to wonder and thanksgiving.

Here is an outline of what these four surveys will include:

- The first survey will focus on the *plan* to send the Messiah.
- The second will focus on the disclosing of the plan to send Messiah: *prophecy*.
- The third will focus on the *person* of Messiah himself, as progressively revealed.

- And the fourth and last survey will focus on the work the Messiah *performs*.

So, plan, prophecy, person, and performance.

1

The Plan to Send Messiah

> "He chose us in Him before the foundation of the world"
> —The Apostle Paul (Eph 1:4)

God has always been, is, and will be. Before he revealed anything of himself to us, he was—the One who revealed himself to Moses in Exod 3 as "I AM WHO I AM."

He always was the Logos (the Word), in the beginning (bereshith) was the Word of God;[1] he spoke before we could speak. Language, the Word of God, existed before the creation of the cosmos. All that he has made, the whole creation, despite its fallen state, declares God's glory.

The way providence works out through history, everything from seasons to human gifts and abilities, reflects the supreme mind of God behind their conception. It is no wonder then when we see such capacity for design that we should also see such evident planning. It should come as no surprise then that the appearing of the Messiah, the centerpiece of the creation, should not be a random and unplanned event, but rather an intricately conceived, precisely prepared, and expertly executed plan. We would also perhaps reasonably expect that this fact would naturally be acknowledged by Scripture, that the plan predated not only Scripture, but the creation itself.

---

1. "In the beginning was the Word, and the Word was with God, and the Word was God" (John 1:1, NIV). "John" is the anglicization of Yohanan—"Gift of YHWH."

A good example of this is found in the verse quoted at the beginning of this section: "He chose us in Him before the foundation of the world" (Eph 1:4). It tells of the existence of choices, a plan, revolving around the person of the Messiah, which preexisted the creation itself. Before the world was made a determination to save it from the foreseeable challenge of evil, by the agency of the Messiah, had been agreed. The plan was conceived in love, as the next verse of Ephesians describes: "In love he predestined us to be adopted as his sons through Jesus Christ, in accordance with his pleasure and will" (NIV). God is good and desires good for all he creates. This purpose of God was a counsel within the Godhead expressed in eternally binding decrees by which his sovereign will, energized by his absolute power, is enacted. Time, space, and matter come into being as the setting in which the divine drama is played out. All this was irreversibly set in motion prior to and independent of any disclosure to human beings.

Naturally when we think of Messiah, we think of him as the man Yeshua ben Yosef, ben David born in Betlechem (Bethlehem) around what some call 1 AD. That references the time when the Messiah appeared in the flesh here on earth in time and space, but it needs to be clear that the office of Messiah had been prescribed before the time of his appearing. That appearing was in fact the incarnation of the second person of the Trinity, the Son. The Messiah comes from heaven to the earth as a willing and fully responsible agent of the divine will, to take on mortal flesh in order to fulfill the purpose for which he is sent. It then is reasonable to say that the world as it is must be established, exactly as it is, as the perfect environment for this event to take place—the entrance of the Creator, into his creation.

But it is not a morally perfect world. Our first parents were made good but were deceived by Satan and went their own way, rebelling against God's one prohibition; a rebellion which has affected all their descendants. So, Messiah comes into a fallen world, a world where death and suffering affect all who live here in consequence of that first sin. This was a deliberate choice. Messiah chose to come to a suffering creation; he comes to save it. While we must be cautious so as not to attribute sin and suffering to the Master of the Universe, so as to make him the author of evil, nevertheless we are saying that the grand design to send Messiah incorporates it.

We can wonder how this might be—that a holy God could make a world in which evil exists. To this we answer that to create a world where love exists (and he is love) there must also exist what we can only call "freedom." Without freedom, love cannot be love; it can only be duty, or involuntary obedience. So, for the sake of freedom an alternative to love must be allowed for. Not to say that it *must* be chosen, but that it must be a real choice. And so it has been chosen by Adam and us all—sin.

So, here is our subject: the plan at which the Messiah is the epicenter, and to which all other plans are subservient. Nevertheless, while we can make these assertions, we cannot do so without reference to Scripture. Prophecy, according to all we have said, is a gradual disclosure of what was already fully formed in the mind of God. For example, we might, in light of all said so far, point to the cry of Messiah himself at the end of his earthly suffering: "It is finished!" What is being referred to if not some aspect of a work he was aware he had to do? Undoubtedly it was an exclamation concerning his imminent death, but more than that an aspect of the plan was complete, an aspect prophesied by Isaiah: "the Lord has laid on Him the iniquity of us all." God's omnipotent love was fulfilling his purpose.

We must also say that as John observed Messiah cry "It is finished" the Spirit has in some measure illuminated him as to its significance. Hence he is led to record this anguish of a dying man. The one convinced that he is the Messiah. The one whom the prophets foresaw would suffer in this way, but one who is also God the Son, who determined before the "foundation of the world" to enter it, to suffer and die a redemptive death, to pay the penalty for the sin of his people so as to reconcile them to God. The opening lines of John's account give ample tribute to the fact that he understood the true identity of the Messiah. What the prophets declared, and the apostles then attested, is now the means by which God graciously enables us to be made aware of what Paul calls this "mystery."

Even the details of who it is that is granted to have this mystery revealed are themselves locked into this scheme. When Scripture talks of election or predestination, whether that refers to Yisrael (Israel) his chosen nation, or Avraham's (Abraham's) seed as his chosen people, or the church as his special possession, or to you or I as his adopted children, then we are being asked to trace this back to our relation to the Messiah. We are categorically told that, in the matter of election for example, the believer has been in love predestined "before the foundation of the world" to be in Christ.

We can therefore say that the events and teachings of Scripture are the consequence of there having been, before the world was made, this plan to send Messiah. Consider one well-known event for example: the story of Purim in the book of Ester (Esther), a book which famously makes no mention of God at all and contains no prophecy. We can nevertheless see the hand of God palpably at work in exceptional, kind, and wonderful ways on behalf of the people of Israel. The necessity to preserve the nation of Israel as the covenant community is imperative, precisely because it is from this community that Messiah has been predetermined to come.

This is an area of inexhaustible study, but I trust it gives some idea of how to proceed with developing it on your own. As a simple rule though, providence—God's actions in history, beginning with creation—is intimately connected to Messiah. It is inseparable in terms of the mind of God and his overarching plans to send him, initially for our salvation and ultimately for the extension of his own glory in time and eternity. In love and grace he works all things to the end he has designed. Think of angels, miracles, the nations, the day of judgment, etc., and consider how these are all part of God's messianic design that every knee should bow, and every tongue should confess that Jesus Christ is Lord.

Question

1. What evidence do you see from Scripture that the creation of the world and the sending of God's Son into it was part of a preordained plan of God? Is anything in history outside of this plan, unforeseen, unexpected, or unplanned?

2

Disclosing the Plan to Send Messiah —Prophecy

"In hope of eternal life, which God, who cannot lie, promised before time began, but has in due time manifested His word through preaching, which was committed to me according to the commandment of God our Saviour"

—THE APOSTLE PAUL (TITUS 1:2–3)

IN THIS STUDY WE see how God determines to reveal his plan, little by little over time—we might call this "progressive revelation." We are centering this study on the appearing of the Messiah for the reasons already given; how his appearing is foretold, and the significance of his appearing as recorded in the writings of the apostles, along with their prophecies of his return. This is the core around which all other revelation is wrapped.

When we talk about the great overarching plan to send the Messiah, promised before the ages began—as the verse from Titus at the head of this chapter mentions—we need to clarify that this is only knowable via what is termed "God's special revelation"; his verbal inspiration of the prophets and apostles by the Holy Spirit, who oversaw its inscripturation so as to secure its preservation intact. This is God's inerrant and authoritative truth, and stands above all and every tradition as the ultimate rule for faith and godliness.

Special revelation covers a multitude of facets, and central to them is the disclosure, in ever-increasing detail, of the plan to send the Messiah, his person, and work. We can therefore expect to find both a beginning and end to this particular aspect of prophecy. There are then early prophecies, and later ones, and we could create as it were a timeline of the gradual disclosure of God's plan to send the Messiah.

So, for example, as a starting point, the fact that the Messiah would be born of a woman (Gen 3:15) was disclosed very early on, but the fact that he would be born in Bethlehem came much later (Mic 5:2). Both facts were planned before the world was even made. Nevertheless, as far as prophecy is concerned, it was not necessary to disclose the exact birthplace of the Messiah until considerably later than the disclosure that he would be born of a woman. That first prophecy put Satan himself on notice of the plan to send the Messiah to defeat him and undo his subversion, and was issued in the hearing of both Adam and Chavva (Eve) for the benefit of them and their descendants. The revelation that God planned to have the Messiah born in Bethlehem only came after the place had already come to exist, and was well established and recognizable, hallowed in particular as the place where King David had been born. This then focused messianic expectation more specifically, not just on the male child of a woman, but on those born in Bethlehem. There are numerous other prophecies as well, each adding further clarity to the details of the plan. The point is, as revelation progresses so it increasingly clarifies until such time as the plan to send the Messiah is abundantly clear, not just in general intention, but in precise detail.

It is therefore possible to trace the development of prophetic disclosure historically from that which came before Moshe (Moses) (to which he gave account in Bereshit) to that which he himself was given to disclose in the other four volumes of Torah, and then subsequently the revelation given via the Ketuvim and Nevi'im. To study this exhaustively is beyond our scope, but by way of example we can return to Bethlehem as a case in point. It is mentioned in Genesis as a preexisting Canaanite town known as "Ephrath," and Yakov (Jacob) approaches it on his return from Aramaea. There his beloved wife Rachel dies in childbirth with Benjamin, his last son (Gen 35:19). So, our introduction to the town is set in the context of the birth of a son to a precious woman, whose father is known as "Israel," and whose name means "son of my right hand," denoting particular favor and blessing. This town is apportioned to the tribe of Yehudah (Judah), who have prophetically been set apart to be the tribe from which royalty will proceed (Gen 49:20). Bethlehem is central to the book of Rut (Ruth), which tells the story of David's immediate ancestors (Ruth 4:17) and begins to link the king and the town. It is also where Shmuel (Samuel) the prophet would later come to anoint him. Among David's early narratives is his love for Bethlehem and the water from its well (2 Sam 23:15)—what comes up from

Bethlehem is precious and so on. Little by little, the gradual sense grows that Bethlehem is a place linked with David's promised descendant, which the prophet Mikah (Micah) confirms by revelation as the place of his birth (seven hundred years before the event).

There are many such examples. We could also investigate the origin of the theme of the plan that the Messiah should be a king from its earliest to last revelations, and how his kingship can be reconciled to his status as a suffering servant, the one prophesied in Yeshayahu (Isaiah) 53:3. So the picture builds up and consolidates from its simple core, the one born of a woman who will bruise the serpent's head, whose heel the serpent will strike. Clearly a triumphant ruler victorious over the agent of temptation, Satan, and yet, one fatally struck by that agent also—a suffering servant. A messianic profile is emerging.

Consequently, in the New Testament writings, especially but by no means exclusively in Matthew, we find a high frequency of passages using phrases of fulfillment. There are a variety of terms but what we are witnessing is a thorough investigation of the Tanakh by the first Jewish witnesses to the Messiah's appearing. They realized retrospectively how the person they encountered perfectly matched the messianic profile. The Messiah would be the Seed of Avraham, and he would be the Ben David, he would be born in Bethlehem, he would leave Egypt, his birth would be signaled by the appearing of a star, and not one of his bones would be broken (John 19:36; see Ps 34:20). I cite here just one or two examples but in his teachings the Messiah himself was concerned to show at every turn how his life and ministry fulfilled the messianic expectations of prophecy, time and time and time again. By way of summary we read: "beginning at Moses and all the Prophets, he expounded to them in all the Scriptures the things concerning Himself" (Luke 24:27).

What we encounter as well in these Gospel accounts is the way that verses in the writings of the prophets, which appear to lead the reader in various and apparently contradictory paths, all seem to be reconciled in the testimony of the apostles. For example, as we have noted, there is a strong theme that emerges through the writings of the prophets that the Messiah would be a great and conquering king (e.g., Isa 9:6–7). On the other hand, however, in an equally evident and traceable fashion, there is a theme that can be identified that the Messiah will be a suffering servant (Isa 53:2–4). These two apparently contradictory profiles of the Messiah are demonstrated in the writings of the apostles to be perfectly harmonized and reconciled in their testimony concerning the Messiah. So those whose expectations of the Messiah were solely invested in him as a conquering king would have been scandalized by the fact that the Messiah suffered as a lowly servant.

It is reasonable to ask then a significant question about the capacity of those who lived in the days preceding the Messiah's appearing. Were they provided with sufficient light to see the day of his coming clearly, and in putting their trust in him who was yet to come, to have been saved for the world to come through that faith? The answer to this must be yes, as Yeshua affirms of Avraham: "Your father Abraham rejoiced to see my day, and he saw it and was glad" (John 8:56). He has always been set forth as the One who overcomes the serpent who tempted our first parents to sin. Likewise, he has always been the One who would be fatally struck by that venomous snake, causing him to suffer in his conquest. There was a gospel to which Adam and Eve were witness which, if believed, was sufficient to save: the same suffering servant and victorious king as Isaiah spoke of. The writer of the letter that has come to be known as the "Epistle to the Hebrews" asserts, "These all died in faith," referring to the saints who lived prior to Jesus' birth (Heb 11:13). That passage describes the hope of the saints of old as expecting citizenship in a city that was yet to be built. So, those who lived prior to the time of the Messiah's appearing would have been saved by their faith in the One to come, revealed in the prophecies concerning him.

To round off this section we have to explore the subject of those who have lived since his coming, believing these same prophets even in our times, hoping in the coming Messiah, yet still denying the apostolic claims that Yeshua from Nazareth is the One. How can a person say they await Messiah, their savior, then deny him when he appears and expect to be saved? No, first that person must reappraise their rejection of Messiah, see the error of their ways and turn from them, and only then, as they turn to Messiah in faith, confessing their sins, can they hope to be forgiven and redeemed.

Questions

1. God's plan of salvation has been progressively revealed starting with his words to Adam and Eve in Gen 3:15. What are the main themes of this progressive revelation?

2. How does it affect you that you are one of the nation to whom all this revelation was given?

3

The Person of Messiah Progressively Revealed

> For He shall grow up before Him as a tender plant,
> And as a root out of dry ground.
> He has no form or comeliness;
> And when we see Him,
> There is no beauty that we should desire Him.
> —the prophet Yeshayahu (Isa 53:2)

IN CHAPTER 1 WE highlighted the fact that Messiah was planned to appear from before the world was even created, and showed that this is explicitly taught in Scripture. We then went on in the second chapter to say that this plan, which in essence was a mystery to us humans, was then progressively revealed via the agency of the prophets whose sayings are recorded in Scripture. Now we are going to look at the complex identity of the actual person of whom the prophets spoke, whom the apostles then attested, and the Messiah himself manifested, all captured in Scripture.

Returning to the beginning, we said that the "Seed ('offspring' in some translations) of the woman" was the earliest recorded prophecy concerning the Messiah. We have already done some exploration of what we should expect about a Messiah from this proto-prophecy. To restate some of the obvious facts, we note that the Messiah will be a true human being, one with a body with its needs and wants, and the social elements, such as emotion, intellect, memory, conscience, and will. Then there is the spiritual aspect of the person: beliefs, thoughts, convictions, etc. These are the kind of elements we must be ready to import into the simple statement that the Messiah is human. In this sense he is quite unremarkable.

In terms of how this person will come into the world, we note the Messiah will be "of a woman," and in that sense appears by the same means as all people do. It sets the Messiah as part of the historical continuum we all find ourselves a part of, one generation leading on to the next. The Messiah is not superhuman.

We can also note from the use of gender that the Messiah will be male. This maleness sets him in distinction from the evident femaleness of his mother. Developing this further, we see that this person, who experiences childhood and humanity, also experiences maleness in distinction from femaleness.

Lastly, if we accept that the striking of the heel is the striking of a mortal blow, then we accept that this declares him to be a mortal man, one who must at some point die. As with these other aspects, later prophets develop this theme, especially Isa 53:5–9. So, a mortal man, a mere mortal we might say. One more man who comes along, is nurtured and raised, grows up, lives, breathes, thinks, feels, acts, and then in time eventually dies. Unremarkable.

All that said, there is more to the Messiah's identity than this. The Messiah's ability to "crush the head" of the serpent needs consideration. He must succeed where Adam failed. He must say no to the serpent's temptations. He must choose the love of God irrevocably and waive the right to ever do otherwise. The words "bruise his heel" appear to indicate this will cost him his life. Here we see something supernatural at work because an apparently ordinary person does an extraordinary thing. Indeed, a thing never done by anyone else, ever; absolutely saying no to sin. What exactly is this telling us about him?

I want to return one last time to the phrase "the seed of the woman" and allow ourselves to be intrigued that the Messiah is so described. It is not that this is problematic, but it is strange given that seed is in the main a reference to the male line in the rest of Scripture. For example, the reference to the seed of Abraham, referring to the Messiah (Gen 12:7; 13:5; 24:7; see also Gal 3:16). The fact that this utterance is delivered by the very mouth of God himself, and Adam is in no way addressed or included in the prophecy, may, with the benefit of hindsight, advise us the father will in no way be "of Adam." The fact it is God speaking could be indicating that the LORD God will be father to the Messiah. If we are looking for an explanation as to his supernatural power, we must look to his paternity. This being so, we must conclude that although he is fully man, he is also, simultaneously, fully God, seeing that his father is the Almighty. Compare this again to Isaiah and we see that the prophet even called the Messiah "Mighty God, Everlasting

Father" (Isa 9:6). Now the ordinary becomes extraordinary; Messiah is God incarnate (Matt 1:23).

The prophets continue to develop the theme of the Messiah's humanity, as well as that of his divinity. One thing they indicate is that this divine-human Messiah shares familial traits with the Lord God. For example, the Lord God is compassionate, slow to anger, and full of mercy. And Messiah is described as suffering great injustice, bearing "the iniquity of us all," being blamed for what we did wrong, yet "He opened not His mouth"—no complaint, petulant whining, or angry outburst. Aside from this we may also move to the kind of signs and wonders that attend the Lord God's presence—miracles, judgments, salvations. These are therefore to be expected in a divine-human Messiah.

The New Testament introduces us to Yeshua, Jesus of Nazareth, and we learn not just of his birth in Bethlehem but his life in Nazareth, his refugee status in Egypt, his submission to parents, his profound commitment to God's law, his share in his people's subjugation to the Romans, his graciousness, his truthfulness, and his extraordinary teaching, miracles, and ultimate saving purpose in his death and resurrection. The conclusion taught by the whole New Testament, and that we are to draw, is that he is the Messiah and Son of God, God himself, manifest in the flesh.

However, the New Testament acknowledges that many of his contemporaries disagreed, as have subsequent generations. This makes us very conscious of how contentious is the matter of the divinity of Jesus Christ. To the rabbis, such claims lead to an idolatry, the worship of a man, a creature, not the Creator; therefore Jesus must be a false Messiah, a deceiver of the people whose name is thereby accursed. This broad and understandable revulsion should make us compassionate when dealing with the widespread rejection of this evident truth taught in Scripture. To say "Jesus is lord" is one thing, to say "he is Lord" is another, but to say "he is Lord" can provoke a significant reaction. But among his own followers it provokes a response, one of worship, as we see from the start with the magi, and was especially so from the time of his rising from the dead (Matt 28:9–10, 16–17; Luke 24:52; Heb 1:6; Rev 22:3). To get it wrong concerning Jesus is forgivable; what is unforgivable is the refusal to admit that one has got it wrong.

Question

1. The Messiah prophesied in Scripture is a complex person. Looking back to when you first learnt about Yeshua, what was unsurprising about his

person to you and what was surprising? Is there anything you still find difficult to accept?

4

The Messiah Who Saves

> I will deliver you from the hand of the wicked,
> And I will redeem you from the grip of the terrible.
> —the Prophet Yirmeyahu (Jer 15:21)

To some extent we have found ourselves doing an extended exposition of Gen 3:15. We have stated that what God declared in this verse was already fully known and planned by him, and what we witness in the declaration of his predetermined counsel is the inauguration of prophecy, disclosing the nature of the person. We now move on to consider the work of the Messiah. God's plan is a salvation plan, and a salvation plan presupposes something going wrong—something very serious indeed if it requires the Maker of heaven and earth to go to such lengths to address it, thereby revealing him to be of unfathomable love and pity.

It must be somewhere here in the problem of evil that the Messiah's work seems to be most necessary. What has been written in my first chapter above reconciles us to the fact that the possibility of evil was a necessary component in the creation insofar as it safeguards a principle, one we tend to hold very dear: the exercise of free will. Without a viable alternative to loving obedience to God, how could we freely express love to God? There must be love as a world without it would be insufferable. The serpent presented a real alternative to love, giving the representatives of humanity real choice, a choice that was exercised once and for all on our behalf. Yes, we can rage against the apparent injustice of it, the misery of having to live with the consequences of what our forebears have done; we may even try to right the wrong, but as each generation knows, history traps us. The consequence is, as the prophet concludes, that "All we like sheep have gone astray" (Isa 53:6). By rights then we can say God has given the option, built into his creation, and we have exercised our freedom of choice and must live now with the painful consequences—that, you must agree, is perfectly just. However, what Moshe was granted to hear, recorded in Exod 34:6–7, was that yes, God is just, but that is not the headline of the revelation—God's principal emphasis was his compassion, mercy, forgiveness, and faithfulness. To be treated as our sins deserve, we can accept as an unhappy fairness—after all, we have rejected God and his ways—but the Scriptures reveal something else, that as the psalmist says, he does *not* treat us as ours sins deserve (see Ps 103:10).

There is something called "grace," what the hymn writer described as "Amazing Grace." The psalmist marvels that there is no direct correlation between what we do and what is done to us, ascribing the cause to God's love for those who fear him (Ps 103:17). It is worth looking at this ancient song of thanksgiving, which states that, "As far as the east is from the west, So far has He removed our transgressions from us. As a father pities his children, So the Lord pities those who fear Him . . . He remembers that we are dust" (Ps 103:12–14). It is clearly stated in Genesis that in the day our ancient parents ate of the fruit, "you shall surely die" (Gen 2:17). But death did not take place immediately as one might expect. In fact, what follows is an essay in grace. The all-knowing God first came out, entered into conversation with them, rebuked the serpent, prophesied his doom, explained the consequences of Adam and Eve's actions to them, prophesied that all is not lost, and even after the expulsion from the garden clothed them and gave them an unexpected measure of prosperity despite the new hardships they faced. That experience of grace is our common experience too. The sun rises day by day, rain falls; irrespective of our moral standing, goodness abounds. We are clearly not being dealt with as our sins deserve.

God being God, this is not even the full extent of this grace, and the psalm we referred to shows us that for those who fear God there is a special grace to be found—full and free forgiveness for our sin and the possibility of a right and good relationship with him (Ps 103:12, 17). This is the subject of atonement; which brings us to the heart of the Messiah's mission. But how can God be merciful without undermining his justice? We have moved the conversation on from that of the "problem of evil" to the "problem of goodness." The fact is that if there is to be not just love but also goodness, then some way of satisfying God's justice must exist, outside of punishing the guilty. Atonement is that way. But God cannot accept atonement that is not equal to the offense. Even the rivers of blood that the God-ordained sacrificial system demanded could not account for the grace shown to the world through the ages. So, like in an accounting system which carries forward, it must be that the full or outstanding balance must be settled at some future time. Which raises the question: What can we offer? The hymn writer Isaac Watts wrote, "Were the whole realm of nature mine, that were an offering far too small." There is the recognition here that nothing can adequately be offered by us in place of our sin. We are lost, it seems.

Lost, it seems, unless God really is more loving and gracious than we dare to imagine. What the sacrificial system foreshadowed, King David's experience typified (Ps 22), and Hoshea (Hosea) and Isaiah prophesied (Hos 13:14; Isa 53), was that God would pay the price for us. This was part of the plan, conceived in the heart of a God who is love. He would take on flesh and live a sinless life, and die in our place, the infinitely holy God suffering in place of the world he has made, a world tainted by sin. This is what the New Testament reveals concerning Yeshua, in the Gospel accounts and the teaching of the apostles' letters. God is abundantly good and his love, goodness, and saving grace can be known. That speaks of the glory of God, and causes the angels to sing, and excites worship here on earth. By satisfying his just wrath against sin, by visiting the punishment for it upon himself in the person of his Son, the Messiah—fully man, able to represent us, and fully God, able to make such an offering sufficient—he has done all that is required to atone for sin and offer mercy to the lost and undeserving. In this we see the wisdom, compassion, grace, and mercy of God which glorifies him forever, in this world and the world to come.

QUESTION

1. Many people doubt the goodness of God. How would you attempt to show from Scripture and experience that he is both good and gracious?

FURTHER READING

Lloyd-Jones, David M. *Ephesians: God's Ultimate Purpose*. Edinburgh: Banner of Truth, 1978.
Vos, Geerhardus. *Biblical Theology*. Edinburgh: Banner of Truth, 1975.
Warfield, Benjamin B. *The Plan of Salvation*. Apollo: Ichthus, 2015.

PART 2

The Bible and Redemption's Story

MARTIN PAKULA

5

The Shape of the Bible

The Bible consists of two major sections, the Tanakh (or Old Testament, OT) and the Brit Chadashah (or New Testament, NT), and the sixty-six books within it were written by various people over about fifteen hundred years. The Bible is not entirely written in chronological order, but it does have a chronology and a storyline to it. My aim is to give you a bird's-eye view of the storyline of the Bible.

(A) THE TANAKH AND THE BRIT CHADASHAH

The Tanakh has three sections: the Torah (the law), Nevi'im (the Prophets), and Ketuvim (the Writings). The word "Tanakh" is an acronym that spells out these three sections: the *T* is for Torah, the *n* is for Nevi'im, and the *k* is for Ketuvim. The English Bible calls the Tanakh the "Old Testament." "Testament" is a word that means "covenant": the pact God made with his people.

The Brit Chadashah, or New Testament, contains twenty-seven books. We can divide these books into four groups or sections: the Gospels, the book of Acts, the Epistles (or letters), and the book of Revelation.

(B) THREE "ERAS"

The books of the Bible were written by different human authors: Moshe (Moses), David, Yeshayahu (Isaiah), Luke, Paul, etc. But each book of the Bible is ultimately authored by God himself.¹ So although David wrote many of the psalms, they can also be said to be written by God through the inspiration of God's Holy Spirit. For example, the book of Hebrews quotes Ps 95 several times. In Heb 3:7 it is ascribed to the authorship of God's Holy Spirit, in Heb 4:3 it is ascribed to God, and in verse 7 of that chapter it is ascribed to David. So we see that the Bible itself understands that whilst this psalm was written by a human author, David, it is ultimately by God, speaking through David by his Holy Spirit; all are true. Thus there is a *dual authorship* to the Bible; each book of the Bible having a human author, whilst the ultimate author is God.

What this means for the whole Bible is that there is a profound unity to all sixty-six books, because they have one ultimate author, God. And this means that God knew where that storyline was heading from the very outset of Bereshit 1:1. The first five books of the Bible are read in synagogue every year, but little else of the Bible. We need to read the Torah and all of the Bible, and to read it within the storyline God has given.

The unified storyline of the Bible finds its fulfillment in the coming of the Messiah (Luke 24:25–27, 44); Jesus (Yeshua) says that the Tanakh is all about him. The one author God wrote it through his human authors, knowing that his Son, the Messiah Jesus, was coming to fulfill all the promises God gave.

So, what is that storyline? Basically there are three eras to this storyline. The first era moves from the beginning of the Bible through to the death of King Shlomo (Solomon). This era covers creation, the fall of humanity due to sin, the patriarchs Avraham (Abraham), Yitzhak (Isaac) and Yakov (Jacob), the exodus from Egypt, the conquest of the promised land, and the installation of kings such as David and his son Solomon. Under Solomon the high point of Yisrael's history in the promised land was reached.

The storyline of the second era goes downhill from there. The kingdom of Israel was split into two after Solomon's death. There were the ten northern tribes, called "Israel," and the two southern tribes, called "Judah," along with the remnant of the tribe of Binyamin (Benjamin). The ten northern tribes lasted only two hundred years and were expelled from the promised land by the Assyrians (722 BC). About a hundred and fifty years later Judah was sent into exile, away from the promised land, at the hands of the Babylonians (586 BC). During this time the prophets spoke of God's forthcoming judgment in the form of the exile, because of Israel's sin. But the same prophets also held out the hope of return from exile, and a glorious

---

1. See chapter 11, (B)(i), (ii), and (iii) for a fuller explanation of God's authorship of the Bible.

new future in which all God's promises would be fulfilled. After the return from exile there would be a new covenant in which God's Messiah would come and bring forgiveness of sins, not only for Israel, but for all nations. The return from exile is recorded in the Tanakh; however it was clear that the fulfillment of God's promises had not yet arrived; they would come to pass in the future.

The third era is the era of fulfillment. God's promises were fulfilled in Yeshua, the Messiah; the promises were fulfilled in part during Yeshua's life, death, and resurrection, and will be consummated at his return. There is also a storyline in the Brit Chadashah: it begins in the four Gospels and continues in the book of Acts, which describes how the good news of Israel's Messiah spread through Israel and then to all nations, resulting in the formation of the church of Jews and Gentiles. God's people now await Jesus' return and the new heavens and new earth, as depicted in the book of Revelation.

These are the three eras of the storyline of the Bible, which we will now describe in a bit more detail.

6

The Torah

THE TORAH, THE BOOKS of Moshe, are the first five books of the Bible: Bereshit (Genesis), Shemot (Exodus), Vayyikra (Leviticus), Bemidbar (Numbers), and Devarim (Deuteronomy).

(A) BERESHIT (GENESIS) 1–11: CREATION, FALL, THE FLOOD, BABEL

The book of Bereshit can be divided into two uneven halves. Chapters 1 to 11 are about the origins of the world and humanity (hence the names "Bereshit," which means "in the beginning," and "Genesis," which means "origin"). Chapters 12 to 50 are about the patriarchs Avraham, Yitzhak, and Yakov (and Yosef [Joseph]).

(i) Creation (Bereshit 1–2)

Bereshit 1 begins with the famous words: "In the beginning God created the heavens and the earth." This is a summary title which tells us that God, in the beginning, made everything. God made the universe—it did not happen by "chance." He made you and owns you and all of creation, for he is its Maker.

The chapter proceeds to describe in a carefully structured format how God made everything. There were six days of creation: on the first three days God created light, then the world and sky, and then the land and seas, and vegetation; on the second three days God filled these three "spaces" with life.

Each of the six days has a repetitive formula, a formula emphasizing that God created all things by his *word* (Gen 1:3, 6, 9, 14, etc.). God simply spoke and things came to be; he is the One who is in complete control of his creation. The repetitive formula also highlights that God's creation is "good" (Gen 1:12, 18, 25), that is, it accords with his purposes. There is no sickness or death because creation was originally made good, very good in fact (Gen 1:31).

On day six, at the climax of creation, God made humankind, which he made in his image (Gen 1:27). The chapter itself explains that being made in God's image results in humanity being God's deputies, as it were, on earth. We represent God, ruling his creation, and male and female are both made in God's image, equal in God's sight, ruling his creation together (Gen 1:26–28).

In chapter 2, verses 1–3 we read that God rested on the seventh day and blessed his creation; this is the origin of Shabbat.

Chapter 2, from verse 4 onwards, narrates the creation story from another angle. The story changes focus, narrowing down to day six and focusing on the creation of humankind; God made a man and put him in a garden paradise, Eden (Gen 2:8). In this chapter humankind is provided with a beautiful paradise garden, and in the second half of the chapter God provides Adam with a wife, Eve, who is his companion (Gen 2:18–25). Here we see how God loves us and provides for all our needs. However, there is one command, in verses 16–17: humankind is free to eat from any tree in the garden except for one—the tree of the knowledge of good and evil.

So at the end of chapter 2, all is right with the world. We have been introduced in the storyline to huge concepts: there is one God, who made us and all the world, and he owns us, and we owe him our lives—our everything. He loves us and provides for all our needs, and we are to care for the world under his leadership. Moreover, at the end of chapter 2, humanity is in right relationship with God, with each other, and with the world. These relationships, however, were now to be tragically shattered.

(ii) The Fall (Bereshit 3)

In chapter 3 of Genesis we are introduced to the devil, appearing in the form of a snake (Gen 3:1).[1] The snake questioned God's goodness in giving the command to Adam and Eve that they should not eat from the tree of the

---

1. Rev 12:9 speaks of "that serpent of old, called the Devil and Satan."

knowledge of good and evil. The snake moved Eve to doubt God's word, and then denied God's word outright, and so Adam and Eve disobeyed God's word—the first act of sin and rebellion against God (Gen 3:1–6).

Verse 5 highlights the nature of sin: "For God knows that in the day you eat of it your eyes will be opened, and you will be like God, knowing good and evil." They will "be like God," able to determine what is good or evil, what is right or wrong; masters of their own destiny. No longer will God be their God, but they will be their own god. The essence of sin is to reject God's rule over us, and to run our life our own way without him.

The harmonious relationships established by the end of chapter 2 are now shattered. At the end of chapter 2 God was in authority over humanity, Adam was in authority over Eve, and Adam and Eve were in authority over the animals and the world. Now these relationships have been inverted and broken. An animal, the snake, led astray the woman; the woman led astray the man; and together the woman and the man rebelled against God's rule.

God's judgment followed (the second half of chapter 3). Humanity was banished from the Garden of Eden; that is, we were banished from God's presence, and from the tree of life (Gen 3:24). The world of suffering and death, with which we are all too familiar, is the result of the fall—the result of humans rejecting God's rightful rule over us.

(iii) The Spread of Sin: The Flood and Babel (Bereshit 4–11)

The next few chapters of Bereshit outline the spread of sin. In chapter 4 there is the famous story of Kayin (Cain) and Hevel (Abel), the children of Adam and Eve. Cain gave in to sin and murdered his brother (Gen 4:7–8), but at the end of the chapter Eve gave birth to a third son, Shet (Seth), to replace the murdered Abel (Gen 4:25).

Chapter 5 traces the line of Adam's descendants through Seth, and the tenth generation from Adam in this line brings us to Noach (Noah) and the flood. The spread of sin became so bad by the start of chapter 6 that verse 5 says: "Then the LORD saw that the wickedness of man was great in the earth, and that every intent of the thoughts of his heart was only evil continually." It's very hard, isn't it, to read this verse and think that we are basically good? In this verse Moshe accurately describes how we all have a sinful nature that turns away from God. We are not basically good, but every intent of the thoughts of our heart is only evil continually. This is not saying that we are evil, like Hitler or a pedophile. But the Tanakh makes it clear that God's standard of goodness is not like ours; God is perfectly holy and good so that his "pass mark" is 100 percent, and we fall very far short of his standard. Falling short of God's standards of holiness is what the Bible calls "sin," which is abhorrent in God's eyes.

Our sinful nature grieves God greatly. As Bereshit 6:6 says: "And the LORD was sorry that He had made man on the earth, and He was grieved in His heart." God does not allow our rebellion against his rule to go unchecked, and so what follows is God's judgment upon humanity. Chapters 6 to 9 contain the story of the flood, a universal judgment in which God put to death all of humanity. It prefigures the final judgment of God and the end of the world.

But there is also grace or mercy. As sin spreads in these early chapters of the Torah, so too does the grace of God shine forth to match it and overcome it. Chapter 6, verse 8 says: "But Noah found grace in the eyes of the LORD," such that God saved Noah, his family, and representatives of all life (Gen 6:18–19). After the flood Noah and all the animals were used by God to restart creation (Gen 8:18–19; 9:1) and Moshe tells us that "God blessed Noah and his sons, and said to them: 'Be fruitful and multiply, and fill the earth'" (Gen 9:1). A new start was made with Noah, which is called a "covenant" in the Tanakh (Gen 9:9). The Hebrew word is *brit*. It involves a commitment from God to his people; in this case, to uphold his creation and never again destroy it with a flood (Gen 9:15).

Humankind is still sinful after the flood (Gen 8:21): Noah gets drunk (Gen 9:20–21) and humanity as a whole rebels against God in the episode of the tower of Babel (Gen 11:1–9); the flood did not change our sinful nature.

The rest of chapter 11 has another genealogy which traces the descendants of Noah through his son Shem (Gen 11:10) down to Avraham (at this point called Avram; Gen 11:26).

(B) BERESHIT (GENESIS) 12–50: THE PATRIARCHS AVRAHAM, YITZHAK, YAKOV, AND YOSEF

(i) The Story of Avraham (Bereshit 12–25)

Genesis 12:1–3 is a very important passage in the whole of the Bible. I like to say that there are two key passages in the Tanakh that unfold the whole storyline. They are Gen 12:1–3 and 2 Sam 7: the promises of God to Avraham and the promises of God to David. The story of the Tanakh is basically the unfolding storyline of how God keeps the promises he made to Avraham and David. Let's take a closer look at Gen 12:1–3.

> Now the LORD had said to Abram:
> Get out of your country,

> From your family
> And from your father's house,
> To a land that I will show you.
> I will make you a great nation;
> I will bless you
> And make your name great;
> And you shall be a blessing.
> I will bless those who bless you,
> And I will curse him who curses you;
> And in you all the families of the earth shall be blessed. (Gen 12:1–3)

In verse 1 God told Avram (Abram) to leave where he was and go to the land God would show him, the promised land of Canaan, and God then promised this land to Abram and his descendants (v. 7). In verse 2 God promised Abram that he would make him into a great nation, which is a promise that Abram will have many descendants, who will become the nation Israel.

In verses 2–3 God also made promises to Abram that concern how he will affect others. Not only will he be a blessing to those immediately around him, but he will also be a blessing to all the families, or nations, of the earth. This is a key promise, which ties these verses to chapters 1–11. We saw in the previous chapters the fall of humankind from paradise due to sin. The plan of God will now advance through Abram so that the fall will be reversed and humanity blessed again, as in the Garden of Eden. But this will now take place through God's promises to one man, Abram, and his descendants; all nations will be blessed through him. The nations of the world will find their way back to God, and back to paradise, through this one man, Abram. God's intention for the world was never to have a chosen people for their own sake, but through them to bless all nations of the world.

The unfolding of these promises to Abram advances the storyline of the Tanakh that now follows. It is handy to remember these three basic promises to Abram by God: people, land, and blessing to the nations. The rest of the book of Bereshit focuses on the promise of people (descendants); the next four books (the rest of the Torah) and the book of Yehoshua (Joshua) focus on the promise of land; the New Testament will speak of blessing going to the nations.

Two important chapters in the story of Abram are chapters 15 and 17, in which God made his covenant with him, which was based upon the promises of Bereshit 12:1–3. In chapter 15, verses 2–3 Abram complained to God that he had no physical heir. In fact, in chapter 11, verse 30 we are told that his wife Sara (Sarai) was unable to have children, a fact which is very important for our storyline. God has promised Abram many descendants, as many as the dust of the earth (Gen 13:16), but Sarai could not have children and so Abram remained childless. How then could God's promises be fulfilled? From a human point of view it was impossible, but in chapter 15, verses 4–5 God promises that Abram will have a child and that his descendants will be as numerous as the stars in the sky.

Chapter 15, verse 6 gives Abram's response to God's promise to him: "he believed in the LORD, and He accounted it to him for righteousness," That is, God counted Abram as right with him—in a right relationship with God, because of his faith in God's promises. Verse 7 onwards of chapter 15 reiterates the promise of land and describes God making his covenant with Abram (Gen 15:18).

Chapter 17 reiterates the covenant promises to Abram (vv. 4–8) and his name is changed to Avraham (Abraham) and Sarai's to Sara (Sarah). The sign of the covenant is added here: that of circumcision. As the rainbow was the sign of the covenant with Noah (Gen 9:16–17), so circumcision is the sign of the covenant with Abraham. God promised him many descendants, and the part of the human body through which descendants are made is literally marked here as a sign of God's promise.

At this point Abraham was still childless at the age of ninety-nine (Gen 17:1). In the following chapter God himself appeared in human form to Abraham, along with two angels, telling him and Sara that they would have a son (Gen 18:1–2, 10, 16–17; 19:1). Yitzhak was born to them (Gen 21:1–7), a birth that was the first fulfillment of the promise that Avraham would have many descendants. There is only one descendant so far, but that's the start of the fulfillment of God's promises. The fact that Sara could not have children is highlighted on purpose; the narrative is making it clear that the fulfillment of the promises is entirely due to God.

Chapter 22 recounts the famous and amazing story of the Akeda, when God tested Avraham by commanding him to sacrifice his only son Yitzhak (Gen 22:1–2). Avraham obeyed God, though at the last second God stopped Avraham from slaying his son (Gen 22:9–12). God spared Avraham's only son, Isaac, providing a substitute in the form of a lamb for a burnt offering. But God did not spare his own Son, Yeshua, who died as our substitute by offering up his own life to God for our sin (Rom 8:32).

God then reiterated his promises to Avraham of many descendants, land, and blessing to all nations (Gen 22:15–18). The story reached its point of highest tension here. God had promised Avraham that he would have many descendants, and had made it clear that this would be through Yitzhak (not through Yishmael [Ishmael]). So if Avraham killed Yitzhak, how could God's promises be fulfilled? It is as if Avraham received his son back from the dead (Heb 11:17–19). Avraham trusted in God, as we saw in chapter 15, and in this episode proved it; his faith was proven by his deeds (Jas 2:21–23).

Before Avraham died (Gen 25:7–10), he made sure to provide for his son Yitzhak. Chapter 24 continues the theme of descendants; Yitzhak would need a wife (and children) and so Avraham sent his servant to his original home country and relatives to find a wife for Yitzhak, who was Rivka (Rebecca). Note verse 60 of chapter 24: the blessing Rebecca's family gave to her was about having many descendants (children). This accords with the theme throughout the second half of Genesis, namely, God's promise to Avraham that he would have many descendants, who would become the nation Israel, through whom all nations would be blessed.

At the end of the story of Abraham we see only a very small fulfillment of God's promises to him: he had one descendant—the fulfillment of the promises was to come in the future. As the book of Hebrews says: "These all died in faith, not having received the promises, but having seen them afar off were assured of them, embraced them" (Heb 11:13).

(ii) The Story of Yitzhak and Yakov (Bereshit 25–35)

We are told in Bereshit 25:20 that Isaac was forty years old when he married Rebecca, and that he was sixty years old when the twins Yakov (Jacob) and Esav (Esau) were born (Gen 25:26). Note again that Rebecca was unable to have children, just like Sarah, but she became pregnant in answer to Isaac's prayer (Gen 25:21). In this way the storyline is making it clear again that God was intervening to fulfill his own promises.

The following chapters focus on Yakov, who inherited the blessings of Avraham. Esau sold his birthright to Yakov (Gen 25:27–34) and then Yakov cheated Esau out of the blessing of his father as well (Gen 27). What is being emphasized is that God's promises, given to Avraham and Yitzhak, will continue through Yakov, not Esau.

Esau, not surprisingly, was angry and wanted to take revenge and so Yakov fled (Gen 27:41–45). His parents sent him to Rebecca's home and family to find a wife (Gen 28:1–2). In chapter 29 we read that Yakov met his cousin Rahel (Rachel) and fell in love with her, so he worked for seven years to marry her, but when the time came for the marriage his uncle Laban deceived him and gave him the older daughter Lea (Leah) instead. Yakov worked another seven years for Rachel to be his wife. The emphasis again, as throughout the story of the patriarchs, is on the fulfillment of God's promise to give them descendants. Yakov now had two wives, Rachel and Leah. Bereshit 29:31—30:24 narrates the birth of eleven of Yakov's twelve sons.

Rachel was unable to have children, like Sarah and Rebecca (notice the pattern?). But at last she conceived and gave birth to a son: Yosef (Joseph; Gen 30:22–24). This section of our story finishes in chapter 35 with the death of Rachel, who died in childbirth whilst giving birth to Yakov's twelfth son, Benjamin. Then verses 23–26 list the twelve sons of Yakov, emphasizing that God is keeping his promises; the promise of many descendants is beginning to take shape.

(iii) The Story of Yosef (Bereshit 37–50)

The story of Joseph shows us how the family of Avraham's descendants ended up in Egypt. Joseph's brothers sold him into slavery (due to their jealousy of him; chapter 37) but in Egypt, after many misfortunes, Joseph rose to second in the land next to Pharaoh (chapters 39–41). After interpreting Pharaoh's dreams concerning seven years of plenty followed by seven years of famine, Joseph was put in charge of storing up grain in the seven good years to provide for Egypt and the surrounding nations during the ensuing famine.

During the famine, Joseph's brothers left the promised land to buy grain in Egypt. They did not recognize Joseph at first, but he finally revealed himself to them (chapters 42–45) and explained how God had sent him to Egypt to provide for his family so that they would not starve during the famine (Gen 45:4–8). Avraham's descendants now numbered seventy (Gen 46:26–27): Yakov, Joseph's brothers, and their families, who all joined Joseph in Egypt, where he took care of them.

The book of Bereshit ends with Joseph's death, and his prophecy that God would bring his people up from Egypt to return to the promised land (Gen 50:24).

(C) THE EXODUS (SHEMOT 1–18)

At the start of the book of Shemot (Exodus), we jump forward in time. Avraham's descendants have now multiplied greatly (Exod 1:7), so at the start of the second book of the Bible the first promise to Avraham has basically been fulfilled: the promise of many descendants, who would be a great nation. But the second promise to Abraham was that his descendants would inherit the promised land. The exodus is all about God fulfilling this latter promise, by bringing the Israelites out of Egypt and into the promised land.

The numerical growth of Israel in Egypt was seen as a threat (Exod 1:8–10) by Pharaoh, who therefore oppressed the Israelites: first with slavery, and then by killing their newborn male babies (to reduce their numbers). One of the male babies born at that time was Moshe (Exod 2:1–2).

(i) Moshe Raised Up as a Savior (Shemot 1–4)

In order to protect this newborn baby Moshe, his mother placed him in a little "ark," which Moshe's sister then placed on the edge of the riverbank and kept watch over him. He was found by Pharaoh's daughter, who took pity on him, and paid an Israelite mother to nurse the baby for her. The nurse, as it happened, was Moshe's mother (Exod 2:3–8). Note the irony: Pharaoh's daughter now paid Moshe's mother to bring him up!

Chapter 2 jumps forward forty years to when Moshe was grown up (Exod 2:11). He saw an Egyptian slave driver beating an Israelite. Moshe killed him, in consequence having to flee for his life to another land. Then in chapter 3, another forty years later, God called Moshe, at the age of eighty, to lead his people out of Egypt and take them to the promised land (3:7–10). God told Moshe right up front his plan: he would harden Pharaoh's heart so that he would not let the Israelites go; then God would bring plagues upon Pharaoh and Egypt, which would eventually force Pharaoh to let God's people go (Exod 3:19–20).

(ii) The Ten Plagues and the Passover (Shemot 5–13)

God sent ten plagues on Egypt. He could have just used one! But he gradually brought his judgments upon Egypt, in the sight of his people Israel, so that they (and the Egyptians) would understand that he is indeed the God of this world (Exod 9:15–16). The plagues showed God's power. They came at God's command and were removed at his command (Exod 8:9–11). They showed that God is in control of his world, and they also showed that God blesses his people, but curses those who curse them (Gen 12:3). The plagues were God's punishment upon Egypt, and his own people were spared from the worst of the plagues (Exod 8:22–23; 9:4).

The final plague was the worst of all: the death of all the firstborn sons (and animals) in Egypt (Exod 11:4–5). This was the plague that finally made Pharaoh give up and allow the Israelites to leave. It is what we remember at seder on the night of Pesach. Chapter 12 describes the final plague itself and the exodus from Egypt. The Israelites, on the night of Pesach, ate the Passover lamb and smeared its blood on the doorframes of their houses (Exod 12:7). Why did they have to put the blood on their doorframes? What does that have to do with the final tenth plague of the death of all the firstborn sons? Shemot 12:12–13 give us the answer. The blood on the doorframes of their houses was a real, but symbolic, gesture. The penalty for sin is death, and blood symbolizes death. When God passed over the houses in Egypt, he executed his judgment, whilst the penalty for sin was paid by all the first-born sons in Egypt but the Israelites were spared God's judgment because the blood atoned for their sins; God's judgment *passed over* them (Exod 12:13, 23, 27). The Israelites went free from slavery, which is recorded in Shemot 12:37–41.

(iii) The Exodus and Journey to Sinai (Shemot 14–18)

In chapter 14 the Israelites arrived at the Red Sea (or Sea of Reeds). Pharaoh once again hardened his heart and chased after the Israelites to get back his slaves, but God parted the Sea of Reeds so that the Israelites could pass through on dry ground, and then he brought the sea back upon the Egyptian army, destroying them in utter defeat (14:15–28). Chapter 15 contains the victory celebration of the Israelites. As God granted them victory over the Egyptians (Exod 15:1–12), so too he would grant them victory over the occupying nations in the promised land (Exod 15:16–17), once they arrived there.

Before the Israelites entered the promised land, however, God brought them to Mount Sinai, where they met with God. Shemot 15:22 through to the end of chapter 18 narrates the two months' journey from Egypt to Sinai, during which God provided food for them on the way, in the form of manna (chapter 16), and he provided water (Exod 15:22–17; 17:1–7). He was teaching the Israelites in the wilderness that he could provide for all their needs.

(D) MEETING WITH GOD AT SINAI (SHEMOT 19–24, 32–34)

The flow of the storyline largely stops at this point. God had rescued the descendants of Avraham from their slavery in Egypt and he would bring them into the promised land, in fulfillment of the promises he made to the patriarchs. But first he brought them to Sinai to enter into relationship with himself. God made a covenant with his people, the nation of Israel, at Sinai. They were there for about a year, before they moved on to the promised land.

The yearlong stay at Sinai takes up the rest of the book of Shemot, all of Vayyikra (Leviticus), and the first ten chapters of Bemidbar (Numbers).

Not until Bemidbar chapter 10 do the Israelites finally move on from Sinai to head out to the promised land (about one year later). In the meantime, these chapters describe the covenant made at Sinai and its laws, which basically spell out the relationship formed between God and his people Israel. The Sinai covenant established the relationship with God that Avraham's descendants possessed already; keeping the law did not bring them into relationship with God. God had *already* saved them in the exodus,[2] and now that they were God's saved people the Sinai covenant spelled out how they were to relate to their Savior God.

(i) The Covenant at Sinai

In chapter 19 the Israelites prepared to meet with God at Mount Sinai (Exod 19:10–11).

The first three commandments concerned specifically their relationship with God. The first commandment calls for exclusive loyalty to God ("You shall have no other gods before me"). The second commandment forbids idolatry: the making of any object by which to represent God; the Israelites were to relate to God through his word, not through images (see Deut 4:15–19). The third commandment forbids the misuse of God's name, which means honoring God's reputation by speaking what is right about him.

The fourth commandment requires the keeping of Shabbat (the Sabbath), by working for six days and resting for one. The fifth through to tenth commandments speak about how we are to love others (the first four were about how we are to love God): we are to honor our parents, not murder, not commit adultery, not steal; we are to honor the reputation of others by not speaking what is false about them; and we are not to "covet" what belongs to others, that is, not even to *think* about taking what belongs to others (which would lead to adultery and stealing). This final commandment concerns even the thoughts of our hearts. Hence Yeshua, in the Sermon on the Mount, says that being angry with someone is equivalent to murdering them in your heart, and that lusting after a woman is equivalent to committing adultery in your heart (Matt 5:21–30). The Ten Commandments spell out in the broadest possible terms how God's saved people in the old covenant were to live to please God and their fellows. If we are honest with

---

2. Note Shemot 19:4 and 20:1. Before the law is given, God reminds his people that he saved them from Egypt. They don't keep the law to be saved: they are *already* saved. The law tells them how to live as God's saved people.

ourselves, we fall far short of these standards of God, for we truly are sinful (have you ever looked at someone lustfully or been angry with someone?!).

After God spoke the Ten Commandments directly to the people, Moshe alone received the rest of the commandments for the people from God, as recorded in chapters 21–23. These commandments are more specific outlining situations and cases that illustrate breaking the Ten Commandments. For example, Shemot 21:28–29 speaks of an owner's bull killing someone. If this had happened before and the owner didn't take precautions to stop it happening again, such negligence was criminal and amounted to murder. Starting a fire in someone's field amounts to theft (Exod 22:6; cf. 22:5).

Shemot 24 describes how the covenant was formalized between God and the descendants of Avraham, the people of Israel. Moshe then went up the mountain to God for forty days and nights, to receive the two tablets of the law on which God himself wrote the Ten Commandments (Exod 24:12, 15–18).

(ii) Breaking the Covenant

Chapter 32 describes how the Israelites broke the covenant while Moshe was on the mountain with God. The people made a golden calf idol, to represent God in his absence, making sacrifices to the idol in worship (32:1–6). Thus they directly broke the second of the Ten Commandments. In response to Moshe's prayer, God forgave his people and the covenant was renewed (Exod 33–34). But we are shown here, straight after the Sinai covenant had been formalized, two important principles. First, that Israel could not keep God's covenant: they immediately broke it and sinned. And, second, God forgives sin.

(E) THE TABERNACLE AND SACRIFICES (SHEMOT 25–31; 35–40; VAYYIKRA/LEVITICUS)

In fact, the forgiveness of sins is inherent in the entire setup of the Sinai covenant. Many of the laws of the Torah revolve around the tabernacle (later the temple) and its sacrifices. The tabernacle had two purposes: it was the place where God dwelt with his people (Exod 25:8), and it was the place where atonement for their sins was made—for example, by the sacrifices of Vayyikra 1:3–4.

The tabernacle itself showed how God could be approached. There were three "inner circles," so to speak. The outer court was where all God's people could come and offer sacrifices, and the altar was there, on which the sacrifices were burnt. "The Holy Place" was the next inner circle, which the priests alone could enter. The final inner circle was "the Most Holy Place," behind the curtain, where God dwelled above the ark (Exod 25:10–22; Lev 16:2). The curtain before the Most Holy Place was a strong visual reminder that God could not be approached by man in his sinfulness; the curtain barred the way into God's presence.[3]

Because of God's holiness and our sinfulness, the other function of the tabernacle was to allow for sin to be atoned for, which was done by the priests burning sacrifices on the altar in the outer court. The first seven chapters of Vayyikra outline the sacrifices that were made at the tabernacle, a system of sacrifices which was visually graphic—there was death and blood. It graphically portrayed the truths that God is holy, that we are unholy (or sinful), and that our sin must be dealt with for us to stay in relationship with our holy God. All these truths point us straight to the Messiah, Jesus.

In the Brit Chadashah it is made clear that Jesus' death on the cross was *the* sacrifice for sin, which atoned for our sins once for all (Heb 8–10). Thus the curtain of the tabernacle was torn in two at his death (Mark 15:38), showing that access into God's presence was now available, since atonement for sins had been fully made. In other words, the sacrifices of the Torah all pointed ahead to the real sacrifice that would deal with our sins, which took place when Jesus died on the cross. Jesus is also called the temple (John 2:19–21), because he is *the* place where God dwells, as God himself in the flesh (John 1:1–3, 14). Not surprisingly, the temple was destroyed and the sacrifices ceased shortly after Jesus' death and resurrection.

(F) IN THE WILDERNESS (BEMIDBAR/NUMBERS)

In the first ten chapters of Bemidbar the Israelites were still at Sinai one year or so after leaving Egypt. They made preparations to leave Sinai and to head out at last to the promised land (Num 10:11–13), and chapters 11–12 describe the short journey.

Chapters 13–14 are watershed chapters. At this point Israel had at last arrived at the border of the promised land and were ready to go in and take it. God had been faithful to his promises to Avraham: his descendants were

---

3. Aaron, Moshe's brother, had four sons. He and his four sons were the first priests in Israel. Two of his four sons approached God, behind the curtain, in the Most Holy Place and, even though they were priests, they were immediately struck down dead (Vayyikra 10:1–2). They bore the guilt of their sins before God and died, for the penalty for sin is death.

numerous and they were a great nation—Israel. And now God would surely give them the promised land.

Chapter 13 describes the mission of the twelve spies, whom God graciously allowed to see the goodness of the promised land. However, in chapter 14 we read that the Israelites were afraid and refused to go in (Num 14:1-4). In consequence God's judgment was that their generation would wander in the wilderness for forty years until they had died out (Num 14:21-35). Their children, the second generation, would be the ones to go into the promised land; thus God would still be faithful to his promises, despite Israel's unfaithfulness.

Not much is said in the Torah about the forty years of wandering in the wilderness. It is recorded in just a few chapters (Num 15-20). By Bemidbar chapter 20, the forty years were over. Sadly, Moshe finally lost his temper with the people's unfaithfulness and was disobedient to God; the consequence was that he would not enter the promised land (20:10-12).

The second generation, whilst they were able to enter the land, were still sinful (Num 21:4-9).[4] However, a turning point is reached in chapter 21. The second generation at this point achieved three victories under God (see Num 21:1-3, 21-35); they conquered the territory to the east of the Jordan and this was a foretaste of conquering the entire promised land.

(G) MOSHE'S FINAL SPEECHES (DEVARIM/ DEUTERONOMY)

The book of Devarim contains Moshe's final farewell speeches before he died, with Israel still on the border of the promised land (Deut 1:1-5). There is no movement as such in the story between Bemidbar 22:1 and the end of the book of Devarim, when the Israelites move into the promised land at last, as depicted in the book of Joshua. Here on the border of the land Moshe preached three sermons, teaching the second generation of Israelites the importance of God's word and his laws, before they entered the promised land.

Chapter 6 for example contains the famous Shema. Verse 4, like many other verses of the Bible, asserts God's unity, his oneness: he is one God and there is no other (also Deut 4:35). Verse 5 asserts what Jesus called the first and greatest commandment: to love God with all our heart, soul, and strength (Mark 12:29-30). This love for God is shown in obedience to

---

4. Note the difference in this story, however. Atonement for sin is provided in the form of the bronze snake. Whoever looked to it in faith was saved (Num 21:9; cf. John 3:14-15).

his commandments, which are to be internalized (v. 6), taught to the next generation (v. 7), and discussed at all times (vv. 7–9). Israel were to love God by knowing his word and obeying it in the promised land.

7

The Prophets (Nevi'im)

Nevi'im, the Prophets, can be divided into two sections: the Former Prophets and the Latter Prophets. The Former Prophets contain the six books that follow the Torah in our English Bible (minus Ruth): Yehoshua (Joshua), Shoftim (Judges), Shmuel (1 and 2 Samuel), and Melakhim (1 and 2 Kings). The Former Prophets are historical books that give us the history of Israel's time in the promised land up until the exile. They are called "prophets" because they tell history from the point of view of the prophets. It is a prophetic history, meaning a history that focuses on God's interactions with his people. The Former Prophets cover the period of Israel's history from their entry into the promised land, around 1400 BC, to their exile from it in 586 BC (about eight hundred years).

(A) THE CONQUEST OF THE PROMISED LAND (YEHOSHUA/JOSHUA)

The book of Joshua continues the storyline from the end of the Torah: the Israelites were on the border of the promised land, ready to go in and take the land by conquest. Moshe had now died, and Joshua took over the leadership of Israel. The book of Joshua falls into roughly two halves: the conquest of the promised land (chapters 1–12), and the division of the land as an inheritance among the tribes (chapters 13–24). The book of Joshua shows how God was faithful to his promises, giving the descendants of Abraham the promised land.

Chapters 3–4 describe Israel crossing the Jordan river and entering the promised land at last. Chapters 6–12 describe the conquest of various cities (such as Jericho, chapter 6), whereby Israel gained control of the whole land. There were areas that still remained to be conquered (13:1), but the land as a whole was subdued.

Chapters 13–19 describe the division of the land among the tribes and emphasize that if the Israelites were faithful to God, they would be able to conquer the rest of the promised land and fully occupy the territories given to each tribe. Chapter 21, verses 43–45 emphasize that God had been faithful, keeping his promises to Avraham in giving them the land.

(B) THE PERIOD OF THE JUDGES (SHOFTIM/JUDGES)

The book of Judges narrates the first period of Israel's life in the promised land. A "judge" is like a king. The word "judge" doesn't mean here a legal judge of a court; it has a wider meaning, such as an "administrator," "governor" or "ruler." The judge was a leader, who often went to war, leading Israel against her enemies. In this sense a judge was like the later kings. But the difference was that the judge's firstborn son did not inherit the role; judges were not hereditary, like kings. God raised up judges as needed.

Chapters 1–2 give a two-part introduction to the book. Chapters 3–16 narrate the stories of the judges themselves. And chapters 17–21 give a two-part epilogue to the book. Chapter 1 outlines Israel's disobedience: they failed to drive out the Canaanites from their tribal territories allotted to them by Yehoshua. The punishment therefore was that God would leave the Canaanites among them. Thus it is important to understand at the outset that Israel's problems with foreign nations, such as the Philistines, were not because of the latter's superior military power, but due to their own disobedience.

Verses 11–19 of chapter 2 are a very important passage in the book of Judges. They outline in summary a cycle that is seen over and over throughout the book. First, the Israelites disobeyed God and then God judged them for their sin (2:11–15). Next in the cycle, usually the people cried out to God in their distress; that is, they turned back to God in repentance (that is missing from the summary of the cycle here). Then God would raise up a judge who saved them from their enemies, leading to a time of peace for the rest of the lifetime of that judge, but then the cycle would start again, as Israel turned their backs on God and disobeyed him again (2:16–19). Thus there was a cycle of: sin, judgment, salvation, and then sin again.

There are six "major" judges and six "minor" ones (only briefly mentioned). The six major judges are: Otniel (Othniel; Judg 3:7-12), Ehud (Judg 3:12-30), Baraq (Barak; Judg 4-5), Gidon (Gideon; Judg 6-8), Yiftach (Jephthah; Judg 10-12), and Shimshon (Samson; Judg 13-16). These men were often greatly flawed, but in the end were men of faith whom God used to save his people (Heb 11:32-34). They point us to Yeshua, who, unlike the judges, was without sin, but like them is a savior of his people—actually, the ultimate savior from sin itself.

The epilogue of the book of Judges shows us how chaotic and ungodly was the time of the judges. However, the book of Ruth presents another side to the story during this time, showing us that God was indeed at work. The book of Ruth is in the Ketuvim section of the Hebrew Bible, but comes next in our English Bibles because it occurs in the time of the judges. The book of Ruth tells the story of Naomi, an Israelite who went to Moab (a neighboring country) because of famine. Her husband and both her sons died there, leaving her with two daughters-in-law, one of whom, Ruth, refused to leave Naomi and came back to the promised land with her; in effect, Ruth became an Israelite. She ended up marrying Boaz and her great-grandson was King David. This shows us that even in the chaotic time of the Judges, with so much disobedience to God, there were still faithful Israelites and even faithful non-Israelites like Ruth. And God achieved his plans through them, bringing about the birth of David, the forerunner and ancestor of the Messiah.

(C) THE BOOKS OF SHMUEL (1 AND 2 SAMUEL): KINGSHIP IN ISRAEL

The books of Shmuel (1 and 2 Samuel) and Melakhim (1 and 2 Kings) give a continuous history from the time of the judges until the Babylonian exile, when Israel was expelled from the promised land. In this period we also move also from judges to kings as the leaders of God's people. This is very important in the Bible's storyline, because the promises of God to Avraham will now be expanded to include promises about God's king (2 Sam 7).[1]

The first seven chapters of 1 Samuel are very similar to the book of Judges. We witness again the classic Judges cycle: Israel sinned (chapter 2); Israel was defeated by a foreign power as punishment for their sin (chapter 4); Israel repented (chapter 7); God raised up a savior/judge to rescue them in the person of Samuel, the judge and prophet (chapter 7).

---

1. The king of Israel is the "messiah" or "mashiach." The word "messiah" means "anointed one," that is, one anointed as king; it is simply a word for God's king.

Chapter 8 jumps ahead in time to Samuel's old age. The Israelites asked him to appoint them a king, because they wanted to be like the nations around them, a request which was viewed as the climax of Israel's sinfulness because of Israel's motives; it was a rejection of God as their king. Yet God granted their request (8:9), and so kings would be part of God's plan from that point on (8:4–9).

Shaul (Saul), from the tribe of Benjamin, was chosen to be the first king (1 Sam 9). Chapters 13–15 outline Saul's disobedience, a man who failed to trust God, even though he was a great military leader who defeated the Philistines and other enemies (14:47–48). The end result was that Saul was rejected by God as his king (15:26).

God did not do away with the kingship, however, but told Samuel to go and anoint David as the next king (16:1–13). The following chapters then narrate a strange time in the history of Israel in which there were two kings: one on the throne (Saul), and one anointed but not yet enthroned (David). The story of 1 Sam 16—2 Sam 4 is about David's sufferings before he took his throne. Saul tried in numerous ways to kill David (1 Sam 18–19), and David ended up fleeing to save his own life; he lived in the wilderness, constantly on the run, during this period. In the end though, Saul was killed in battle and David was made king (2 Sam 5:1–5). The section of 1 Sam 16—2 Sam 4 is a long and important section of the storyline, one in which David had to suffer before taking his throne as king. In this he prefigured Jesus, who often taught the same: that the Messiah must suffer before taking his throne. Many of David's psalms were written during this period, as their headings attest, and describe his trust in God during his period of suffering (for example, Pss 52–59).

Once David was made king, he proceeded to capture Yerushalayim (Jerusalem) and he brought the ark of God into the city (2 Sam 5–6). David then planned to build a special house for the ark—a permanent tabernacle, called the "temple." However, God told David not to build the temple yet; his son Solomon would build it instead (7:1–13). In a play on words, God said that although David would not build God's *house*, God would build a *house* for David (7:11b); that is, God would make a lasting *dynasty* for him. Second Samuel 7 is one of the most important chapters in the Tanakh. From now on, there would be always be a king in the line of David, ruling over Israel (7:13–16); and one day a perfect, righteous king in the line of David would come—the Messiah. Chapter 7 then has two key promises: that David's son would build the temple and that he would rule over Israel and his descendants after him (the Davidic dynasty).

David then proceeded to conquer the surrounding nations, bringing peace to the promised land and God's people (2 Sam 8–12). Sadly, David then showed that he was not the Messiah himself. Whilst David was a great king, he was also a sinful man like us. He committed adultery with Bathsheba and murdered her husband to cover up his sin (chapter 11), for which he repented, but God's punishment for his sin was that adultery and murder would now plague his family (12:9–12): David's son Amnon raped his half sister Tamar (13:1–20); his son Avshalom (Absalom) murdered Amnon and usurped David's throne (13–15), but Absalom was killed in an ensuing battle and David retook his throne (18–19). However, David was a broken man, shattered over the loss of his son Absalom (2 Sam 18:33—19:7). Although David is held up as an ideal king to follow in the books of Melakhim, his story shows his sins and flaws. He trusted in God very much, as his psalms in particular show, but he was a sinful man like us. He himself could only hope that one of his descendants would be different (Pss 2, 110; Mark 12:35–37).

(D) THE BOOKS OF MELAKHIM (1 AND 2 KINGS): FROM SOLOMON UNTIL THE EXILE

(i) The Reign of King Solomon (1 Kgs 1–11)

The books of Kings continue the storyline straight on from the books of Samuel. King Solomon, David's son, took the throne of Israel after the death of David (1 Kgs 1–2) and God granted him great wisdom (chapter 3). Solomon's main achievement was the building of the temple (chapters 5–8) but he also established a kingdom that covered a large area from the Euphrates river in the north to Egypt in the south.

At this point in the storyline we have reached a high point, because the promises to Avraham were almost all fulfilled within the history of Israel under King Solomon. The promises to Avraham were that his descendants would be a great nation, that they would inherit the promised land, and that they would be blessed and all nations would be blessed through them. The promises to David also were that his son would sit on the throne and build the temple. Almost all these promises had now come to fruition. Israel was a great nation, ruling over the surrounding countries and at peace. She fully possessed the promised land (1 Kgs 4:20–21, 25). David's son sat on the throne and had built the temple (8:14–21). Israel was blessed. There were even hints that the nations would now be blessed through them (such as the visit of the queen of Sheba; 10:1–13).

Sadly, however, Solomon abandoned God later in life (1 Kgs 11:1–13). Blessing did not come to the nations through Israel; that would only come later. Thus the promises were yet to be fulfilled. After the death of Solomon, Israel was split into two and there was a loss of land, empire, and glory. From the high point of Israel's history under King Solomon, things then went downhill . . .

(ii) The Divided Kingdom (1 Kgs 12–16)

You may recall that I suggested the Bible can be broken up into a storyline of three eras. We have now finished our overview of the first era and will commence our overview of the second era. From this point on Israel's fortunes in the promised land steadily declined until they were ejected from the land. Under Solomon's son, King Rechavam (Rehoboam), Israel was split into two. The northern ten tribes were known as "Israel" and the southern two tribes (Judah and Benjamin) were known as "Judah." Rehoboam ruled only over Judah. The northern tribes set over them another king, Yarovam (Jeroboam). Since the temple was in Judah's territory, in Jerusalem, Jeroboam proceeded to install a new religion in the north; although it was based on God's true religion as revealed in the Torah, he set up golden calves in the north and south of his territory as an alternative to the temple in Jerusalem, and the people of Israel offered sacrifices to them. He hoped that this would stop the Israelites of the ten northern tribes from going to Jerusalem and thereby reverting to the Davidic kingship (1 Kgs 12:25–33).

The rest of the books of Kings give a history of the kings of the north and the south. The kings of the north are universally seen as evil kings, because they continued in the sinful idolatry that Jeroboam had set up (for example, 15:26, 34). The northern ten tribes never repented of the false religion that they had set up, contrary to the Torah.

The kings of the south were in the line of David. Some were good kings; some were unfaithful to God; but God had promised that the Davidic dynasty would continue (2 Sam 7; cf. 1 Kgs 15:3–4).

At this point I will mention the prophets. God spoke to individual Israelites, telling them his will, which they then spoke to God's people. Such individuals are called "prophets." Avraham was called a prophet (Gen 20:7), Moshe was a prophet (Deut 18:15–18), and other prophets are mentioned throughout the books of Samuel and Kings. At this stage, the words of the prophets were not written down in books, like the later prophets were, but they were great prophets nonetheless, such as Eliyyahu (Elijah) and Elisha, who appear in the second half of 1 Kings through to the first half of 2 Kings. God warned his people, through these prophets, to repent. The Israelites needed to return to God and obey him. Failure to do so would result in a reversal of the promises to Abraham: they would become fewer in number, be conquered by their enemies, and be ejected from the promised land. These punishments were known as the "covenant curses," inflicted on God's people for persistent disobedience and rebellion against him (Lev 26 and Deut 28).

(iii) The End of the Northern Ten Tribes (1 Kgs 16 to 2 Kgs 17)

In the northern ten tribes, King Ahab married a princess of Tyre (a foreign nation to the north) named Jezebel (1 Kgs 16:29–31). She introduced her own foreign god, Baal, into Israel and God's people worshiped this god. Elijah was sent by God to confront his people with their sin and call on them to return to God (1 Kgs 17–18). He was able to show them that God is the only true God and that Baal is a fictional god (18:22–39) so that eventually Baal worship was purged from the north (2 Kgs 9–10). In the south Baal worship briefly gained a foothold before being purged from there too (2 Kgs 11).

The ten northern tribes, however, never repented of their idolatry. Jeroboam introduced his calf idols into Israel around 930 BC and the northern kingdom only lasted about two hundred years after that. God sent prophets to warn them to turn back to him, but they would not listen (2 Kgs 17:13–17).

In the first half of the eighth century BC there was a growing period of stability in the north and the south during the long reign of Jeroboam II (2 Kgs 14:23). By the mid-eighth century BC the borders of the land were probably once again the same as they were under the kingdom of Solomon and there was peace. Internationally, the superpower Assyria was gaining ascendancy and had subdued the surrounding nations. The prophets warned the northern tribes that God would send the Assyrians to defeat them and take them away from the promised land unless they repented (for example, Hos 9:3; 10:6; 11:5).

The first two of the writing prophets (prophets who have their words written down in books named after them), Amos and Hosea, spoke at this time against the sins of the north, calling on God's people to repent.[2] They

---

2. The prophets whose words were written down in books named after them are called the "Latter Prophets." The Latter Prophets section of the Tanakh contains the "big three" prophetic books of Yeshayahu (Isaiah), Yirmeyahu (Jeremiah), and Yechezkel (Ezekiel), and the twelve "minor" prophets that our English Old Testament's finish with: Hoshea (Hosea), Yoel (Joel), Amos (Amos), Ovadya (Obadiah), Yona (Jonah), Mikha (Micah), Nachum (Nahum), Chavaqquq (Habakkuk), Tzefanya (Zephaniah), Chaggay (Haggai), Zekharya (Zechariah), and Malaki (Malachi). Those twelve books are called "minor" prophets not because they are less important than the big three, but because

spoke of the great social and moral decay during this time. Despite the outwardly healthy appearance of life in Israel during this prosperous period, internally Israel was in an advanced state of decay. The poor were oppressed by the wealthy (Amos 2:6–7; 5:11; 8:4–6); the people were religious, but it was not the true worship of God (4:4–5; 5:21–24). Israel, the northern tribes, probably took God's blessings upon them as a sign of his favor. However, their disobedience would soon result in judgment; the prophets Amos and Hosea pronounced the coming judgment of God upon them.

Hosea speaks movingly of God's covenant with his people as a marriage. God loves his people, but they had been unfaithful, like an adulterous wife (Hos 1–3). God yearns for his people to come back to him and love him; he does not want to bring his judgment upon them, but because of their stubborn refusal to return to God they would be sent into exile to Assyria (9:10—10:8). Yet there was still hope for the future, because God would keep his promises to his people, despite their sin (1:10—2:1; 14–23; 11:8–11).

And so the Assyrians came. In 724 BC they invaded the land and in 722 BC the capital of the north, Samaria, fell and the people were taken to Assyria in exile (2 Kgs 17:3–6). The Tanakh makes it clear that all this happened to Israel because of their sin (2 Kgs 17:7, 13–15, 18, 23).

(iv) The Exile of Judah (2 Kgs 18–25)

Second Kings 17 makes it clear that Judah was not much better than her northern sister Israel (17:13, 19); thus the downfall of the northern tribes anticipated also the downfall of Judah. Judah did not fall to the Assyrians at this time because King Ahaz, an evil king, had paid tribute and become their vassal (16:2–4, 7). That is, he didn't trust in God, but simply gave in to the enemy. However, Ahaz's son Hizkiyya (Hezekiah) was one of the godliest kings of Judah, who reigned in Judah after the fall of the north and sought to throw off the shackles of the Assyrians (18:3–7); he trusted in God. Sennacherib, king of Assyria, threatened to destroy Jerusalem and the temple (18:17–35)[3] but Hezekiah refused to give in and the prophet Isaiah backed him. Isaiah prophesied that Jerusalem would be saved and the Assyrian army was subsequently annihilated by an epidemic sent by God (19:30–36).

The period between the death of Hezekiah and the fall of Jerusalem was exactly one hundred years (686–586 BC). Hezekiah's son Menashshe (Manasseh) reigned for fifty-five years (2 Kgs 21:1) and was the exact

---

the books are much smaller in size.

3. This was in the year 701 BC.

reverse of his father: he was the worst of all the kings of Judah. He sacrificed his son and followed the pagan practices of the nations; in fact he is said to have done more evil than the Canaanites who were previously in the land (21:2–11). As a result, God pronounced judgment on Judah: Jerusalem would be destroyed and the people would go into exile (21:12–15).

Manasseh's grandson Yoshiyyahu (Josiah), like Hezekiah, was one of the most godly kings ever to reign over Judah. Chapters 22–23 focus largely on Josiah's reforms. Around this time the great Assyrian Empire was losing its power and Josiah was free to conduct his reforms—he got rid of all the foreign religious worship practices in Judah—and because of his godliness the exile was delayed until after his death (22:18–20).

It seems that Josiah's reforms were successful, but, sadly, they did not last. Only four more kings would come before Judah fell. Three of these four kings were sons of Josiah and one was his grandson; they were all said to be evil kings, who did not follow in his ways.

Towards the end of the seventh century BC the Assyrians were no longer an empire[4] and the Babylonian Empire was on the ascendancy. The Babylonians came three times to Judah and they took over the promised land in 605 BC (2 Kgs 24:1, 7). At this time they carried some of the leading people into exile to Babylon, among them Daniyyel (Daniel). The book of Daniel, in the Ketuvim section of the Tanakh, describes how he and his friends lived during exile in Babylon: they fitted in with Babylonian society but would not compromise in their obedience to God.

When the king of Judah rebelled against his Babylonian overlords, the king of Babylon, Nebuchadnezzar, marched against the promised land and took it over in 597 BC (2 Kgs 24:10–16). The king, the royal family, and many of the leading citizens were deported to Babylon, among them the prophet Ezekiel. When the next king of Judah rebelled against the Babylonians, they came and laid siege to Jerusalem in response (25:1–2). After about a year and a half the city fell (25:3–4); one month later the Babylonians came and destroyed the temple, the palace, and the walls of the city, taking most of the people into exile (25:8–12) whilst leaving only the poorest in the land.

We should pause at this point to consider God's promises made to Avraham and David. Since the middle of the book of 2 Kings it has been like

---

4. The Latter Prophets such as Isaiah spoke against the Assyrians. However, two books are entirely devoted to them. In the eighth century BC the prophet Jonah was sent to preach God's judgment against the Assyrian capital, Nineveh. His book describes their mass repentance upon Jonah's preaching. It was a foretaste of how the gospel would go to the nations, including even the enemies of God's people (cf. Isa 19:23–25). In the seventh century BC, maybe a century later, the prophet Nahum, however, declared that God's judgment had come at last upon the Assyrians for their cruel oppression of the surrounding nations (as indeed it had).

watching a movie going backwards. The land promised to Avraham's descendants shrank in size, as it was conquered little by little (2 Kgs 10:32–33); and then it was lost altogether in the exile. The people, likewise, promised to be as numerous as the sand on the seashore, steadily dwindled in number until only a remnant of Judah was left. The blessing promised to them was apparently undone, and the covenant curses of the Torah came upon them instead (Lev 26, Deut 28). The promises to David of a temple for God and a king on the throne also appeared to have been undone—the temple was destroyed and the king taken into exile. But how could this happen? Does not God keep his word? Doesn't he keep his promises? Was this the end of God's people and kingdom? To answer these questions we turn now briefly to the message of the Latter Prophets.

(E) THE LATTER PROPHETS

Just as there were prophets like Amos and Hosea who warned the northern tribes before they fell,[5] so too there were prophets who warned the people of Judah before they went into exile. The prophet Ezekiel was taken into exile in the deportation of 597 BC, and he prophesied to the exiles in Babylon for the next eleven years, while Jerusalem and the temple still stood. He warned them that God's judgment would fall upon Jerusalem and the temple, as indeed it did. Other prophets such as Habakkuk and Zephaniah likewise prophesied the fall of Judah at the hands of the Babylonians. Jeremiah spoke extensively about the judgment of God to come upon the people of Judah over a long period of time (Jer 1:1–3). God had warned his people for decades (in fact, for centuries) about the covenant curses: punishment for disobeying him and rebelling against him.

These prophets not only spoke about God's judgment but also spoke of restoration after the judgment of God. God would indeed punish sin, but sin would not thwart his overall purposes; God would still keep his promises to his people, *despite* their sin. Moshe in the Torah spoke of the exile of God's people and their restoration after exile.[6] This return from exile was described in terms of a new heart for God's people: God would circumcise their hearts so that they would now obey God in the promised land (Deut 30:1–6; 10:16; 31:20–21). For if God merely returned the people physically to the land, they would sin and disobey him once more, and be sent into exile again. The prophets spoke of a new covenant in which God would

---

5. I mentioned them in chapter 7 (D) (iii).

6. Moshe spoke about these things around 1400 BC, some 800 years before their time.

forgive his people their sins and change their hearts so that they would obey him. You can read what God says about this new covenant in Jer 31:31–34 and Ezek 36:24–28 (and 11:17–20).

In fact Jeremiah prophesied that the exile would be temporary, lasting seventy years (Jer 29:10). The exile was a temporary punishment; God would indeed still be faithful to his promises.

In addition, the prophet Isaiah spoke of a new exodus in which God's people would return to the promised land through the wilderness (Isa 40:3–5; 43:16–19). Just as God's people were saved from Egypt and brought into the promised land, so they would also be saved from Babylon and brought back to the promised land—as indeed they were.

Isaiah also spoke of the Messiah, who would be born of a virgin (Isa 7:10–14) and would be a perfect king in the line of David, ruling forever (Isa 9:2–7; 11:1–9). He spoke of the Messiah as the Servant of God. Whilst the Servant of God was at first identified as Israel (Isa 41:8–10), Israel failed in her service of God (Isa 42:18–25) so that Israel as the Servant narrowed down to a faithful remnant within Judah (1 Kgs 19:18; Isa 10:21–22); but even that faithful remnant, who trusted in God, was not without sin. In the end the Servant of God was an individual, who was without sin, and who would bring justice and salvation to the nations, in fulfillment of the promises to Abraham (Isa 49:5–6). Yet he would be put to death, though he was without sin (Isa 53:8–9), the prophet revealing that his death was in the plan of God, for the servant died in the place of Israel to pay the penalty of death that they deserved for their sins (Isa 53:4–6). The sacrifices at the temple had shown Israel that only blood atones for sin (Lev 17:11).[7] The Servant of God would shed his blood and die for Israel's sins, taking the punishment of sin, namely death, upon himself in their place, to bring them forgiveness of sins (Isa 53:5, 11). This is the way in which God would forgive the sins of his people in the new covenant when they were restored to the promised land after the exile.

So, the Latter Prophets warned God's people of his judgment that was coming in the form of the exile, but they also held out great hope that after the exile God's people would be restored to the promised land, and forgiven all their sins in a new covenant through the death of the Messiah in their place.

---

7. The rabbis today deny that God would ever use a human sacrifice to atone for sin. Of course human sacrifice as a means of appeasing God is forbidden in the Tanakh (Devarim 18:10). However, God does indeed, strangely, use such a sacrifice to atone for sin (2 Sam 21:1–14). This points us to the Messiah who would atone for all our sins (Isa 53:4–6).

(F) AFTER THE EXILE: THE RETURN TO THE PROMISED LAND

As Jeremiah prophesied, the exile lasted approximately seventy years. The Babylonian Empire fell in 539 BC to the Persians and Medes. King Cyrus of the new Persian Empire allowed God's people to return to the promised land in 538 BC.[8]

The books of the Bible that cover this last period of the Tanakh (after the exile) are: the final three of the Latter Prophets (Haggai, Zechariah and Malachi) and the books of Ezra and Nehemiah in Ketuvim.[9]

When the exiles returned in 538 BC, they began rebuilding the temple. They immediately rebuilt the altar and resumed the sacrifices (Ezra 3). However, opposition to the rebuilding of the temple brought it to a halt (Ezra 4), until 520 BC, which is when the prophets Haggai and Zechariah (his contemporary) spoke to the returned exiles to encourage them to get on with the work of rebuilding the temple, which was finally completed in 515 BC (Ezra 6:14–15).

At this stage of the history of God's people, after the return to the land, things looked rather grim: they were small in number, struggling, under a foreign power (the Persians), and none of the glorious promises of the prophets seemed to be coming true. Into this situation the postexilic prophets spoke. They encouraged the returned exiles and made clear that God's promises would yet come true in the future.[10]

The last part of the storyline of the Tanakh occurs in the fifth century BC. Ezra 7–10 and the book of Nehemiah speak of a later period, after the building of the second temple, in the mid-fifth century BC, when Ezra and Nehemiah came to Jerusalem. Ezra came in 458 BC (Ezra 7) to teach God's word to the postexilic community. He confessed the sins of the people (Ezra 9) and called on them to turn back to God. The people, after the exile, had not been living God's way (shown by their intermarriages with foreign peoples around them, which was contrary to the law; Ezra 10).

Nehemiah came to Jerusalem thirteen years later in 445 BC, and he saw to the rebuilding of the walls of Jerusalem. He and Ezra joined forces to teach God's word (Neh 8). They called on God's people to obey God in the land; in particular, to see to the upkeep of the temple by giving tithes, to keep the Sabbath, and not to intermarry with foreigners (Neh 10). At the end of the Tanakh, at about 430 BC, it records that God's people after the

---

8. The Cyrus decree can be read in Ezra 1:1–4 (also 2 Chr 36:22–23).
9. The book of Ester (Esther) also takes place after the exile.
10. See especially Hag 2:6–9 and Zech 9–14.

exile were disobeying God in these precise areas (shown in Neh 13 and in the prophet Malachi, who prophesied around this time). They still needed a new heart and God's Spirit to move them to obey him. The new covenant and true restoration had still not come; nor would it come, until about 450 years later, when the Messiah Yeshua arrived.

8

The Writings (Ketuvim)

BEFORE WE MOVE ON to the Brit Chadashah and speak of the Messiah Jesus, let me mention briefly the third and last section of the Tanakh: Ketuvim (the Writings). The books within Ketuvim are: Tehillim (Psalms), Mishlei (Proverbs), Iyyov (Job), Shir HaShirim (Song of Songs), Rut (Ruth), Ekha (Lamentations), Kohelet (Ecclesiastes), Ester (Esther), Daniyyel (Daniel), Ezra-Nechemya (Ezra and Nehemiah), and Divre Hayyamim (1 and 2 Chronicles). These books of the Tanakh mostly do not advance the storyline of the Bible but they fit *within* the storyline (except for Ezra and Nehemiah, discussed in the previous section).

Psalms are the songs of praise to God, many of which were written by King David. David's son Solomon was given wisdom by God and he wrote much of what is called the "wisdom literature" in the Bible. The latter includes Proverbs and perhaps Song of Songs and Ecclesiastes (or parts of them). Proverbs explains how to live life well in this creation: the wise person fears God and lives according to reality as it is built into God's good creation. The books of Job and Ecclesiastes examine life in this world when it accords more with the fall rather than with God's good creation. That is, sometimes the righteous suffer and are not blessed by God for their wisdom and obedience. We may not even know why this is so, but God knows why.[1]

The story of Ruth, as mentioned previously, takes place during the time of the judges. Lamentations, by tradition attributed to Jeremiah, was written during the exile. It is a series of lamentations about the suffering of God's people due to the fall of the temple and Jerusalem. The story of Daniel, as

---

1. See Job 1–2.

The Writings (Ketuvim)

also mentioned previously, also occurs during the exile. Esther takes place during the period of the Persian Empire after the return from exile. Here we read of an attempted genocide of God's people which was overturned by God and celebrated thereafter in the festival of Purim. And, finally, 1 and 2 Chronicles is a history of David and Solomon and their descendants, the kings of Judah, down to the exile, in parallel with the books of Samuel and Kings.

These books are an important part of the Tanakh, but they fit largely *within* the storyline of the Bible.

Questions

1. Avraham and David are the two pivotal persons in the development of the promise in God's plan of salvation in the Tanakh. What promises were made to them and how were they fulfilled? Does anything remain to be fulfilled?
2. How do the three eras in the Bible's storyline connect with the covenants God has made?
3. What different types of literature are there in the Tanakh? How do these differences affect how you interpret their message?

9

The Brit Chadashah (New Testament)

We come now to our third and last era of the storyline of the Bible: the fulfillment of the promises to Avraham and David.

(A) THE GOSPELS

After several hundred years of silence in which God's purposes seemed to be in abeyance, John the Baptist was born (Luke 1:5–25, 57–80). His prophetic ministry as an adult was to proclaim that the long-awaited Messiah would now come and that Israel needed to turn back to God and be ready for him (Luke 3:1–18).

The Gospels tell the story of the coming of the Messiah Yeshua. There are four Gospels: Matthew, Mark, Luke, and John. The first three Gospels are very similar to each other, and although John contains some similar stories (especially Jesus' death and resurrection) his account is quite different to the other three. The Gospels tell the story of the birth, life, miracles, teachings, death, and resurrection of Yeshua but only Matthew and Luke mention his birth, celebrated at Christmas. Mostly the Gospels focus on the final three years of his life, and particularly the last week of his life leading up to his death.

John's Gospel tells us that Jesus existed from all eternity; he was with God and is God (John 1:1–3, 14). All creation came to be through him (John 1:3, Col 1:15–17), and at one point in the history of our world he came to earth as a man; Jesus is God in the flesh.[1] Matthew's and Luke's Gospels

---

1. Col 1:19, 2:9; Heb 1:3.

trace Jesus' ancestry back to Abraham and King David (Matt 1:1-17, Luke 3:23-38); that is, Jesus was descended from David, as the Messiah, and came to fulfill the promises of God to Abraham, especially bringing blessing to all nations.[2]

The Gospels emphasize how the coming of Jesus fulfilled the prophecies of the Tanakh about the Messiah: Jesus was born of a virgin[3] in Bethlehem;[4] he was the suffering servant prophesied by Isaiah;[5] the accounts of his death on the cross in the Gospels are filled with comments on the fulfillment of prophecies in the Tanakh.[6] There are many other prophecies fulfilled that could be mentioned here, but space does not permit.

Jesus' teaching can be summed up as announcing that the kingdom of God, God's rule, had arrived with him (Mark 1:14-15). Daniel had spoken of the coming kingdom of God, and Jeremiah revealed God's new covenant, all ushering in the long-awaited restoration of Israel. Jesus was announcing that with him all the promises of the prophets would now be fulfilled and God's kingdom would come. Mark records how Jesus taught in the synagogues (Mark 1:21-22)—the substance of his teaching was that the kingdom of God had come, and that people needed to repent and believe (Mark 1:15).

Matthew and Luke give much more detail than Mark about Jesus' teachings. Matthew chapters 5-7 are a famous record of Jesus' teaching, called the Sermon on the Mount.[7] Here Jesus made it clear that he had come not to overthrow but to fulfill the Tanakh and all that it said (Matt 5:17). He also made it clear that it wasn't enough just to know what the Tanakh says; the true person of God would actually follow and obey what it says (Matt 5:19-20). Jesus made it clear that trying to get around the laws of Moshe would not do (Matt 5:20; 6:1-8, 16-18); perfect obedience is God's standard. Sin comes from within us (Mark 7:20-23) and we all desperately need forgiveness of our sins (Mark 2:17, 10:45). Only those who think they are OK as they are would not be forgiven (because they rejected God's forgiveness freely offered to them).

Jesus performed many miracles. These mainly consisted of healing people of their afflictions and diseases (Matt 8-9)—pointing to the coming

2. Gal 3:8-9, 14.
3. Isa 7:14 and Matt 1:20-23.
4. Mic 5:2 and Matt 2:1-8.
5. See especially Isa 53 and Matt 8:17.
6. Such as him being pierced for our sins (Zech 12:10 and John 19:37), his clothes being divided up (Ps 22:18 and Mark 15:24, see also other parts of Ps 22), and none of his bones being broken (Exod 12:46 and John 19:36), etc.
7. See also Luke 6:17-49.

time in the perfected kingdom of God when there would be no illness but perfect health, as at the beginning in the Garden of Eden. Jesus' miracles were like sermon illustrations, showing what the perfected kingdom of God would be like; he even raised the dead (Mark 5:35–42, Luke 7:11–15, John 11)—in God's kingdom there would be no more death but eternal life.

But there was opposition to Jesus as he taught and healed (Mark 3:6). He was popular with the crowds of Jews who followed him, and so the leaders of the Jews became jealous (Mark 15:10). Jesus also had mercy on people of all backgrounds: Jews who were prostitutes, traitors, and disreputable were all healed and forgiven by Jesus if they repented; this offended the leaders of the Jews (Mark 2:13–17).

It was not immediately obvious to people at the time that Jesus was the Messiah; even his followers took quite a while to realize the truth. The crowds of Jews who followed Jesus certainly thought that he was someone special; they believed he was a prophet (Mark 6:14–15; 8:27–28) but Jesus was far more than a prophet—as Peter, one of the apostles, at last confessed that Jesus was the Messiah (Mark 8:29–30).

After this, Jesus taught his followers what it meant for him to be the Messiah, and what it meant for them to follow him (Mark 8:31–38). The Jewish people of Jesus' time believed that the Messiah would be a conquering king, like David, but Jesus knew that the true conquering king, like David, first had to suffer before taking his throne. So, Jesus "began to teach them that the Son of Man must suffer many things, and be rejected by the elders and chief priests and scribes, and be killed, and after three days rise again" (Mark 8:31). His followers were to likewise deny themselves and take up their cross (Mark 8:34).

In the end, one of Jesus' disciples, Judas, betrayed him to the Jewish leaders, who handed him over to the Roman authorities (Matt 26:14–16, 47–48). The charge against him was . . . being the Messiah! Jesus was claiming to be the king of the Jews, a rival to the Roman emperor (John 18:28—19:16). The penalty was death by crucifixion. Jesus was put to death according to the charge of being the king of the Jews (John 19:17–22). But as Isa 53 said, he was put to death, though an innocent man, for our sins and in our place, to bring us forgiveness with God.

The story of the Gospels does not end here. Jesus, on the third day, rose from the dead (Mark 16:1–7); then he was seen alive by many witnesses (Luke 24; 1 Cor 15:1–8).

(B) THE BOOK OF ACTS

The book of Acts was written by Luke. It continues from his Gospel account with the history of the early church after the death and resurrection of Yeshua. It tells the story of the Yeshua's followers, especially Saul of Tarsus (Paul), and the spread of early Christianity, first among the Jews and then even among non-Jews (Goyim or Gentiles). The letters that make up most of the rest of the Brit Chadashah fit into the storyline of the book of Acts; those of Paul were largely sent to churches that he founded, as described in Acts.

The book of Acts starts in Jerusalem with a small group of Jesus' closest followers who were witnesses to his ascension (Acts 1:12–15). Jesus died and rose from the dead at Pesach, and some weeks later at Shavuot the new covenant at last arrived (Acts 2). God sent his Holy Spirit to convict his people of the truth and bring them forgiveness of sins. Thousands of Jewish people now turned to God as they put their trust in Jesus (Acts 2:37–41; 6:7). Subsequently some of the Samaritans (like half-Jews) turned to God and put their trust in Jesus (Acts 8:4–8, 25). Finally, Saul (Paul) was converted (Acts 9:1–19) and was appointed to take the good news of Jesus to non-Jews (Acts 9:15). Much of the book of Acts explains how Paul traveled across the Roman world taking the good news of Yeshua to both Jewish and non-Jewish people. Many Jews were saved, fulfilling God's promise to the fathers, and so were many Gentiles, demonstrating God's mercy for all, so that churches were formed everywhere—a story which continues to this day as the gospel reaches all nations. The promises of God to Abraham, that the nations would be blessed through his descendants, were finally being fulfilled as the message of Jesus the Jewish Messiah was accepted even by non-Jews.

(C) THE EPISTLES

The Epistles (or letters) were written to early churches and individuals by the apostles (Yeshua's leaders who were eyewitnesses of his life, death, and resurrection). The churches they write to are referred to in the book of Acts. The letters of Romans, 1 and 2 Corinthians, Galatians, Ephesians, Philippians, Colossians, and 1 and 2 Thessalonians were written by Paul to the churches of those cities or regions, most of which churches were founded by him. First and Second Timothy and Titus are letters by Paul to individuals of those names who were Paul's helpers in establishing the early churches.

Hebrews is a letter written to Jewish believers, although we are uncertain who the author was. The letters that follow were not written to individuals or churches, but to Christians in general. They were written by James the brother of Jesus, and the apostles Peter, John, and Jude: James; 1 and 2 Peter; 1, 2, and 3 John; and Jude.

These letters explain, often to new believers, what the Christian message is and how to live God's way in the light of it. The letter to the Romans is Paul's great explanation of the good news of Jesus.[8] Other letters explain many issues confronting Christians, including being persecuted for the faith. They explain how the promises of the Tanakh are fulfilled in Yeshua, whilst some promises, like the resurrection of our bodies, await his return (Ezek 37:1–14 and 1 Cor 15:35–58).

(D) THE BOOK OF REVELATION

The book of Revelation was written by the apostle John to seven particular churches (in an area that is within modern Turkey). It takes the form of a vision given by the risen Lord Jesus to John, showing him what will happen to the churches in his time, whilst also looking forward into the future until the return of Jesus. The book ends with Jesus' return and his final victory over evil. Then will come the new Jerusalem, the new heavens and earth, where there will be no more suffering or death, but eternal life with God (Rev 21:1–4).

QUESTIONS

1. The central focus of each of the four Gospels is the Lord Jesus. What are the main similarities and differences in their presentation of him and his ministry?

2. What is the purpose of the book of Acts?

3. Each of the New Testament letters was written with a specific aim in mind. State that aim for each one in a single sentence.

4. What is the purpose of the book of Revelation?

---

8. Chapters 9–11 of Romans is the key place in the Berit Chadashah that explains God's plan for his Jewish people.

FURTHER READING

Goldsworthy, Graeme. *The Goldsworthy Trilogy*. Milton Keynes: Paternoster, 2001.
Longman, Tremper (III), and Raymond B. Dillard. *An Introduction to the Old Testament*. Grand Rapids: Zondervan, 2006.
Machen, J. G. *The New Testament: An Introduction to Its Literature and History*. Edinburgh: Banner of Truth, 1976.
Roberts, Vaughan. *God's Big Picture*. Leicester: InterVarsity, 2002.

BOOK TWO

Doctrines of God's Revelation

Paul Morris

PART 3

God

It should come as no surprise that these studies in theology should start with God. When God brought Yisrael out of Egypt and prepared them to be his people in the land he had promised them, he did not lead them straight there. His first priority for them was to reveal himself in his majesty, power, and glory at Sinai, and then show them how he was to be known, approached, and worshiped through the construction of the mishkan (tabernacle). Only when that was done, and Pesach celebrated, were they ready to move forwards with their God.

God is the high and holy One who inhabits eternity. In Isaiah he reveals, "For as the heavens are higher than the earth, So are My ways higher than your ways, And My thoughts than your thoughts" (Isa 55:9). We are created beings, and unless our Creator reveals himself to us he is incomprehensible. We are sinners, with hearts and minds darkened by sin, widening the gulf between us. We must come humbly to learn of our great God; we are on holy ground.

God is; he can be known because he has revealed himself. He has told us what he is like and has names which underline that revelation. These are the themes we will consider in Book Two, Part 3.

10

God's Existence

God is the only self-existent, independent being. He declares of himself to Moshe: "I AM WHO I AM." It is from the verb "to be" that the divine name YHWH is derived. God is because he is. The Scriptures never seek to explain or prove God's existence; it is a simple, stated fact, as in Bereshit 1:1, "In the beginning God . . ." Scripture not only asserts his existence but also declares that humans know that he exists through what he has made—what we often term "nature" (Ps 19:1–3; Rom 1:20). However, the universal human response, due to sin, is to suppress this knowledge and refuse to honor God or be thankful (Rom 1:18, 21). Humans also know that there will be a reckoning for this behavior, "who, knowing the righteous judgment of God, that those who practice such things are deserving of death, not only do the same but also approve of those who practice them" (Rom 1:32).

Humanity is not in a position of neutrality on the question of God's existence; human nature is in rebellion. Hence we can observe all the false, man-made, and demonic religions of the world, through which humans recognize the divine and the supernatural, but believe and respond as they please. Agnosticism and atheism are also willful and sinful responses to what is known.

Hence people will not believe purely on the basis of rational proofs, although such proofs may have a value in opening the mind to consider what God has revealed. This is not a book of apologetics, hence such proofs will not be considered in detail but some are listed briefly below.

- Israel's unique history among the nations, the miracles, the moral teaching, their national preservation in their land, and the diaspora.

- The record in Scripture of fulfilled prophecies, especially in the life of Messiah Yeshua.
- The life of Jesus, his perfection, miracles, death, and resurrection.
- The continuance of the Christian church despite the many pronouncements of her imminent demise.
- The changed lives of Christians, especially virulent opponents like Saul of Tarsus.
- Humans' inbuilt sense of purpose, requiring a Creator with a purpose.
- The design in nature, especially the human body, argues for a designer.
- Our ability to think, reason, and plan, and to contemplate ourselves, all point to a nonmaterial spirit within us, necessitating a Creator spirit.
- Our inner sense of moral values, many of which are universally held, implies a transcendent ground for such values.
- The unsatisfactory nature of the explanations of human experience given by false religions and nontheist philosophy.

Whilst traditional Judaism would agree with much that is written here about God's existence, as is shown by the synagogue liturgy, and which has had a beneficial effect on the Jewish people, there have been those on the fringes, like the Kabbalists, who are so concerned to preserve the mystery of God's existence that they have come perilously close to a dualism by the distinction they make between God as he is in himself and God as he becomes manifest to his creatures, the former being impersonal and the latter personal. We do indeed have to say that we do not know, and cannot know, all there is to know about God, but we must not say that there is something essential about God's nature, further to what we understand and experience of him through his self-revelation, that can never be known by us. We can truly know God; and he is perfectly revealed in his Son, Yeshua.

> Oh, clap your hands, all you peoples!
> Shout to God with the voice of triumph!
> For the Lord Most High is awesome;
> He is a great King over all the earth. (Ps 47:1–2)

Scriptures

Gen 1:1; Exod 3:14–15; Job 33:14–18; Ps 53:1–2; Isa 40:18–26; 43:9–13; 45:1–13; Dan 4:34–35; John 15:22–24; Acts 14:14–17; 17:22–31; Rom 1:18–32; 2 Cor 4:3–4; 1 Thess 1:9–10; Heb 11:6.

Questions

1. Apart from Scripture, what evidence is there for God's existence?
2. What evidence do you see for humans' suppression of their awareness of God's existence?
3. What influences led you to believe in God's existence?

Further Reading

Keller, Tim. *The Reason for God*. London: Hodder & Stoughton, 2009.
Macleod, Donald. *Behold Your God*. Fearn: Christian Focus, 1995.
Strobel, Lee. *The Case for a Creator*. Grand Rapids: Zondervan, 2014.

11

God's Revelation of Himself

WE ARE GOD'S CREATURES and dependent upon him to tell us about himself. We need revelation from him and also his enabling to understand that revelation and respond to it properly. It is reasonable to suppose that our Creator would wish to do this for us, and the testimony of the Scriptures of the Old and New Testaments is that this is precisely what he has done. He has told us all we need to understand to come to know him and enjoy him forever, and promised his Spirit's help to all who seek him. God has revealed himself in two main ways: in creation (general revelation) and in the Scriptures (special revelation).

(A) GENERAL REVELATION

The natural world is a clear evidence to us of God's existence, his power, glory, and intelligent rule. David writes:

> The heavens declare the glory of God;
> And the firmament shows His handiwork.
> Day unto day utters speech,
> And night unto night reveals knowledge.
> There is no speech nor language
> Where their voice is not heard. (Ps 19:1–3)

And Paul teaches, "since the creation of the world His invisible attributes are clearly seen, being understood by the things that are made, even His eternal power and Godhead" (Rom 1:20). This revelation is clear because to deny it is, according to David, to be a fool, i.e., to fail to live according to reality

(Ps 14:1). Furthermore, a person's moral nature, and sense of a reckoning to come, reveals that God is righteous and punishes disobedience, as Paul explains, "And do you think this, O man, you who judge those practicing such things, and doing the same, that you will escape the judgment of God?" (Rom 2:3).

All this tells us something about our Creator but it leaves us with the thought that there must be so much more to know. On top of which our sense of his displeasure with us means we especially need to know how to be restored to his favor. General revelation is insufficient; the Scriptures are the further, special revelation, he has given.

(B) SPECIAL REVELATION

Here we need to distinguish between how the revelation was given in history and how it was recorded.

(i) Special Revelation Given

The giving of special revelation has been a process, using a variety of means over a long period of human history, as Hebrews tells us, "God, who at various times and in various ways spoke in time past to the fathers by the prophets, has in these last days spoken to us by His Son" (Heb 1:1–2). This tells us: the principal vehicle of God's revelation is words, the principal recipient has been Israel, and the process has come to its climax in the words of God's Son, Yeshua the Messiah. We have already examined the story of God's unfolding of revelation in Israel's history; here we will underline the *how* of it, and then how it was recorded.

The Scripture accounts are clear that people heard spoken words from God so that time and again we read, "And God said," or some such phrase. Here are some examples: to Adam, "And the Lord God commanded the man"; to Noach, "And God said to Noah"; to Avraham, "Now the Lord had said to Abram"; to Moshe, "Then the Lord spoke to Moses, saying"; to Natan (Nathan) and David, "the word of the Lord came to Nathan, saying, 'Go and tell My servant David.'"

Interestingly, we never read this sort of phrase in association with Messiah Jesus because he is the Word of God—"And the Word became flesh and dwelt among us" (John 1:14); all that he spoke was God's word. All subsequent audible spoken revelation was from him; for example to Paul, "Then the Lord said, 'I am Jesus, whom you are persecuting'" (Acts 9:5), or to John, "I, Jesus, have sent My angel to testify to you these things in the churches" (Rev 22:16). Indeed, the One who spoke to Adam, Noach, Avraham, Moshe, Nathan, and David is the same One who was incarnate among Israel and spoke subsequently to men like Paul and John. He is, and has always been, the Word of God, as we read of him in Proverbs where he is revealed as wisdom personified:

> The LORD possessed me at the beginning of His way,
> Before His works of old.
> I have been established from everlasting...
> Rejoicing always before Him,
> Rejoicing in His inhabited world,
> And my delight was with the sons of men. (Prov 8:22–23, 30–31)

From the very beginning he has always been the communicator for God with humanity.

The means of this communication has varied. We read of God speaking in a vision (Zech 1:7–17) or in a dream (Gen 12:12–13), but often we are not told the details, only that "God said." God spoke to Moses by a voice from the pillar of cloud at the door of the tabernacle in the wilderness (Exod 33:7–11), and many centuries later Peter, James, and John heard that same voice from a cloud when Jesus was transfigured before them: "This is My beloved Son. Hear Him!" (Mark 9:7) That was the last appearance of the cloud of God's presence, because a new stage in God's purposes had been reached, what Hebrews calls the "last days," when God spoke through his incarnate Son.

We also read in the Tanakh of a visible appearance of God in human form, known as a "theophany." For example, the appearance of the Angel of YHWH to Manoach (Manoah) in Judg 13:3, 18, and the commander of the army of the LORD to Joshua in Josh 5:14, 15. In both cases it is clear that the person speaking is divine, to be approached as the LORD himself. To Moses God says of the Angel of the LORD, "My name is in Him" (Exod 23:20–21, cf. 13:21). This was surely a great mystery at that time, but now, with all the subsequent revelation of the new covenant, we understand this person to be the preincarnate Son of God, who by these appearances gave hints of his coming incarnation to instruct us and lead us in God's will.

Jewish sources, like the Targums, often use the term "Memra" when Scripture records a creative, direct word of God manifesting God's power in the world. For example, in Ps 33:6 we read, "By the word of the LORD the heavens were made"; the Targum would have "Memra" for "word of the LORD." Similarly, when God speaks directly to a man, as in Gen 3:9, the Targum has "the voice of the Memra" instead of "God." In apocryphal and rabbinic literature the Memra is sometimes viewed as a personified agency.

Such Jewish sources have discerned something mysterious about the word of the Lord in the Tanakh, which only becomes clear in the new covenant: that God has always revealed himself to us through his Son, who is the Word of God.

It is important to ask how it was that those who heard God's word were convinced it was indeed God speaking. It is clear that the utterance they heard carried with it a sense of divine authority. God's word, spoken directly by him, inevitably has a sense of God. When he spoke by a human instrument, like Israel's prophets or Jesus' apostles, we are told it was the working of God's Spirit to invest the words with divine authority. Of the prophet Yahazi'el (Jahaziel) we read, "Then the Spirit of the Lord came upon Jahaziel . . . And he said . . . 'Thus says the Lord to you'" (2 Chr 20:14). And of Peter, speaking the truth to Israel's rulers, we read, "Then Peter, filled with the Holy Spirit, said to them, 'Rulers of the people and elders of Israel'" (Acts 4:8). The Spirit is not always mentioned but how else, for example, can we explain the people of a pagan city like Nineveh repenting at Jonah's preaching?

We need to note the place of miracles in this history of revelation. It is important to remember that they did not occur frequently but YHWH granted them at special moments, either at the beginning of a new epoch in his purposes or at a crucial moment in them. We might say, to use a military metaphor, they helped to establish a bridgehead, and then the more regular work went on without miracles. Israel's conquest of Canaan is an obvious example. At the commencement a great miracle is granted—the collapse of the walls of Yericho (Jericho)—but that was not the pattern for the conquest of all the remaining cities; regular warfare was necessary. At the inauguration of the Mosaic and new covenants there were many remarkable miracles, by which God demonstrated that a new era had begun. The miracles alerted people to God visiting his people in an unusual way for a very specific purpose. Also, the miracles demonstrated something of the nature of the new era, underlining the authority of the covenant's mediator (Moshe and Yeshua respectively). Miracles were also evident at times of calling God's people back to faithfulness, as in the ministries of Elijah and Elisha. The miracles were an encouragement to faith and gave insight into the nature of the development in God's purpose, as John wrote, "And truly Jesus did many other signs in the presence of His disciples, which are not written in this book; but these are written that you may believe" (John 20:30–31).

> The voice of the Lord is powerful;
> The voice of the Lord is full of majesty. (Ps 29:4)

> Oh how I love your law!
> It is my meditation all the day. (Ps 119:97)

SCRIPTURES

General revelation: Ps 19; John 1:9; Acts 17:24–30; 24:24–25; Rom 1:18–32.
Special revelation given: Gen 12:1–3; Exod 31:12–18; Josh 5:13–15; 1 Kgs 18:20–39; 2 Chr 28:11–12; Ps 19:7–11; Jer 1:4–10; Zech 3; Luke 1:26–38; John 1:18; 6:63; 14:26; 2 Cor 12:1–7; Eph 3:3–5; Heb 1:1–2; Rev 22:6–8.

QUESTIONS

1. Why is general revelation insufficient? What is its value?
2. Jesus is called the Word in John 1:1; what does this tell us about his role in all of God's special revelation?

FURTHER READING

Entries on "Revelation" in:
Packer, James, and David F. Wright, eds. *New Dictionary of Theology*. Leicester: InterVarsity, 1988.
Wiseman, Donald, ed. *New Bible Dictionary*. 3rd ed. Leicester: InterVarsity, 1996.

(ii) Special Revelation Recorded

We need to underline at the start of this section that the style of God's written revelation is not a systematic statement of truth but a collection of historical accounts, poems, pithy sayings, discussions, reflections, prophecies, apocalyptic writings, and letters. We should be grateful to God that in his wisdom he has revealed truth in a most interesting, challenging, humbling, and inexhaustible way.

God's people have always claimed that the Holy Scriptures of the Old and New Testaments are his unique and only written revelation to humanity. That is not bravado or a marketing ploy; it is what those Scriptures claim for themselves. In the Old Testament there are many, many places where the words are prefaced by "Thus says the Lord" or "God said." God's commission to Jeremiah makes clear that the prophet's words are God's words: "and the LORD said to me: 'Behold, I have put My words in your mouth'" (Jer 1:9). There are of course many words which are not recorded with "Thus says . . ." but they are to be viewed as equally authoritative due to the author's status. For example, Joshua adds the words of a covenant (Josh 24:26), Samuel wrote instructions for the behavior of royalty (1 Sam 10:25), and David clearly states in his instructions to Solomon regarding the construction and ordering of the temple that this has been divinely revealed to him (1 Chr 28:11–13).

What of the way the New Testament refers to the Old Testament writings? Messiah Jesus was emphatic that nothing in their pronouncements could ever be broken; they all had the status of divine truth (John 10:35). His reference to all three sections of the Tanakh—"the Law of Moses and the Prophets and the Psalms" (Luke 24:44)—indicates that the entire collection of writings then extant, our Old Testament, was unbreakable—God's words. The apostles taught the same: Peter described David as a prophet and treated his writing as having divine authority (Acts 2: 29–30), and he understood the writings of the prophets as the product of God's activity (2 Pet 1:20–21). Paul described the Scriptures, by which he would have meant the Tanakh, as inspired by God (2 Tim 3:16). We will look more closely at this inspiration in the next section but Paul's view of the Old Testament is clear—it is all God's word.

Likewise, the New Testament views itself as the word of God. Yeshua the Messiah viewed his own words as divinely authoritative: "The words that I speak to you are spirit, and they are life" (John 6:63) and "I do nothing of Myself; but as My Father taught Me, I speak these things" (John 8:28). Jesus invested his apostles with divine authority: "whatever you bind on earth will be bound in heaven" (Matt 16:19; 28:19–20). To ensure the accuracy of what they taught, he promised to remind them of all they had heard, to give them a fuller understanding of it, and to reveal future things (John 14:26, 16:13). The apostles viewed their own writings as Scripture. Peter accepted Paul's letters as equal to "the rest of the Scriptures" (2 Pet 3:15, 16), and Paul understands his own teachings to be "the commandments of the Lord" (1 Cor 14:37). In 1 Tim 5:18 Paul quotes two texts, one from Deut 25:4 and the other from Luke 10:7, describing them both as "Scripture." He sees no difference between the Old Testament writings and the Gospel accounts; all are God's word. All this is Christianity's view of the Scriptures and, with regard to the Old Testament Scriptures, the Jewish religious leadership and devout Jews have traditionally taken the same view.

The Gospels sometimes give us an insight into the faith of what I would call non-establishment Jewish people of those days: devout Jewish individuals like Mary, Zacharias, Elizabeth, Simeon, Anna, Andrew, Philip, and Nathaniel. What is clear is that their faith is based on the Tanakh, which they trust absolutely. Mary says, "As He spoke to our fathers, To Abraham and to his seed forever" (Luke 1:55), and Zacharias says, "As He spoke by the mouth of His holy prophets, Who have been since the world began . . . To perform the mercy promised to our fathers" (Luke 1:70, 72). We may deplore the status given to human traditions during that period, but their emphasis on the Scriptures, which had been revived by Ezra and came to pervade the life of Israel by the time of Yeshua, is something for which we should be grateful. It prepared the way for the coming of Messiah, and for faith in him among many in Israel. The interaction of Yeshua with the religious leadership shows they also had the same reverence for the Tanakh that he had; those writings were God's word. This view of the Tanakh has stood firm in traditional Judaism ever since: "The traditional Jewish view of revelation is that the whole Bible was conveyed by God to man,"[1] a view usually expressed by the phrase "Torah Min Ha-Shamayim" (Torah from heaven). This understanding is beautifully exhibited in synagogues at the close of the Shabbat morning service every week by the singing of Tehillim 29.

The authority with which Scripture speaks, and its own view of itself, comes to readers with convincing power. The miracles, and especially the resurrection of Yeshua, are witnessed historical events that lock in Scripture's claim to be God's revelation. Added to the convincing effect of hearing the words of Scripture is the witness of God's Spirit to their truth. Jesus promised to the apostles, "But when the Helper comes, whom I shall send to you from the Father, the Spirit of truth who proceeds from the Father, He will testify of Me" (John 15:26). Men and women may resist Scripture's claim to be God's revelation but those who believe find that the indwelling of God's Spirit leads to a permanent inner witness to the truth of the written word: "He who believes in the Son of God has the witness in himself" (1 John 5:10), and "But the anointing which you have received from Him abides in you . . . and just as it has taught you, you will abide in Him" (1 John 2:27).

> I have rejoiced in the way of Your testimonies,
> As much as in all riches. (Ps 119:14)

---

1. Jacobs, *Jewish Theology*, 199.

SCRIPTURES

Deut 31:9; 1 Sam 10:25; 2 Sam 23:1–2; Ps 45:1; Jer 36:1–4; Luke 1:1–4; 1 Cor 14:37; 2 Pet 1:12–15; 3:1; Rev 1:10–11.

QUESTIONS

1. How do we know the Scriptures of the Old and New Testaments are the word of God?
2. Knowing the Bible is God's word, how does this affect your reading of it? What place do you give to prayer, meditation, confession, and praise as you read?

FURTHER READING

Jensen, Peter F. *The Revelation of God*. Leicester: InterVarsity, 2002.
Packer, James. *God Has Spoken*. London: Hodder, 1979.

(iii) Inspiration

It stands to reason that if God has revealed himself to us, then he would ensure that what he has revealed is accurately recorded, otherwise the whole process falls to the ground. The Bible tells us the story of that unfolding revelation, and so we can be confident that the One who gave it by varied means has ensured that the books of the Bible are a precise account of this revelation. The claims and proof within the Bible that its revelation is from God demonstrate that the record of it is an accurate one. The Scriptures themselves tell us something of the process God used to ensure accuracy, and the word we use to describe this is "inspiration."

The word "inspiration" is taken from Paul's words in 2 Tim 3:16, "All Scripture is given by inspiration of God, and is profitable for doctrine, for reproof, for correction, for instruction in righteousness." The Greek word is *theopneustos*, meaning "God-breathed," and it occurs only here in the New Testament. Paul is using a familiar biblical metaphor for a direct action of God, usually involving his creative word, for example in Ps 33:6, "By the word of the LORD the heavens were made, And all the host of them by the breath of His mouth." The Greek word might be better translated "expired" but that has unhelpful connotations, and the English word "inspired" is familiar as a term which points to an influence upon the writer; "inspired" conveys the meaning well. Similar claims are made by Yeshua for the written words of Scripture where he says, referring to the words in a psalm, "the Scripture cannot be broken" (John 10:35), and again in Matt 22:43 where he refers to Ps 110:1 as written by David "in the Spirit."

There is a strong element of mystery about the divine inspiration of Scripture because it is quite obvious that the personalities of the different authors shine through the text. The writing style of Isaiah is quite different to that of Hosea, and Paul's is quite different to John's. Not just that, but the social background, education, and natural gifts of the writers are varied. Both Jeremiah and Paul are described as prepared by God from before birth (Jer 1:5, Gal 1:15) but they were obviously very different men. God ensured a wide variety in the authors so that Scripture could be easily related to by people of all types in all walks of life. This underlines that "God-breathed" does not mean dictation; God's inspiration of the authors was more mysterious than that. Dictation would override human personality but that is something which obviously did not happen. In some cases an author had to engage in research and study to be able to write an account, as when Luke tells us, "Inasmuch as many have taken in hand to set in order a narrative of those things which have been fulfilled among us" (Luke 1:1). This was not dictation but guidance of the human mind such that the research Luke did and the words he chose were words chosen by God; we may call it "supervision." This means the words themselves were inspired, not just the thoughts or ideas which they contain.

Paul uses the words "*all* Scripture" in 2 Tim 3:16, indicating there are no books, or parts of books, which are not God-breathed in every word. This does not mean that everything recorded is in itself truth. For example, we read that God rebuked Job's comforters for speaking error about God Job 42:7). What this indicates is that all the words were inspired so as to achieve God's purpose for Scripture, so that it is profitable for doctrine, reproof, etc., and sometimes it is necessary to have accurately expressed erroneous statements to achieve that. But that does not create uncertainty because Scripture itself ensures in context that we know that an erroneous statement is being made.

There are a number of deductions to be drawn from the divine inspiration of Scripture. Firstly, that Scripture is clear (the *perspicuity* of Scripture). This does not mean all parts are equally straightforward to understand but it asserts that Christians are not in need of a professional class of teachers without which they are hopelessly at sea in trying to understand the Bible. Undoubtedly teachers are important but Scripture also asserts that ordinary believers can read the Bible and understand its central message and much besides with the help of God's Spirit. In the context of discerning error, John writes, "But the anointing which you have received from Him abides in you, and you do not need that anyone teach you" (1 John 2:27). Jesus points to this activity of God as the explanation for the ordinary people coming to hear him: "It is written in the prophets, 'And they shall all be taught by God.' Therefore everyone who has heard and learned from the Father comes to me" (John 6:45). Throughout Scripture God has revealed truth to ordinary men and women—even the apostles were counted such (Acts 4:13). Being with Yeshua was the key for them, and it is he who continues to teach us through the Scriptures by his Spirit. It is remarkable that this clarity of the Scriptures is not impaired by their antiquity. This is primarily because they deal with the human condition, which is unchanging. Although the books of Scripture were products of their own day and contain metaphors and allusions we do not use now, there are very few which cannot be understood today.

Secondly, the inspiration of the Scriptures underlines their *sufficiency*. When we see all that God has done to give us a sure revelation of his truth, it is tantamount to blasphemy to assert we need teaching from another source to supplement Scripture. And yet there have been and are church denominations and teachers who assert that their additions or insights are necessary for salvation or a complete Christian life. We will consider this more under the section "Ultimate Authority." This sufficiency of Scripture is something which ordinary believers have acknowledged over the centuries. As they have sought to obey God, they have not been reduced to confusion—feeling a strong necessity to look elsewhere—but they have found that the Scriptures have taught, led, and guided them sufficiently. Of course, there are areas of life where Scripture does not give detailed instruction, for example, the church gatherings we organize, and in such matters we have freedom and we are to use our common sense.

Thirdly, the inspiration of the Scriptures, their perspicuity and sufficiency, assures us that they are *their own interpreter*. Again, this does not deny the value of teachers but they are not so essential that we are lost without them. All believers have the promise of Yeshua that his teaching ministry continues: "And I have declared to them Your name, and will declare it" (John 17:26). If we need help with how to interpret the Old Testament we can find it in the way the New uses the Old Testament texts. This is not always easy but the point is that help is available within Scripture. In 1 Cor 2 Paul disavows words of human wisdom in conveying God's truth. He speaks of "comparing spiritual things with spiritual" with the aid of the Holy Spirit. This refers to a process of induction by which we compare one Scripture passage or verse with another to arrive at a proper understanding. We will see this especially when we consider God's triunity; for although there is no one individual text which states this doctrine in its fullness, yet if we bring together relevant texts and compare them we can draw out the biblical teaching.

Fourthly, the inspiration of the Scriptures asserts that their teachings are *true*, so that they do not mislead the reader and are at no point mistaken; "Every word of God is pure" (Prov 30:5). Their teaching is frequently in conflict with the thinking of the day but it is Scripture which is true. Connected to this is the *inerrancy* of Scripture, that is, all it records is free from error, whether doctrine, ethics, history, etc. It is not a textbook of all subjects but this freedom from error does go beyond matters of faith and practice; it extends to all it records. The claims that there are errors and contradictions in Scripture are, when carefully examined, seen to be misunderstandings or misinterpretations of the text. It is well to remember that many things once confidently asserted to be errors have since been shown to be true by further historical, scientific, and archaeological discoveries.

It needs to be stated that all these assertions about the text of Scripture are only applicable to the original documents, as penned by the original authors—documents that we no longer possess. That sounds like a get-out clause but there is good reason for the loss of the originals; they were actually used, not stored away in a vault for safekeeping. They wore out by use and age, and had to be replaced by copies. As the faith spread more copies were needed, so there are many, many copies but no originals. This does not reduce all the above to uncertainty. There are many famous documents of the past whose originals we do not possess but whose account no one would doubt. In the case of some, like the record of some of Caesar's exploits in *Gallic Wars*, we have only nine or ten good copies, made nine hundred years after the original. With the Magna Carta we have four copies of the original, which were made in the same year (1215). With the Scriptures we have some five thousand Greek manuscripts in whole or in part and the best of these date to within three hundred years of the originals, and one small papyrus fragment of John was circulating in Egypt about forty years after John wrote it. Comparing the copies leads to certainty regarding the authenticity and integrity of the books of the NT. No vital doctrine of Scripture is affected in the very few places where there is reason for doubt about the precise wording of the text.

> Your word is very pure;
> Therefore Your servant loves it. (Ps 119:140)

Scriptures

1 Kgs 22:1–28; Isa 61:1; Mic 3:8; Matt 22:43; Acts 1:16; Rom 3:2; 1 Cor 7:40; 2 Tim 3:14–17; Heb 3:7; 1 Pet 1: 10–12; 2 Pet 1:21; Rev 2:11.

Questions

1. Choose a few authors of Scripture from the OT and NT and demonstrate the differences of personality, background, and style of the authors.
2. What causes you to marvel when you consider God's inspiration of the authors of Scripture?
3. Which apparent errors in the Bible have been drawn to your attention? Write out how you have responded to some of them.
4. What view of the Scriptures were you brought up to believe? How has your view changed?

Further Reading

Edwards, Brian. *Nothing but the Truth*. Darlington: Evangelical, 1978.
Young, Edward J. *Thy Word Is Truth*. Edinburgh: Banner of Truth, 1972.

(iv) The Books of Scripture—the Canon

How did the sixty-six books of our Bible come to be there? Much of the process is unrecorded but the end result is not; it is called the "canon of Scripture." The word "canon" comes from a Greek word which was borrowed from a Semitic one having the root meaning of "reed," i.e., a means of measurement, in this case which books to include. A point that cannot be overstated is that it was not the formation of the canon which gave the books of Scripture their authority, but rather the books were included because their authority was already recognized by God's people—leaders and led equally. For example, when the people of Israel heard Moshe read the Torah which God had given him, they acknowledged the words as the Lord's words. They recognized their divine authority (Exod 24:7). Paul expected the same recognition of the divine authorship of his words by those who read his letter (see 1 Cor 14:37). The authority of those who wrote the books was recognized as from God; people such as lawgivers, prophets, and apostles. It involved a witness of the Spirit, much as Christians today recognize God speaking in his word preached. Difficulty was experienced concerning a few of the books, whose authorship was uncertain, or due to statements of doctrine which seemed to be at variance with the teaching of accepted books, but when these were resolved acceptance followed. No book was ever included concerning which significant numbers of God's people had doubts. A comparison with apocryphal writing of both Testaments quickly shows the difference between human works (however valuable) and those inspired by God's Spirit.

(a) The Old Testament Canon (Tanakh)

The process of recognition and collection of the books of the Tanakh is not recorded, except for the obvious fact that the five books of Moses were accepted from earliest times. Rabbi Isidore Epstein (principal of Jews College, London, 1945) asserts that canonization began before the Babylonian exile. It is highly likely it was completed soon after the return because the rabbis have generally held that inspiration ceased soon after that time. The rabbinical discussions at Yavneh (post 70 AD[2]) reaffirmed the books of the Hebrew Bible which we have today. The records show that those discussions added nothing and removed nothing from what was already acknowledged as canonical. We can have no doubt that when the Lord Jesus referred to the Scriptures it was the same collection of books that Yavneh listed not many years later. In Luke 24:44 he referred to the traditional Jewish threefold division of Scripture—the law, the Prophets, and the Psalms ("Psalms," as the largest book of the Writings (Ketuvim), stood for all of them). His reference in Luke 11:51 to the first and last recorded martyrs (Abel and Zechariah) indicates his stamp of approval on all the books of the Hebrew Bible from Genesis to 2 Chronicles (2 Chronicles being the last book of the Hebrew Bible). Whilst Jesus differed with Israel's spiritual leaders on many things, there was never any dispute over the books of Scripture, and Jesus quotes from all but four of them. The Old Testament is the Tanakh of the synagogue, the Scriptures Yeshua used.

(b) The New Testament canon

We are much more aware of the history of how the New Testament books were collected into a canon but, even so, much has been left unrecorded.

---

2. It is recognized that some are more familiar with CE rather than AD, but AD will be used throughout this book.

God's Revelation of Himself

The Lord Jesus promised his apostles special guidance to teach all he had taught them, and to give them fuller revelation (John 14:26; 16:13–14). They went out with the gospel, people believed, and churches were formed. Some of them wrote letters to those churches, especially Paul, and such writings were immediately recognized as authoritative. That's not to say there were no difficulties from imposters even then, as 2 Thess 2:2 makes clear. Then, as the early witnesses died out, the four Gospels came to be written, each at a separate location. Mark's was first, then Matthew's, then Luke's (with Acts), and then John's. At the end of the first century some collecting together of the writings began. The four Gospels, called "The Gospel," were first, Acts being kept separate though of equal authority with Luke. Then the thirteen letters of Paul were collected into "The Apostle." Around this time the other universally recognized documents were: 1 Peter, 1 John, Revelation, and Hebrews. The main test applied was apostolic authorship, or written by "apostolic men," that is, men like Mark and Luke who were close companions of the apostles. Of course, there were fraudulent documents which used the names of apostles or their associates, like the *Gospel of Thomas* and the *Gospel of Mary* (of *Da Vinci Code* fame). These usually had a doctrinal axe to grind, and when their errors were detected by comparison with established writings they were rejected. Other documents, like the *Shepherd of Hermas*, were not so much fraudulent as of a lower order, and some of these were recommended for reading, although not recognized by God's people as having that same stamp of divine authority as the accepted writings. There were doubts about some genuine writings either due to uncertainty over apostolic authorship or their content seeming to differ from more established writings. The cast-iron ones (called *homologoumena*) were the four Gospels, Acts, Paul's thirteen letters, Hebrews, 1 Peter, 1 John, and Revelation (although a few had doubts about Hebrews and Revelation over authorship and content respectively). The ones which the majority accepted, but concerning which a significant minority had doubts (called *antilegomena*), were James, Jude, 2 Peter, 2 John, and 3 John.

One of the earliest lists is called the Muratorian Canon, created about 175 AD. Eusebius, in the early fourth century, listed all in the *homologoumena*. In 367 AD we have the first list of books identical to the twentyseven we have in our Bibles today, compiled by Athanasius, bishop of Alexandria. The first church council to list the same twentyseven books was the Synod of Hippo in 393 AD. Three hundred years may seem a long time to come to a conclusion, but too much can be made of this. The vast majority of the books were accepted by all the churches within fifty years of the death of the last apostle, John. The rest were circulating and accepted as authoritative by the vast majority of Christians not long after. The process can be summarized:

- 50–100 AD, all twentyseven New Testament books written;
- 100–200 AD, writings collected and read in churches;
- 200–300 AD, process of examination and comparison with the many spurious writings;
- agreement obtained by 400 AD.

When account is taken of the many churches involved, how widespread they were, how slow communication was then, and the large number of spurious documents in circulation, it is not surprising it took so long to finalize the process. Since that time, no book has been excluded from the canon and no book has been added.

> I will worship toward Your holy temple,
> And praise Your name
> For Your lovingkindness and Your truth;
> For You have magnified Your word above all Your name. (Ps 138:2)

Scriptures

The Old Testament: Exod 24:4–7; Deut 31:9–26, Josh 24:26; Ezra 7:6, 14; Neh 8:1–3; Prov 25:1; Isa 8:16; 34:16; Jer 36:1–4, 32; Dan 9:2; Luke 24:27, 44; Acts 28:23; Rom 16:25–26.
The New Testament: 1 Cor 7:10; 14:37–38; 2 Cor 10:8–11; Col 4:16; 2 Thess 2:15; 3:17; 1 Tim 5:18; 2 Pet 3:15–16; Rev 1:1–3; 2:1; 22:8–10, 18–19.

Questions

1. What is meant by the "canon of Scripture"? Outline the process by which the OT canon and the NT canon came about.
2. Apostolic authorship is a key factor in authenticating NT documents. Why is this, and how do we account for the inclusion of Mark, Luke, Acts, and Hebrews?

Further Reading

Bruce, F. F. *The Books and the Parchments*. Glasgow: Pickering & Inglis, 1971.

———. *The New Testament Documents*. Leicester: InterVarsity, 1971.

(v) The Relationship between the Testaments

What has been written so far about God's special revelation recorded in the Scriptures underlines the unity of the Old and New Testaments. The revelation in the Old looks forward to Messiah's coming and a fuller revelation, as the Samaritan woman said to Jesus, "'I know that Messiah is coming' (who is called Christ). 'When He comes, He will tell us all things'" (John 4:25). The revelation in the New Testament constantly looks back to the Old Testament, as Paul wrote, "Christ died for our sins according to the Scriptures" (1 Cor 15:3). The Bible is a unified book, despite its fundamental division into two testaments, and the fulcrum of that division is Messiah Jesus, as Luke tells us, "And beginning at Moses and all the Prophets, He expounded to them in all the Scriptures the things concerning Himself" (Luke 24:27). The most fundamental factor in the unity of the testaments is, therefore, God's plan of salvation in his Son, fulfilled in Yeshua.

But the plan of salvation has a goal—the rescue from sin of multitudes of people, granting them forgiveness and leading them to live holy lives for God as they await the return of Jesus in glory. How should they then live? The problem is that an obedient lifestyle under the Mosaic covenant was significantly different from one under the new. So, how does the authority of the Old Testament as God's word operate in the life of a believer in Messiah Jesus, Jew or Gentile? We can only consider this briefly here, but it is appropriate to do this as part of our consideration of the authority of God's self-revelation. To consider this question it will be helpful to step back a bit and consider God's covenants. God, in his dealings with humanity, has entered into covenants, or agreements, that establish a relationship between him and us. The difference from our idea of an agreement is that in God's covenants he states all the terms and calls us to acceptance, or as in the case of Noah, simply makes promises; it is not a negotiation. All his covenants are full of promises to us, and in them he calls us to loving obedience. It is all of his grace.

This was so at the very beginning, when Adam and Eve were promised life as they obeyed the Lord. In the Old Testament period, the main covenants to consider are those with Avraham, with all Israel through Moshe and with David. In the New Testament, the covenant is the new covenant made by Messiah Jesus, offered first to Israel and then to all. It is helpful to view the covenant with Abraham as the foundation covenant, and the Mosaic and the new as administrative covenants. This can be seen in the way both the Mosaic and the new refer back to Abraham. When Israel was suffering in Egypt and God was about to initiate their deliverance, we read in Shemot, "So God heard their groaning, and God remembered His covenant with Abraham, with Isaac and with Jacob" (Exod 2:24). Paul's words in Gal 3:14 show how he connected the blessings which come through Christ (and his new covenant) to the blessing promised to Abraham: "that the blessing of Abraham might come upon the Gentiles in Christ Jesus." The promises to Abraham are the bedrock of the two covenants which God has used to administer the lives of his people in two different eras. The Mosaic covenant was for his people living together in the land of Canaan as an earthly, national theocracy. The new covenant was for his people, Jew and Gentile, scattered throughout the world as a spiritual nation, a spiritual theocracy. They are united in aim, a life of holiness, but they differ in the stage on which they are set.

Those who have believed in Yeshua, Jew and Gentile, are living under the administration of the new covenant which began when he inaugurated it with his first Jewish disciples: "this is My blood of the new covenant, which is shed for many for the remission of sins" (Matt 26:28). As with the Mosaic covenant, the crucial element to this inauguration was a blood sacrifice to atone for the sins of those who entered. The first believers were all Jewish, as we read in the opening chapters of Acts; they entered by faith and then the Gentiles heard of Christ crucified and also entered through faith in his blood. They were both part of a new body which Paul calls the "one new man from the two" (Eph 2:14–15). Their life of obedience is regulated, or administered, by the teachings of Jesus and his apostles.

All this meant the Mosaic covenant came to be seen as "old" and was termed the "old covenant," or "Old Testament" (2 Cor 3:14). This does not mean it has no further use because it still guides and inspires new covenant believers to a holy life. Yeshua said, "till heaven and earth pass away, one jot or one tittle will by no means pass from the law till all is fulfilled" (Matt 5:18). This fulfillment takes place in a number of ways, and one of them is in the righteous lives of believers, as Paul wrote: God's Son came, "that the righteous requirement of the law might be fulfilled in us who do not walk according to the flesh but according to the Spirit" (Rom 8:4). This is an ongoing fulfillment. The key phrase is "righteousness of the law" and it indicates there is a righteous principle in all the commands of the law of Moses which we are to discern and practice. For example, when we sin we cannot fulfill the law by confession and bringing a sin offering, but we can fulfill its righteousness by confession and trusting the death of Messiah Jesus for the cleansing of our sin (see 1 John 1:8—2:2). Also, the law has much to say about welcoming a stranger and fulfilling the righteousness of that command is not difficult to understand—our churches are to be places where those who are different from the majority due to race, social background, or lifestyle are made to feel welcome, not shunned as an alien influence. As we observe the LORD's dealings with Israel, or as we read the encouragements and warnings of the prophets, or the praises and laments of the psalmists, we learn righteous principles and apply them to our lives. The old is always being fulfilled in the new until Yeshua returns and creates a new heaven and a new earth.

It is of value at this point to note how the traditional rabbinic interpretation of the new covenant of Jer 31:31–34 differs from that of the New Testament. It is usually viewed as a promise of a new day for the exiles who returned from Babylon, who would rebuild the temple, reinstitute the worship of God according to the existing Mosaic pattern, and observe the Mosaic law from their hearts, rather than being content with no observance, or only outward observance. In this teaching, the new covenant is not especially connected with the coming of Messiah. The Christian faith agrees with the rabbinic stress on a renewed observance of the righteousness of the law in the new covenant but is deeply concerned that the rabbis overlook the context of its announcement—the failure of the Mosaic law due to Israel's sin. This clearly indicates a replacement of the Mosaic and points to new conditions in which to keep the law's righteousness. The new covenant is not a small matter, like a promise made to an individual such as Pinehas (Num 25:12), but it is made with the whole house of Israel and the house of Judah (Jer 31:31). It points to a new era in God's plan of salvation, and who could inaugurate such if not Messiah?

Finally, we can see the fundamental unity of all God's covenants in that, at one time or another, they are all described as everlasting (Gen 9:16; Isa 24:5; Gen 17:7; 1 Chr 16:17; 2 Sam 23:5; Isa 61:8; Heb 13:20). Now, in its form, the Mosaic was not everlasting, because the temple has gone. But in its goal, and the goal of all covenants for the salvation of sinners—to fit us for life with God forever—there is an obvious underlying continuity. The result for all who believe under any covenant is an everlasting one. This underlines the fact that the differences between old and new are only in degree, and not fundamental. Forgiveness and hope were experienced under the old, but not enjoyed to the same degree as in the New Testament, due to the knowledge of Messiah's resurrection and the indwelling of the Spirit. A regenerate heart and righteous life were enjoyed under the old, but failure was more frequent until the Spirit indwelt believers in the new covenant era. A clearer understanding of God's being and his salvation came under the new through the revelations given to Messiah's apostles and prophets (Eph 3:5, "prophets" here refers to New Testament prophets), but the mysteries they spoke of were not totally unheard-of ideas. In other words, those mystery truths were embryonic in the old in some form or another, but not fully understood until the light of the new was shone upon them. A text which underlines this is Rom 11:25–26, where Paul speaks of a mystery but then quotes Isaiah to underline it. As one wise man put it, "the new is latent in the old, the old is patent in the new."

> Blessed is the Lord God of Israel,
> For He has visited and redeemed His people . . .
> To perform the mercy promised to our fathers
> And to remember His holy covenant. (Luke 1:68, 72)

SCRIPTURES

Deut 18:15–19; Jer 31:31–34; Matt 5:17–19; 7:12; 22:34–40; Luke 10:25–28; John 8:56; Rom 3:1–2, 31; 13:8–10; 2 Cor 3; Gal 3:15–29; Eph 2:11–22; Heb 8.

QUESTIONS

1. What unites the Old and New Testaments?
2. How do we know the old covenant has "vanished away"? (Heb 8:13)

FURTHER READING

McComiskey, T. H. *The Covenants of Promise*. Leicester: InterVarsity, 1985.

(vi) Scripture Authority and Other Authorities

Authority is the power to require obedience, and for all humanity the Scriptures are God's supreme authority because in them his requirements are revealed. However, there are other "authorities" or "helps," recognized by Scripture, by which believers are better able to understand the Scriptures, and we will consider three of them. Yet believers are always to be on their guard against exalting them above Scripture, which is always their supreme and uncontested authority.

(a) Reason

Human reason can never be a final authority, due to the limitations of human knowledge and the corrupting influence of sin upon the human heart, mind, and will. Nevertheless, there is a valid place for reason in understanding Scripture. For example, to compare Scripture with Scripture to derive doctrine, or to arrive at an application of the truth in our lives, or to express a doctrine in words and then assess it; all of these require the use of human reasoning powers. When believers engage in such activities they do so prayerfully, looking to God for his Spirit's aid, and their reasoning powers are used, not set aside. What must be avoided is the use of reason to judge what is acceptable in Scripture, something known as "liberal Christianity," which is a false use of human reasoning power.

(b) The Community of God's People

Under the Mosaic covenant the community was Israel; under the new covenant it is the church. "Church" may be understood as a local body of believers, or a national or international body, or believers throughout the ages. God has always raised up leaders among his people to teach and interpret his word, whether prophets and priests under the Mosaic covenant, or apostles, prophets, evangelists, pastors, and teachers under the new. Such people had authority, but an authority which is under God and Scripture (Eph 4:11; Titus 2:15; 1 Cor 5:4–5). It is under Scripture because it is God's word that brought his people (Israel or church) into being, not the other way around. Hence the ministry of those recognized and ordained to teach has always been highly valued (Heb 13:7), and not lightly set aside. However, where the instruction has been in conflict with Scripture it should be rejected, having no power to bind the conscience. This experience of valued or rejected teaching can be observed in both the Mosaic and new covenant period, in Israel and the church. In the Mosaic there were false prophets (Jer 29:31–32), and those who made their traditions equivalent to Scripture's teachings (Isa 29:13–14). No doubt, there was much valuable teaching of the God's word in the Old Testament period, especially post-Babylon (see Ezra 8:1–8 for example). The Old Testament Apocrypha gives us some insight into what was being discussed and taught in the intertestamental period, but its value is limited now that Messiah has come.

Today we have the inspired understanding and application of the Old Testament Scriptures in the pages of the New Testament. The same experience of valued or rejected teaching has happened under the new covenant, whose writings warn against false prophets and human traditions (Matt 24:11, 1 Tim 4:1–3), yet those writings also give the church an important place in upholding the truth of Scripture: "the church of the living God, the pillar and ground of the truth" (1 Tim 3:15). Hence, we should value creeds and church councils, great teachers of today and from earlier days, and the decisions of church bodies, and not treat them lightly; but all to be tested by Scripture.

The above paragraphs focus on the teaching of truth but the need for organization has led to the establishment of traditions, both in Israel and the church; traditions which were intended to facilitate the worship and service of God's people. History teaches that they have a tendency to ossify and often end up hindering or opposing what they were designed to support, and churches and denominations are undoubtedly guilty at this point. God's people of the new covenant constantly need to be reassessing their practices.

At this point brief mention should be made of the oral law of traditional Judaism, which is the rabbinic claim that not only did Moshe receive the written laws recorded in Scripture but he also received also oral ones, and the latter have been handed down via leaders and are the basis of the Talmud today: "Moses received Torah from Sinai and handed it on to Joshua, and Joshua to the Elders, and the Elders to the Prophets, and the Prophets to the men of the Great Assembly" (the opening words of *Pirke Abot*, the final section of *Nezikin*, the fourth order of the Talmud.) Rabbi Jonah, in explaining "Torah" in this quotation, states that it refers to both the written and the oral Torah: "It is written, 'And I will give Thee the tables of stone, and the law and the commandment' (Exodus 24:12): *the law* refers to the written Torah; *the commandment* refers to the Oral Torah."[3] What Rabbi Jonah fails to do is give the full quotation of Exod 24:12 (JPS), "And I will give Thee the tables of stone, and the law and the commandment, which I have written, that thou mayest teach them." Clearly, both *law* and *commandment* refer to written law. It is highly likely that traditions of religious practice were indeed handed down orally, and such a process has value; the danger is when they are made equal to or above the written law. This is just what has happened in traditional Judaism, even though there is no mention in the books of Moshe or elsewhere in Scripture of an authoritative oral law.

Yeshua's rebuke to the Jewish leadership in Matt 15:3–14 stands today, because rabbinic Judaism's leadership has continued to place their

---

3. Goldin, *Living Talmud*, 43.

traditions equal to and above Scripture. This can be seen, for example, in the explanation by Rabbi Louis Jacobs for viewing the command to kindle the Hanukkah lights as a command of God, as discussed in the Talmud (*b. Sabb.* 23a): "we have here the germ of the idea that indirect commands through the experience of Israel and the institution of its sages are also divine commandment."[4] This gives people the power to bind the conscience; something only God's written word can do. Although Jewish believers in Yeshua remain part of Israel, they are not under the authority of the teachings and traditions of its religious leaders, who have rejected Yeshua, maintaining that their oral law is equal to the written law (Matt 15:14).

All this has application to the messianic movement, which stresses the value of Jewish traditions for Jewish believers. Jewish believers may choose to observe Jewish religious traditions which are not in conflict with new covenant teaching, but only as a valued human tradition, not as an authoritative command of God for today. There will be more on this subject later in the book.

(c) Inner Revelation

Christians sometimes speak of an inner voice or a strong impression, or a vision or dream. All these are something they alone have experienced, not being outwardly perceived, but inwardly. Such are usually understood as an inward work of the Holy Spirit, and there is a danger of making such equal to and additional to Scripture. Such experiences do exist in the New Testament—Philip heard a voice (Acts 8:26–40) and Paul had a vision (Acts 16:6–10)—but even in those special times they were rare, not everyday experiences, and it should be noted that they were given in particular or difficult circumstances. Such experiences need to be distinguished from the normal workings of the human mind, and only heeded in conjunction with other forms of teaching and guidance, especially Scripture. They are subject to the testing of others (1 Cor 14:29), who can only judge by Scripture. There should be no written recordings of such things, as if they are a written revelation equal to Scripture. When such things are given undue prominence, rather than their occasional function of guidance or teaching or encouragement (e.g., 1 Cor 14:31), then there is a great danger of self-delusion, and believers should be on their guard, because Satan is always active to mislead. Scripture is supreme and is always sufficient to learn and to judge all things.

---

4. Jacobs, *Jewish Theology*, 207.

Remember now your Creator in the days of your youth . . . The words of the wise are like goads, and the words of scholars are like well-driven nails, given by one Shepherd. (Eccl 12:1, 11)

SCRIPTURES

Isa 8:20; Matt 7: 15–20; Mark 7:9–13; 1 Cor 12:28; 2 Cor 11:13–15; Gal 1:6–9; 2 Tim 3:1–9; Heb 13:7; 2 Pet 2:1–2.

QUESTIONS

1. Are the Scriptures of the Old and New Testaments the supreme authority in your life? Describe practices and experiences in your life which demonstrate this.
2. What is the place of church teaching, reason, and special leadings of the Spirit in helping believers to submit to Scripture's authority?

FURTHER READING

Lloyd-Jones, D. M. *Authority*. Edinburgh: Banner of Truth, 1984.

(vii) Interpreting Scripture (Hermeneutics)

Scripture is not a list of truths about God followed by another list of dos and don'ts for humanity. It is truth conveyed in a varied patchwork of literary styles, written over many centuries by different authors in very different days to our own. It needs to be understood in its original context and applied to us now. This is not an easy task, and the history of Scripture interpretation shows it has many pitfalls. But we can be sure God has not deliberately made things difficult for us; indeed it shows his desire to treat us not as semi-automatons but as individuals made in his own image who should love and serve him with understanding.

There is a long history of interpretation in the teaching experience of Israel and the New Testament church. Before the Babylonian exile, King Yehoshafat (Jehoshaphat) sent out judges to teach (2 Chr 19:4–11), and after the return Ezra began a tradition of careful explanation of the text (Neh 8:5–8). Ezra's example placed the interpretation and teaching of Scripture at the center of Israel's religious life alongside the temple, and one consequence of that was the focus on Scripture observable in the pages of New Testament among the scribes and Pharisees. They developed rules of interpretation; for example, Hillel's seven *middoth*. The writings of the New Testament also give many examples of Scripture interpretation through the way it uses the Old Testament Scriptures, setting a template for subsequent generations of the church to follow.

Running parallel to this interpretative work of the church, Jewish teachers have continued to interpret the Scriptures for the people of Israel, as seen in Talmud, midrash, etc. Not all of this has been positive. The best interpreters have sought the literal meaning of the text, and this was the approach used by the Jewish interpreter Rashi, and revived among Christians at the time of the Reformation. Christians speak of the historical-grammatical method; the Jewish term being "peshat." Jewish interpreters often developed an extreme letterism—an excessive focus on the detail of the words which lost sight of the simple meaning of the text. They also sought a deeper meaning, not obvious in the text itself, asserting there could be many of these, which led to what is known as "midrash" (or derash). It became little more than "a kind of peg in Scripture on which to hang an idea."[5]

Christian interpreters have not been immune from letterism or using Scripture as a peg for their ideas. Both Jewish and Christian interpreters have sometimes taken an allegorical approach, which has usually led to fanciful interpretations. Such have done little harm when God's way of salvation was the guiding light, but the allegorical approach has also been used to support opposition to Scripture's true message. A particular irritation with the Christian allegorical tradition for Jewish believers is that it often lacks any interest in the real history of Israel. The four points which follow present the traditional Protestant approach, which has drawn on the best in the history of Scripture interpretation.

(a) The Right Attitude

Our basic confidence is that the Bible is sufficient for the life of faith and, hence, is its own interpreter—it contains all we need to guide us as interpreters. God gives his people the things they need to properly interpret his word: regenerate hearts, the promised aid of his Spirit (John 14:16), reason and common sense, the teaching ministry of leaders, and fellowship with his people.

---

5. Jacobs, *Jewish Biblical Exegesis*, x.

(b) The Right Approach

Although the Bible is a unique book, it is still literature. It should be interpreted literally, i.e., according to the straightforward sense intended by the author to his original hearers or readers. This is known as the "historical-grammatical method," which takes account of the normal meaning of words in their literary context. It is not literalistic (or letterism), hence it takes account of different literary forms such as prose, poetry, metaphor, imagery, parable, allegory, fable, and apocalyptic, and of the historical and cultural setting. The big picture also needs to be kept in view. So we have to ask, how does our passage relate to God's unfolding plan of redemption in Messiah?

Scripture makes clear that God has so arranged his plan of redemption that events, persons, and institutions in the Old Testament anticipate Messiah's days. Because of this a text may be interpreted in a way that transcends its original setting. The traditional word for this is "typology," but some prefer to speak of "patterns." For example, Adam is a type of Messiah (Rom 5:14), as is David (Ezek 34:23–24; Luke 1:32); the exodus from Egypt is a type of Messiah's deliverance (Luke 9:31), and the institution of temple, priesthood, and sacrifice is a shadow of Messiah and his atoning and intercessory work (Heb 8:1–5; 9:11–15). Although the modern Jewish mind pays little attention to types, traditional Jewish teaching does; for example, the messianic titles "Messiah ben Joseph" and "Messiah ben David," coined by the rabbis, are typology. Likewise, the tradition of Elijah's cup at the seder indicates the Passover deliverance and is understood as a type of Messiah's deliverance, because it is a rabbinic teaching that Messiah comes at Passover time and is announced by Elijah (as per Mal 4:4–5). Now that Messiah Jesus has come, giving a full revelation of God's way of salvation, the types and patterns in the Old Testament stand out much more clearly, although they were not unrecognized during Old Testament times.

Typology has its subspecies, and terms like "types," "shadows," "patterns," "fuller meaning," and "allegory" are used to describe how the earthly life of God's people in the Old Testament finds fulfillment in New Testament spiritual realities. Some of these terms are used interchangeably but, in general, it may be said that "types" refer to persons (like David) who portray Messiah and his salvation, "shadows" refer to institutions (like the priesthood and tabernacle), and "patterns" refer to historical events (like the exodus). "Fuller meaning" is a term for an interpretation which looks back at an Old Testament text and sees in it a messianic reality only dimly presented in the original. Such an interpretation is sometimes referred to as "a filling-up of the text." Examples would be to preach the gospel from Gen 3:15 or to teach lessons of holiness from the Levitical food laws.

A particular example of fuller meaning is "allegory," a term used when a gospel lesson is being drawn from a story in the Old Testament where more than one character or event is in view, for example in the Abraham and Sarah, Hagar and Ishmael episode (see Gen 21:1–13, Gal 4:21–31). It is more complex than a type or a pattern. Two general points need to be made. Firstly, allegorical interpretation is very rare in the NT, so it should be used sparingly. Secondly, allegorical interpretation is one that is open to abuse, making connections to Messiah which are not in the Old Testament text at all, only in some superficial similarity of language or form. A safeguard is to remember that although allegory transcends the meaning to the original hearers, it is not divorced from the significance of the original event in God's plan at the time it happened.

(c) The Right Confidence

Scripture interprets Scripture. The Scriptures reveal a divine plan, and therefore they are a unity, so that all books and texts are in harmony with one another. Hence books and texts can be elucidated by other books and texts. It is important to understand the place and purpose of a book in the overall narrative of God's plan, and endeavor to understand the purpose of a passage within the book. Get help from passages elsewhere with a similar theme. Interpret earlier passages, especially difficult ones, in the light of later ones, with their fuller revelation. The New Testament is the authoritative interpretation of the Old, and its many Old Testament quotations give principles which can be applied to other texts. A warning: it is common today to read of "the Jewish view," as if information drawn from Jewish sources gives a necessary extra insight for Christians who have only listened to Christian teachers (mostly Gentiles). Such insights from Jewish people (who are not Christians) may have value but, first and foremost, we need to remember that we have the Jewish view in the New Testament, all its authors being Jewish (except Luke), and it is sanctioned by the Lord Jesus, the Jewish Messiah.

The Holy Spirit interprets Scripture. Yeshua promised the Spirit to enlighten: "when He, the Spirit of truth, has come, He will guide you into all truth" (John 16:13). This was something the disciples had already experienced: "You have hidden these things from the wise and prudent and have revealed them to babes" (Matt 11:25). Jesus reveals in his prayer to the Father that he would continue to do this for all believers (John 17:26). Teachers should be heard and respected, but illumination of truth to the soul is always a work of the Spirit. We should therefore study God's word prayerfully and in anticipation.

(d) The Right Goal

Our purpose in studying God's word is to know him and his will, and so be more like him and pleasing to him. Likeness to Yeshua is our aim and prayer. Hence our efforts to understand the meaning of a text in context must lead to the question, what does it mean for me today? We should beware of a desire to simply acquire head knowledge, and be careful to avoid a contentious spirit.

> Your testimonies are wonderful;
> Therefore my soul keeps them. The entrance of Your words gives light;
> It gives understanding to the simple. (Ps 119:129–130)

SCRIPTURES

Deut 5:1–4; Ezra 8:5–8; Ps 78; Ezek 34:23–24; Dan 8:8; Matt 5:17–48; 22:29–32; Luke 24:27; John 5:45–47; Acts 17:2; 1 Cor 10:11; 2 Cor 1:20; 2 Tim 2:15; 1 Pet 1:10–12; 2 Pet 1:20; 3:16; 1 John 2:27.

QUESTIONS

1. What are the different types of literature in the Bible? Do you have a preference for any particular type?
2. How does historical-grammatical interpretation and application of a text differ from the typological? Illustrate from the life of Joseph.
3. In Hebrews 1–2 how is the author using the OT texts?
4. What application is there to your own life from Luke 13:10–17?

FURTHER READING

McCartney, Dan, and Charles Clayton. *Let the Reader Understand*. Phillipsburg: Presbyterian and Reformed, 2002.
Ramm, Bernard. *Protestant Biblical Interpretation*. Grand Rapids: Baker, 1985.

12

The Knowledge of God (Knowability)

GOD EXISTS AND HE has revealed himself to his creatures, so we can know about him and it is his desire that we should; this is traditionally termed his "knowability." Nevertheless, it is important to understand that our knowledge of him is not full; only God himself knows all there is to be known about him and his activities in his creation. Isaiah tells us, "His understanding is unsearchable" (Isa 40:28). Yet what we do know from his word is true and that which lies beyond us is in no way inconsistent with what is revealed. There will always be more to learn; and we can learn because, Paul tells us, there is One who can search the things of God and reveal more to us: "But God has revealed them to us through His Spirit. For the Spirit searches all things, yes, the deep things of God" (1 Cor 2:10). Furthermore, there is a glorious day coming when what we can know now will seem dimness and greyness compared to our knowledge then, as Paul puts it. "For now we see in a mirror, dimly, but then face to face. Now I know in part, but then I shall know just as I also am known" (1 Cor 13:12).

It is not God's desire that we should only know about him but know him relationally, as in a relationship between persons. God is a person; he is a free personal spirit; he is not a mere force but has intelligence, will, affections, and self-awareness, and he communicates by words. When we study more of his triunity of nature we will explore further how relationship is at the core of his being. Such an understanding preserves us from cold, metaphysical speculation or mindless mysticism, both of which either deny he is a person or cannot conceive of intelligent communication between humans and the divine. Some may protest that all these Scripture expressions that use our terms to refer to God are mere anthropomorphisms; they are God adapting himself to his creatures, but they do not tell us what he himself is actually like in his essence. The Scriptures never lead us to think in such a way; they never give the impression that our limitation as creatures means we cannot perceive the true nature of God's character, but it is the full extent of his characteristics (for example in the outworking of his love and his justice), their height and depth, their glory, that we can only dimly perceive. As Job said of the mysteries of God's natural world (pointing to the mysteries of his moral government), "Indeed these are the mere edges of His ways, And how small a whisper we hear of Him!" (Job 26:14).

Some of the means God has used to reveal himself underline the reality of personal relationship. Firstly, God communicates with us by words, and he utters them with the expectation of a response from us which will lead us to knowing him. God spoke to Adam in the garden, "Where are you?" (Gen 3:9). He spoke to Moshe, "God called to him from the midst of the bush and said, 'Moses, Moses!' And he said, 'Here I am'" (Exod 3:4). Secondly, he has appeared in human form (a theophany), and spoke, for example, to Joshua, "No, but as Commander of the army of the Lord I have now come" (Josh 5:14). Thirdly, he has made covenants in which he brings humans into a committed and intelligent relationship with himself, as with Yisrael through Moshe at Sinai: "Then he took the Book of the Covenant and read in the hearing of the people. And they said, 'All that the Lord has said we will do, and be obedient'" (Exod 24:7). Fourthly, he encourages us to pray, to ask things of him: "Trust in Him at all times, you people; Pour out your heart before Him" (Ps 62:8); and Yeshua said to his disciples, "Until now you have asked nothing in My name. Ask, and you will receive, that your joy may be full" (John 16:24). Finally, and preeminently, God as a God of relationship is revealed by the incarnation of his Son, Messiah Jesus, who came to make that relationship a possibility and a reality: "And this is eternal life, that they may know You, the only true God, and Jesus Christ whom You have sent" (John 17:3).

The liturgy of the synagogue leaves one in no doubt that traditional Judaism believes we know about God and that he desires a relationship with his people. Christians can say amen to most of the statements and petitions in the liturgy. However, the relationship envisaged in the liturgy is primarily in terms of God with Israel as a whole, so that the idea of an individual, personal relationship is reserved for especially blessed and holy people in Israel's Bible history. It is not something contemplated for the average Jewish person today. Yeshua taught something better, and gave his life as a sacrifice so that sinners may have a personal relationship with the living God.

> Whom have I in heaven but You?

And there is none upon earth that I desire besides You. (Ps 73:25)

Scriptures

Gen 2:16–19; 3:9–10; 18:17–33; Exod 33:11, 18–23; Ps 62:8; Jer 9:24; 31:34; John 17:3; 16:23; 1 Tim 6:16.

Questions

1. Do you have a personal relationship with God through Yeshua? How did that first come about, and how is your relationship with God expressed now?
2. Assuming God's existence, is it reasonable to expect to know about him and to accept limits to our knowledge? Give your reasons.
3. How would you encourage seekers after God to believe God desires a personal relationship with them?

Further Reading

Macleod, Donald. *Behold Your God*. Fearn: Christian Focus, 1995.
Packer, J. I. *Knowing God*. London: Hodder & Stoughton, 2005.

13

God's Names and Nature

(A) GOD'S NAMES

God's names are part of his self-revelation and tell us the nature of his being and character. They were all revealed in the context of Israel's Old Testament and New Testament history, and had particular significance in the setting in which they were given. They reveal attributes of his being which cannot be communicated to us (such as almighty power) and also attributes which can (such as graciousness). Our approach here will be to briefly mention the most significant names and what they indicate, and then draw out the meanings and implications in the next section—God's nature. As most of these names first appear in the Old Testament, we will focus on the Hebrew words but draw attention to the New Testament usage later in the section. The names can be broadly classified into: general names, God's covenant names in Old and New Testament, and God's unique New Testament name.

(i) General Names

This term is used because many of these words are not used as names in the traditional sense of indicating a particular person. However, they have the sense of a name when their use points to God as the one and only God, in distinction to false gods.

(a) *El* is a general Semitic word with the root idea of strength and might. It is used about two hundred times of the true God (e.g., Gen 31:13) and in other ways about fifty times (e.g., Exod 34:14). The compound forms of *El* are used to make clear that the one true God is being referred to, and in a particular way; for example, El Elyon, God Most High. This speaks of God as the One above all powers and authorities and appears nearly thirty times, first in Gen 14:8 in the Melchizedek-Abraham encounter. It is a popular usage in the synagogue.

(b) *El Olam*, the Everlasting God, speaks of the One who is eternal, the One who has no beginning and no end (Gen 21:33). "The Eternal" is a title for God among the Orthodox.

(c) *El Shaddai*, God Almighty, which will be considered below under "God's Covenant Names."

(d) *Eloah* is derived from El and conveys the same truth—God as all-powerful and infinite. It is mostly used in the book of Job, e.g., 29:2.

(e) *Elohim* is the plural of Eloah and is the preeminent word for God in the Hebrew Bible. It is the first word used for God in Gen 1:1 and occurs about 2,300 times of the true God and about 250 times in another sense (e.g., Exod 21:6, Judges; Job 38:7, sons of God [angels]; Exod 20:3, other gods). It speaks of God as the Creator and provider, the supreme deity. Elohim is El in a preeminent sense. The plural is one of majesty. It usually occurs with singular verbs or adjectives, underlining both his majesty and his oneness.

(ii) God's Covenant Names in Old and New Testaments

By this is meant those names which God especially associates with a particular stage in the development of his covenant relationship with Israel. They are El Shaddai, YHWH, and Yeshua. El Shaddai was especially used in the patriarchal period, YHWH in the Mosaic, and Yeshua in the messianic. Each name does not in itself reveal all about God that is unfolded in each period, but it points to that within God's character which undergirds the further revelation given in the period. Exod 6:2–3 illustrates: "I appeared to Abraham, to Isaac, and to Jacob as God Almighty, but by My name LORD [i.e., YHWH] I was not known to them." Now, the patriarchs did in fact know the name YHWH, but the making of the covenant with Abraham was especially associated with the name God Almighty (El Shaddai) (see Gen 17:1–2 and 28:3, 35:11, 43:14, 48:3, 49:25). The covenant promised abundant offspring, a land, defense, and blessing. The name El Shaddai, God Almighty, teaches his absolute power, above all power, and hence underlines his ability to deliver on those promises. In the New Testament it is a name which appears especially in the book of Revelation, underlining that God is able to fulfill all his plans for his people and the whole creation.

The name YHWH (Heb. יהוה) is linked to the revelation to Moshe in Exod 3:14. When Moshe asks God's name, God declares it using the verb "to be"—I AM THAT I AM, or I WILL BE THAT I AM. So YHWH has the meaning "He will be." The thought is that he alone has self-existence; he is; he is present, and never changes. He is; he does not become. In the context of the covenant it points to his power and determination to be faithful to his promises. He reveals himself to Moses as the One who will now deliver from Egypt and take Israel to the land he has promised (Exod 6:5–8). This deliverance shows what he later declares to Moses in Exod 34:6–7: his goodness, graciousness, and mercy, alongside his determination not to leave sin unpunished.

The name YHWH is compounded with other words to express how YHWH delivered or provided. For example, YHWH Ropehah, ("YHWH your healer," Exod 15:26); YHWH Jireh ("YHWH will provide," Gen 22:14); YHWH Nissi ("YHWH is my banner," Exod 17:15); YHWH Shalom ("YHWH is peace," Judg 6:24); YHWH Tsidkenu ("YHWH our righteousness," Jer 23:6).

What is the correct pronunciation of YHWH? Out of reverence for God and his name, it became forbidden to speak it, and hence the original pronunciation was lost. Whilst such an attitude in Israel was commendable, it was surely a loss. God gave his people his name as a sign of growing intimacy in his relationship with them, and it was surely designed to be used. It is fair to say that God's people were hesitant to address him solely by the word YHWH, such that YHWH is almost always preceded by "O" in direct speech, or by "Lord" (i.e. "Lord YHWH," which is always written in English Bibles as "Lord God," see Gen 15:2). The diminutive of YHWH is written as YAH in English Bibles and expresses endearment, underlining intimacy, but it is usually accompanied by YHWH, underlining awe (Isa 26:4). The uncertainty over pronunciation led to the use of Adonai (my Lord), which is familiar in the synagogue. Why Adonai? Presumably because it expressed both covenant intimacy and the personal submission required. English Bibles have Lord for YHWH in the Old Testament to make it clear it is the divine name יהוה in the text. In the New Testament the writers followed the LXX example, which uses *Kurios* for YHWH, written as "Lord." Some Christians believe the name should still be used and so "Jehovah" or "Yahweh" may be encountered in some translations of the Bible.

The name *Yeshua*. The familiar name "Jesus" is derived from the Greek word *Iesous*, the word used for Joshua in the LXX. Joshua is the name Moses gave to Hoshea Ben Nun. In Hebrew it is *Yehoshua*, meaning "YHWH-Savior" or "YHWH saves," the meaning attached to the naming of Jesus by an angel (Matt 1:21). Yeshua is a later, contracted form of Yehoshua, in common use after the return from Babylon (see Ezra 3:2, Heb. *Yeshua*); it is the Hebrew name of Messiah Jesus. It was not a new name in Israel, just as YHWH was already known to Moses, but it points to a new and fuller understanding of God's character as the savior of sinners. The life and death of Yeshua reveal a God who saves, not just by power but by personal sacrifice and suffering. In Yeshua God reveals himself as a God of love in a way previously unimagined and unknown. The fact that the word "Yeshua" contains an abbreviated form of YHWH underlines the continuity with what God has already revealed of himself to Israel—his name is always YHWH (Exod 3:15)—but Yeshua provides a fuller revelation of his character, one who saves by personal sacrifice.

(iii) God's Unique New Testament Name

The name "the Father and the Son and the Holy Spirit" (Matt 28:19) comes from the lips of Yeshua. The singular word "name" makes it clear that the union into which his disciples are baptized is a union with the one and only God, the God of Israel, but the full mystery of his being—the three persons in the one God—is stated clearly. This will be considered in more detail as we proceed, but here we note that this is a name of God. As with the other names, it reveals to us those truths of his being which he brings to light in this particular covenant era. This name tells us that there are three persons—the Father, the Son, and the Holy Spirit—in the one God, something which is beyond our comprehension. Hints of this truth exist in the Old Testament, but it is only under the new covenant that they are clearly revealed.

> I will extol You, my God, O King;
> And I will bless Your name forever and ever.
> Every day I will bless You;
> And I will praise Your name forever and ever. (Ps 144:1–2)
>
> Who shall not fear You, O Lord, and glorify Your name?
> For You alone are holy.
> For all the nations shall come and worship before You,
> For Your judgments have been manifested. (Rev 15:4)

Scriptures

See in the text of "God's Names" above for the many Scripture references.

Questions

1. How did the names of God prepare God's people for the revelation which followed?
2. What name/s did you use for God before coming to faith in Yeshua, and which do you use now? What does this indicate of the change in your thinking?

Further Reading

Girdlestone, Robert B. *Synonyms of the Old Testament*. Peabody, MA: Hendrickson, 2000.

(B) GOD'S NATURE

To write and read of God is an awesome exercise for us, his creatures. But it can be done, and he wants us to do it, for he is seeking a humble people who love and worship, fear and enjoy him. For that, we need to think of him as he truly is.

God's nature is thought of in terms of his attributes. We can only think of them one by one, but it is important not to isolate one attribute from any other, as if they are simply separate parts of his being. God's whole being is gracious, all powerful, etc., and each attribute qualifies others, e.g., his wisdom is infinite. God's attributes describe his essential being; they are not somehow distinct from an irreducible essence of God.

God's revelation of himself as the "I AM" points us to a classification of attributes. God existed before he chose to create the visible and invisible worlds, and so we may consider separately those attributes of his being which are unrelated to his creation, and then those which are manifested through his relationship to it. However, in making this distinction we need to remember that all we know about God is revealed to us in the context of his created world.

Note: the consideration of God's triunity will come at the end of this consideration, but it is everywhere assumed and is occasionally referred to.

(i) Unrelated Attributes

God is a *spirit*; he has no body or parts (John 4:24). Scripture uses anthropomorphisms to describe his actions (e.g., the arm of the Lord), but none are to be taken literally. God has *personality*; he is not mere impersonal force. He has mind, will, and affection, and within the triune Godhead there is communication (Rom 11:34; Heb 2:4; 2 Sam 12:24-25; John 17:24). Examples of God's affections are: love between persons of the Godhead, his pleasure in his people's obedience (Isa 62:4), his grief at suffering (Gen 6:5-6), and his anger at disobedience (Ps 2:5, 12). Such affections in God are manifested according to his will and not forced by anything outside of himself; God is *free*, and acts exactly as he pleases according to his nature (Eph 1:11). God is *infinite*, which is an attribute closely related to freedom, and it is not an easy concept for finite creatures to grasp. God's infinity is best thought of qualitatively—that his love is infinite means that it has no defect, no weakness, and no limit. If God's infinity is to be thought of quantitatively, it is not so much a spatial concept, but one of energy—he never grows weary but is boundlessly active (Isa 40:28). God is *eternal*; "from everlasting to everlasting, You are God" (Ps 90:2); he has no beginning or end and his being is not constrained by the fixity of time as we experience it, for with him a day is as a thousand years and a thousand years as a day. He is therefore *immortal*, and he alone; having life without end is his by nature. God is *unchangeable* (immutable); all his attributes are completely constant, as Malachi reveals, "I am the Lord, I do not change" (Mal 3:6). This quality leads to his faithfulness and covenant consistency. He is *self-sufficient*; he is in need of nothing from outside of himself. He did not create the world because of a need he felt, but solely for his glory and good pleasure, and our good.

Only in two places in Scripture do we read "God *is* . . .": he is *love* (1 John 4:8, 16) and he is *light* (1 John 1:5), and it is important to consider them together. *Love* and *light* (understanding) lie at the heart of God's being as Father, Son, and Holy Spirit. The unity of the persons is expressed in their love for one another and their perfect knowledge of one another (Mark 1:11; John 3:35; 14:31; Gal 5:22). God's self-sufficient, Trinitarian life before ever the world was made was one of perfect love and perfect understanding (John 17:24; 1 Tim 6:16).

When we survey all attributes considered so far, we understand what is meant by his *holiness*: God is the Holy One of Israel. In Isaiah's vision (6:1-3) the Lord is seen high and lifted up, and the seraphim declare his holiness by uttering the word three times; he is the thrice-holy God. Here holiness points to his otherness from all else. Similar words are used in Rev 4:8, where his holiness is connected to being the One who was, is, and is to come. All the preceding unrelated attributes underline his otherness. He is spirit, free, infinite, eternal, immortal, unchangeable, self-sufficient, love, and light and he alone has such qualities. His holiness confronts us with his *glory*, his majesty, and his sheer Godness. God's glory has a visible manifestation (Ezek 1:28; Rev 1:14–16) which points to the majesty of his character. Moshe asked God to show him his glory and God said, "I will make all my goodness pass before you" (Exod 33:18–23; 34:5–8), and the same is said of the glory of Jesus (John 1:14). The word "glory" points to "weightiness"; it is something which overwhelms, bringing both awe and delight. Ultimately, the fullness of his glory is seen "in the face of Jesus Christ" (2 Cor 4:6), revealing in greatest clarity his triunity, his perfection, his love, mercy, and justice.

In all that is written above, there is little difference between Christianity's understanding and that of traditional Judaism, except in the matter of God's triunity. The Scriptures of the Old Testament have led Judaism's teachers to the same understanding of God's unrelated attributes as Christian teachers using both Old and New Testaments. Christian churches do differ on doctrine but those who hold to the historic creeds are of one mind on what is written here and below on God's nature.

(ii) Related Attributes

These are those attributes which are manifested through God's relation to his creation. Consideration will be given to the more overarching attributes, e.g., omnipresence, and then those which reveal God as a relational being towards creatures made in his image.

Note: Many theological books will have something in their section on God which considers God as Creator, sustainer, and ruler. I have included that in Part 2: God's Creation.

(a) God's Attributes in Relation to All He Has Made

God is present everywhere in his creation (*omnipresent* or *immanent*). There is nowhere that he is not. He is in the seen and unseen realms; he is in the realm of the living and of the dead, for "all live to Him" (Luke 20:38). He is fully present everywhere—not partially here and partially there. All things everywhere rely on him for their existence and continuance: "in Him all things consist" (Col 1:17). There is a moral dimension to this. For example, in Ps 139 David reveals his awareness that all his actions were seen, and there was no place of escape. Because God is everywhere, he sees all and will one day judge all actions of all humans (Rev 20:12–13); similarly, he knows all the griefs of his people (see Ps 56:8). None of this means God *is* his creation, or that nature is God (pantheism). He is *transcendent*, which is another way of expressing his holiness. He is external to the world, not somehow tied into what he has made.

Scripture sometimes speaks of God's presence as manifested in a particular location. It was visibly manifested in the tabernacle and the temple (the Shekinah, Exod 33:8–14; 1 Kgs 8:6–13) and finally on the Mount of Transfiguration (Mark 9:7). Invisibly, his presence is manifested in the hearts of believers in Jesus (John 14:16–18, 21) and in their gatherings (Matt 18:20). He does not choose to manifest himself everywhere in such a special manner, but he is nonetheless present everywhere. Such manifestation is in grace and is relational towards those with whom he has entered into a covenant. Traditional Judaism teaches such a view of God as transcendent and immanent. Its rejection of Messiah means it has forfeited the opportunity to experience his indwelling in the heart and his presence in gatherings for worship despite all that is uplifting in the synagogue. Mystical Judaism has perhaps sought to make up for this felt lack by thinking of the created world as an emanation from God so that "all is filled with the essence of His pure unity"; this errs in the direction of pantheism.

God is *all-powerful* (*omnipotent*). Israel owes its beginnings to this, as God counters Sarah's doubts with, "Is anything too hard for the LORD?" (Bereshit 18:14), and also Israel's survival, as God vows her return from Babylonian captivity: "I am the LORD, the God of all flesh. Is there anything too hard for Me?" (Jer 32:27). That same chapter promises a changed Israel, and that too requires omnipotence: the miraculous conception of the Savior, "For with God nothing will be impossible" (Luke 1:37), and the miraculous work of regeneration, "for with God all things are possible" (Mark 10:27). In the affairs of humankind and the work of salvation the omnipotent God can do what we can barely imagine.

God is *all-knowing* (*omniscient*). This not only means that, due to his omnipresence, he is aware of everything in his creation at any moment in time, but that he knows all that has been and will be. All that has been in the lives of humans is, as it were, recorded in the books: "And the dead were judged according to their works, by the things which were written in the books" (Rev 20:12). This extends to the intents and thoughts of the heart (Gen 6:5, Luke 5:22). The many prophecies in Holy Scripture of future events demonstrate God's foreknowledge of all that will be, whether a particular event in an individual's life (John 21:18–19) or detailed developments in the affairs of nations (Dan 11). God's foreknowledge is not in any way limited by contingencies which have yet to occur; all is determined by the "counsel of His will" (Eph 1:11); his own plan and purpose covers all that has been, is, or will be. Does this mean humans are not responsible for their actions? Clearly not, or God could not justly judge the world. God knows us, our circumstances, the influences upon us, and our weaknesses, all of which contribute to a decision we freely and responsibly make; yet he knows exactly what we will do, and he knows this of all his creatures. Without this there could be no certainty about God's plan of salvation. This leads on naturally to the next attribute, God's sovereignty.

God is *sovereign*. It is not without significance that Israel's substitute for the divine name YHWH was "Adonai," my Lord. God's lordship is the consequence of all his attributes, such as his power, presence, knowledge, and wisdom, and it defines the attitude which he expects in his creatures: one of submission to his rule, a submission which should be marked by gratitude and love as they perceive his goodness. He alone is God, and there are no others (Isa 45:5), and all authority which exists is under him (Rom 13:1; Col 1:16). His will is the final cause of all things (Isa 46:9–10) and the Scriptures mention these things in particular: creation (Isa 40:28; Ps 148:5), providence (Ps 104:30), salvation (Eph 1:4; Rom 8:29), life and destiny (Rom 8:28; 15:32; Dan 5:23; Isa 37:26–27), life's details (Matt 10:29), natural disasters and upheavals (Gen 6:13; Lev 26:14–39; Rev 6), the sufferings of Messiah Yeshua (Acts 2:23), the sufferings of God's people (Ps 44:22; 119:67; Phil 1:29), and sufferings to awaken sinners to repentance (Job 33:14–30).

As people observe history and present experience, they have often been overwhelmed by negative perceptions, so that life is mainly suffering, or it is pointless, and they are at the mercy of forces which are either irresistible or unchangeable. This is unbelief. God's lordship is revealed as good towards his creation, and yet not to be resisted without consequences. Those who seek him will find him, and experience his mercy and kindness (Rom 2:6–11; Ps 52:1; Isa 55:6–7; Matt 7:7–8; Job 5:8). These things are abundantly clear in both the Old and New Testaments, and traditional Judaism and Christianity share these convictions.

(b) God's Attributes as a Relational Being towards His Rational Creatures

Under this heading are considered those attributes which are manifested especially in God's intercourse with his rational creatures, whether in a fallen or unfallen state. Two scriptures reveal the core of God's nature: "God is *love*" and "God is *light*" (1 John 4:8; 1:5). From these two qualities emerge all the attributes considered in this section. When God's relationship with humans in sin is considered, there appears to be a tension between these two core attributes. If God is light, he hates and turns away from all that is dark, all which fails to conform to his perfect righteousness. How then can his love be manifested to the unrighteous? His love has determined that the judgment sinners deserve will be suffered by himself, in the person of his Son. Thus he may justly forgive the guilty and shower his love upon them, giving them everlasting life with himself (John 3:16).

God Is *Light*

This means he is the touchstone of all that is true; there is no shadow of turning with him, no change concerning what is right and wrong (Jas 1:17). He is *truthful* in all his dealings with his creatures (Ps 25:10; 1 John 5:6). All that he says and promises can be relied upon fully (Ps 91:4; 2 Sam 7:28; John 17:17). Because God is light, his essential being is *righteous*; it is impossible for him to be otherwise. Yeshua addressed his Father as "righteous Father" when he considered returning to him from this fallen world (John 17:25). The world is unrighteous and struggles to be otherwise; God is intrinsically and always righteous. All his ways are right (Ps 145:17). There is a connection here to his holiness, because sinful humans inevitably feel impure and unrighteous when confronted by God's otherness (Isa 6:1–5). The heart of the gospel is a provision of righteousness for repentant sinners (Rom 1:17; 3:21–24). God's righteousness leads to his *justice*, his righteous will exercised in the world (Deut 32:4). This is exercised in: temporal punishments (2 Chr 25:20), a giving over to sin (Rom 1:24–32), vindicating deliverance (Ps 76:9; Dan 6:22), temporal rewards and blessings (Ps 18:20), and in final rewards and punishments (2 Cor 5:10–11). When God's righteousness is resisted and opposed, his response is *wrath*, his holy revulsion towards all unholiness. If he was not wrathful, he would not be truly holy. God's wrath is not to be likened to the rash anger of humans when they are crossed (Luke 9:53–54). It is a steadfast opposition to evil (Ezra 8:22; John 3:36), which may be manifested in a steady way over a long period (Rom 1:18, 24) or in an isolated event (Num 11:33). It is not easily aroused to action against persons because of his desire to bless and do good (Ps 103:8; Exod 32:10 "let me alone"). Humans may question God's justice in the light of all the injustice in his world but this is to be understood in the light of what is considered next.

God Is *Love*

His love is preeminently seen in his mercy to sinners through the giving of his Son to pay the price for their sins (John 3:16). *Mercy* is God's kindness towards sinners in their various needs. Its especial focus is forgiveness of sins (Exod 34:7; 1 Pet 1:3), but it also refers to his general kindness to those who are helpless in their circumstances (Ezra 7:28; Luke 10:27). God is *good* (Ps 86:5); his love leads him to be *good* to all (Ps 145:9; Matt 5:45). He does not judge every sin immediately but is *long-suffering* towards rebels (Ps 103:10). The presence of evil in the world is not deliberately planned by God as an inherent necessity; it is a violation of his goodness (Gen 2:16–17; Jer 7:31; Jas 1:13). God is *faithful*, which is often expressed as steadfast love (Dan 6:26). This is especially manifested in his covenant commitments to his people (Ps 89:34; Neh 1:5; Heb 13:20), which are expressed as unbreakable promises (Heb 6:13–18). The history of Israel and the church is abundant evidence of his faithfulness to the weak, backsliding, and undeserving. Because of this covenant commitment, he is a *jealous* God (Exod 20:4–5) who is angered by his people's unfaithfulness and determined to keep them for himself (Zech 1:14–15). God's love is *wise*, giving his people that which is best for them, not spoiling them with blessings they are not yet ready to receive (Prov 30:7–9), and allowing them to be tested to make them better (Job 23:10; John 15:2). But this should not be misunderstood; he is ready to bless and is not niggardly; he encourages his people to ask (John 16:24; Zech 10:1). God's love means he is *gracious*, a word which speaks of showing kindness to those who deserve the opposite: "The LORD is gracious and full of compassion, Slow to anger and great in mercy" (Ps 145:8). It is a term which is greatly used in the New Testament, where the rich meaning of it is revealed through what Messiah has done for undeserving sinners—to forgive them and then bless them with eternal life (Eph 2:5–7). In the synagogue liturgy there is great emphasis on the mercy and kindness of YHWH in his dealings with Israel.

> Ascribe greatness to our God.
> He is the Rock, His work is perfect;
> For all His ways are justice,
> A God of truth and without injustice;
> Righteous and upright is He. (Deut 32:3–4)
>
> Oh, give thanks to the LORD, for he is good!
> For His mercy endures forever. (Ps 106:1)
>
> Blessing and honor and glory and power
> Be to Him who sits on the throne,

And to the Lamb, forever and ever! (Rev 5:13)

Scriptures

Unrelated attributes: spirit (Exod 20:4; John 4:24); personality (Ps 94:9–10); free (Isa 40:12–14; Eph 1:9, 11); infinite (Isa 40:28; Jer 23:24); eternal (Pss 90:2; 102:24–27; Isa 40:28) immortal (1 Tim 1:17; 6:16); unchangeable (Ps 102:24–27; Mal 3:6); self-sufficient (Ps 50:7–12); holy (Lev 19:2; Isa 6:1–3; 1 Pet 1:15–16); loving (Deut 33:3; Zeph 3:17; 1 John 3:1; 4:8–16); glorious (Exod 15:11; Rev 21:22–23).

Related attributes: omnipresent (Ps 139:2; Acts 17:24–28); transcendent (Isa 40:12–15); omnipotent (Job 42:2; Matt 19:26); omniscient (Ps 33:13–15; Heb 4:13); sovereign (2 Chr 20:6; Rev 4:11); truthful (Ps 86:15; Isa 65:16); righteous (Gen 18:25; John 17:25); holy (Lev 19:5; Ps 99:3; Isa 1:4; 1 Pet 1:15–16); just (Deut 32:4; Zeph 3:5; Rev 15:3); wrath (Deut 9:7; John 3:36; Rom 1:17; Rev 16:1); merciful (Ps 103:2–18; Isa 63:9; Jas 5:11); good (Ps 33:5; Matt 5:45; Acts 14:7; 17:25); faithful (Deut 7:9; Lam 3:22–23; Phil 1:6; Titus 1:2); jealous (Exod 20:5; 1 Cor 10:22); wise (Dan 2:20; 1 Tim 1:17; Jude 25); gracious (Exod 34:6; Joel 2:13; 1 Pet 2:3); loving (Deut 10:15; Jer 31:3; John 3:16; Rom 5:8; 1 John 4:16).

Questions

1. Write a sentence or two in which all the unrelated attributes of God (section (i)) are mentioned, stating as far as is possible their relationship to each other.

2. Write a prayer of praise which expresses all God's related attributes (section (ii)) and try to include thoughts of how these truths strengthen you as a Christian.

3. If God's righteousness demands retribution, is he loving? How would you explain this apparent incompatibility? What other apparent incompatibilities are there in God's attributes?

4. It is said that the doctrine of God is a great strength to his people in their struggles. Think of some of those struggles, and state which attribute/s would be most helpful to strengthen faith.

5. Is God a person you desire to know as much as you possibly can? What are you doing to achieve that?

Further Reading

Macleod, Donald. *Behold Your God*. Fearn: Christian Focus, 1995.
Packer, J. I. *Knowing God*. London: Hodder & Stoughton, 2005.

(C) GOD'S UNITY AND TRIUNITY

When Yeshua was asked what was the greatest commandment, he replied with the words of Moses in Deut 6:4–5, "Hear, O Israel, the LORD our God, the LORD is one. And you shall love the LORD your God with all your heart, with all your soul, with all your mind, and with all your strength" (Mark 12:29–30). These words are known as the "Shema," and are well known to all Jews, being recited twice daily by the devout, taught early to children, recited on a person's deathbed and also by martyrs as they prepare to die for their faith. Here is the great text of Jewish monotheism, which for Jesus was the greatest commandment of all. Thus Jesus saw no contradiction between the divine unity he underlined in this encounter and what he also taught of God's triunity. This truth is a particular challenge to Jewish believers because of the familiar and strong opposition of Judaism to any suggestion of plurality in God, and because of the tension between Jews and Christendom,[1] of which this doctrine has been a catalyst and a painful reminder. And yet the doctrine of God's triunity ought to be seen as a wonderful filling out of what Israel already knew. YHWH had shown them his love and truth in his acts towards them but this further revelation reveals how the same love and truth are the essence of YHWH's inner being, an eternal relationship of love and truth between three persons in the Godhead. Here is the pinnacle of God's glory.

(i) In the Tanakh

All God's revelation is progressive and so we would expect to find hints of his triunity in the Old Testament. I say "hints" and not "clear teaching" because the OT stress is on God's unity so as to ward off the prevalent idolatry, polytheism, and dualism of the religions surrounding Israel. Here are the main hints in the Tanakh.

Yisrael was more than God's people or his servants; they were his son: "Then you shall say to Pharaoh, 'Thus says the LORD: Israel is My son, My

---

1. This term is used to describe those lands in which Christianity, in one form or another, became a national religion, leading to most citizens being viewed as Christians when by and large they were little more than baptized Gentiles.

firstborn" (Exod 4:22). God was their father, and this points to a being who is by nature a father, not one who began to be a father when he adopted Israel. He has always been a father, having an only begotten Son.

Plural terms are used for God, either in his name or the verbs associated with him, as in Gen 1:26, "Let Us make man in Our image," which might be a plural of majesty but it may be something more, which would be consistent with a plurality in the Godhead when that later revelation is given. The use of *echad* and not *yachid* for "one" in the Shema is significant because it allows for plurality; this is because *echad* was sometimes used to indicate a composite unity, as of a man and his wife in Gen 2:24. It would seem that Maimonides sought to avoid this implication when, in the second principle of Judaism's faith, he used *yachid* for "one," which points to uniqueness and singleness.

The very first act of God, his creation described in Gen 1:1–3, involves a creative will, a command by word and a Spirit who is active. One God most certainly, but these different aspects of the creative action are indicative of something more.

The Angel of the LORD is one who is distinct from God but also identified with him; "My name is in Him" (Exod 23:21, see also Exod 3:2–6). Proverbs 8:22–31 pictures "wisdom" as an entity distinct from God but always with him, and especially communicating his truth to his creatures. The term "Spirit of God" is an unusual term and seems superfluous. In Isa 63:14 we read, "As a beast goes down into the valley, And the Spirit of the LORD causes him to rest"; but why not just write that the LORD causes him to rest? The use of the term "Spirit of God" raises the thought of his distinctiveness.

Some of the messianic prophecies identify Messiah with God, for example Ps 2, in which he is begotten of YHWH; and Isa 9:6, where his name includes terms like "wonderful" and "mighty God."

Isaiah 48 is a passage where all three persons seem to be mentioned distinctly, particularly in verse 16:

> Come near to Me, hear this:
> I have not spoken in secret from the beginning;
> From the time that it was, I was there.
> And now the Lord GOD and His Spirit
> Have sent Me.

The chapter is a prior revelation of the return from Babylon, but the words of verse 16 appear to be spoken by another, one like "wisdom" in Prov 8:22–31, a being always with God, and they seem to indicate he is the One who will bring about this purpose of God, sent by the LORD and his Spirit. These words take our thoughts to the Angel of the LORD previously mentioned. Three persons seem to be in this text.

Traditional Judaism has not been deaf to these hints. For example, in the Talmud (Sanhedrin 38b) the rabbis call the Angel of the LORD mentioned in Exod 23:20, 21 "Metatron" (Heb. for "guide") and observe that his name is even as his master. Rashi, in his commentary on this text, points out that the words "even as his master" are used because the numerical value of Metatron (314) is the same as that of Shaddai (the Almighty). Nevertheless, it is fair to note that the rabbis are emphatic that, despite all this, Metatron is in no way equal to YHWH.

(ii) In the New Testament

Within the Gospels there is a progressive unfolding of this truth, principally in terms of the incarnation of the Son, and then in terms of his relationship with God the Father and the Spirit. The term "triunity" (or "Trinity") is not found in Scripture because nowhere is the whole doctrine stated in a single explicit statement with a name for it included, but that is so of many doctrines. Christian (and Jewish) teachers have, by the method of induction from different texts, discerned a teaching of Scripture and often coined a term to denote it; "triunity" is one such.

Jesus' disciples gradually became aware through his character, words, and miraculous deeds that he was someone very special (Mark 4:41). They became convinced he was the Messiah and Son of God (Mark 16:16) and, after his resurrection, that he was God incarnate, leading them to worship him (Matt 28:16, 17; see also John 20:28). As their awareness was developing, Jesus taught clearly about his unique relation to the Father, underlining his equality of nature. His enemies understood this and sought to stone him (John 8:57–59; 10:31–33). He told his disciples that only he could reveal the Father (Matt 11:27), and of his oneness with the Father: "I and My Father are one" (John 10:30, also 14:11). He spoke of the Spirit as the One who would show believers all that is the Son's, all of which was given to him by the Father, who gave him all that is the Father's (John 16:13–15). All this demands an equality of the three persons.

The first express statement of the three persons in the one God, where the three persons are mentioned as one name, is in Matt 28:19: "the name of the Father and of the Son and of the Holy Spirit." There are several other statements where all three persons are mentioned as involved in a particular action of God: the baptism of Jesus (Matt 3:13–17), Jesus' prayer for the gift of the Spirit to indwell believers (John 14:15–23), the first giving of the Spirit at Shavuot (Acts 2:32–33), receiving God's triune blessing via an apostle (2 Cor 13:14), the Christian's experience of God's love (Eph: 3:16–19), and God's eternal plan of salvation (Eph 1:1–14).

There are certain points we need to explore further, which have received clarification through the discussions within the church since the earliest days; discussions which have especially helped to defend the church's teaching against misunderstandings and denials which have emerged from time to time. Those errors have often been prompted by a desire to conform to the religious ideas of others, or to express the teaching in a way more acceptable to human reason. This has usually led to emphasizing YHWH's unity at the expense of his triunity, or his triunity at the expense of his unity. However, we must note that in seeking to understand what the Scriptures teach on God's triunity we are more than ever faced with mystery. It is a truth which cannot be grasped by our powers of reasoning but is spiritually discerned by revelation from God's Spirit, as Jesus said, "I will pray the Father, and He will give you another Helper . . . the Spirit of truth . . . At that day you will know that I am in My Father, and you in Me, and I in you" (John 14:16–20).

(iii) Aspects of the Doctrine

There is one God and his name is one (Zech 14:9). He is of one substance, which is undivided despite there being three persons in the Godhead. Hence, the three persons are not the result of dividing the divine essence into three but the divine substance is fully present in each of the three persons; each person is therefore fully divine. The Father is God (Matt 6:8; 7:21; Gal 1:1); the Son is God (John 1:1–18; Rom 9:5; Heb 1:8–10); the Spirit is God (Mark 3:29; 1 Cor 6:19; 2 Cor 3:17). The Athanasian Creed (circa eighth century) expresses it thus: "We worship one God in Trinity, and Trinity in Unity; neither confounding the Persons: nor dividing the substance." The three persons are each distinct persons in the sense of being self-conscious and self-directing. However, there is never any sense of a tension of opposing wills; a reality underlined by John's expressions: "God is love" and "God is light." The nature of YHWH, fully indwelling each person, is one of love and complete knowledge, underlining to us the unclouded unity of the persons. The Father loves the Son and the Spirit; the Son loves the Father and the Spirit; the Spirit loves the Father and the Son (Mark 1:11; John 3:35; 10:17; 14:31; Rom 15:30). The Father is light (Jas 1:17); the Son is light (John 8:12); and the Spirit is light (John 16:7–15). The names "Father," "Son," and "Holy Spirit," are not in any way to be understood as different aspects of, or different designations used by, a single-person God; something temporarily adopted in connection with particular actions in his work of redemption.

The titles "Father," "Son," and "Holy Spirit" surely give us insight into their eternal relationships within the Godhead. This is not easy to discern from the New Testament because the mention of the three persons is so often related to their activity in salvation and not exclusively in terms of their eternal modes of subsistence. It seems to this author that the expression "only begotten" underlines that whilst the Son is "God of God" (John 1:14, 18) the title "Son" implies some form of subordination to the Father, not in nature but in order of relation. In the same way the Holy Spirit is also subordinate to the Father because he is said to proceed from the Father and the Son (John 14:26; 15:26). These relations are eternal and part of the very nature of YHWH as he has always been; the One who is, was, and is to come, the unchanging One (Exod 3:14; Rev 1:4; 4:8). The Son and the Spirit are not lesser divinities brought into being by God for the purpose of our salvation. That would be to deny their equality of nature with the Father.

Both the unity and the triunity of God are underlined in his activities. His unity is underlined in those texts in the NT and the Tanakh which refer to the activities of the one God without any mention of a particular person. For example: in creation (Rev 4:8, 11), in sustaining the world (Rom 11:36), and in saving sinners (Jude 25). But his triunity is underlined by the involvement of each of the three persons in these same three activities. In creation the Father was active (1 Cor 8:6), as was the Son (John 1:3), as was the Spirit (Gen 1:2). In sustaining the world the Father is active (1 Cor 8:6), as is the Son (Heb 1:3), as is the Spirit (Ps 104:30). In salvation the Father is active (Eph 1:3, 4; Rom 6:4), as is the Son (John 3:16; 1 John 1:7), as is the Spirit (Rom 8:13–16).

And yet the NT does present them as having different roles in the detailed outworking of these activities. One way to underline that is to state that only the Son died for sin, not the Father or the Spirit. One text which expresses these different roles is 1 Pet 1:2, where Peter describes believers as "elect according to the foreknowledge of God the Father, in sanctification of the Spirit, for obedience and sprinkling of the blood of Jesus Christ," which can be summarized like this: the Father planned redemption and sent his Son to achieve it; in obedience the Son accomplished it, and the Spirit was sent by the Father and the Son to apply the redemption to the lives of God's people. Paul expresses this difference of roles at greater length in Eph 1:3–14.

From the very earliest days of the new covenant there have been assaults on this doctrine, usually via an attack on the full deity of Jesus, and the NT has examples of the apostolic response in Col 2:9 and 1 John 2:23. It is still so today, and it has to be said that any teaching which fails to speak of Jesus the Son and the Holy Spirit as possessed of the fullest deity, coequal and coeternal with the Father, is not to be tolerated. Such teachings deny to the Son and the Spirit their true glory, and fail to proclaim the ineffable majesty and glory of the God whose unity is a triunity—that of the Father and the Son and the Holy Spirit.

In conclusion it should be noted that YHWH's way of salvation is indissolubly linked to his triunity. How can there be substitutionary propitiation if two persons are not involved? And how can the suffering substitute bear the full intensity of divine wrath if he is not also divine? Regeneration, sanctification, and glorification are essential to our salvation, but if the Spirit who works such things is not God then how can it be said that God is our Savior (Titus 1:3)? Salvation in every part is the work of a God who is love and who has always loved in the divine life of the three persons. We can but marvel, worship, and be filled with thanks.

> Now to Him who is able to keep you from stumbling,
> And to present you faultless
> Before the presence of His glory with exceeding joy,
> To God our Savior,
> Who alone is wise,
> Be glory and majesty,
> Dominion and power,
> Both now and forever.
> Amen. (Jude 24–25)

SCRIPTURES

Unity: Exod 20:2–3; Deut 6:4–5; Mark 12:29–30; 1 Cor 8:4–6.

Plurality and Persons in the Godhead

OT anticipation: Gen 1:26; 16:7–13; Exod 23:21 with Exod 3:2–6; 31:3; Ps 2:7; Prov 8:22–31; Isa 6:3–8; 9:6; 11:2; 48:16; 61:1.

The Father (God absolutely): John 17:3; Eph 1:3–6; Gal 1:1.

The Son (the only begotten and image of God): John 1:14; Rom 9:5; Col 1:15; Heb 1:2–6.

The Spirit (proceeding from the Father and the Son): John 15:26; 1 Cor 2:10–11; 2 Cor 3:17.

Father, Son, and Spirit (plurality in unity in one text): Matt 28:19.

Relations of the Persons

Mutual honor (John 15:26; 16:13–15); coordination (Eph 4:4–6; 1 Pet 1:2); differing roles (Father: Eph 1:4, 9–11; Son: Eph 1:7; 1 Tim 2:5; Heb 7:28–8:2; Spirit: John 3:5–8; Eph 2:18; 2 Thess 2:13).

Questions

1. How is God's oneness and unity taught in both the OT and NT?
2. What indications are there in the OT that God is a triunity?
3. Collect references in the NT relevant to the doctrine of God's triunity and express the doctrine in your own words.
4. Demonstrate from NT references the different roles of the divine persons in the work of salvation.

Further Reading

Macleod, Donald. *Behold Your God*. Fearn: Christian Focus, 1995.
Reeves, Michael. *The Good God*. Milton Keynes: Paternoster, 2012.
Warfield, Benjamin B. *Biblical and Theological Studies*. Phillipsburg: Presbyterian and Reformed, 1968. See pp. 22–60 on the Trinity.

PART 4

God's Creation

In this second part of Book Two we begin by looking at what Scripture teaches about the world God has made, and how he sustains and governs it. Then we focus on the creation of humankind, the fall into sin, and all the consequences of that for humans and God's created world.

14

God the Planner

WHEN WE MAKE SOMETHING it is normal to have an idea in our head what we want the end result to look like and how we will go about it. The texts in Scripture which contain the words "before the foundation of the world" indicate God had a very clear, detailed plan and purpose in mind when he created the world. There will be further examination of this truth in subsequent parts of this book but we will consider the subject briefly now; it is often referred to as "God's decrees."

It was especially the plan of God the Father to create an eternal kingdom for the blessing of those who loved and obeyed his Son; "Then the King will say to those on His right hand, 'Come, you blessed of My Father, inherit the kingdom prepared for you from the foundation of the world" (Matt 25:34). Paul describes such people as chosen: "just as He chose us in Him before the foundation of the world, that we should be holy and without blame before Him in love" (Eph 1:4, see also Rev 17:8). The elect are a gift from the Father to his beloved Son, who will be with the Son in the final glory of God's kingdom (John 17:24). Elsewhere this relationship is spoken of in terms of a bride to a husband (Rev 21:2; Eph 5:25–27). God planned their salvation by the death of his Son before the world began (Rev 13:8, see 1 Pet 1:19–20). The plan of God unfolded through God's choice of Abraham, the election of Israel, the Messiah as God's elect one, and finally the people of the new covenant as God's chosen ones. This leaves us in no doubt that before God made the world he planned for the consequences of the fall, for the salvation from sin of a great multitude who were known to him individually and given to his Son, that his Son would be incarnate and die for those he had been given by the Father, that all those given and saved would surely arrive in God's eternal kingdom and never sin again, and that they would enjoy the very blessedness of God with God the Father, the Son, and the Spirit in God's eternal kingdom.

The questions this raises about humans' free will and God's justice are examined elsewhere, especially in Part 4, chapter 19, under "The Creation of Humankind"/"Human Freedom" and "The Fall of Humankind"/"Divergent Teachings"; and in Part 5, chapter 27, under "From Life to Death"/"Election." However, at this point it should be kept in mind that the God who is love planned for an innumerable multitude of redeemed sinners to be with him forever living in an intimate relationship of love—the height, depth, and breadth of which they have come to appreciate through the cross. We can but marvel and worship.

15

God the Creator

"In the beginning God created the heavens and the earth," and Scripture makes clear in many places that this work was his alone and he created (Heb. *bara*) the seen and the unseen world out of nothing: "All things were made through Him; and without him nothing was made that was made" (John 1:3, see also Ps 102:25; Isa 40:26; Rev 4:11). This truth should lead humans to worship (Ps 95:6). God did not use some form of existing material: "the things which are seen are not made of things which are visible" (Heb 11:3). If he had, it would be questionable if it was fully under his control. He did not make the world out of himself, as if it is an extension of his being. If that was so, then evil had its origin in him and must be somehow good. Does scientific theory hold to a cosmic beginning? In the past it has not done so, but among the cosmological models today the big bang theory points to a cosmic beginning.

The creation account in Gen 1 has been a source of debate within both Judaism and Christianity, a debate which revolves around the interpretation of the passage. Did God create the universe in six consecutive twenty-four-hour periods, through six decrees, or was it six eras of indeterminate length initiated by him, or is it all just a picture, the details not to be taken literally? None of these different views necessarily aims to minimize the truth that God created the world out of nothing. The text undoubtedly has a poetic form, but that does not mean it is not describing literal events in a precise time frame. It needs to be noted that the language is popular, designed to be intelligible in all ages, and that it assumes the viewpoint of the reader as an observer. In other words, it is not a scientific treatise.

This author's conviction is that the first view is correct. Our term "twenty-four hours" was not one in use in Moses' time, and is in a sense a technical term, but the wording "the evening and the morning were the first day" is a very precise way, in the language of observation, of saying "twenty-four hours." The establishment of the Sabbath in Israel's life was modeled on the rest which took place on the seventh day, and is explained in literal terms: "for in six days the Lord made the heavens and the earth" (Exod 20:11). This is in conflict with some scientific theories but it is worth remembering two things: scientific theories are constantly being modified, and science can only observe and draw deductions from what can be seen; but the six days of creation are not observable and no doubt involved processes which are not happening today. It is part of God's glory that his ways are not our ways and his act of creation should lead us to marvel, as Gen 1:31 records: "Then God saw everything that He had made, and indeed it was very good."

God has also created an invisible supernatural world (Ps 148:2; Col 1:16), inhabited by beings with non-material bodies (Heb 1:7) who are very numerous (Ps 68:17; Rev 5:11). Most are described as angels (messengers), two of whom are mentioned by name, Michael and Gabriel, the former being described as the archangel (Jude 9). There are "holy ones" and "watchers" (Dan 4:17). We also read of beings close to God's throne, represented to us in vision form: cherubim (held fast ones, Gen 3:24; Isa 37:16; Ezek 10), seraphim (burning ones, Isa 6:2), and living creatures (Ezek 1; Rev 4:4). They are God's servants who worship him, execute his will, reveal truth, and serve the redeemed (Heb 1:14, see also Ps 148:2; 104:4; 91:11; Dan 4:17; 9:20–22; 10:10–11:1); and on occasions served the Savior himself (Luke 1:26; 22:43; 24:23). There is a danger that, being out of sight, they are out of mind, but sufficient information is revealed for us to know they have an important role in God's purpose of salvation for which we should be grateful. Yet the paucity of information tells us we are not to pry beyond what has been revealed, which some early Christians did (Col 2:18), and have done so since, and this is especially in the area of evil spirits.

The evil angels were not made evil, but fell into sin: "And the angels who did not keep their proper domain, but left their own abode, He has reserved in everlasting chains under darkness for the judgment of the great day" (Jude 6); they oppose God's purposes (Gen 3:1–5; Zech 3:1; Dan 10:10–11:1; Rev 16:13–14), and are led by Satan (adversary) (Rev 12:9). They have been conquered by Jesus at the cross (Col 2:14–15) and will be punished in hell forever (Matt 25:41). The danger of an obsessive interest in the activity of evil spirits is that believers may go beyond what Scripture tells us of our interaction with them. There is a warfare which requires us to be strong against demonic activity: "Put on the whole armor of God, that you may be able to stand against the wiles of the devil" (Eph 6:10–20). In the regular activities of the Christian life the believer will be resisted by evil forces and sometimes know special attack (Eph 6:16). There may be encounters with the demon-possessed which may require confrontation and casting out (Acts 16:16–18). The point is that it all happens in the normal course of Christian life and service. There is no hint in Scripture of believers taking the initiative to seek out evil spirits and confront them. Our task is to seek out people, and to minister the gospel to them; in such activity it may well be that evil, in the form of evil spirits, will confront us but we are to oppose them: "Resist the devil and he will flee from you" (Jas 4:7, see also 1 Pet 5:9).

> Bless the LORD, O my soul!
> O LORD my God, You are very great:
> You are clothed with honor and majesty,
> Who cover Yourself with light as with a garment,
> Who stretch out the heavens like a curtain.
> He lays the beams of his upper chambers in the waters,
> Who makes the clouds His chariot,
> Who walks on the wings of the wind,
> Who makes His angels spirits,
> His ministers a flame of fire.
> You who laid the foundations of the earth,
> So that it should not be moved for ever. (Ps 104:1–5)

SCRIPTURES

Plan and election: Gen 12:1–3; Exod 3:6–10; Isa 42:1; John 6:37, 44; 17:2; Acts 2:23; Rom 8:28–30; 11:5–7; Eph 1:11; 2:10; 2 Thess 2:13; 2 Tim 1:9; 1 Pet 2:4.

Creation: Gen 1:1—2:3; Job 26:13; Ps 90:2; Isa 40:26; John 1:3; Rom 1:25; 1 Cor 8:6; Rev 10:6.

Creation ex nihilo: Ps 33:6; Rom 4:17; Heb 11:3.

The invisible world: Gen 28:12; 1 Chr 21:20; 2 Chr 32:21; Job 38:7; Ps 91:11; Zech 1:9; Matt 2:19; Luke 15:10; Acts 10:3; Heb 1:4; Rev 8:6.

Fallen spirits: Isa 14:12–15; Ezek 28:11–15 (Satan under imagery of king of Tyre); 2 Cor 11:14; 1 Tim 4:1; 2 Pet 2:4; Rev 12:7.

Questions

1. How comprehensive was God's plan for the world before he created it?
2. What is the scriptural doctrine of creation, and how should it contribute to scientific investigation?
3. How do you interpret Gen 1–2?

Further Reading

Berkouwer, G. C. *Divine Election*. Grand Rapids: Eerdmans, 1960.
Blocher, Henry. *In the Beginning*. Leicester: InterVarsity, 1984.
Calvin, John. *Institutes of the Christian Religion*. Peabody, MA: Hendrickson, 2007. See chapters 21–24.
Garner, Paul. *The New Creationism*. Darlington: Evangelical, 2009.
Lennox, John. *God's Undertaker: Has Science Buried God?* Oxford: Lion, 2009.
Wilkinson, David. *The Message of Creation*. Leicester: InterVarsity, 2006.

16

God the Provider and Ruler

THE WORLD HAS NO built-in ability to sustain or renew itself, neither is it solely dependent on humans for the ordering of its affairs. Rather, God himself actively preserves it, sustains it, and renews it, operating in all that occurs and directing all to the end he has determined. There is no such thing as blind fate or chance. This extends to all that is inanimate and animate, all persons, events, and activities, of individuals and governing bodies. Concerning God the Son it is written, "in Him all things consist" (Col 1:17), and the Son is now "upholding all things through the Word of His power" (Heb 1:3). Ephesians 1:11 tells us that God "works all things according to the counsel of His will," and Acts 4:28 teaches that human evil plans can only be "whatever Your hand and Your purpose determined before to be done." Psalm 33 reveals God's directions of the affairs of nations (vv. 10–12, 16–17) and his forming of every individual (v. 15). Psalm 104 describes his ordering of and providing for the natural world of animals, sea creatures, and humankind (vv. 10–23), summarized by verse 30: "You renew the face of the earth."

Due to the fall, humans have a tendency to focus on what God forbids, but Scripture emphasises his goodness in all his sustaining and renewing activity: "The earth is full of the goodness of the LORD" (Ps 33:5, see also Ps 104:28; Matt 5:45; Acts 14:17). In this sense God is described as the Father of all humanity (Mal 2:10; Acts 17:29); as a father to a son or daughter, so he cares for all his creatures.

God's government of the universe works through all he has made, visible and invisible, but Scripture is primarily concerned with humankind. His rule of humankind is not arbitrary, but according to moral laws based on his righteous nature, "The Lord is righteous in all His ways, gracious in all His works" (Ps 145:17). His righteousness might lead us to expect an inflexible application of his law, but his graciousness means he may choose to act in mercy rather than deserved judgment, and hence his ways are not easily traced, for he shows mercy to whom he wills and punishes whom he wills (Rom 9:18). His raising up and putting down of nations is based on his sovereign will but it is not unrelated to their response to the revelation they have (Jer 18:7–10). Likewise with individuals; he knows all their thoughts and actions and aids the obedient:

> Behold, the eye of the Lord is on those who fear Him:
> On those who hope for His mercy,
> To deliver their soul from death,
> And to keep them alive in famine. (Ps 33:18–19)

He punishes the disobedient: "Therefore God also gave them up to uncleanness" (Rom 1:24, see also vv. 18–32). The grand purpose of God's government is his salvation purposes in Messiah and he orders the decisions of rulers to that end (Isa 44:28; 45:1).

What evidence is there that a supreme being is acting in all these ways? What can be observed and deduced? Firstly, we can assert that the orderliness of nature, leading to the provision of humanity's needs for life and happiness, is a witness to God's power and goodness: "Nevertheless, He did not leave Himself without witness, in that He did good, gave us rain from heaven and fruitful seasons, filling our hearts with food and gladness" (Acts 14:17).

Secondly, humans know that they are only able to control the world and nature to a limited extent, and throughout history they have looked outside of themselves for help. This is evidence of humankind's religious nature, and it connects to humankind's moral nature because people naturally attribute good or bad events to good or bad behavior. In all this, humans have a sense of a superintending providence at work (Rom 1:21–23).

Thirdly, humans are sensible of the same power at work in their individual life and destiny. We simply are not the "captains of our soul," able to direct outcomes in our experience to exactly our desired end. We are all subject to "the slings and arrows of outrageous fortune," and it is natural for us to cry out to deity when in mortal danger.

Fourthly, the fulfillment of the Bible's prophecies regarding future events powerfully confirms what humans know concerning the divine providence. For example, God's promises to Abraham, Isaac, and Jacob have all come true, against all odds. From one man grew the people of Israel. Scripture and history record how they were enslaved by a superpower but were miraculously delivered from its grip; later they were saved from many superior enemies and returned from a national captivity by another superpower, Babylon. The people of Israel have survived all attempts to annihilate them during the last two thousand years of dispersion, and are again established in the land God gave to Abraham; a remarkable story. As the Marquis d'Argens said to Frederick the Great in 1779, when he was asked for one single irrefutable proof of God, "Yes, your Majesty, the Jews." In the Jewish Scriptures great events of nations are spoken of long before they occur (Isa 45:1–7), and a great person is described who will enter human history to save it from its sins (Gen 3:15; Isa 9:6–7; 52:13–53:12); a role most remarkably fulfilled in the perfect life, teaching, miracles, divine power, suffering, death, and resurrection of Abraham's descendant, Yeshua of Nazareth. Multitudes throughout the world now worship him.

God's providence has a goal and it centers in his Son. He has given him a people, a bride, and he directs human history to the end of gathering that people to his Son from Israel and all the nations, "that in the dispensation of the fullness of the times He might gather together in one all things in Christ, both which are in heaven and which are on earth—in Him" (Eph 1:10). People, made in God's image, sense that life has a purpose but only find it by seeking the God of providence. For those who find, God providentially works the circumstances and events of their lives so that they more and more conform to the likeness of his Son (Rom 8:28).

When causality in providence is considered we observe God acting without human agency: "Fire and hail, snow and clouds; Stormy wind, fulfilling His word" (Ps 148:8), and also through human agency (Isa 45:13). Certain questions inevitably arise when considering the latter, so that the truths concerning God's providence and government are often seen in tension with other truths, such as human freedom or the existence of evil. As creatures we cannot hope to resolve all such tensions, and our underlying attitude should be that of David in Ps 131:1–2:

> LORD, my heart is not haughty,
> Nor my eyes lofty.
> Neither do I concern myself with great matters,
> Nor with things too profound for me.
> Surely I have calmed and quieted my soul,
> Like a weaned child.

However, some things can be stated. Human freedom of choice is a reality, and God, who is just in all his ways, holds men and women accountable for their choices. Those choices are part of God's working of all things. He controls the myriad events which surround and influence our choices so that his will is done. He can both soften and harden hearts so that the choice made is both his will and their will (Exod 4:21; 8:15; Neh 2:4–6). To be clear, this control of God extends to the evil choices humans make, which are part of God's government. God's predetermination in human evil choices and actions is proactive without being responsible for human sin, for example the death of Messiah at the hands of wicked people: "Him, being delivered by the determined purpose and foreknowledge of God, you have taken by lawless hands, have crucified, and put to death" (Acts 2:23, see also 4:28). Many prefer to speak of God's permissive will in such contexts to make clear that God is not the author of evil, but those who do so do not intend to deny that the actions are predetermined by God. To resolve the tension, some have posited the idea that, as God is concerned more to be generous and sensitive than controlling, he is ready to change his plans to suit people's responses; that is, he does not directly influence their choices. Such thinking brings God down to our level and overlooks that he is both sensitive and compassionate in all his works, even when he judges those who are disobedient (Ps 145:17; Jer 32:37, see also Rev 3:14–22).

Evil confronts us with mystery in God's providence (2 Thess 2:7) but we should never use it to minimize human responsibility to choose the good and refuse evil. It is God's set purpose to remove evil, through the work of Messiah and his return in glory. He has entered our world, suffered, and died to defeat it. Evil can in no sense be viewed as good, or somehow emerging from God, an error which some forms of religious mysticism, both Jewish and non-Jewish, have fallen into as they have speculated as to the origin of evil.

The final comment to be made concerns the apparent injustice of God's providence. Because God is gracious much sin is left unpunished, leading people to doubt God's justice. However, humans are aware there is a judgment to come (Rom 1:32—2:6), which may give comfort through knowing all will be set to rights, but it should also alarm, knowing that sin will be judged.

God's rule and providence is directing history to the point where the people of his Son will be delivered from all evil and its consequences (Rev 21:1–4); the natural world will also be delivered (Rom 8:19–22), and there will be a judgment of all who have ever lived (Rev 20:11–15). The glory of God's grace and justice in his providence and government will then be clearly seen by all (Rom 3:19; see also Rev 15:3–4; 21:4–5).

Traditional Judaism comes to very similar conclusions to the above as it wrestles with the mystery of God's providence in all his works. At no point is there any fundamental difference with that Christian thinking which is faithful to the biblical revelation. The New Testament revelation only amplifies and underlines what can be understood through a study of the Tanakh; it does not diverge, as is underlined by these words of the redeemed in Rev 15:3–4:

> They sing the song of Moses, the servant of God, and the song of the Lamb, saying:
> "Great and marvelous are Your works,
> Lord God Almighty! Just and true are Your ways,
> O King of the saints!"

17

Miracles

As stated above, God actively upholds the natural world himself, moment by moment, and its regularity is due to his will. Miracles occur when he acts in the natural order in a way that is obviously outside what humans ordinarily observe; e.g., a rod turned into a snake, a day lasting longer than twenty-four hours, an ax-head floating, water turned to wine, a body resurrected from death. Other events which are often described as miraculous may not be so obviously different to the normal, but their timing is so startling as to make them stand out from the usual: "As for me, being on the way, the Lord led me to the house of my master's brethren" (Gen 24:27, see vv. 10–28). Similarly, when a divine revelation interprets a startling event as an unusual interposition of God, it is usually described as miraculous (Isa 37:33–37).

God's miracles have a purpose: they are a personal blessing to those who experience them (Luke 8:26–39), they signify a particular truth of God (John 9:39–41), and they authenticate God's messenger (Exod 4:1–5; John 20:30–31). Miracles are not as common in the biblical accounts as is often thought, but mostly cluster around significant moments in the development of God's redemptive purpose; e.g., the exodus, the rescue of Israel from apostasy (Elijah and Elishah), the life and ministry of Messiah, and the birth of God's new covenant people. Scripture discourages seeking miracles as an end in themselves (Matt 12:38–39).

The Jewish nation could be called the "miracle nation," for without miraculous activity they would have remained enslaved in Egypt. By the standards of any other nation Israel's history is one full of miracles; a privileged people. And this is not easily forgotten, for the one central festival which almost all celebrate, and of which surely none are ignorant, is Pesach, celebrating that deliverance from slavery to freedom, which would never have happened without the abundance of miracles that weakened the grip of their superpower oppressors. Nor is the miraculous in Yeshua's ministry among Israel, especially his resurrection, a thing which is easily set aside. God's miracles among his people Israel speak loudly, to them and to the whole world, of the God who is there and who acts for his people.

Not all miraculous, supernatural phenomena are of God; there are counterfeits. Satan has power to work such as part of his purpose to lure humans away from the truth: "And then the lawless one will be revealed . . . with all power, signs, and lying wonders" (2 Thess 2:8–9). The test of all such supernatural phenomena is whether the miracle worker leads people to God's truth or away from it (Deut 13:1–3). Such deceptions are not to be taken lightly; Jesus warned against their power to mislead: "For false Christs and false prophets will rise and show great signs and wonders to deceive, if possible, even the elect. See, I have told you beforehand" (Matt 24:24).

There is an unnecessary tension between scientific observation and belief in miracles. Science deals with the observable and repeatable in the natural world, and can only draw conclusions about it because of the regularity of God's upholding of it. If God chooses to act contrary to the regular then such divine activity is not usually subject to scientific scrutiny but is verified by what is called the "tests of history," that is, the evidence of reliable witnesses. The refusal of many to believe in miracles is not due to the lack of evidence, or a scientific theory as to their impossibility, but the intuitive fear that if there are miracles then there is a God, a person to whom humans know they are accountable for their sins.

Should we expect miracles in the life and ministry of the church today? The link between the miraculous and special moments in God's plan of redemption would indicate not (Exod 4:1–5). Likewise, the link of miracles to the ministry of the apostles, as signs of their unique authority, would also indicate not (2 Cor 12:12). However, Paul writes of a working of miracles through some in Corinth as a gift of the Spirit (1 Cor 12:10). There is no biblical reason to assert that the gifts of the Spirit are no longer given, but there is historical reason for saying they are rarely experienced. The miraculous has recurred from time to time in church history, yet always in extraordinary circumstances and not as part of the regular life of the church. The sovereign Spirit does occasionally work such in special times. In saying this, it must never be forgotten that the greatest and most fruitful of miracles should be a constant feature in the life of every church—the miracle of regeneration—souls being born again of the Spirit to new life in Messiah. Unbelievers may try to explain away the miraculous in Scripture but a changed life, filled with peace, joy, and righteousness, and tested in the ups and downs of life, is an irrefutable evidence of God miraculously at work. Surely this is the greater work Jesus referred to when he said, "Most assuredly, I say to you, he who believes in Me, the works that I do he will do also; and greater works than these he will do, because I go to My Father" (John 14:12).

18

Prayer

Prayer will be considered more fully in a later section, but some comment on prayer in the context of God's providential determining of all things is necessary. Prayer is not getting God to change his mind, or getting him to do something he had not planned to do; rather, it is something he uses to bring about what he has planned. It expresses trust in him, and it brings us more in line with his mind and will; it is involvement in his eternal purpose, and brings him glory. Prayer is an immense privilege because it draws us into the forwarding of God's plans and purposes. This is because answered prayer is that which is according to his will: "Now this is the confidence that we have in Him, that if we ask anything according to His will, He hears us" (1 John 5:14–15).

Scripture teaches us many things which are within his will for this world, for example holiness for his people, the salvation of sinners, and the care of his creation. As we pray for such things we know he will answer, and his answer will be part of his plan and purpose. It is a mystery, but we must remember that prayer is a divine exercise in which we look to God's Spirit to prompt us (Eph 6:18), and the Spirit knows the mind of God. Prayer is used to bring about change, as when Moshe interceded for Israel's preservation (Exod 32:11–14), but Moshe's words show how his prayer was informed by God's revealed will for Israel and a concern for God's glory. This encourages us to study God's word to know what he has revealed so we may pray according to his mind.

In a similar way Abraham's prayer was used of God for Lot's deliverance from the destruction of Sedom (Sodom) (Gen 18:16–33). He interceded on the basis of God's character (v. 25) and was heard. The Lord's words "Shall I hide from Abraham what I am doing?" indicate God's desire to involve his people in the forwarding of his purposes through prayer. We may not always know the sort of detail Abraham knew in this passage, but the Spirit can lead us because he does know: "Likewise the Spirit also helps in our weakness. For we do not know what we should pray for as we ought, but the Spirit Himself makes intercession for us with groanings which cannot be uttered" (Rom 8:26–27).

And yet there are many times when we desire to see a situation change to be more in line with God's revealed will, and we pray, and our prayer appears to be unanswered; sometimes the answer is "no" or "not yet." Paul received a "no" and Yeshua explained why: "My grace is sufficient for you, for My strength is made perfect in weakness" (2 Cor 12:9). This example makes it clear that a "no" is for our good. Often God delays his answer—a "not yet." For example, the faithful of Israel's prayed for centuries for Messiah's coming (Ps 14:7; Isa 62:1–3), and they must have been tempted to think that their prayers were unheard; but at the set time he came. Their prayers were used in the development of God's plan and his providential government of the world for his purposes (Dan 9:20–23; 10:12). This underlines that it is not necessarily wrong to persevere in prayer when prayer seems to be unanswered (see Luke 18:1–8). If it is in God's will, he will enable us to persevere. There is a mystery about prayer, and it should humble and thrill God's people to be involved in his purposes in such an intimate way.

> The LORD is gracious and full of compassion,
> Slow to anger and great in mercy.
> The LORD is good to all,
> And His tender mercies are over all His works. (Ps 145:8–9)

> O You who hear prayer,
> To You all flesh will come. (Ps 65:2)

SCRIPTURES

Providence and rule: Gen 45:7–8; 2 Kgs 19:28; 2 Chr 16:9; Neh 9:6; Pss 76:10; 115:3; 136:25; Dan 5:23; Amos 3:6; Matt 6:26; 10:29–30; Acts 17:28; Phil 2:13.

Coming Savior: Gen 49:10; Deut 18:15–19; Pss 2:6–9; 110; Isa 7:14; 9:6–7; 52:13—53:12.

Miracles: Exod 7:3; 14:21, 31; 1 Kgs 17:14–16; 2 Kgs 2:19–22; Ps 145:4–6; Matt 9:29; 13:58; 17:19–21; Luke 7:9–10; John 2:11; 9:6–7; Acts 2:22; 2 Cor 12:12.

Prayer: 2 Chr 7:14; Matt 21:22; 26:39; John 15:7, 16; 16:23–24; Acts 4:25–26; 2 Cor 12:8–10; Jas 1:5, 6–8; 4:2, 3; 1 John 1:9; Rev 6:11.

Questions

Providence and rule

1. What is meant by the providence of God? How extensive is it, and how does this teaching impact your daily life?
2. Give some instances in Scripture where evil was used to forward God's purposes, drawing attention to God's activity and human responsibility.

Miracles

1. What is a miracle, and what are God's purposes in the miraculous? Should we expect miracles as in the days of the apostles?

Prayer

1. Discuss what it means to pray "according to God's will." How does this help us to deal with unanswered prayer?

Further Reading

Berkouwer, G. C. *The Providence of God*. Grand Rapids: Eerdmans, 1952.
Blocher, Henry. *Evil and the Cross*. Leicester: Apollos, 1994.
Carson, D. A. *How Long, O Lord?* Leicester: InterVarsity, 2006.
Helm, Paul. *The Providence of God*. Leicester: InterVarsity, 1993.
Lewis, C. S. *Miracles*. Glasgow: Collins, 2012.

19

Humankind: Creation and Fall

(A) THE CREATION OF HUMANKIND

(i) Beginning

The creation of humankind stands out from the rest of creation because it involved particular deliberation by God: "Let Us make man in Our image, according to Our likeness" (Gen 1:26). Humankind is therefore unique. The greater detail of Gen 2:7 underlines this: "And the LORD God formed man of the dust of the ground, and breathed into his nostrils the breath of life; and man became a living being." The first man had a physical and a spiritual nature; he was one united being made up of body and soul. Eve was made from him in a separate act of God (Gen 2:21) but in such a way that her essential equality and similarity of nature is recognized because the word for "woman" (Heb. *ishah*), as in English, is derived from the word for "man" (Heb. *ish*).

The rest of Scripture views the creation of humankind by God as an historical event (1 Chr 1:1; Mal 2:10; Matt 19:4), underlining that there is a unity to the human race (Gen 5:1–2; Ps 8:5–8; Acts 17:26). It is incorrect to speak of different races if by that we imply distinct origins, or different cradles of development. There is only one race, the human race, with one common origin in Adam and Eve. The differences between groups of humans are due to many factors but those which are derived from their physical nature all derive from the original gene pool within the first pair, Adam and Eve.

The reader should be aware of other theories of human origins, such as: progressive creation, theistic evolution, and evolution, the last of which rules out a Creator, and the others seeking some integration of the Genesis account and the theory of evolution. It is not the purpose of this book to discuss the issues raised, but the Further Reading section below mentions suitable apologetic works. I have given my reasons earlier in this book for accepting the Bible's account of a six-day creation.

(ii) The Use of "Man" for the Human Race

It has become the norm for "humanity" or "humankind" to be substituted for "mankind," because to use "man" as a generic word for a race which contains male and female implies some sort of superiority for males, which has become unacceptable. The subject of male/female relations and roles will be considered later but it ought to be stated here that "man" is used in the creation account to refer to the whole race. The word for "man" in Hebrew is *adam* and in Gen 1 and 2 it usually has the definite article (Heb. *haadam*) and refers to the first man, who came to be called Adam. Different Bible versions turn *adam* into the name Adam at different points in the narrative, but always by Gen 5:1. When there is no definite article (*adam*) then it is either being used of a human male or of the human race in general. For example, in Gen 5:1–2 we read, "in the day that God created man [*adam*], He made him in the likeness of God. He created them male and female, and blessed them and called them Mankind [*Adam*] in the day they were created" (cf. Gen 1:27). *Adam* is elsewhere used in distinction from woman (*ishah*; Gen 2:22, 25). It is therefore not inappropriate to use the word "man" or "mankind" of the whole human race. This does not mean other generic terms are incorrect, like "humanity," and I will vary the terms I use, but the use of "man" as a generic term indicates a special role for the first man from the beginning of creation, before ever the fall occurred.

(iii) Purpose

Man is the pinnacle of God's earthly creation, as one made in his own image. Adam and Eve are given dominion over God's creation—"have dominion over the fish of the sea," etc., etc. (Gen 1:28)—which included naming all the animals (Gen 2:19–20). They are also told to "fill the earth and subdue it" (Gen 1:28), which implies a stewardship of God's world, and is confirmed by the words, "the Lord God took the man and put him in the Garden of Eden to tend and keep it" (Gen 2:15). As Ps 8:6 expresses it, "you have put all things under his feet." Humans are not therefore of equal value with animals and birds; they alone are made in God's image and have authority over all other living creatures. People are therefore to act towards God's creation as God would: to care for it and make it productive and beautiful. It does not belong to humans, to do as they please, but they are to rule and develop it as under God, its owner.

Humans are also social creatures—"it is not good that the man should be alone"—and so God created Eve as a wife for Adam, and hence the most basic social unit is husband and wife and their offspring. The command to fill the earth (Gen 1:28) indicates God's plan for a large human race which would inevitably develop many forms of social interaction. So, although marriage and procreation are the obvious means of filling the earth, it is not the sole form for satisfying the human need for social interaction. History and present experience demonstrate the myriad ways that humans gather to socially interact in twos or two thousands, and their freedom to do so without interference is seen as a basic human right and dignity.

The highest form of personal relationship humans are designed to enjoy is fellowship with their Creator; God speaks words to Adam and Eve immediately after their creation. They are told what they can and cannot eat (Gen 1:29; 2:16–17). A relationship develops as God brings the animals to Adam for naming, and then creates Eve and brings her to him (Gen 2:19–22). Genesis 3:8 indicates a daily time with God for Adam and Eve, a developing relationship which held no fear, and which was clearly designed to remain forever by the provision of the tree of life, of which they could freely eat (Gen 2:9, 16). As one Christian catechism asks, "What is the chief end of man?" and answers, "To glorify God and enjoy him forever." His desire was to create myriads of others to enjoy his own blessedness. No doubt, if humans had continued in obedience to God, growing in knowledge of him and themselves, they would have been raised to a fixed state of life, an eternal life with God forever which could not have been lost.

It is interesting to consider what might be the ideal way for the social nature of humans to develop. In Israel's development from Avraham, who walked with God, we see an interesting example of what happens when a nation develops, creating a strong sense of bond and social cohesion. Living in one location strengthens the sense of identity and increases care for one another through working together. Having God at the center of family and also national life lifts personal and communal life above the petty and mundane, and gives comfort in all losses. Into this security outsiders should be welcome, whether they come for employment, out of need, or in admiration. There is room for a multiplicity of such societies.

(iv) In God's Image

God declares man to be made in his image: "Then God said, 'Let Us make man in Our image, according to Our likeness; let them have dominion . . .' So God created man in His own image; in the image of God He created him; male and female He created them" (Gen 1:26–27). Obviously, this does not mean that all we know of God is to be seen in man. That can only be said of God's Son, who is "the express image of His person" (Heb 1:3). But being made in God's image is meaningful. Negatively, we can say that this does not point to some similarity of form; God is a spirit.

Positively, we can think of humans as distinct from all other earthly life forms because of this image of God, and hence they have *special dignity and value*; to kill a man is condemned because he is in God's image (Gen 9:6). The use of the word "our" in "our image," and the mention of male and female, points to *community and communication*. God communicates and speaks words, and humans have an innate power of speech by which they communicate thoughts. This is essential to community, and reflects the divine community in God's triunity. Humans' highest expression of community is their fellowship with God, which underlines how precious they are in God's sight. God is creative, and humans possess that *capacity of creativity* to a remarkable degree. Just think about the myriad paintings, stories, poems, songs, and artifacts people have created, yet developed around a limited number of themes! Humans are *evaluative*, an essential quality for developing and ruling God's world. And as God's creation is ordered, so men and women are able to *create order and develop plans*. All this is done in a rational way involving discussion and logical conclusions. Humans are *self-conscious*, and this is part of God's image, and something animals lack—they do not ask questions of themselves as to who they are and what is their purpose. Humans were created *righteous*, and Adam and Eve grew in moral strength initially by refusing to eat the forbidden fruit and eating of the tree of life. This indicates humankind has an inbuilt *hope of immortality*, something only those with a moral faculty, an obedient life, and a relationship with God are able to anticipate.

The fall has not eradicated the image of God in man. Righteousness is lost, and a natural obedience, but Scripture speaks of man subsequent to the fall as a creature in God's image: "For a man indeed ought not to cover his head, since he is the image and glory of God" (1 Cor 11:7, see also Gen 9:6). Hence the characteristics mentioned above are not lost but they are all defaced and debased due to sin. That humans remain precious in God's sight, and able to have a hope of immortality, is abundantly shown in the gospel, and it is the gospel which takes "man in God's image" onto a higher plane, for it recreates believers in the image of the heavenly man, God's Son (1 Cor 15:49; Col 3:10). Amongst other things this adds a dimension of love and light unknown to Adam before the fall.

A purely material understanding of humans, which can be investigated by the scientific method, fails to explain several human characteristics. We are persons and not just physical objects, and the Human Genome Project tells us nothing about what it means to be a human person. Humans have a mind, which all the study of the brain's physical aspects fails to fully explain. Humans live by ethical principles, with much similarity between tribes and peoples; a purely material view of humanity struggles to explain what drives this.

Concerning those aspects of man's creation covered so far, the teaching of traditional Judaism is very similar. However, there is a difficulty in that books of Jewish theology mainly focus on man in the context of observing Torah, rather than a close examination of his nature. That said, traditional Judaism emphasizes humans as God's special creation, made in his image, made to know him and obey his laws, and having responsibility for his earthly creation. This accounts for a strong sense of human responsibility in the Jewish community.

(v) Human Nature

(a) Body, Soul, and Spirit

The Scriptures speak of humans as being made up of body, soul, and spirit. The word "body" or "flesh" is always used of that material part of our nature, originally made of the dust of the earth (Gen 2:7), and which, due to sin, returns to dust (Eccl 12:7). The word "soul" is used in two ways. Firstly, to describe us as living beings without making any distinction between our material and immaterial nature, as of Adam: "and man became a living being" (i.e., soul, Heb. *nephesh*). It is used in a similar way of animals, without implying they have an immaterial nature: "Then God said, 'Let the earth bring forth the living creature [soul, Heb. *nephesh*], according to its kind'" (Gen 1:24). David uses the term in this way in 2 Sam 4:9: "As the LORD lives, who has redeemed my life [*nephesh*] from all adversity." Similarly in the New Testament: "and that day about three thousand souls [Gk. *psyche*] were added to them" (Acts 2:41). Secondly, the term is used of the immaterial part of our nature alone, distinguished from the material body, as in this passage about punishment of Assyria: "And it will consume the glory of his forest and of his fruitful field, both soul and body"; or in this New Testament text: "do not fear those who kill the body but cannot kill the soul" (Matt 10:28; see Isa 10:18). It is probably fair to say that in the Old Testament the word "soul" (*nephesh*) is mostly used to describe the whole person, a unity of the material and immaterial. In the New Testament it is certainly used in that way but there is a more frequent use of the word "soul" for man's immaterial nature, and this is perhaps due to the more intense focus on the inner life in the New Testament.

Scripture also uses the word "spirit" (Heb. *ruach*, Gk. *pneuma*). It is not used in either the Old Testament or the New Testament as a word to describe the whole person, both material and immaterial. In the Old Testament it may refer in a precise way to the immaterial part of our nature, as in Eccl 12:7, "And the spirit will return to God who gave it," but it more usually refers to the dominant force at the core of a person's being: "Create in me a clean heart, O God, and renew a steadfast spirit within me." And so "spirit" refers to man's inner life, towards God and towards man. The New Testament uses the word "spirit" in a similar way. It may refer to man's immaterial nature, as in 1 Cor 2:11, "For what man knows the things of a man except the spirit of the man which is in him," or it may refer to what drives him: "And being fervent in spirit, he spoke and taught accurately the things of the Lord" (Acts 18:25).

All this leads some to the conclusion that humans are three parts: body, soul, and spirit (tripartite); but others conclude we are two parts: body and soul (bipartite). The latter understand the word "spirit" as used either interchangeably with "soul" when referring to the immaterial part of man, for example, "With my soul I have desired You in the night, Yes, by my spirit within me I will seek you early" (Isa 26:9, see also Luke 1:46–47), or as referring to the inner life of the whole person, for example, "I had no rest in my spirit, because I did not find Titus my brother" (2 Cor 2:13). However, those who hold to three parts refer to 1 Thess 5:23 and Heb 4:12 as pointing to three distinct parts: "and may your whole spirit, soul, and body be preserved blameless at the coming of our Lord Jesus Christ."

Whichever view is taken, certain points must be maintained. Humans are a unity before God; the body is not an impediment to the spiritual life and should be honored as a creation of God. It is in the body that humans live to God, love him, obey him, and will be judged by him. The body is forever, and will be raised from the dead. Humans are not conscious of being a three-part being, hence any distinction between soul and spirit is one of differing aspects of the same essence, which is the immaterial part of human nature. This immaterial part lives apart from the body after death, in relation with God and other creatures, and is therefore the essence of the person (Luke 20:37–38; Rev 6:9–11; Gen 15:15).

This author believes a case can be made for the word "spirit" being used in a few NT texts for what is created anew at regeneration. Yeshua said, "That which is born of the flesh is flesh, and that which is born of the Spirit is spirit" (John 3:6). Something new is created within a human when they come to faith, and Paul speaks of believers as new creatures (2 Cor 5:17). Using a different metaphor, Peter and John speak of regeneration as God's seed placed in a person (1 Pet 1:23; 1 John 3:9). It is therefore plausible to conclude that the two texts which speak of "soul" and "spirit" as distinct (1 Thess 5:23 and Heb 4:12) are using the word "spirit" to refer to that which is born anew in the soul. There will be more on this later in the section on the regenerating work of the Spirit. Again, it is important to note this is not a consciously distinct part of a whole human person. Hebrews 4:12 indicates it is very hard to distinguish soul from spirit, so that the spirit should be seen as a new divine principle suffusing every part of the soul, affecting every one of its parts and actions. Those parts are described using various terms: "heart," "affections," "mind," "understanding" and "will." The conclusion of this view would be that humans are bipartite but the regenerate person has born within them a new spirit which enables them, body and soul, to live for God.

Traditional Judaism affirms that man is body and soul (or spirit), as Isidore Epstein writes: "although composed of two different elements, the earthly body and the heavenly soul, man is a unity. Judaism rejects the dualistic idea of a pure spirit imprisoned in a body which is impure and hostile to the immaterial and spiritual."[1]

(b) The Origin of the Soul

The creation of the first man is described in two stages in Gen 2:7. He is formed from the dust of the ground but only has life through a direct act of God breathing into him the breath of life. Subsequently, all humans come into existence through the process of reproduction and the origin of their immaterial nature, the soul or spirit, is hidden from us. One view is that God creates each soul distinctly and unites it to the physical nature formed in the mother at some point after conception. Another view is that both soul and body are transmitted from the parents. The importance of this subject relates to the teaching of Scripture on original sin and its transmission to all of Adam's progeny, which will be discussed later in Part 4.

Traditional Judaism views each soul as a special creation of God, as shown by an old rabbinic prayer recited daily, "O my God, the soul which

---

1. Epstein, *Judaism*, 141.

Thou gavest me is pure; Thou didst create it."[2] *Gilgul* is a term of mystical Judaism which refers to the preexistence of souls and their reincarnation after death. It has no basis in Scripture, was unknown both in the Judaism of the Second Temple Period and in the Talmud, and was opposed by Jewish philosophy.[3] It is mentioned here because of the increasing influence of mystical Judaism upon traditional Judaism.

(c) Human Freedom

Adam was created free to obey or disobey God's will, which was initially expressed by one command in Gen 2:16–17—to freely eat of all the trees in the garden but not of the tree of knowledge of good and evil. He was not immune from temptation as the Genesis account demonstrates, but he was under no compulsion to disobey; Adam's defense after his sin was not that God had made him prone to sin. God's punishment of his disobedience would have been unjust if he was not absolutely free to obey or disobey. That is not the situation of humans subsequent to the fall, as we shall see.

(d) Human Immortality

Only God has immortality; he is the self-existent One (1 Tim 6:16). Humans do not have this by nature, as is plain from the existence of the tree of life (Gen 2:9). They were free to eat of it (Gen 2:16) and it was the means of receiving God's sustaining power. It kept them in a perfect life in God's presence. When they disobeyed they were barred from it, leading to decline and death. Therefore immortality was not an inherent characteristic for them. However, although immortality is not inherent for humans, God has designed us for it; to live in his new heavens and new earth forever (Rev 21:1–5). Hence, the word "immortality" for humans is always linked to the hope of the gospel as in 2 Tim 2:10: "our Savior Jesus Christ, who has abolished death and brought life and immortality to light through the gospel." "Immortality" is not an appropriate word for those who die under God's wrath. They suffer God's judgment forever, in a condition which could best be described as "eternal mortality."

2. Montefiore and Loewe, *Rabbinic Anthology*, 312.
3. Scholem, *Kabbalah*, 344.

(vi) Humankind as Male and Female

"It is not good that man should be alone" (Gen 2:18, 21–23); these words indicate that God made humans for relationship. Men and women are equals by nature, both made in God's image (Gen 5:1–2), equally responsible before God (Gen 3:16–19), responsible to honor one another (Prov 31:10–11, 28–31; 1 Pet 3:7; 1 Cor 11:11–12), and destined for eternal equality (Luke 20:34–36). The marriage of a man and a woman—modeled on Messiah's relationship to his people—should be one of mutual love (Eph 5:28, 33; Song 7), mutual affection (1 Cor 7:3), mutual sharing of authority over each other's bodies (1 Cor 7:4), and a commitment to a lifelong union (Matt 19:6). This does not mean the unmarried are unfulfilled or second best. Unmarried people may experience deep and fulfilling relationships with friends on a natural level. Jesus himself was single and enjoyed fulfilling relationships which were important to him (John 11:3, 11; 21:20; Luke 22:28; Matt 26:37–38). For single Christians there is further relational fulfillment because of spiritual oneness with other Christians. For those, like Paul, with the gift of singleness, this may lead to greater usefulness in service, but to insist on it for Christian ministry, as some churches do, has been detrimental (e.g., the Roman Catholic priesthood).

Traditional Judaism also has a high regard for marriage: "R. Jacobs said: He who has no wife lives without good, or help, or joy, or blessing, or atonement."[4] This is underlined by the tradition of a husband reading Prov 30 to his wife on Shabbat, and by the Orthodox insistence that a rabbi be married. However, attitudes to women are ambivalent, as indicated in the blessing of one official Orthodox prayer book, "Blessed art thou, O Lord our God, who has not made me a woman." This is usually explained away by pointing out that a woman's responsibilities in the home have made it impossible to insist she attend to the various religious duties which occurred at fixed times, and hence she missed out. That may well be so but it could have been better phrased. The rabbis of the past were men of their times and Loewe best sums up their view of women as "halfkindly, halforiental."[5]

Men and women were created by God to have different roles, particularly in the marriage relationship, which is the context of their creation. This can be seen before the fall: Adam was created first, with Eve as his helper (Gen 2:7, 18–23); the human race was named "Mankind" (Heb. *adam*) not "Womankind" (Gen 5:2; NKJV) (see earlier discussion); Adam represented the whole race and was spoken to first after the fall, even though he did not

---

4. Quoted from Genesis Rabbah, Bereshit 18:2, in Montefiore and Loewe, eds., *Rabbinic Anthology*, 507.

5. Montefiore and Loewe, eds., *Rabbinic Anthology*, 510.

sin first (1 Cor 15:22; Gen 3:9). In this relationship of two, Adam was to lead.

The New Testament underlines this by Paul's likening of the husband/wife relationship to that of Messiah and his church: the husband is the head of the wife as Messiah is the head of his people (Eph 5:23). This is not popular teaching today, and it cannot be explored in depth here, but further reading is recommended at the end of this section.

The effect of the fall and God's curse was to distort the roles and functions which existed before the fall, not to add new ones. The man works the ground and the woman bears children, but now it is much harder. A new element of tension enters the relationship due to sin's desire for autonomy and control. The man will lead by "rule," indicating an authoritarian style of leadership. She responds with "desire," which probably indicates two conflicting feelings: a desire to have a meaningful husband/wife relationship, and a desire to exert some sort of control in it (see the use of the Hebrew word *teshuquah* in Gen 3:16; 4:7; Song 7:10). Such things are not difficult to observe both in history and the present.

The effect of the gospel is to restore the relationship to its prefall functioning. For example, in marriage husbands are to love their wives (Col 3:18–19; 1 Pet 3:1–7) and wives are to submit to a husband's leadership with respect (Eph 5:22–33; note: the word for "submit" is not the same as the word for "obey" used in regard to children in Eph 6:1, and is appropriate for equals with different roles). The strife for control should be banished by the grace in the gospel.

A brief word on sexual relations at this point. God's word sanctions sexual relations only between a man and a woman and within a committed marriage relationship (Gen 2:24; Matt 19:4–5). Other expressions of sexual relationship, homosexual or heterosexual, are forbidden (Exod 20:14; Matt 5:28; Lev 18:22–23; Rom 1:26–27; 1 Cor 6:9). The Bible views sexual relations within marriage as God's gift to strengthen their love and oneness (1 Cor 7:3; Song of Songs); a love and oneness which is likened to the union of a believer and Messiah Yeshua (Eph 5:31–32; 1 Cor 6:16–17), who is the bridegroom of his people, the bride (John 3:29; Rev 19:6–9).

The subject of male and female roles is not confined to the subject of marriage and Paul's teaching in 1 Tim 2:11–15 demonstrates this. As the apostle to the Gentiles, ministering in cultures with little or no history of biblical norms, he was confronted with the need to give teaching on this issue. But as this is often seen as negative, we should first consider what the New Testament has to say about male/female equality in Messiah. They are equal in status as sons of God due to their union with the Savior (Gal 3:26–28). They both formally enter the new covenant through baptism, which is a rite for women as well as men, which was not the case with circumcision under the old covenant. Women may exercise gifts of the Spirit such as prophecy (1 Cor 11:5), and it is expected that the Spirit will be poured out in equal measure on men and women (Acts 2:16–21). Paul's letters refer to many women engaged in crucial ministries in the church (e.g., Rom 16:1, 6; 1 Tim 3:11; see also 2 John). However, as Paul addresses aspects of the subject of men and women in church life in 1 Tim 2:8–15 he is clear that a woman is not to teach or have authority over men, and his reasons are not connected to any passing cultural justification but to God's creation order and man's fall, things which continue to affect male and female roles despite the passage of time and the coming of the gospel. It is also relevant to note that all of the apostles of the Messiah were men (Matt 10:2–4), and church elders were men (1 Tim 3:2; Titus 1:6). None of this prohibits women from teaching and leadership roles among women, or even of teaching men in need of one-to-one help (Acts 18:26).

Traditional Judaism has always insisted on male leadership but, due to contemporary pressures, it has become a subject of debate within what might be called the left wing of Orthodoxy, where some synagogues appoint female educational and spiritual leaders but not rabbis. Conservative/Masorti, Reform and Liberal Judaism have long had women rabbis.

Does this have any implications for male/female role relationships outside of the church and outside of marriage? The New Testament does not directly address the subject. It needs to be remembered that the arena of such relationships is the fallen world, under the curse, which means that men will seek to rule and women will be caught between a desire towards them and a desire to subvert their rule. The gospel is salt and light and ought to influence men and women in society to act in a way that more closely resembles God's original design for their relationship. This should mean that the Christian message will influence men in general to be less overbearing and more honoring of women, and women to express their fundamental equality with men in an honoring and respectful manner. Whatever the state of male/female relationships in a culture, Christian men and women should act in a way that honors members of the opposite sex with whom they interact.

> I will praise You, for I am fearfully and wonderfully made;
> Marvelous are Your works,
> And that my soul knows very well. (Ps 139:14)

Scriptures

Created by God: Gen 1:26–27; 2:7, 21–23; 5:1–2; Deut 4:32; Isa 45:12; Mal 2:10; Mark 10:6; 1 Cor 15:45; 1 Tim 2:13; Rev 10:5–6.

In God's image: Gen 1:26; 5:3; 9:5–6; 1 Cor 11:7; Jas 3:9.

Human nature: Gen 1:31; 2:25; 12:5; Pss 16:10; 31:5; Eccl 7:29; 12:7; Matt 22:37; Luke 12:4; Acts 2:43; 1 Cor 5:5; 2 Cor 5:1–10; 12:2; 1 Thess 5:23; Heb 4:12.

Adam's headship affects all humans: Ps 8:4–8; 1 Cor 15:20–22.

Male and female: Gen 2:18, 22–23, 24; 5:2; Prov 31:10–31; Song of Songs; Matt 19:6; Luke 20:34–36; 1 Cor 11:11–12; Eph 5:22–33; Col 3:18–19; 1 Tim 2:11–15; 1 Pet 3:7.

Questions

1. What does Scripture teach about human origins? Is there any conflict with the understanding of human origins you were taught prior to becoming a believer?
2. What does it mean that Adam was made in God's image, and how does that affect us?
3. Do you believe mankind to be bipartite or tripartite? Give your reasons.
4. Why did God create humans?
5. What did freedom mean for Adam and Eve before their fall?
6. Men and women are different. What difference does it make?

Further Reading

Blocher, Henry. *In the Beginning*. Leicester: InterVarsity, 1984.
Council of Biblical Manhood and Womanhood website, www.cbmw.org.
Garner, Paul. *The New Creationism*. Darlington: Evangelical, 2009.
Machen, J. G. *The Christian View of Man*. Edinburgh: Banner of Truth, 1965.
Smith, Clair. *God's Good Design*. Sydney: Matthias Media, 2012.
Strachan, Owen, and Gavin Peacock. *The Grand Design*. Fearn: Christian Focus, 2016.
Strobel, Lee. *The Case for a Creator*. Grand Rapids: Zondervan, 2014.

(B) THE FALL OF HUMANKIND

Having considered the creation of humans we now need an in-depth consideration of human sin to see why we humans so desperately need a savior and salvation.

(i) The Fall—the Sin of Adam and Eve

Bereshit 3 presents the fall as a real space/time event, and the New Testament takes the same view (1 Tim 2:13–14; Rom 5:12). Although God's forbidding of the tree of knowledge of good and evil presented a moral pressure upon Adam and Eve, God allowed something more: the entry into the world of a sinister and evil creature who sought to turn them away from God.

Scripture reveals little on the origin of evil in God's world, although there are hints at Satan's fall under the imagery of the fall of two great powers, Babylon and Tyre, in Isa 14:12–15 and Ezek 28:11–19. Scripture's concern is with human responsibility and man's need of salvation and does not encourage speculation. However, regarding evil's origin, we can state emphatically that God is not the author of sin; he abhors it. It may help to view the origin of evil as similar to the way in which its activity increases, something which is due to God giving humans up to themselves (Rom 1:24, 26, 28; Isa 59:2; Jer 33:5). God does not create anything or actively promote anything evil so that sin, from God's perspective, is seen as essentially negative; it is a turning away from him. The origin of evil can perhaps be seen in the same way.

The nature of the first temptation was to take a wrong view of God. Instead of viewing him as the good God who had created a world for them to enjoy and rule, with the benefit of fellowship with him, they were encouraged to see him as restrictive in his provision, and desiring to keep them from a greater knowledge which would free them from his control (Gen 3:2–5). They swallowed the lie, and humans have done so ever since. It is clear that Adam and Eve were responsible for their behavior and, in the light of their upright natures and God's abundant goodness, their disobedience was willful in the extreme. God's subsequent judgment underlines their full responsibility.

(ii) The Fall—Its Consequences Stated Generally

God approached Adam and Eve gently, giving them opportunity to repent (Gen 3:8, 9, 11) but no repentance was forthcoming, only criticism of God, the serpent, and one another (Gen 3:12–13). God's judgment on them is pronounced: childbearing will be much harder, tension will enter their relationship, and producing food will become toilsome; all to be followed by physical death (Gen 3:16–24). Worst of all, they will be banished from the place where God manifested himself to them—an expression of their spiritual death. All this was to affect their offspring and chapters 4–6 of Bereshit trace the early story of God's judgment and human decline into wicked living: fratricide, bigamy, vengeance and murder, intermarriage between the godly and ungodly; all summed up in Gen 6:5, "Every intent of the thoughts of his heart was only evil continually." It appeared that there was no possibility of recovery. There was of course, but not by humans left to themselves. It is plain from all this history that sin has not deprived humans of their essential makeup of heart, mind, and will, but all is corrupted. Nor have they lost the capacity for a relationship with God, but their sin has erected a barrier which only he can remove.

(iii) The Nature and Extent of Sin

"Sin is a lack of conformity to the moral law of God in state, disposition and act."[6] This section will unpack these words. Of course many humans have never possessed God's law written, but Paul tells us it is "written in their hearts, their conscience also bearing witness" (Rom 2:15). Humans have a basic awareness of God's moral requirements, which should lead them to live morally upright lives. The people of Israel have been especially privileged because to them God's nature and righteousness was clearly revealed in writing: "to them were committed the oracles of God" (Rom 3:2). But all have failed to live up to what they know, so that Jews and Gentiles are "all under sin" (Rom 3:9) and all "fall short of the glory of God" (Rom 3:23; see also 3:19), leading to one simple fact—all die. Sin is universal in its extent and reigns in human nature.

The nature of sin is best explored by the main words used in Scripture and translated sin in English versions. We will consider four of the Hebrew words used for sin:

- *Asham* (e.g., Gen 26:10), which points to the guilt which sin incurs.
- *Chataah* or its cognate *chet*, which describes sin as failure, missing the mark (e.g., Exod 32:30).

---

6. D. M. LloydJones in a sermon, "Consequence of the Fall," available at www.mljtrust.org.

- *Pesha*, which describes sin as transgression or rebellion (e.g., 1 Sam 25:28).
- *Avon*, which is often translated "iniquity" and points to sin's perversity (see Gen 15:16).

In the Greek the same understanding of sin is underlined by the five main words used in the New Testament:

- *Hamartia* is the most frequently used and refers to error, missing the mark (e.g., Mark 2:10).
- *Anomia*, speaks of lawlessness, from which we get the word "antinomian" (e.g., 1 John 3:4).
- *Adikia*, describes sin as unrighteousness (e.g., 1 John 5:7).
- *Parabasis*, views sin as transgression (e.g., Heb 2:2).
- *Diastrepho*, describes sin as acting perversely (see Matt 17:17).

In summary, sinful human behavior is a failure to meet God's standard, a willful transgression of a known requirement, and a deliberate perversion of what is known to be right. Because of this the sinner is unrighteous and guilty in God's sight. Sin will affect other humans, but it is first and foremost an offense against God (Ps 51:4).

Sin affects every part of human nature so that no part of human existence is free from its dominion. Paul describes humans as "slaves of sin" (Rom 6:17, 20) and no person described as a slave can claim freedom over any aspect of their life. The very core of our being, the seat of all affection and motivation—the heart—only pours forth evil according to Yeshua, "out of the heart of men, proceed evil thoughts, adulteries, fornications, murders, thefts, covetousness, wickedness, deceit, lewdness, an evil eye, blasphemy, pride, foolishness" (Mark 7:21–23). As Jeremiah summarizes, "The heart is deceitful above all things, And desperately wicked" (Jer 17:9). The mind, the thought processes of humans, is governed by sin, which Paul states in Rom 8:7: "the carnal mind is enmity against God" (see also Gen 6:5). The will is enslaved to sin, which is Isaiah's explanation for Israel's disobedience and troubles, "For they would not walk in His ways, Nor were they obedient to His law" (Isa 42:24), a sentiment repeated by Yeshua: "How often I wanted to gather your children together, as a hen gathers her chicks under her wings, but you were not willing!" (Matt 23:37, see also John 5:40). In Rom 8:7–8 Paul sums up human hopelessness and powerlessness because of indwelling sin: "the carnal mind is enmity against God; for it is not subject to the law of God, nor indeed can be. So then, those who are in the flesh cannot please

God." Note: to be "in the flesh" is human nature estranged from the divine life, to be unregenerate and without the Spirit (see Rom 8:9 and John 3:6).

This powerlessness in sin is so great that when humans are faced with God's law, rather than repenting they find it stirs up sinful thoughts within them (Rom 7:7–11), leading to their death. In sin they are no match for Satan, who will ensure death seizes them (Heb 2:14). Three words are often used to describe sin's consequences for humans. There is the *guilt* of sin; they have broken God's law and that incurs guilt in his sight. There is the *pollution* of sin, which infects every part of their being and degrades them morally. There is the *power* of sin, which keeps them in a sinful life, and is so deceptive that humans either justify it or make light of it.

"Total depravity" is the theological term used to describe this fallen, hopeless condition, but it needs to be used with care. It does not mean that humans are as bad as they can be in practice, but it refers to every part of their nature being corrupted and under the dominion of sin; they have a sinful nature. God in his grace prevents people from becoming as bad as they could be so that his image within them, though tarnished, ensures some good behavior, as Yeshua put it: "If you then, being evil, know how to give good gifts to your children" (Luke 11:13). Such behavior enables "the world to go around" but does nothing to change the human condition, which Jesus describes here as evil, and in which humans cannot please God.

(iv) The Transmission of Sin

The term frequently used for this is "original sin," referring both to Adam's first sin and its effect on all humanity. Scripture is clear that sin is in some manner hereditary. Adam was made in God's image, but his own offspring were born in his image and likeness, i.e., fallen and under God's curse (Gen 5:3). David expresses this in Ps 51:5: "in sin my mother conceived me"; and Paul points to the impact of Adam's sin upon all his descendants: "For as in Adam all die" (1 Cor 15:22). It is not difficult to observe this work of sin in humans from their earliest years.

Adam stood as our representative, our federal head, in much the same way as an ambassador in a foreign court acts for his nation, making decisions in which citizens play no part but which affect their lives. In Rom 5:12–21 Paul makes this federal headship clear by his sustained contrast between Adam and Messiah. As fully as Messiah stood for his people, providing them with a righteousness, so Adam stood for all his descendants, and his sin is viewed as theirs by virtue of their organic union with him.

How this original sin and its corrupting effect is transmitted to all humans is connected to imputation. In Rom 8:13 Paul states that sin is not imputed when there is no law, but people still died from the time of Adam to Moses. Hence the death of those who had received no law can only be because Adam's transgression of the command not to eat of the tree of knowledge of good and evil was imputed to them, with the consequence of corruption, judgment, and death.

Some object that all this appears unjust on God's part, but humans need to beware of acting as God's judge. He has chosen to constitute humanity as a race descended from one man, and that the one man should stand for all who were in him. His sin became theirs, the thought being that we would all have acted in the same way, not of necessity but in willful rebellion.

This raises the question of present freedom. Humans are free in all sorts of ways and circumstances. They freely make decisions regarding many aspects of their lives but in the moral realm that is not so. They know what they should do, but they prefer sin, choose it, and willfully disobey God despite the alarm bells of their own conscience and an awareness of judgment to come. Human behavior has all the appearance of a death wish. Our responsibility in God's moral universe is very real: "whatever a man sows, that he will also reap" (Gal 6:7).

(v) Divergent Teachings

Before concluding this consideration of the fall by examining God's judgment on sin, it is important to consider other explanations of the human condition, and for two reasons. Firstly, to be mistaken about the cause will inevitably mean being mistaken about the solution, leading to disastrous and eternal consequences. Secondly, erroneous teachings exist within the fold of Christendom and the newcomer needs to be alert; new Jewish believers may not be aware of the exact nature of such errors in the churches, although Jewish history and experience will have shown them something is wrong somewhere, so they need to be equipped to detect churches unfaithful to Scripture.

However, these errors are not a reason to turn away from churches altogether, as if this is a Gentile problem from which Jewish believers are immune. The same tendency to error existed among the Jewish people in the days of both the Mosaic and the new covenants. For example, churches have erroneously recognized other religions as somehow saving, which is a serious error; likewise Solomon introduced idolatry into Israel. Churches have placed their traditions above the Scriptures, just as both Isaiah and Yeshua condemned in Israel in their day (Isa 29:13-14; Matt 15:3-9). Some among the early believers in Yeshua taught another gospel when they stressed the need for Gentile believers to be circumcised and keep Moses' law (Gal 4:9-10; 5:2-4; 6:13-15; 1:6-8, see also 2 Cor 11:13-22). Churches have also played down the supernatural, wanting only a reasonable religion, and the Sadducees of Yeshua's day did the same (Acts 23:8). Churches have played down the seriousness of sin, emphasizing God's benevolence, and Israel's false prophets often did the same (1 Kgs 22:5-18; Jer 23:14-17). The continuance of sin among God's people, and the work of Satan, ensure that errors will continue to arise, as Paul warned: "Now the Spirit expressly says that in latter times some will depart from the faith, giving heed to deceiving spirits and doctrines of demons" (1 Tim 4:1). The important thing is to be able to discern error and join with those who hold to the truth.

Outside the major religions camp, humanism and New Age will be briefly mentioned. Humanism views humankind as able to overcome its worst tendencies by the use of reason, developing a liberal attitude to others and their values, and having a confidence in science to improve us and our world. Such things are obviously not without value but, bearing in mind the human desire for perfection, humanism seems to have made little progress; as the dictum goes, "History teaches us that history teaches us nothing." In fact, societies based on humanistic communism have been guilty of some of the worst behavior towards their own people that history has ever witnessed.

New Age teaching hopes for human perfectibility via perceiving the oneness of all things, thus inspiring adherence to the positive mindset of seeing themselves and all things as God, a thinking which has a ring of Gen 3:5 about it. The teaching of karma plus reincarnation offers a hope of perfectibility, but history shows things have changed very little over many millennia. The actual experience of those who follow New Age ideas is a depressing one: constant failure in trying to deny or overcome the self.

Within the religious camp we will consider Roman Catholicism, Orthodox Christianity, liberal Christianity, and Judaism. A teaching arose within the church of the fifth century which contended that God could only justly demand what humans could perform, so people must be free to choose good or evil. Humans were therefore viewed as Adam before the fall, having no sinful nature, and the only effect of Adam's sin being the force of bad example. Variations of this thinking, known as "Pelagianism," have found their way into churches. Roman Catholicism describes man in sin thus: "The first man, Adam, sinned and lost supernatural life and because of this loss incurred other weaknesses too. We find this weakness and loss in all of us who are Adam's descendants";[7] and, "What is original sin? Original sin is that guilt and stain of sin which we inherit from Adam, who is the origin and head of all mankind."[8] It is clear that Roman Catholicism upholds the doctrine that Adam's sin affects us all, but the actual effect upon Adam's descendants is insufficiently grave; it is a "weakness," a "loss," and a "stain," words which do not reflect the New Testament teaching of enslavement to sin and blindness to spiritual truth (Rom 6:17; 1 Cor 2:14). Hence, one Roman Catholic theologian can write, "Even in the fallen state, man can, by his natural intellectual power, know religious and moral truths."[9]

Orthodox Christianity makes a distinction between the image of God and God's likeness in humans, and teaches that the likeness is lost due to sin but the image remains, though corrupted. The image is made up of free will, reason, and moral sense. Hence human will is not totally bound by sin and people can cooperate with God to move towards a renewal of God's likeness: "God wanted sons and daughters, not slaves. The Orthodox church rejects any doctrine or grace which might seem to infringe on human freedom."[10] Here we see a variation of Pelagianism, such that the will is not totally corrupted but retains some power to cooperate with God. Also, Orthodox churches reject the teaching that Adam's descendants inherit his guilt; i.e., our guilt is only due to our own sins. It is interesting that the booklet "What Orthodox Christians Believe"[11] makes no mention of original sin or a sinful nature in its section on sin (p. 5).

Liberal Christianity is a name which mostly refers to the effect of liberalism within Protestant churches. But it has also affected Roman Catholicism and Orthodox Christianity. Liberalism places reason over revelation with the result that doctrines which are less palatable to fallen man's sensitivities, or do not appear to fit with modern scientific discoveries, are downplayed or jettisoned. For example, liberal Christianity rejects such truths as Scripture's inerrancy and eternal punishment. On the matter of human sin, most liberals reject the idea of Adam as a real historical person and hence they reject the imputation of Adam's sin. Humans are not totally depraved but still have the power to freely choose to go God's way.

Judaism predates Pelagianism but has much in common with it. There is no doubt that Judaism takes sin seriously, recognizes its power to destroy so much that is good in human life, and teaches the reality of divine

---

7. Catholic Inquiry Centre, *Life of Faith*.
8. Catholic Truth Society, *Catechism of Christian Doctrine*.
9. Ott, *Fundamentals of Catholic Dogma*, 233.
10. Ware, *Orthodox Church*, 221.
11. "What Orthodox Christians Believe."

retribution, before and after death. And yet it does not take sin seriously enough, and hence, as we shall see later, its remedy is inadequate. Judaism's struggle is with the effect of Adam's sin on his descendants; do we have a nature which is "totally depraved"? Judaism's answer is no; it denies original sin in the sense that Adam's sin has led to spiritual death and a corrupt nature for all his descendants. It teaches that his sin brought only physical death on all, and by the introduction of disobedience into human life brought about an environment in which obedience to God's ways is so much harder. But people still have the power to choose the good and reject the evil, so redemption is by penitence and God's mercy: no savior is necessary.[12] Man is to be viewed as a moral being pulled in two different directions but only his actions, thoughts, or words can be sinful, not the desires of his heart: "It is not a sin to feel lust, but it is sinful to act in an immoral way . . . [it is] simply human nature, ugly and unpalatable though it may be."[13] The pull in the evil direction is called the *yetzer ha-ra* and the pull to good is the *yetzer ha-tov*. Strange to say the *yetzer ha-ra* is called very good in a rabbinic midrash[14] because it is "identified with the force in man which drives him to gratify his instincts and ambitions,"[15] and hence it is what leads humans to build a house, marry, have children, do business, etc., and is especially identified with the sex instinct. Yet it is seen as an evil inclination because it can so easily lead to wrongdoing. It is understood to have originated in God's initial act of creation: "Raba said: Though God created the yetzer ha-Ra, he created the law, as an antidote against it."[16] Therefore, diligent attention and obedience to the Torah is the antidote. No one is ever free from the *yetzer ha-ra* in this life and its power is to be taken seriously, as Jacobs remarks: "the idea that man's heart is evil from his youth is found in the Bible."[17]

How does Judaism's teaching concerning the two inclinations relate to humans as body and soul? A person's soul, which is seen as pure, is the seat of the *yetzer ha-tov*, but the body is the seat of the *yetzer ha-ra*. This appears to present a human being as a pure spirit imprisoned in a body which is impure and hostile to the immaterial and spiritual, but traditional Judaism denies this is so. Hasidic Judaism, influenced by mystical teachings such as Kabbalah, seems at times to veer closer to this dualism, which sees the

12. Epstein, *Judaism*, 142–43.
13. Brawer, *Judaism*, 56.
14. *Mid. Gen R.* 9:7.
15. Jacobs, *Jewish Theology*, 244.
16. *b. Bab. B.* 16a.
17. Jacobs, *Jewish Theology*, 247.

body as somehow hostile to the spiritual. Naftali Brawer writes: "The soul is the little bit of godliness that we possess," and "The purpose of the soul is to re-fine the body." But, according to Brawer, a human being has another soul, an animal soul: "It is from the animal soul that all the negative traits, tendencies and appetites come . . . On the one hand is the divine soul with its agenda to elevate the body spiritually. On the other hand is the animal soul with its own agenda to enjoy life to the utmost. More often than not these two agendas clash."[18] Whilst it is fair to say we all recognize the sort of inner tension he describes, it is important to remember he is describing not only the inner experience of the whole human race now, but that of Adam and Eve when they were first created. Hence, both traditional and mystical Judaism can be said to be in conflict with God's statement at the completion of creation, "Then God saw everything He had made, and indeed it was very good" (Gen 1:31), because to have created people with such an inner conflict could not have been "very good," and the Bible gives no support for such thinking. Such teachings of Judaism are designed to resist any idea of people having a sinful nature due to Adam's sin.

Here is the root of the tension between Judaism and the gospel—that human pride which insists on self-salvation through obedience to God's Torah. As a matter of interest Brawer has not stated a significant detail in hasidic theology, which is that all are now created with an animal soul, but the divine soul, which God breathes into humankind, is only realized in a human when they rise above the purely earthly and, better still, occupy themselves with Torah and its commandments.[19] This implies only a Jewish person is likely to receive a divine soul, and this is confirmed in a statement about Gentiles from the hasidic leader Rabbi S. Zalman: "The souls [animal souls] of the nations of the world, however, emanate from the other, unclean qelipot, which contain no good whatever."[20] By contrast, the Jewish animal soul emanates from a realm of both good and evil. So, according to Zalman, whilst a Jewish person has some potential to rise higher, the Gentile has none.

All this implies that God made humankind faulty, as R. Aibu said referring to Gen 6:6: "God said, I made a mistake that I created the evil yetzer in man, for had I not done so, he would not have rebelled against me."[21] Worse still, it implies that God is the author of evil. However, Judaism would reject such a notion. The reality is that Judaism's determination to reject the

---

18. Brawer, *Judaism*, 58.
19. Scholem, *Kabbalah*, 155.
20. Zalman, *Liqqutei Amarim*, 23.
21. *mid. Gen R.* Bereshit, XXVII, 4.

teaching of original sin and the corruption of our nature leaves it struggling to explain the origin of the inclination to evil in our nature and the sheer power of it. This in turn leads to great confusion regarding the rightness of natural desires because Judaism fails to clearly understand that whilst such are genuine and good they are always corrupted by our sinful nature. It seems to this author that unnecessary psychological disturbance may result from such confusion when coupled to a strong desire to please God.

(vi) The Punishment of Sin

Scripture reveals God is a God of wrath, which refers not to a vindictive spirit but rather to his steadfast and righteous hostility to evil. The punishment of sin is to be seen as the vindication of God, the One who gave humans his holy commands. His wrath is most clearly seen in the punishment of his Son in our place. The Father laid on the Son what sin deserved, resulting in separation ("My God, my God, why have you forsaken me?") and death ("and Jesus cried out with a loud voice and breathed his last"). God does punish sin in the here and now, the most obvious example being the universal experience of death because, "all have sinned and fall short of the glory of God" (Rom 3:23). Sometimes he punishes nations (Jer 18:7–10), and sometimes his punishment is seen in giving people up to their sins (Rom 1:24–32). His punishment in a general way can also be seen in the upheavals of nature, disease, and famine, which are all part of the curse (Rev 6:15, 16). It may even be seen in the lives of individuals, for example in the life of King Uzziyyahu (Uzziah), who sinned by offering incense and was punished with leprosy (2 Chr 26:16–21), or King Herod, who died horribly because he took God's glory to himself (Acts 12:20–24).

Yet it must be said that in such instances we have an inspired comment in Scripture, and that is not possible today. God may still do such things, but it seems to this author that the person's conscience, aided by God's Spirit, is the best judge of what is happening, not the opinions of others. Jesus warned against rushing to judgment when others suffer (Luke 13:1–5), cautioning that such events should be taken as an encouragement to repentance, as all are sinners and could easily suffer such troubles.

God will punish forever those who have not repented of their sins. This will be discussed in detail in a later section, so it is simply stated here. The prophet Isaiah speaks of the fire that is not quenched (Isa 66:24), Yeshua spoke of everlasting punishment (Matt 25:4–6), and Paul wrote of everlasting destruction from the presence of the Lord (2 Thess 1:8–9). It is a fearful thing to fall into the hands of the living God (Heb 10:31). It is always a mark of false religion that it belittles or waters down this Scripture teaching. Liberal forms of Christianity teach universalism; i.e., that there is no everlasting punishment, but that all will be forgiven, and non-traditional forms of Judaism take a similar view. There is much variation in the teaching of the ancient rabbis, but it seems that traditional Judaism now accepts two realities for Jewish people: firstly that "All Israel has a share in the world to come,"[22] and secondly that those who have been wicked spend twelve months in Gehenna, a place of punishment.[23] Regarding the righteous of all nations, traditional Judaism teaches they also inherit the world to come.

> The sting of death is sin, and the strength of sin is the law. But thanks be to God, who gives us the victory through our Lord Jesus Christ. (1 Cor 15:56–57)

SCRIPTURES

The fall (and original sin and sin's transmission): Gen 3: 5:3; Job 31:33; Ps 51:5; Eccl 7:29; Hos 6:7 (ESV); Luke 3:38; Rom 5:12–19; 1 Cor 15:22; 2 Cor 11:3; 1 Tim 2:13.

The nature and extent of sin: Gen 3:6; 6:5, 12, 13; 8:21; 1 Kgs 8:50; Pss 14:1–3; 51:3–4; Isa 59:12–15; 64:6; Jer 17:9; Matt 5:21–22; 27–28; 15:11; Rom 3:23; Eph 2:1–3; 2 Pet 2:19; 1 John 1:8.

The effects of sin: Gen 3:17–24; 4:6–8, 23–24; 6:5–7, 13; 19:1–12; 26:10; Exod 9:34–35; 10:7; 1 Kgs 14:7–11; Eccl 9:3; 11:7–8; Isa 59:1–11; 65:11–16; 66:22–24; Jer 18:9–10; Matt 25:31–32, 46; Rom 1:18–32; 8:19–23; Gal 4:19–21; 2 Thess 1:6–10; Jas 5:1–6; 2 Pet 3:5–10.

Conscience: Rom 2:14–15; 9:1; 13:5; 1 Cor 8:4–13; 1 Tim 1:19; 4:2; Heb 9:6–10; 1 Pet 3:16–21.

QUESTIONS

1. Describe the nature of Adam's sin. What were its immediate consequences? Do you see those in our world today?
2. What is our relationship to Adam, and how has his sin affected his descendants?
3. What is meant by the expression "total depravity"?

---

22. *b. Sanh.* 90a.
23. Epstein, *Judaism*, 143.

4. Describe the various aspects of the nature of sin.

5. What understanding of sin did you grow up with? In what way was it deficient?

6. Many think they are good enough for God. How would you show them they are not?

7. All humans have a conscience which convicts them of moral failure. How accurate is it?

FURTHER READING

Blocher, Henry. *Original Sin*. Leicester: Apollos, 1997.
Guinness, Os. *The Dust of Death*. Leicester: InterVarsity, 1973.
Hallesby, Ole. *Conscience*. Leicester: InterVarsity, 1950.
Hitchens, Peter. *The Rage against God*. Grand Rapids: Zondervan, 2010.
Luther, Martin. *The Bondage of the Will*. Translated by J. I. Packer and O. R. Johnston. Cambridge: James Clark, 1957.
Murray, John. *The Imputation of Adam's Sin*. Grand Rapids: Eerdmans, 1959.
Venning, Ralph. *The Plague of Plagues*. Edinburgh: Banner of Truth, 1965.
Zacharias, Ravi. *The End of Reason: A Response to the New Atheists*. Grand Rapids: Zondervan, 2008.

PART 5

God's Salvation

AFTER CONSIDERING THE HOPELESS condition of humans in sin it is good to turn to God's remedy, his salvation through his Son, Messiah Jesus, and the work of the Holy Spirit. But it will be good to begin by a reminder that humankind's falling to sin did not catch YHWH by surprise; his salvation was planned and then promised. The next paragraph is a brief reminder before proceeding with our study.

Salvation was planned from before the foundation of the world: "He [Messiah] indeed was foreordained before the foundation of the world" (1 Pet 1:20; see also Rev 13:8; Matt 25:34). It was then promised, and those promises were recorded in the Scriptures. From the beginning of the Tanakh to its last prophet God promises a deliverer (Gen 3:15; Ps 110:1, 4; Mal 3:1). Year after year, century after century, Israel's faithful hoped in such promises so that many, like Zacharias, were prepared and full of hope when the time came:

> Blessed is the Lord God of Israel,
> For He has visited and redeemed His people,
> And has raised up a horn of salvation for us
> In the house of His servant David,
> As He spoke by the mouth of His holy prophets,
> Who have been since the world began. (Luke 1:68–70)

Traditional Judaism continues to hold firmly to YHWH's promise: "I believe with perfect faith in the coming of the Messiah, and, though He tarry, I will wait daily for His coming."[1]

Likewise, the Spirit was promised:

> For I will pour water on him who is thirsty,
> And floods on the dry ground;
> I will pour My Spirit on your descendants." (Isa 44:3, see also Ezek 36:27; Joel 2:28)

There is little in the New Testament to tell us about the expectation Yeshua's disciples had of the promised Spirit, although a religious ritual of their day did incorporate this hope into the daily temple services during Succot. Water was brought up from the Pool of Siloam and poured out at the base of the altar while the words of Pss 113–118: were recited. It was on the seventh day of the feast, most likely at this exact moment, that Jesus cried out, "If anyone thirsts, let him come to Me and drink . . . But this He spoke concerning the Spirit" (John 7:37, 39).

It is also important before we enter into this study of Messiah to underline that every aspect of God's plan of salvation is linked to Messiah. From before the foundation of the world to its consummation in glory, all is described as being "in Christ." This paragraph mentions those many aspects, and every text quoted connects them to being in Christ or in him. All of the redeemed were chosen and intended by God for holiness before time began (Eph 1:4; 2 Tim 1:9). This was entirely God's initiative, inspired by his love (1 Cor 1:30; Rom 8:39), and through this divine purpose in Christ the whole material and spiritual universe will be brought to a united wholeness, and the principalities and powers in heavenly places will understand the manifold wisdom of God (Eph 1:10; 3:11). Salvation in Messiah fulfills all the covenant promises of the Tanakh (Gal 3:17; 2 Cor 1:20) and creates basic spiritual realities such as redemption, reconciliation, sanctification, and freedom from condemnation (Rom 3:24; 2 Cor 5:19; 1 Cor 1:2; Rom 8:1). Salvation is experienced by being "in his life" (see Rom 5:10; 1 Cor 15:22), so that believers become new creatures, are seated in heavenly places, and are under "the law of the Spirit of life in Christ Jesus" (2 Cor 5:17; Eph 2:6; Rom 8:2). Believers are brought into one body, being united and equal in him, so that differences of Jew and Gentile, male and female, etc., have no consequence for entry to the body or status within it (Rom 12:5; Gal 3:28; 6:15); Gentile believers are fellow heirs with Jewish ones so that being in Christ is all that matters (Eph 2:13; 3:6). Every aspect of the believer's

---

1. The twelfth of the Thirteen Principles of the Faith recited at the Shachrit Service (Morning Service).

spiritual experience is connected to being in Messiah: spiritual growth (1 Cor 3:1; Col 1:28), rejoicing (1 Cor 15:31; Phil 3:3), spiritual liberty (Gal 2:4), peace (1 Pet 5:14), thankfulness (1 Thess 5:8), faith and love (1 Tim 1:14), grace (2 Tim 2:1), boldness (1 Tim 3:13), good conduct (1 Pet 3:16), triumph in ministry (2 Cor 2:14), bringing others to new birth (1 Cor 4:15), and in suffering (Phil 1:13; 2 Tim 3:12). Believers who have died are secure for they are "in Christ" (1 Thess 4:16), and all have a certain hope through the promise of life, the coming upward call, and hope of glory (2 Tim 1:1; Phil 3:14; 2 Tim 2:10). In summary, Paul tells us: "Blessed be the God and Father of our Lord Jesus Christ, who has blessed us with every spiritual blessing in the heavenly places in Christ" (Eph 1:3). All these spiritual realities will be explored further in what follows in the two sections "God's Messiah" and "God's Spirit."

SCRIPTURES

Union with Messiah: John 17:24; Rom 3:24; 5:10; 8:1; 12:5; 1 Cor 1:2; 3:1; 4:15; 15:22, 31; 2 Cor 2:14; 5:19; Gal 2:4; 3:28; 6:15; Eph 1:3, 4, 10; 2;6; 3:11; Phil 1:13; 3:14; 1 Thess 5:8; 1 Tim 1:14; 3:13; 2 Tim 1:1, 9; 2:1; 1 Pet 3:16; 5:14; Rev 17:8.

QUESTION

1. Is there any blessing of salvation which comes to us apart from Messiah? What are our spiritual blessings "in Christ"?

FURTHER READING

Reeves, Michael. *Christ Our Life*. Milton Keynes: Paternoster, 2014.

God's Messiah

OUR AIM IN THIS section of "God's Salvation" is to look at Yeshua, who he is and what he has done to save and bless sinners. We will consider him as God's promised Messiah and then look more closely at his humanity, his deity, his person, and then his work of atonement. All that has been written so far makes clear why humanity needs a savior; Jesus is that One.

20

Yeshua the Promised Messiah

THE MESSIAH IS PROMISED by God in Scripture as one who will deliver humanity from its rebellion against God with all its consequences, something which began when the first man and woman, Adam and Eve, disobeyed God's command. The deliverer would be descended from the woman, truly human, and as subsequently revealed he would be descended from Abraham, Judah, and David (Gen 3:15; 12:3; 49:10; 2 Sam 7:12–13). Yeshua was all of these things, an Israelite of the royal line (Luke 3:23–38; Matt 1:1–16). He is the manifestation of God's merciful love towards his rebellious world (John 3:16).

(A) PROPHET, PRIEST, AND KING

As God's revelation unfolds within Israel it becomes clear that the promised deliverer will fulfill Israel's three anointed leadership roles—prophet, priest, and king. Moshe first reveals him as a *prophet*, one of Israel who will speak perfectly God's truth and must be heard by Israel or they will suffer the consequences. He will learn from God, honor the law, reveal hidden things, take truth to all the earth, be wise and understanding, bring life-changing good news, and like Moshe and the prophets suffer rejection (Deut 18:15–19; Isa 50:4; 42:21; Ps 78:2; Isa 49:6; 11:2; 61:1–3; 49:4; 50:6; Ps 22:16–18). Yeshua was such a prophet: one of the people, a unique teacher ("No man ever spoke like this Man!"; John 7:46), one of integrity ("You are true, and teach the way of God in truth"; Matt 22:16), warning Israel of the need to heed his words. He honored the law, taught with compassion, and proclaimed the good news of the kingdom and sins forgiven. He worked miracles and his prophecies have been and are being been fulfilled; he also suffered rejection (John 12:48; Matt 5:17–18; Mark 6:34; 1:14–15; Matt 9:2; Luke 8:22–56; 21:20–24; John 6:66; Matt 26:57–68; 27:15–31). He continues in this office now, since his ascension: "I have declared to them Your name, and will declare it" (John 17:26; see also Luke 10:22; Acts 1:1; Rom 9:23–24), for in him "are hidden all the treasures of wisdom and knowledge" (Col 2:3).

Messiah's role as a *priest* should not be surprising because Avraham and the other patriarchs offered sacrifices, acting as priests for the family. To David it was revealed that the Messiah would be a priest, but not of the Levitical order under the Mosaic covenant; rather Messiah would be of the earlier order of Melchizedek. Therefore Messiah must offer a sacrifice which will provide atonement, and he must intercede for the people before YHWH, being one of them and able to empathize with them; these things Isaiah predicted of Messiah (Gen 12:7–8; 14:18–20; Ps 110:1–4; Isa 52:13—53:12, especially 53:10–12). Jesus fulfilled all these things. He was truly a man and able to sympathize with those he represented (Heb 2:17; 5:1–2); and being appointed by God to this priestly role, he interceded for them as one who sat where they sat (John 10:17–18; 14:31; 17). Having lived a perfect life which fulfilled all the demands of God's law, he offered himself without spot to God for his sheep, giving his life a ransom for many on the cross at Golgotha (John 8:29, 46; Heb 9:14; John 10:14–15; 17; Mark 10:45; 15:33–38). His resurrection demonstrates God's acceptance of his sacrifice (Acts 13:37–39). Now exalted to God's right hand he is the divine advocate who intercedes for his people (1 John 2:1; Heb 7:25; 5:7–9).

Messiah's is a ruler, a *king*. The prediction of one to crush the serpent's head points to one of strength and rule, and Yakov understood him to be a ruler of the people. The promise to David places Messiah on David's throne to rule Israel, a reign which will extend to all the world and forever. The nature of his reign is not like the kingdoms of this world; it is a reign based on truth and righteousness, and his people are those who keep God's word. He extends his rule and salvation to all the world, and he also acts in judgment to discipline his people and to punish God's enemies (Gen 3:15; 49:10; 2 Sam 7:12–13; Ps 2; Isa 11:1–10; Dan 7:13–14; Zech 9:9–10; Ps 45:6; Isa 42:3; 66:2; Prov 3:11–12; Ps 110:5–7). Yeshua is such a king. He was born king of Israel as the heir to David's throne, recognized as ruler and king of Israel by Jew and Gentile, and his preeminent concern was for righteousness and truth among his followers: "My mother and My brothers are these who hear the word of God and do it" (Luke 8:21; Matt 2:1–2; 21:9; John 1:49; Matt 8:5–10; 27:37; 5:20; John 18:36–37). His resurrection proclaims his victory over sin and death and the demonic (Heb 9:28; 1 Cor 15:54–55; Col

2:15), and declares him to be YHWH's Son and king Messiah (Rom 1:4; Acts 2:32–33). After his resurrection he ascended to the right hand of the Father in glory, where he now rules all things in heaven and on earth, gathering in his people from all nations, and acting in judgment to discipline his people and to punish God's enemies (Acts 2:36; Eph 1:22; 1 Pet 3:22; Rev 19:16; Matt 28:19–20; Rev 2; Acts 13:11; 1 Thess 2:16; 2 Thess 2:11–12; Rev 6:1–17). One day he will return in glory and be recognized as king by all who have ever lived: "that at the name of Jesus every knee should bow" (Phil 2:10); he will be admired by his people and feared by those whom he will punish (2 Thess 1:10; Rev 6:15–16; 2 Thess 1:7–9).

(B) THE FULFILLER OF PATTERNS

People, institutions, and historical events in Israel are a pattern of the person and ministry of the promised Messiah; those mentioned above are three examples, but a few more will be mentioned here. Avraham, Yizthak, and Yakov were men through whom God revealed himself in their day, and Yeshua was preeminently so (John 1:51). Joseph and David were both leaders who suffered and knew rejection before they ruled, as did Jesus. The exodus of Israel from Egypt and their time in the wilderness was experienced by Jesus, who came out of Egypt as a child and was tempted in the wilderness as a man. He was the true Israel, perfectly performing all that Israel was commanded to do, and fulfilling all that the sacrifices, the priesthood, and the tabernacle portrayed of the way into the presence of the living God. As Moshe mediated a covenant, so Jesus mediated a new covenant with the house of Israel. Yeshua is the lamb of Pesach, who protects his people from judgment, the One whose Atonement Day blood on Golgotha grants entrance into the holiest place; he is the firstfruits of God's world harvest and the Succah for blessing and protection in the wilderness of this fallen world. Much more could be written and can be found in the Further Reading section (Hos 11:1; Matt 2:15; 4:1–11; Isa 49:3; 42:21; Heb 8:1–2; Matt 26:26–28; Eph 2:11–20; John 1:29; Heb 9:24–25; Acts 26:23; John 17:11–15).

(C) THE ONE WHO MAKES ISRAEL A BLESSING TO THE WORLD

God promised Avraham, "And in you all the families of the earth shall be blessed" (Gen 12:3), and Messiah fulfills this by restoring Israel to God and subsequently becoming a light to the Gentiles. Through Yeshua many in

Israel turned from transgression and those who were restored, men such as Paul and Barnabas, fulfilled this purpose of YHWH by taking the message out: "I will also give you as a light to the Gentiles, That you should be My salvation to the ends of the earth" (Isa 49:6). Israel continues to fulfill this role through the word of God, revealed to and recorded by Israelites and now read throughout the world due to the work of believers in Jesus (Isa 59:20; Acts 13:46–47; John 4:22).

(D) MESSIAH MORE THAN A MAN

The Hebrew Scriptures point to a Messiah who is more than a man. He will defeat a supernatural foe, the serpent Satan; he is called "Son of God"; and David spoke of him as his lord long before Messiah appears in history. He appears in Daniel's vision on the clouds of heaven and he is born of a virgin. He is described as the Angel of the Lord by Malachi, the angel of whom Moshe writes, "My name is in Him" (Exod 23:21; Gen 3:15; Ps 2:7; Matt 26:63; Ps 110:1; Dan 7:13–14; Isa 7:14; Mal 3:1). There are texts which describe Messiah in divine terms but it is doubtful they were understood to teach Messiah's deity before Jesus came. In the same way that Jesus' faithful disciples could not grasp his teaching about his coming death and resurrection until it happened, so those faithful ones who lived before Messiah could not grasp this teaching in the Tanakh concerning his deity before he came. It was a mystery yet to be revealed: "and without controversy great is the mystery of godliness: God was manifested in the flesh" (1 Tim 3:16). Isaiah and Jeremiah give names to the coming Messiah which are descriptive of who he is: "Immanuel" (God with us, Isa 7:14); "Wonderful, Counselor, Mighty God, Everlasting Father, Prince of Peace" (Isa 9:6); and "YHWH Tsidkenu" (the Lord our righteousness, Jer 23:6). Psalm 45, which exults in the glories of Messiah and his bride, describes him thus: "Your throne, O God, is forever and ever; A scepter of righteousness is the scepter of your kingdom" (Ps 45:6). Jesus did not hesitate to assert he was more than a man: "I have come down from heaven, not to do My own will, but the will of Him who sent Me" (John 6:38). What this means—his deity—will be considered further in the sections which follow.

As has been noted before, this is not a book of apologetics (such books are mentioned in the Further Reading section), so there is no attempt here to answer the objections of those who reject what is written above; however some note must be made of those who agree and disagree. Whilst this book disagrees with significant teachings of the Roman Catholic Church and the Orthodox churches, it is right to note that those churches would not dissent from all that is written above. Liberal forms of Christianity do differ, especially regarding Jesus' miracles and virgin birth, and some deny his deity. Cults or sects which have split off from the mainstream Christianity of the ancient creeds, like the Jehovah's Witnesses, likewise reject his deity. Traditional Judaism would agree with much that is written, holding on, often in the face of persecution, to the messianic hope of a coming king and great teacher who will turn Israel and the world to a love of YHWH and his laws. But the teaching of Messiah's deity and priesthood, truths which are not peripheral but fundamental to salvation, have been rejected, which has led to a parting of the ways for Jews who follow Yeshua and those who do not.

21

Yeshua—His Humanity

THE ABOVE LOOKS AT the messianic expectation and how Yeshua began to fulfill those hopes in his earthly ministry; here we go into more detail on his true humanity, something about which there is little disagreement. He was one like us, and although he was different—sinless and having a divine nature (which will be considered next)—there was nothing lacking in his humanness. Even in the days of the apostles some sought to undermine this truth because it was thought to detract from spirituality, ideas that today are referred to as "gnostic," but the apostles firmly rebutted them: "in Him dwells all the fullness of the Godhead bodily," and "every spirit that does not confess that Jesus Christ has come in the flesh is not of God" (Col 2:9; 1 John 4:3).

Like us all, Yeshua has forebears; he has a genealogy from Adam, Avraham, and David, which places him firmly as human and one of the Jewish nation (Matt 1:1–16; Luke 3:23–38). He was conscious of his Jewishness and, when necessary, made a point of it, as in his conversation with the Samaritan woman: "You worship what you do not know; we know what we worship, for salvation is of the Jews" (John 4:22). He came into this world through a normal birth after growth in his mother's womb (Luke 1:31; 2:6–7; Gal 4:4) and grew to maturity like all others, increasing in physical size, and undergoing a learning process so as to increase in knowledge and wisdom: "And the Child grew and became strong in spirit, filled with wisdom; and the grace of God was upon Him" (Luke 2:40). His family life was a normal one, growing up with brothers and sisters, and he was known in his community as one like everyone else, so we can assume a normal social life

(Mark 6:3; Luke 4:16, 22), participating in life's special events with others (John 2:1–10). He valued close friendships (John 13:23; 11:1–3).

He lived under the Mosaic law, and although he ignored those manmade rules with which others had surrounded it, he honored Moshe in his teaching and his instructions to others: "go your way, show yourself to the priest, and offer the gift that Moses commanded" (Mark 7:10; Matt 8:4; 23:2). He observed the Sabbath, attended synagogue, and traveled to Jerusalem for festivals (Luke 4:16; 2:41; Mark 14:16; John 10:22; Gal 4:4). His extensive knowledge of the Scriptures demonstrates his disciplined study of them, added to which he made the effort in his youth to learn from the teachers of his day (Matt 22: 23–46; Luke 2:46).

Jesus experienced the whole range of human emotions. He showed love, anger, compassion, amazement, joy, and sorrow (Mark 10:21; Luke 7:11–15; Mark 3:5; 6:6; Luke 10:21; 18:23), and experienced emotional stress (Mark 14:33; Matt 26:37–38). No one who lived close to him for those three years of his public ministry recorded the slightest doubt about his being truly human even though he was exceptional: "And the Word became flesh and dwelt among us" (John 1:14). Jesus experienced all the usual physical needs, eating and drinking with others and at times knowing hunger, thirst, and tiredness (Luke 7:36; John 4:6–7; Matt 21:18–19).

Jesus was sinless due to his unique conception, what is commonly termed the "virgin birth"; he did not have a human father, and hence Adam's sin was not imputed to him. His close associates saw no sin in him and even his enemies could make no accusation when asked to do so (1 Pet 3:18; John 8:46). However, he experienced temptation to sin (Luke 4:1–13), and although it was not possible for him to actually sin, the temptation was real. The fact that he did not have a fallen nature did not mean he felt temptation less keenly. Temptation to sin comes through the natural desires (Jas 1:14), whether mental, emotional, or physical, and the pressure is to satisfy them in a way other than how God has directed; Yeshua knew all that was natural as one with body and soul. There was also a particular temptation associated with his ministry because it involved immeasurable self-sacrifice. He knew forty days and nights of personal pressure from Satan, and in Gethsemane he sweated drops of blood resisting sin (Luke 22:39–46). Scripture is clear: he "was in all points tempted as we are, yet without sin" (Heb 4:15).

There is a mystery about Yeshua's knowledge in his encounters with others, which will be explored later under the mystery of his two natures: there were times when he needed information from people (Mark 9:21) and there were times when he had supernatural awareness (John 1:48). In a similar vein he, like all Israel's prophets and leaders, needed the anointing of the Spirit (Luke 4:14). Being God's only begotten Son did not mean he could minister without any need of the Spirit's divine enabling; he was a truly human servant of YHWH.

Jesus lived by faith, trusting his Father at all times: learning from him, experiencing his direction in ministry, praying to him, obeying him, and submitting to the hard calling which was his as the suffering servant (John 15:15; 5:19; Luke 6:12–13; John 6:38; Luke 22:42).

Everything considered so far relates to his life before his resurrection and ascension and it may be tempting to think that after those events he was somehow different, and perhaps remote and less human, but the accounts teach otherwise, for example in his tender comforting of Mary Magdalene: "Jesus said to her, 'Woman, why are you weeping? Whom are you seeking?'" (John 20:11–15). And after his ascension we read of him: "Jesus Christ is the same yesterday, today, and forever," and, "For we do not have a High Priest who cannot sympathize with our weaknesses" (Heb 13:8; 4:15).

All these points about his humanity led Paul to describe him as the "last Adam" and the "second Man" or the "heavenly Man" (1 Cor 15:45–49). These designations point to Yeshua as truly a part of the human race and yet signaling its end (last Adam), and the one who begins a new humanity, a heavenly one (second man). His true humanity was crucial to both of these roles.

We can only marvel that the One who had existed from all eternity, through whom the worlds were made, became a babe, a child, a youth, and a man, living among his own people Israel, living in our fallen and corrupt world so as to save us, and has now taken that Jewish humanity to glory (Phil 2:5–11).

> Blessed is the Lord God of Israel,
> For He has visited and redeemed His people,
> And has raised up a horn of salvation for us
> In the house of His servant David. (Luke 1:68–69)

Scriptures

Yeshua the Promised Messiah

Gen 3:15; 12:3; 49:10; 2 Sam 7:12–13; Matt 1:1–16; Luke 3:23–38.

Prophet: Deut 18:15–19; Pss 22:16–18; 78:2; Isa 11:2; 42:21; 49:4, 6; 50:4, 6; 61:1–3; Matt 5:17–18; 9:2; 22:16; 26:57–68; 27:15–31; Mark 1:14–15; 6:34; Luke 8:22–56; 21:20–24; John 6:66; 7:46; 12:48; 17:26; see also Luke 10:22; Acts 1:1; Rom 9:23–24; Col 2:3.

Priest: Gen 12:7–8; 14:18–20; Ps 110:1–4; Isa 52:13–53:12; Mark 10:45; 15:33–39; Heb 9:14; John 10:14–15; 17; Heb 7:25; 5:1–2; 7–9.

King: Gen 3:15; 49:10; 2 Sam 7:12–13; Pss 2; 45:6; 110:5–7; Prov 3:11–12; Isa 11:1–10; 42:3; 66:2; Dan 7:13–14; Zech 9:9–10; Matt 2:1–2; 5:20; 8:5–10; 21:9; 27:37; 28:19–20; Luke 8:21; John 1:49; 18:36–37; Acts 2:36; 13:11; Eph 1:22; 1 Thess 2:16; 2 Thess 2:11–12; Rev 2; 6:1–17.

Patterns: Isa 49:3; 42:21; Hos 11:1; Matt 2:15; 4:1–11; 26:26–28; John 1:29; 17:11–15; Acts 26:23; Eph 2:11–20; Heb 8:1–2; 9:24–25.

Makes Israel a Blessing: Gen 12:3; Isa 49:6; 59:20; Acts 13:46–47; John 4:22.

More than a Man: Gen 3:15; Exod 23:21; Pss 2:7; 45:6–7; 110:1; Isa 7:14; 9:6; Jer 23:6; Dan 7:13–14; Mal 3:1; Matt 14:43; 26:63; John 6:38; 10:30–39; 20:28; 1 Tim 3:16.

Yeshua—His Humanity

Matt 8:4; 21:18–19; 22:23–46; 23:2; 26:37–38; Mark 3:5; 6:3, 6; 7:10; 10:21; 14:16, 33; Luke 1:31; 2:6–7, 41, 46; 4:1–13, 14, 16, 22; 6:12–13; 7:11–15, 36; 10:21; 18:23; 22:39–46; John 1:48; 2:1–10; 4:6–7; 5:19; 6:38; 8:46; 10:22; 11:1–3; 13:23; 15:15; 20:11–15; 1 Cor 15:45–49; Gal 4:4; Phil 2:5–11; Col 2:9; Heb 4:15–16; 13:8; 1 Pet 3:18; 1 John 1:3.

Questions

Yeshua the Promised Messiah

1. Did Yeshua fulfill the requirements of the Mosaic law for a prophet? How is his prophetic function fulfilled today?

2. How does having Yeshua as our priest help us to live the life of faith?

3. How is Messiah ruling now?

4. What is Messiah's most important work and why?

5. What was it that convinced you that Jesus was the promised Messiah?

6. What individuals, institutions, and historical events of Israel are a pattern fulfilled by Yeshua? How has he fulfilled them, or will yet fulfill them?

Yeshua—His Humanity

1. Why was it necessary that Messiah was truly human?
2. What convinces you that Yeshua was truly human?
3. How is an awareness of Jesus' true humanity a help to those undergoing the trials of this earthly life? Give some examples from your own experience.

Further Reading

Yeshua the Promised Messiah

Brown, Michael. *Answering Jewish Objections to Jesus*. Vol. 1, General and Historical. Grand Rapids: Baker, 2000.
———. *Answering Jewish Objections to Jesus*. Vol. 2, Theological. Grand Rapids: Baker, 2000.
———. *Answering Jewish Objections to Jesus*. Vol. 3, Messianic Prophecy. Grand Rapids: Baker, 2003.
———. *Answering Jewish Objections to Jesus*. Vol. 4, New Testament. Grand Rapids: Baker, 2007.
———. *The Real Kosher Jesus*. Lake Mary, FL: Charisma Media, 2012.
Edersheim, Alfred. *The Life and Times of Jesus the Messiah*. Peabody, MA: Hendrickson, 1988.
Fairbairn, Patrick. *The Typology of Scripture*. Los Angeles: HardPress, 2019.
Habershon, Ada R. *Study of the Types*. Grand Rapids: Kregel, 1974.
Jukes, Andrew. *Types in Genesis*. Grand Rapids: Kregel, 1976.
Santala, Risto. *Messiah in the New Testament in the Light of the Rabbinical Writings*. Jerusalem: Keren Ahvah Meshihit, 1992.
Van Groningen, Gerard. *Messianic Revelation in the Old Testament*. Grand Rapids: Baker, 1990.

Yeshua—His Humanity

Jones, Mark. *Knowing Christ*. Edinburgh: Banner of Truth, 2017.
Ware, Bruce A. *The Man Christ Jesus*. Wheaton, IL: Crossway, 2012.

22

Yeshua—His Deity

The Scriptures assert the startling fact that a man walked this earth in the land of Israel who was God incarnate among us, come to do what could not be done by a human or any supernatural created being, to save us from the consequences of our willful rebellion against YHWH; his name was Yeshua, which stands for "YHWH saves." YHWH had come among his people in a unique and personal way.

(A) YESHUA—YHWH'S ONLY BEGOTTEN SON

(i) Oneness with YHWH the Father

The description "only begotten Son" communicates his oneness of nature with God: "The only begotten Son, who is in the bosom of the Father, He has declared Him" (John 1:18). A son may be subordinate to his father but he is equal in being and nature, something Jesus asserted by the words, "I and My Father are one," which the Jewish leaders rightly understood as a claim to identity of nature with God (John 10:30, 33). The phrase is not meant to indicate God gave birth to God, as if the Son had a beginning, but to describe the relationship of the second and first persons within the Godhead of YHWH, an eternal relationship of Son to Father, a mystery which creatures will never fully fathom. He spoke of his relationship to the Father before he came into the world, of his dwelling in heaven with the Father even whilst in this world, of his constant awareness of the Father's love for him and his for the Father, of the love of the Father for his Son in desiring he should be equally honored, and of his returning to the Father (John 1:2;

6:38; 3:13; 15:10; 14:31; 5:23; 16:10, 28). It is because he is the divine Son that he, and he alone, can perfectly reveal the Father to us: "no one knows the Son except the Father. Nor does anyone know the Father except the Son, and the one to whom the Son wills to reveal Him" (Matt 11:27). All this makes clear that Yeshua had a divine nature as well as a human one.

There are many places where the term "Son" or "Son of God" appears, referring to him as the divine Son within the Godhead (e.g., Acts 9:20; Rom 1:3; Heb 1:1-2; 1 John 5:12). However, two exceptions are worth considering. Firstly, he was called "Son of God" because his human nature was conceived by the miraculous working of God (Luke 1:35). Secondly, he was also called "Son of God" because of his resurrection. In Acts 13:33 Paul refers the words of Ps 2:7, "You are My Son, Today I have begotten You," to Yeshua's resurrection, because it was a begetting to new life and ministry as the risen Messiah.

(ii) Likeness to YHWH

The divine name in the Greek form, *Kyrios* (Lord), as used in the Septuagint, is applied to Yeshua in a unique and exalted way in the New Testament, especially by Paul: "No one can say Jesus is Lord except by the Holy Spirit" (1 Cor 12:3). Old Testament passages that refer to YHWH are attributed to Yeshua, such as the use of Joel 2:32 in Rom 10:9, 13, where faith in the Lord Jesus is equated with calling on the name of YHWH (see also John 12:41 and Isa 6:10; Phil 2:9 and Isa 45:23-25). Yeshua used the divine name of himself: "Most assuredly, I say to you, before Abraham was, I AM" (John 8:58); and his hearers understood the claim he was making and sought to kill him. All this was received and believed by devout people of Israel, for whom YHWH had no equal, but who had come to see Jesus as his incarnation through his Son.

YHWH is One who jealousy guards his glory and will give it to no other (Isa 42:8). But Jesus is described as "the Lord of glory," something he shared with the Father before the world was created; a glimpse of which was seen by three disciples on the mount of transfiguration (1 Cor 2:8; John 17:5; Matt 17:2). Their glory is shared because their nature is one.

John speaks of another aspect of Yeshua's glory: "we beheld His glory, the glory as of the only begotten of the Father, full of grace and truth" (John 1:14); it is a glory of character. For John this was one preeminent means of perceiving the deity of Yeshua. YHWH's description of himself in Deut 34:6 stresses his grace, goodness, truth, forgiveness, and justice, and Jesus was full of these things. The comment has been made that no one could have invented Jesus, so he had to have existed, and that is correct. Nobody could know what God in the flesh would be like unless he appeared. But when he did he must be exactly like what was revealed of YHWH. If Jesus' words and actions are carefully considered, it will be seen how he was always gracious and truthful, good to all and forgiving, demanding righteousness without fear or favor. Comparing him with Israel's exemplary men underlines this, for although they exhibited traits to follow, they also manifested failures to avoid: Avraham dissembled, Yakov deceived, Joseph was priggish, David committed adultery, Solomon slid into idolatry, etc., etc. Good men who had weaknesses. Yeshua was a good person who had none whatsoever; truly the glorious Son of YHWH.

(iii) He Does What YHWH Does

YHWH created and upholds the universe, saves sinners, judges evil, hears prayer, and receives worship. Jesus is described in the same terms. The world came into being through him and he sustains it (John 1:3; Heb 1:3); he saves sinners and punishes evil (Matt 9:2; 1 Tim 1:15; John 5:22; Matt 25:31-46); he hears prayer and receives worship (Acts 7:59; Heb 4:14-16; Matt 14:33; John 9:38; Matt 28:17; Rev 5:12). All these things are unthinkable for a created being, however glorious.

(B) YESHUA—THE WORD OF YHWH

God is a communicating God—within the Godhead and to his creation. When we read in the account of the creation "God said . . ." John the apostle tells us that those words are the work of the person within the Godhead called the Word: "In the beginning was the Word . . . All things were made through Him" (John 1:3). John also tells us, "the Word was with God, and the Word was God." This is a development of what Proverbs tells us about personified "wisdom":

> The LORD possessed me at the beginning of His way,
> Before His works of old . . .
> Rejoicing always before Him,
> Rejoicing in His inhabited world,
> And my delight was with the sons of men" (Prov 8:22, 30–31)

John goes on to speak more of Yeshua: "And the Word became flesh and dwelt among us" (John 1:14). He comes to bring about God's new creation as God's living Word.

As the Word of God Yeshua spoke God's words, so that all he taught was the truth of God (John 12:50; 6:63). Hence he spoke with authority, as his hearers recognized (Matt 7:28, 29; Luke 4:32), and all he taught was consistent with what had already been revealed (Matt 5:17; Rom 10:4); he gave the authoritative interpretation of earlier revelation (Matt 5:17–48; Luke 20:37–38, 41–44) as well giving as new revelation (Matt 13:1–52). As God's living Word he expected absolute obedience and devotion to everything he taught (Matt 28:20).

He spoke words of command with divine authority when casting out demons, healing the sick, raising the dead, commanding nature, and forgiving sins (Mark 1:27; Luke 4:39; Mark 7:34; John 11:43–44; Matt 8:26; 9:1–8). He taught that these works were direct evidence of his being the unique Son of God (John 10:31–38), one with the Father. Although some opposed him, there were many who marveled: "We never saw anything like this!" (Mark 2:12). And those words underline a significant difference between Jesus and the miracles of Moshe and the prophets before him: they called upon God to act; Jesus simply gave commands as God would to his creation—because he was the Word of God made flesh.

(C) YESHUA'S SELF-CONSCIOUSNESS OF HIS DEITY

Jesus was fully aware of who he was from an early age (Luke 2:49). In his ministry he spoke of his unique relation to God as Son to the Father (John 5:17–30), especially by his use of the intimate word "Abba" to address him (Mark 14:36). He was aware of his preexistence (John 17:5). He said he was the "Messiah," using the precise term, and by his frequent use of the term "Son of Man" (John 4: 25–26; Matt 26:63–65). The supernatural voice appearing at his baptism (Mark 1:9–11) and on a few other occasions was not because he had doubts but to encourage him in his human nature at crucial points in his ministry.

(D) YESHUA'S RESURRECTION AND EXALTATION

His resurrection declares him to be the divine Son because it establishes as true all that he said about himself, which includes his deity. His ascension in a cloud signified his deity, and his exaltation to God's right hand to rule all things (Ps 2:7–9), putting an end to all other rule, authority, and power (Acts 1:9–12; 2:32–33; 1 Cor 15:24–28), underlines his equality of nature and authority with YHWH, as One who does what YHWH alone does.

(E) DIRECT NEW TESTAMENT STATEMENTS OF DEITY

Yeshua's deity is most usually understood from his relationship to YHWH, and doing the works that only YHWH could do. However, there are direct statements, which are mostly in the Epistles, written to deal with errors which were creeping into the churches and to clarify the teaching for believers. Some are quoted above but there are others, such as: "Christ came, who is over all, the eternally blessed God" (Rom 9:5); "our great God and Savior Jesus Christ" (Titus 2:13); "our God and Savior Jesus Christ" (2 Pet 1:1); "we are in Him who is true, in His Son Jesus Christ. This is the true God and eternal life" (1 John 5:20); "who, being in the form of God, did not consider it robbery to be equal with God, but made Himself of no reputation" (Phil 2:6–7).

(F) DOXOLOGIES, GREETINGS, AND BENEDICTIONS

Doxologies are exclamation of praise and worship and some are addressed to Jesus: "And the Lord will deliver me from every evil work . . . To Him be glory forever and ever" (2 Tim 4:18); others are addressed to the Father and the Savior equally:

> Blessing and honor and glory and power
> Be to Him who sits on the throne,
> And to the Lamb, forever and ever!" (Rev 5:13)

In all Paul's letters he greets his readers with the phrase "God our Father and the Lord Jesus Christ" (e.g., Rom 1:7, see also 2 John 3), a phrase which could only be appropriate if they are equal. A similar point can be made from the way the benedictions at the close of two of Paul's Epistles join together the Father and Messiah Jesus: "The grace of the Lord Jesus Christ, and the love of God, and the communion of the Holy Spirit be with you all" (2 Cor 13:14; see also Eph 6:23).

23

Yeshua—His Two Natures and One Person

Jesus had a perfect and complete human nature and an undiminished divine nature, and his person was that of the eternal Word of YHWH. As we contemplate such a One, we can only be filled with wonder at the wisdom and power of God, for we face something beyond our comprehension. And yet it is legitimate to seek to understand as much as Scripture reveals as long as we approach humbly and with reverence. This has been attempted throughout church history, and light has been given but also mistakes have been made, some inadvertently and some with a desire to make the nature of the Savior more accessible to human reason. Because of this the church has needed to carefully put into words the revelation of the New Testament so as to prevent false teaching and to edify believers.

An early error among Jewish believers became known as "Ebionism," which denied the deity of Yeshua whilst continuing to assert his messiahship, especially his kingly rule. The pressure upon Jewish believers today to dilute Yeshua's deity in some way is very real due to the opposition from Judaism and the community in general, and some on the fringes of the messianic movement have succumbed, but the glory of YHWH incarnate among his people must always be upheld; God became man by taking to himself a human nature.

Arianism was a similar denial, one which had a far wider impact on the churches, and which taught the Word was a created, though exalted being; it led to strenuous debates throughout the fourth century. The Council of Nicea in 325 AD restated the biblical teaching on Christ's deity and subsequent conflicts were finally resolved at the Council of Constantinople in 381 AD. A key phrase in these statements was "one substance" (Gk. *homoousios*), referring to the Son as of one substance with the Father in the Godhead. It is tempting to look back at these debates and see it as all rather arid and the language of the statements as Gentile, but precise wording in the language of the day was necessary to preserve the purity of the gospel; faith in a Savior who is less that the Father's only begotten Son is not acceptable to him.

Subsequent discussion looked more carefully at how the human and divine natures were united together and in union with the person of the divine Word. Here is great mystery and the errors made then are repeated in churches today. Some understood Yeshua to be the Word in a human body; that is, the Word was in place of the human soul but that meant Yeshua was not truly human. Others so insisted on the separation of the human and divine natures that Yeshua appeared not to be an integrated person. Still others considered Yeshua to have a composite nature, made from his human and divine, but then he was neither truly man nor truly God. The Council of Chalcedon in 451AD was convened to create a statement which would define the biblical teaching. Two significant phrases are of interest: "hypostatic union," which asserts the union in the one person of the full human nature and the full divine nature of Yeshua; and "communion of properties," which underlines that each nature retains its essential properties yet with a true communion between the two natures such that the properties of each are truly communicated to each other. The key wording at Chalcedon regarding the two natures in Yeshua was: "without confusion, without change, without division, without separation."

To explain the apparent limitations in Yeshua, some point to the wording "made Himself of no reputation" in Phil 2:7, considering that although Yeshua had a true divine nature yet he made latent certain divine attributes. There seems little evidence for this and the text points more to making himself insignificant. He was always fully God and never ceased to be the One who, for example, was "upholding all things by the word of His power" (Heb 1:3). It seems better to understand these limitations in the way expressed by Jesus: "Most assuredly, I say to you, the Son can do nothing of Himself, but what He sees the Father do; for whatever He does, the Son also does in like manner" (John 5:19). This theme is strongly emphasized in John and points to that eternal aspect of the relationship within the Godhead whereby the Father initiates and the Son follows, except that the incarnation has led to a true human dependence on the Father whereby the God-man Yeshua depends on knowledge and direction received from the Father. This can be summarized by saying Yeshua possessed deity but it was not fully expressed because his life, being a life of service on earth, was lived in the main through his human nature.

This leaves the question of the self-consciousness of Yeshua. Was this no more than that of the Word? Or was it that of the Word plus a full human self-consciousness? The former makes Yeshua less than a true human and the latter makes him two persons, neither of which fit the biblical evidence. A better understanding of this mystery is that Yeshua's human self-consciousness had no separate existence of its own but existed only by virtue of hypostatic union with the Word. This preserves Yeshua's true and full humanity, but his essential self is that of the Word, the second person of the Godhead. We can but be amazed that the divine person who made himself of no reputation for us still has, and will forever have, that true human nature in which he became of no reputation, a true human nature that was derived from Abraham and David; his self-consciousness being forever taken into hypostatic union with that of a true human nature. "Jesus Christ is the same yesterday, today, and forever" (Heb 13:8). This is surely the greatest of all the works of God. What can we do but be filled with wonder, love, and praise?

> Therefore God also has highly exalted Him and given Him the name which is above every name, that at the name of Jesus every knee should bow, of those in heaven, and of those on earth, and of those under the earth, and that every tongue should confess that Jesus Christ is Lord, to the glory of God the Father. (Phil 2:9–11)

Scriptures

Yeshua's Deity

The only begotten Son of YHWH: Matt 9:2; 11:27; 14:33; 17:2 (see Isa 42:8); 25:31–46; 28:17; John 1:2, 3, 14; 3:13; 5:22, 23; 6:38; 8:58; 9:38; 10:30, 33; 12:41 (see Isa 6:10);14:31; 15:10; 16:10, 28; 17:5; Acts 1:9–12; 2:32–33; 7:59; 9:20; Rom 1:3, 4; 10:9, 13 (see Joel 2:32); 1 Cor 2:8; 12:3; 15:24–28; Phil 2:11; 1 Tim 1:15; Heb 1:1–2, 3; 4:14–16; 1 John 5:12; Rev 5:12.

The Word of YHWH: Matt 5:17–48; 7:28, 29; 8:26; 9:1–8; 13:1–52; 28:20; Mark 1:27; 2:12; 7:34; Luke 4:32, 39; 20:37–38, 41–44; John 1:1–3 (see Prov 8:22, 30–31); 1:14; 11:43–44; 12:50; 6:63; Rom 10:4.

His self-consciousness: Matt 26:63–65; Mark 14:36; Luke 2:49; John 4: 25–26; 5:17–30; 17:5.

Direct NT statements: Rom 9:5; Phil 2:6–7; Titus 2:13; 2 Pet 1:1; 1 John 5:20.

Doxologies, etc.: Rom 1:7; 2 Cor 13:14; Eph 6:23; 2 Tim 4:18; 2 John 3; Rev 5:13.

Two natures and one person: John 6:51; 8:57–58; Phil 2:5–8; 1 Tim 2:5; Heb 1:3; 13:8; 1 John 1:1–3.

Questions

1. What in the accounts of the four Gospels convinces you of the humanity and deity of Jesus of Nazareth? Do you detect any difference of emphasis in the four accounts?
2. What first convinced you that Yeshua was God with us?
3. How would you convince a Jewish friend of the identification of Yeshua with YHWH?
4. How do errors concerning Yeshua's person undermine our hope of salvation through him?

Further Reading

Systematic Theology

Bauckham, Richard J. *God Crucified*. Milton Keynes: Paternoster, 2002.
Lewis, Peter. *The Glory of Christ*. Milton Keynes: Paternoster, 1992.
Macleod, Donald. *The Person of Christ*. Leicester: InterVarsity, 1998.
Warfield, Benjamin B. *The Person and Work of Christ*. Phillipsburg, NJ: Presbyterian and Reformed, 1989.

Biblical Theology

Letham, Robert. *The Message of the Person of Christ*. Leicester: InterVarsity, 2013.

Historical Theology

McGowan, Andrew T. B. *The Person and Work of Christ*. Milton Keynes: Paternoster, 2012.

24

Yeshua—His Work of Salvation

Here we come to the heart of God's plan of salvation; here "Mercy and truth have met together; righteousness and peace have kissed" (Ps 85:10)—at the cross of Golgotha and the empty tomb.

(A) SALVATION BY ATONEMENT IN THE TANAKH

From the very beginning the Lord taught fallen humans the need for a covering for their sin to make possible a relationship with the Holy One. Adam and Eve were given clothing from a dead animal, the patriarchs always approached with a burnt offering, and Israel's deliverance from Egypt required the death of a lamb in each household. When Israel's approach to YHWH was established through the tabernacle and priesthood with a system of sacrifices and offerings, his purpose was clear: he desired fellowship with his people, providing a specific offering, the peace offering (Lev 3), to express it. The great obstacle to it was their sin and his just wrath against it; they deserved death. YHWH the merciful, loving, and gracious God provided the solution, which he had planned from before the foundation of the world—a substitute would pay the penalty. At that time he ordained animal sacrifices which made atonement so that sin was covered from his sight and he was reconciled to the sinner; a price had been paid to set them free from God's judgment. The word "atonement" is the principal word in the Old Testament and Judaism that is associated with sacrifice for sin; the Hebrew word means "to cover" but the English word ranges more widely and expresses the end result: at-oneness, reconciliation with God. It should be noted that the New Testament does not use a word meaning "cover," and that is surely because the sacrifice of Messiah does much more than cover sins; it removes them altogether.

Three sacrifices in particular stressed God's initiative in providing atonement. Firstly, the Passover lamb was an initial offering which underlined God's willingness to take people as his people once their sin was covered. Secondly, the first offering—instituted as soon as the tabernacle was erected and the priesthood consecrated—was the daily burnt offering (Exod 29:38–46), which was to continually burn on the altar. It acted as a permanent covering of sin for the nation, leading to God's promise in verse 45 of the same passage: "I will dwell among the children of Israel and will be their God." Thirdly, the offerings of Yom Kippur were a provision "to make atonement for the children of Israel, for all their sins, once a year" (Lev 16:34); an annual cleansing of the nation in which the people themselves played no part, it was all the work of the priests, and especially the high priest.

The sacrifices the people were to bring were a response to this gracious provision of God. The burnt offering was an expression of dedication to him, the peace offering for fellowship with him, and the sin and trespass offerings to restore fellowship after a breach caused by sin. There is no doubt that there were many faithful Israelites who understood God's grace and responded in faith and humble thanks (e.g., Avraham; see Rom 4:1–25), but it is equally true that many made that common human error of thinking their religious activities earned God's favor, so that prophets like Isaiah and King David needed to expose the hopelessness of such endeavors (Isa 64:6; Ps 51:7).

All these sacrifices pointed forward to that which was to come through Messiah. Being animal sacrifices, they could not bear the weight of God's anger against a sinful human being made in his image (Heb 9:9; 10:1–4). That is not to say it was all a charade. YHWH had promised mercy to Israel, to those who approached him in his way, and he forgave the truly penitent, but it was on the basis of what was to come (Heb 9:15). Moshe and the prophets gave further revelation which taught Israel that the promised deliverer would indeed be the one to make atonement (Deut 32:43; Ps 110:4; Isa 52:13—53:12; Jer 23:6; Dan 9:24; Hos 13:14; Zech 3:6–10). That atonement was made by Messiah Yeshua on the cross; effective both backwards in history from the cross and forwards from it into the future; there is no other means of atonement (Rom 3:25; John 14:6). We will now consider what the New Testament teaches about that great event, which fulfilled all that YHWH had taught Israel.

(B) YESHUA AS PRIEST

Hebrews 5:1–11 teaches us the qualities God requires in his priest. He must be one in nature with those he represents so as to be able to sympathize with them, he must have a sacrifice to offer, and he must be appointed by God. The writer of Hebrews teaches that all these things were so of Yeshua. He was truly man and was perfected for a priest's role by his experience of faith and of learning obedience in times of suffering (Heb 2:17–18; 5:7–9); he was appointed by God (Heb 5:10; 7); and had a sacrifice to offer (Heb 9:11–12).

There is no need here to elaborate on *Yeshua's humanity*; that has already been clearly stated. His ability to sympathize can be seen in passages like Matt 9:35–38; 20:32–34; Luke 7:11–15; 19:41–44; John 11:32–38.

It is important to elaborate on *the priesthood to which Jesus was appointed*; he was of the order of Melchizedek (Heb 5:6, 10; 6:20—7:28) and not of Levi. The argument in Heb 7:1—10:18 demonstrates the weakness of the Levitical priesthood because of the following:

- There was no oath of God involved;
- There were many priests due to their mortality;
- Their ministry was a shadow of something substantial;
- The covenant they served under was to be replaced;
- Ceremonial access to God was limited to once a year; and
- The sheer repetition of the sacrifices indicated they were not actually removing guilt.

A priest was needed who would make one sacrifice, once for all, and whose nature made it possible for him to be part of an everlasting priesthood. Hebrews 7:1–3 argues that Melchizedek is presented in Scripture as a model for the coming Son of God by having no record of his parentage, beginning or end of life, and being named "king of peace" and "king of righteousness." Thus his priesthood is an everlasting one with no weaknesses, fulfilled in the person and ministry of YHWH's Son, Yeshua. He is the one who is able to mediate with God for his people and to intercede for them forever: "For the law appoints as high priests men who have weakness, but the word of the oath, which came after the law, appoints the Son who has been perfected forever" (Heb 7:28). What greater priest could be desired by a sinner approaching the Almighty?

The offering of Yeshua is himself: "Who his own self bare our sins" (1 Pet 2:24, KJV). He understood himself to be the promised Servant of the Lord who would pay the price to set sinners free from guilt: "For even the

Son of Man did not come to be served, but to serve, and to give His life a ransom for many"—words of Mark 10:45 which accurately paraphrase Isa 53. He was the good shepherd who laid down his life for the sheep, who in love died for his friends, paid the price for ungodly sinners, shedding his own lifeblood, and suffering rejection to the point of death that sinners might be accepted (John 10:11; 15:13; Rom 5:6–10, Heb 9:14; 13:12). All this took place on the cross, where Yeshua freely offered himself to the Father as a sacrifice. The different aspects of his sacrificial death will now be explored further.

(C) THE SACRIFICIAL DEATH OF YESHUA

The New Testament words which express the fulfillment of Old Testament themes can be divided into two broad categories: those which are objective and connect to sin as lawbreaking, and those which are subjective and connect to God as the offended one.

(i) Imputation, Punishment, Redemption

Sin is the breaking of a command of God. Adam and Eve disobeyed the command not to eat of the tree of the knowledge of good and evil (Gen 2:16–17; 3:6) and that sin has been imputed to all Adam's descendants, as Paul wrote: "in Adam all die" (1 Cor 15:22). Furthermore, God has made his requirements known to all (Deut 27:26; Rom 2:14), leading to the conclusion, "There is none who does good, No, not one" (Ps 14:3). Every breach of a known requirement increases guilt before God so that Paul pronounces, "that every mouth may be stopped, and all the world may become guilty before God" (Rom 3:19). God's law demands that all transgression and guilt are *punished*: "the soul who sins shall die" and "the wages of sin is death" (Ezek 18:4; Rom 6:23). YHWH is not a God who can overlook sin without compromising his very being and character; he has said he will punish and he will. This would appear to leave sinners with absolutely no hope; guilt is guilt and the passage of time may dim its memory to us but not to the One who sees and knows all things through all time. But YHWH's determination to punish has gone hand in glove with his revelation of a way of escape for sinners through another bearing their punishment, a substitutionary sacrifice which satisfies the demands of his law. By such means the Lord is just and the One who forgives; he is vindicated as a lawgiver and as a savior. Yeshua is God's means of salvation. The sin of the guilty was *imputed* to him and he was treated as a transgressor, which is expressed in the New

Testament by language such as "made sin" and "bore our sins"; for example: "For He made Him who knew no sin to be sin for us" (2 Cor 5:21, see also 1 Pet 2:24; Heb 9:28). Another way this is expressed is by the word "curse." The curse that the law pronounces on the guilty was placed upon Yeshua: "Christ has redeemed us from the curse of the law, having become a curse for us" (Gal 3:13). At Golgotha he was made a curse. We can only be filled with awe and thanks; "Hallelujah" is a good Hebrew response!

The concept of *redemption* comes under this heading because it involves the payment of a price to release those who cannot escape the situation in which they are held captive, that is, paying the penalty demanded by the law (see Gal 3:13 in the above paragraph). It has sometimes been thought the price is paid to Satan, understood to be the person intended by the word "Azazel" in Lev 16:8, 10: "And Aaron shall cast lots over the two goats, one lot for the LORD and the other lot for Azazel." This is the ESV translation, where the Hebrew word is transliterated "Azazel," but in other versions the word "scapegoat" is used, which aims to express the actions described later in Lev 16:21–22. It is likely that the name Azazel refers to Satan, but the action of sending the live goat into the wilderness for Azazel should not be understood as a payment to Satan but as a declaration to him that his power is broken; sin is atoned for, and he can accuse no longer. This concept is expressed of Yeshua's sacrifice: "having wiped out the handwriting of requirements that was against us, which was contrary to us. And He has taken it out of the way, having nailed it to the cross. Having disarmed principalities and powers, He made a public spectacle of them, triumphing over them in it" (Col 2:14–15). Yeshua paid the ransom price, the shedding of his blood, to release sinners from the law's demands and the wrath to come (Eph 1:7; 1 Pet 1:18–19; 1 Thess 1:10). The believer is set free from Satan's power and sin's bondage, to love and serve God (John 8:34–36).

(ii) Propitiation, Expiation, Reconciliation

The breaking of God's requirements is more than disobeying a code; it is being an enemy of God, a rebel, and it is an affront to him personally; he is deeply offended and justly angry. Here we consider the more subjective side of atonement. That God is a God of wrath is everywhere taught in Scripture (Exod 22:24; Ps 110:5; John 3:36; Eph 2:3); he is angry not just with sin but with sinners. This is the significance of the word "vengeance"; it expresses the personal element of judgment and it is something God reserves for himself as the offended one (Deut 32:5). But it must be remembered that YHWH's wrath is not like a man's, lashing out without restraint; his requires what could be called an effort so as to overcome his reluctance to show it due to his heart of mercy: "Now therefore, let Me alone, that my wrath may burn hot against them" (Exod 32:10). Scripture describes the death of Yeshua as a *"propitiation"* because his sacrifice for sinners appeases God's wrath against them (Rom 3:25; 1 John 2:1; 4:10[1]). This is why the Savior shrank at the contemplation of the cross, for it was not just a place of death for sin in a legal sense but a place of experiencing the full force of divine wrath and displeasure against sinners, and he knew what that meant (Luke 22:42–44; 12:5). The experience caused that cry of dereliction to burst from his lips, "My God, My God, why have You forsaken Me?" (Mark 15:34). Here is the importance of his deity; only a divine person could bear the divine wrath. Here also is the immeasurable love of YHWH; that he gave his Son, and the Son came willingly, knowing the agony and grief of soul that would be involved in dying in the place of sinners.

"*Expiate*" is a word that is sometimes used to describe the removal of sin without reference to the concept of appeasing God's anger. There has been a tendency with some theologians to focus mainly on expiation and minimize or deny propitiation but Scripture has both emphases. This is well illustrated by the two goats of Yom Kippur ritual: one is killed, portraying God's wrath and the need for propitiation; the other is sent away into the wilderness with Israel's sins upon it, portraying the removal of sin from God's sight, expiation (Lev 16:7–10, see also Ps 103:12; Jer 31:34; Col 2:14).

The outcome of Yeshua's sacrifice of propitiation is that God is *reconciled* to sinners. Too often reconciliation is seen principally in terms of a sinner's change of heart but it is firstly a change in God's position: "God was in Christ reconciling the world to Himself, not imputing their trespasses to them, and has committed to us the word of reconciliation" (2 Cor 5:19, see also Rom 5:10; Eph 2:16). This verse presents judgment on hold and reconciliation offered because of the acceptable sacrifice of Jesus. It is God taking the initiative in Messiah to deal with the enmity between him and his sinful creatures, first of all by reconciling himself to them through the removal of sin at the cross. This has detailed and universal proportions. For example, even when death is caused by accident there must be atonement because God's creation is polluted, and in the case of the manslayer that was by the death of the high priest (Num 35: 9–34, especially 25, 28). In Col 1:19–20

---

1. The Greek word used in these texts is the same word as is used in the LXX's translation of the Hebrew word for "atonement" into Greek, a Greek word that does not mean "cover" but expresses the concept of appeasing anger. Sometimes the same word is translated "mercy seat" with reference to that part of the ark of the covenant in the holy place, as in Heb 9:5, the place where God was appeased.

God is spoken of as reconciling the whole universe to himself through the blood of the cross; it is all polluted by the rebellion of demons and humans.

(D) YESHUA AS MEDIATOR

A mediator is a person who can act as a bridge between two parties in conflict, seeking to bring them together. In salvation terms the parties are God and rebellious humans, and Yeshua is the God-appointed mediator: "For there is one God and one Mediator between God and men, the Man Christ Jesus, who gave Himself a ransom for all" (1 Tim 2:5). Three things are vital for salvation's mediator: appointment by the offended party, the payment of the price to redeem offenders from their just deserts, and being a fellow human, a true representative. Yeshua fulfilled all these things. Messiah as mediator has different imagery to that of a priest, drawing more on a concept of warring parties, but the qualifications are the same.

In Hebrews, Yeshua as Mediator is in covenantal terms, "He is also Mediator of a better covenant, which was established on better promises" (Heb 8:6). A new covenant is required because it actually cleanses from sin and because it hangs out a welcome sign, so to speak, by comparison to the first covenant (Heb 9:11–15; 12:18–24). Jesus inaugurated this covenant with his disciples at his final Passover meal (Matt 26:26–28). It was a covenant that was later offered to all Israel in the preaching of the apostles and enjoyed by those who put their faith in its Mediator, Jesus.

(E) THE NATURE AND EXTENT OF YESHUA'S ATONEMENT

In connection with the sacrificial death for sin of Messiah Yeshua, Scripture speaks in both the plural and singular, of sins and sin: "Himself bore our sins in His own body on the tree," and "He made Him who knew no sin to be sin for us" (1 Pet 2:24; 2 Cor 5:21, see also 1 John 2:2). The use of the singular points to the *qualitative* aspect of atonement; sin is heinous in God's sight; its quality of rebellion is infinite and required an infinite person, God's only begotten Son, to bear its just punishment. The use of the plural encourages believers to know that nothing has been missed; the punishment that all sin deserved was meted out upon the Savior. There is no sense that Jesus should have suffered more if, so to speak, an unexpected person believes; the atonement is not *quantitative*.

This inevitably leads to the question, for whom did Yeshua die? For the whole world or only for those designated as his people? Verses can be presented which appear to support both: "For there is one God and one Mediator between God and men, *the* Man Christ Jesus, who gave Himself a ransom for all," and "Christ also loved the church and gave Himself for her" (1 Tim 2:5–6; Eph 5:25). Calvin's dictum is helpful: "sufficient for all, efficient for the elect." The qualitative nature of the atonement ensures it was sufficient for all, and hence the free offer of the gospel to all is genuine, but the intention of God was the salvation of a people he had given to his Son before the foundation of the world (John 10:29; 17:24; Eph 1:4; John 10:14–15). This means that when Yeshua offered himself he had those whom the Father had given him upon his heart: "the Son of God, who loved me and gave Himself for me" (Gal 2:20); something vividly portrayed by the names of the sons of Israel engraved on the twelve stones of the breastplate and the two shoulder stones of the ephod of Israel's high priest. This underlines the special love of God for his people, their union with Christ in eternity and time, Christ's representation of them in particular, and hence the certain achievement of his offering for them. The theological term for this is "particular redemption." The term "limited atonement" has been used but it seems less suitable because it appears to deny the sufficiency of Messiah's death for all. For a believer to realize that Jesus died for them—having his or her name on his heart, rather than them simply being one of a great number—is a deeply enriching, assuring, and humbling thought, filling the heart with wonder, thankfulness, and love.

Among those within Christianity and Judaism there are those who agree and disagree with the above teaching on Messiah's work of atonement. The Roman Catholic Church and the Orthodox churches would be in general agreement on the person and work of Jesus, although, as will be examined later, they differ on its application to sinners. Liberal forms of Christianity, if they do understand the cross as a sacrifice, will diminish or deny God's wrath; and some deny the substitutionary nature of Golgotha altogether and assert Yeshua's death as an example of self-giving love, inspiring his followers to live the life God requires. All forms of Judaism accept the sinner's need of atonement but reject the notion of atonement for sin by a substitutionary sacrifice of Messiah. There is no doubt within traditional forms of Judaism that God is understood to be a righteous God who is angry with sinners and will punish sin, but emphasis is placed on his mercy and his willingness to forgive the penitent as the means of expiation: "R. Abba b. Kahana said: On New Year God judges His creatures, and finds merit in them, as it says, 'As I live I desire not the death of the wicked' (Ezek xxxiii,11)."² According to Jewish teaching, atonement can only be obtained after a process of repentance involving the recognition of sin: "Now that the Temple is no longer standing, he [Maimonides] asserts, repentance itself atones for all sins."³ More on the obtaining of atonement and forgiveness under Judaism is related in the next part of the book.

Generally speaking, Judaism does not deny the death of Yeshua, but the accuracy of the Gospel accounts is disputed, especially the accounts of his trial. The more traditional would say his death was deserved because he profaned God's name, although many would be less harsh and see him as just another false Messiah, of no more interest that all the others. Among the less traditional many would acknowledge his worth as a teacher but one who came into conflict with the Jewish authorities because of his more radical teaching, and with the Roman authorities because he was perceived as a threat, and who had him put to death. But God's view is otherwise:

> Therefore God also has highly exalted Him and given Him the name which is above every name, that at the name of Jesus every knee should bow, of those in heaven, and of those on earth, and of those under the earth, and that every tongue should confess that Jesus Christ is Lord, to the glory of God the Father. (Phil 2:9–11)

SCRIPTURES

Atonement in the Old Testament

Gen 3:21; 12:7; Exod 12:3–7; 40; Exod 29:38–46; Lev 1–9, 16; Deut 32:43; Ps 110:4; Isa 52:13—53:12; Jer 23:6; Dan 9:24; Hos 13:14; Zech 3:6–10; Rom 3:25; 4:1–25; Heb 9:9; 10:1–4.

Yeshua as Priest

Heb 5:1–11; 2:17–18; 5:7–9; 9:11–12.

Sympathetic: Matt 9:35–38; 20:32–34; Luke 7:11–15; 19:41–44; John 11:32–38.

Appointed: Heb 5:6, 10; 6:20—7:28.

---

2. Montefiore and Loewe, eds., *Rabbinic Anthology*, 236; quoting from Pes. R. 166b.
3. Cohn-Sherbok, *Jewish Faith*, 78.

Offering: Mark 10:45; John 10:11; 15:13; Rom 5:6–10, Heb 9:14; 13:12; 1 Pet 2:24.

Yeshua's Sacrificial Death

1 Cor 5:7; Eph 5:2; Heb 9:26; 10:1–10.

A substitute by imputation: 1 Cor 5:21; Gal 3:13; 1 Pet 2:24; Heb 9:28.

Redemption: John 8:34–36; Rom 3:24; Gal 3:13; Col 2:14–15; Eph 1:7; 1 Thess 1:10; 1 Pet 1:18–19.

Propitiation: Matt 27:46; Luke 22:42–44; 12:5; Rom 3:25; Heb 9:5; 1 John 2:1; 4:10.

Expiation: Lev 16: 21–22; 1 Sam 3:14; Ps 103:12; Jer 31:34; Col 2:14.

Reconciliation: 2 Cor 5:19; Rom 5:10; Eph 2:16; Col 1:19–20.

Yeshua as Mediator

Matt 26:26–28; 1 Tim 2:5; Heb 8:6–13; 9:11–15; 12:18–24.

Nature and Extent of the Atonement

John 10:14–15, 29; 17:24; 2 Cor 5:21; Eph 1:4; 5:25; Gal 2:20; Col 1:19–20; 1 Tim 2:5–6; 1 Pet 2:24; 1 John 2:2.

Questions

1. What does the Old Testament reveal about the why and how of atonement?
2. Why were animal sacrifices inadequate?
3. How would you convince a Jewish friend that the Old Testament points forward to atonement by the promised Messiah?
4. What are the qualifications for a priest of YHWH and how has Yeshua fulfilled them?
5. Discuss the various scriptural terms associated with the death of Jesus.
6. Show that the message of the cross was central to the preaching of the apostles.

7. What actually happened to Jesus on the cross that makes him the Savior of the world?
8. What evidence does Scripture offer that Jesus truly died and rose again from the dead?
9. What qualifies Jesus to be the Mediator of the new covenant?
10. For whom did Messiah die?

Further Reading

Systematic Theology

Calvin, John. *Institutes of the Christian Religion*. Vol. 2, 15–16. Peabody, MA: Hendrickson, 2007.
Denney, James. *The Biblical Doctrine of Reconciliation*. Eugene, OR: Wipf & Stock, 2018.
———. *The Death of Christ*. Carol Stream, IL: Tyndale, 1951.
Letham, Robert. *The Work of Christ*. Leicester: InterVarsity, 1993.
Lloyd-Jones, D. M. *Romans 3:20—4:25—Atonement and Justification*. Edinburgh: Banner of Truth, 1970.
Morris, Leon. *The Cross in the New Testament*. Milton Keynes: Paternoster, 1965.
Murray, John. *Redemption Accomplished and Applied*. Grand Rapids: Eerdmans, 2015.
Packer, J. I., and Mark Dever. *In My Place Condemned He Stood*. Wheaton, IL: Crossway, 2007.
Stott, John R. W. *The Cross of Christ*. Leicester: InterVarsity, 1986.

Historical Theology

McGowan, Andrew T. B. *The Person and Work of Christ*. Milton Keynes: Paternoster, 2012.

God's Spirit

The word "spirit" in both Old and New Testaments can be translated as spirit or wind or breath (Heb. *ruach*, Gk. *pneuma*; see Gen 41:18; 8:1; Luke 1:47; Matt 14:24). However, when it is connected to God, i.e., Spirit of God, it points to the agency by which God executes his purposes in the world. The Old Testament looks forward to a much greater working of the Spirit in God's purpose of redemption, and the teaching of the New Testament demonstrates how abundant and manifold it is.

In the Tanakh God's Spirit is referred to by four terms: "the Spirit of God," "the Spirit of the Lord," "the Holy Spirit," and "the Spirit"; and the same four terms are also used in the New Testament, where "Spirit of the Lord" is written "Spirit of the Lord" (e.g., Luke 4:18 quoting Isa 61:1). The New Testament adds many other terms, giving further indications of his nature and manifold functions: "Spirit of your Father," "Spirit of the living God," "Spirit of his Son," "Spirit of Jesus Christ," "Spirit of Christ," "Spirit of Jesus," "Spirit of truth," "Spirit of promise," "Spirit of grace," "Spirit of life in Christ Jesus," "Spirit of adoption," and "Spirit of him that raised up Jesus from the dead." As Jesus spoke of his return to glory, he pointed to the Spirit as "another Helper, that He may abide with you forever—the Spirit of truth" (John 14:16–17). The Greek word translated "helper" (or counsellor or comforter) is *paraclete* and indicates an advocate who comes alongside. All that Yeshua had been to his people the Spirit would be.

25

The Person of the Holy Spirit

Although the Spirit is only referred to four times as "Holy Spirit" in the New Testament, it is the term used as his principle title in theological writings. This is because it is the term used by Jesus in God's unique new covenant name—the Father, and the Son, and the Holy Spirit (Matt 28:19)—and because it points to his principle work in salvation, producing holiness in God's people to prepare them for a life with God for eternity.

(A) THE HOLY SPIRIT IS A PERSON

The Old Testament revelation stresses YHWH as the one and only God, in contrast to people's many false gods, and this truth needed to become firmly rooted in Israel before revelation was given of God's triunity. Hence the distinct personhood of the Spirit is not clear in the Tanakh but it is certainly hinted at. The very mention of the Spirit of God performing works, rather than simply describing God as doing them, hints at the Spirit as more than a divine influence. The use of the definite article, especially when there is no other term attached, i.e., "the Spirit" rather than "the Spirit of God," hints at his personhood (see Num 27:18; Isa 32:15). The Spirit's intelligence and will is indicated by his actions (see Exod 31:3; Job 33:4; Isa 11:2; 1 Chr 28:12) and points to personhood. In the New Testament his person becomes clear by the use of the pronoun "he," even though the Greek word for spirit is neuter: "But the Helper, the Holy Spirit, whom the Father will send in My Name, He will teach you all things" (John 14:26). The Spirit can be grieved (Eph 4:30), which is only so of a person, and Yeshua's reference to the Spirit as another helper or advocate, one like himself, points clearly to the Spirit as a person (John 14:16). The Spirit is most certainly not a mere influence or an "it." As the Spirit of Christ Jesus, he reveals the Savior to us, something only a person can do.

(B) THE HOLY SPIRIT IS A DIVINE BEING

The truth of his personhood combined with titles such as "Spirit of God" point to his full deity. One who is another helper or advocate, one who would be to the disciples all that the divine Son had been, must himself be a divine person. YHWH alone is holy and the use of "holy" in the name Holy Spirit indicates his divinity.

There are New Testament texts where the Holy Spirit is said to speak words which are attributed to YHWH in the Old Testament (e.g., Acts 28:25–27, quoting Isa 6:9–10). Likewise, Scripture attributes actions which can only be divine works to the working of the Spirit, for example, renewing the earth and renewing sinners: "You send forth Your Spirit, they are created; And You renew the face of the earth" (Ps 104:30) and "unless one is born of water and the Spirit, he cannot enter the kingdom of God" (John 3:5). Similarly, he maintains the divine life of righteousness (Rom 8:13), resurrects the dead (Rom 8:11), brings into God's presence (Eph 2:18), and reveals God's truth (1 Cor 2:10). There are verses in the New Testament where the Spirit is linked to other divine persons in a way which is only appropriate if he is a divine person, for example: the baptismal formula of Matt 28:19, the doxology of 2 Cor 13:14, and Peter's summary description of the work of salvation in 1 Pet 1:2.

This teaching of Scripture concerning the Spirit's deity underlines he is a Trinitarian person, coequal with the Father and the Son in the Godhead, and proceeding from the Father and the Son, as discussed in the earlier section on God's triunity.

During the early centuries of the church the deity and person of the Holy Spirit were affirmed without controversy and clearly stated by various councils such as Nicea (325 AD) and Chalcedon (451 AD). The medieval churches upheld the statements of such councils and the Roman Catholic and Orthodox churches which emerged from the medieval period have continued in the same vein. The early forms of Protestantism which grew out of the Reformation have all upheld this teaching. The influence of liberalism within Protestantism from the nineteenth century onwards has led to the view among some that the Spirit is an influence, not a person.

Traditional Judaism makes little mention of the Spirit and when it does it is emphatically against any idea that he is a distinct person from God or within God, "but the fact remains that all Jewish thinkers have rejected Trinitarianism as incompatible with monotheism as Judaism understands it."[1] However the "Holy Spirit" as an influence on the devout is recognized. The Holy Spirit inspired the Ketuvim (Writings),[2] and what the righteous accomplish is said to be by the Holy Spirit.[3] Kabbalists stress the importance of *devekut*, cleaving to God, which is a state of mind that is attained when a person constantly remembers God and his love and never removes their thoughts from him; to such the Holy Spirit is given.[4]

(C) THE HOLY SPIRIT—GOD'S EXECUTOR

In all the purposes of God, the Spirit is the executor. To summarize: he was active in the creation of the universe, renews the world daily, and gives life to all creatures. He reveals God's truth, inspires God's messengers, and illuminates the minds of hearers. He empowered the Messiah in his ministry and energizes his people in their service. It is the Spirit's work to awaken sinners, draw them to Yeshua in faith and repentance, regenerate them, sanctify them, and enable their communion with God.

---

1. Jacobs, *Jewish Theology*, 26.
2. Jacobs, *Jewish Theology*, 199.
3. Montefiore and Loewe, eds., *Rabbinic Anthology*, 677.
4. Scholem, *Kabbalah*, 175.

26

The Spirit and Messiah

(A) THE WORK OF THE SPIRIT IN MESSIAH'S LIFE AND MINISTRY

This work of the Spirit is insufficiently taken account of, such that Jesus' ministry is often explained solely in terms of his being both divine and human, but the work of the Spirit was crucial to his being our forerunner. Yeshua's dependence on the Spirit in his life of faith is an example to us who have the same need. Messiah's work was always a Trinitarian work, for "in Him dwells all the fullness of the Godhead bodily" (Col 2:9), but a Trinitarian work in which the second person had also become truly human, so that in his human nature he heard from the Father (John 5:19, 30) and spoke and acted as truly human in the power of the Holy Spirit (John 3:34; 6:63).

The Tanakh anticipates a Messiah endued with power by God's Spirit: "The Spirit of the Lord shall rest upon Him" (Isa 11:2, see also Isa 61:1; Ps 2:2; Isa 42:1). In these texts the whole scope of his work is anticipated, such that the Spirit will enable Messiah to act with wisdom, understanding, and righteousness; he will preach good news, heal the brokenhearted, console mourners, proclaim liberty, inaugurate the plan and purpose of God, bring truth and justice and shalom to the nations, and punish rebels. The New Testament records how these predictions began to be fulfilled. Although the Spirit was at work in Jesus before his public ministry began—he was conceived by the Spirit's power and knew, like John the Baptist, the work of the Spirit from his earliest years (Luke 1:35; 2:40, see also Luke 1:15)—it was especially at his baptism that he was anointed with the Spirit without measure for his work as the Servant of the Lord (Mark 1:9–10; John 3:34). Luke expresses the place of the Spirit in his entire ministry: "Then Jesus returned in the power of the Spirit to Galilee" (Luke 4:14). The Spirit guided him (Matt 4:1) and cast out demons through him (Matt 12:28, see also Acts 10:38). His teaching and miracles were evidently of YHWH and the people recognized it (Luke 4:14–15; John 3:34; 7:46; Matt 9:18; Luke 7:11–16). He was raised from the dead by the Spirit's power (Rom 1:4) and by that same power ascended to the Father's right hand (Eph 1:19–20), from where he rules as the God-man by the Spirit (Rev 1:4; 3:1, "the seven Spirits of God" being symbolic of the manifold and perfect work of the Spirit).

(B) MESSIAH'S SPIRIT

Among the titles of the Spirit listed earlier were Spirit of the Son, Spirit of Jesus Christ, Spirit of Christ, and Spirit of Jesus (Gal 4:6; Phil 1:19; Rom 8:9; Acts 16:7 in ESV). His work in salvation is always to apply Messiah's redemptive work and to point to him. Jesus said of the Spirit, "He will glorify Me, for He will take of what is Mine and declare it to you" (John 16:14). The Spirit's presence is in place of Yeshua as another helper but he does not manifest himself but rather Yeshua: "I will not leave you orphans; I will come to you" (John 14:18). An important implication of this is that all claims to a work of the Spirit can be simply tested—is Jesus being exalted? Being Messiah's Spirit is underlined by the fact that the Spirit was not given until Jesus had completed his work and was glorified (John 7:39; Acts 2:32–33). The goal of the Spirit's work is to create a people who are a dwelling place for God (Eph 2:19–22).

> Who has directed the Spirit of the LORD,
> Or as His counsellor has taught Him?
> With whom did He take counsel, and who instructed Him . . .
> To whom then will you liken God? (Isa 40:13–14, 18)

SCRIPTURES

Person of the Holy Spirit: Exod 31:3; Num 27:18; 1 Chr 28:12; Job 33:4; Ps 104:30; Isa 11:2; 32:15; Matt 28:19; John 3:5; 14:16, 26; Rom 8:11, 13; 1 Cor 2:10; 2 Cor 13:14; Eph 2:18; 4:30; 1 Pet 1:2.

God's Executor: Gen 1:2; Ps 104:29–30; Isa 42:1; Luke 4:14; John 3:5; 16; Rom 8:15; 1 Cor 12:7; Gal 5:16; Eph 2:8; 2 Tim 3:16; 1 Pet 1:2, 11.

The Spirit in Messiah's ministry: Ps 2:2; Isa 11:2; 42:1; 61:1; Matt 4:1; 12:28; Mark 1:9–10; Luke 1:35; 2:40; 4:14; John 3:34; 6:63; Rom 1:4; Rev 1:4; 3:1.

Messiah's Spirit: John 7:39; 14:16; 16:13–14; Acts 2:32–33; 16:9; Rom 8:9; Gal 4:6; Eph 2:19–22; Phil 1:19.

Questions

1. Does the Old Testament present God's Spirit as a person?
2. What is the New Testament evidence that the Spirit is a divine person?
3. The Messiah is God's anointed one; how is this seen in the life of Jesus of Nazareth, and what do we learn from Jesus' need of the Spirit?
4. The Spirit is called "the Spirit of Christ"; why does he have this title?

Further Reading

Ferguson, Sinclair B. *The Holy Spirit*. Leicester: InterVarsity, 1996.
Goodwin, Thomas. *The Work of the Holy Spirit*. Edinburgh: Banner of Truth, 1979.
Jackman, David. *Spirit of Truth*. Tain, UK: Christian Focus, 2007.
Jones, Mark. *Knowing Christ*. Edinburgh: Banner of Truth, 2017. See chapter 7.
Morris, Leon. *Spirit of the Living God*. Leicester: InterVarsity, 1960.
Smeaton, George. *The Doctrine of the Holy Spirit*. Edinburgh: Banner of Truth, 1959.

27

The Work of the Holy Spirit in Our Salvation

(A) FROM DEATH TO LIFE

IN THIS SECTION OUR focus is the work of the Spirit in converting a person from sin to God, and the status they receive. It is a work in which the individual's heart and mind is fully active but it is all under the influence and power of the Spirit or no change will ensue.

(i) All of Grace

Israel's condition after the return from Babylon was precarious, with enemies opposing their welfare and the rebuilding of the temple. Zerubbabel was encouraged to focus not on human power but on the Spirit, through whom the work would be done, and celebrated with cries of "Grace, grace to it!" (Zech 4:6–7).

So it is with the new covenant: the building of believers into a holy temple in the Lord is a work of grace. Grace is favor shown to those who deserve the opposite, and sinners are exactly that, having nothing to commend them to God, so that they can only appeal to God's kindness and mercy. Believers are only made acceptable due to God's grace—"to the praise of the glory of His grace, by which He made us accepted in the Beloved" (Eph 1:6)—and when Paul describes God's work of making dead sinners alive he draws out the obvious implication, "by grace you have been saved" (Eph 2:5). Indeed, the conception, purchase, and experience of salvation is all God's grace, "For the grace of God that brings salvation has appeared to all men" (Titus 2:11). This raises questions of human freedom and responsibility, which will be considered in what follows. One thing is quite clear from experience: humans freely choose to reject Christ or accept him; however, for those who do accept Scripture teaches that the power to do so is a gift of God's grace.

(ii) Election

The reason why any person comes to faith in Jesus through the work of the Holy Spirit is because of God's election: "He chose us in Him before the foundation of the world" (Eph 1:4). Choice by God can be seen from the earliest days of his unfolding purpose, for example through these words of Moshe: "The LORD delighted only in your fathers, to love them; and He chose their descendants after them" (Deut 10:15, see Gen 12:1–3; Exod 3:6–10; Acts 13:17). It is a choice of Israel which remains to this day: "God has not cast away His people whom He foreknew" (Rom 11:2). It was also a choice of individuals within the offspring of Abraham: "the older shall serve the younger" (Gen 25:23, see Gen 28:10–15; Rom 9:10–12). Israel's Messiah was chosen of God—"My Elect One in whom My soul delights!" (Isa 42:1)—and Yeshua is so described: "chosen by God and precious" (1 Pet 2:4). God's new covenant people are similarly described: "But you are a chosen generation" (1 Pet 2:9, see also Mark 13:20). Such words are not only a description of the church as a whole but also extend to every individual member: "Therefore, brethren, be even more diligent to make your call and election sure" (2 Pet 1:10, see also Rom 8:33; Acts 13:48).

This teaching confronts us with mystery in God's working, something to which believers must always be ready to submit. It does not encourage fatalism or indolence—Peter makes it plain that diligence in godly living is a means of believers assuring themselves they are indeed among God's elect (2 Pet 1:10–11). It is not a doctrine which arises in gospel preaching; hearers are never encouraged to ask themselves if they are elect but to see themselves as sinners who need to repent and trust the Savior. God's election does not diminish human responsibility: those who continue to rebel and are one day punished will only have themselves to blame; those who repent and are saved will recognize their will was not forced, yet they will understand that but for God having chosen them to salvation they would never have believed. The means by which he works to achieve this in his elect will be considered as we proceed.

The main objection raised to this teaching centers on the word "foreknowledge" and asserts that this refers to God knowing beforehand who would repent and hence choosing them. Election is therefore not an initiating action of God, but his recognition of an action by humans. It is difficult to see why such should be revealed in Scripture as it carries no practical weight; it certainly does not forward humility in God's people. The objection fails to recognize a particular use of the word "know" or "foreknow" in Scripture. To know a person often points to relationship, more than a simple awareness, as can be seen in the use of the Hebrew word *yada*, "to know," for sexual union (Gen 4:1); likewise for God's personal choice of a prophet (Jer 1:15) and of national Israel (Amos 3:2).

The Greek has a more specific word, *prognosis*, translated "foreknowledge" (or "foreknow"). This word is used of God's foreknowledge or foreknowing in five places. Two of them refer to his knowledge before the foundation of the world that his Son would die for sinners (Acts 2:23; 1 Pet 1:20), and there can be no doubt they point to his having planned it beforehand—certainly not a fact of future history that he was simply aware of. The other three texts refer to his election or choice of people. In Rom 11:2 we read, "God has not cast away His people whom He foreknew," and as in Amos 3:2 the reference is to his particular relationship with Israel. It was not simply that he knew about them but that they were specially known to him; they did not choose him but he chose them. To assign a different meaning to "foreknow" in Rom 8:29 and 1 Pet 1:20, where it is used of his foreknowing believers in his Son, requires some strong evidence from the context. The opposite is the case in Rom 8:29, 33, where all the stress is on everything being according to God's purpose (v. 28). In 1 Pet 1:20 the stress is on the activity of each person of the Trinity in the experience of believers: Jesus' blood cleanses, the Spirit sanctifies, and the Father has chosen. To suggest the Father's foreknowledge is simply awareness negates a dependence on the divine that the text expressly declares concerning the Son and the Spirit; it would be inconsistent.

The difficulty this teaching raises is whether the corollary is true: that God chose people for condemnation. This is undoubtedly a difficult subject and the answer is not to be determined by any human logic aiming at a watertight system of doctrine, but by Scripture. Three texts are especially relevant. Peter, referring to the disobedient, writes, "to which they also were appointed" (1 Pet 2:8); Jude, referring to unsaved, sensual people in the churches, writes of them, "who long ago were marked out for this condemnation" (Jude 4); and Paul, referring to those who reject God, wrote,

"What if God, wanting to show His wrath and to make His power known, endured with much longsuffering the vessels of wrath prepared for destruction" (Rom 9:22). It should be clearly noted that all the persons in view are fully responsible for their disobedience to the truth revealed to them; in that sense their sin has prepared them for destruction, not any action of God. Note the careful wording of Rom 9:22–23, where it is specific that God prepares his people beforehand for glory, but in verse 22 it is not said God prepares for destruction; that is, it is sin which prepares for destruction. The activity of God towards them is that they are not chosen in his Son; they are passed by; the theological term is "reprobate." As God orders all things in this world according to his will yet is not the cause of sin, nor the author of evil, nor in any way to blame, so in his divine decrees no person is chosen and predestined to sin such that God is to blame for their condition.

It should be noted that Scripture has relatively little to say on the subject of reprobation compared to election to salvation; its emphasis is on the glory of God's grace. The teaching of election in Scripture is to magnify God and his grace, to give him the glory due to him as sovereign in all matters pertaining to salvation. This is revealed to keep believers humble, but also to uplift them as they understand the particular love God has always had towards them in his Son, giving them a firm conviction that the one who initiated their salvation will complete his work and bring them to be with him forever (Eph 1:1–6).

(iii) The Spirit Prepares and Enlightens

Before anyone comes to faith in the Savior, the Spirit works to prepare them. The traditional theological term is "prevenient grace," meaning predisposing grace. Every believer can look back at things that awakened them to the serious issues of life. For scriptural examples think of the following varied experiences: God asking questions of Adam and Cain: "Where are you?" "What have you done?" The sin of Joseph's brothers came back to haunt them and Moses' attention is drawn to God by an unusual event; similarly Peter is convicted of sin by something striking. A jailer is awakened by believers singing in jail! As Elihu puts it:

> Behold, God works all these things,
> Twice, in fact, three times with a man,
> To bring back his soul from the Pit,
> That he may be enlightened with the light of life. (Job 33:29–30)

In one way or another such awakening experiences will be accompanied by the witness of God's truth and at that point the Spirit will be at work to add his witness. That may be through creation (Ps 19:1–4), the reading of God's word (Ps 19:8), or persuasive preaching: "the Gentiles, to whom I now send you, to open their eyes, in order to turn them from darkness to light" (Acts 26:17–18). At all such times in human experience the Spirit is at work: "when He has come, He will convict the world of sin, and of righteousness, and of judgment" (John 16:8, see also John 15:26–27). However, not all believe but, as in the parable of the sower, many don't give it a second thought, or their response is only emotional, or their initial enthusiasm is stifled by other interests. However, the true believer, not just intellectually but from the heart, understands the word and responds in faith. Lydia is an example: "The Lord opened her heart to heed the things spoken by Paul" (Acts 16:14); and Yeshua said of Peter's confession, "flesh and blood has not revealed this to you, but My Father who is in heaven" (Matt 16:17). Yeshua's miraculous healing of the blind signifies this work in the human heart; we are born spiritually blind but he gives sight to perceive spiritual realities and believe on him; it is a work of the Spirit.

As we move on to consider the acts of both people and God which are essential to the beginning of the Christian life, a few points need to be made. It is of value to distinguish the different aspects such as conversion, regeneration, justification, etc., but it must be remembered they are all part of a unitary process, each taking place at the time when saving faith in Yeshua is first exercised. Scripture has no statement in which a full order is given, although Rom 8:30 justifies us in thinking there is an order. The order in which the different aspects are considered below is a practical one, focusing on the believer's conscious experience at conversion and immediately after. At the end of this consideration the place of regeneration vis-à-vis faith and repentance will be discussed.

(iv) The Effectual Call

There is a call of God to all people to repent and trust his way of salvation but not all believe; as Jesus said, "many are called, but few chosen" (Matt 20:16). Scripture speaks of a call which is effective such that believers are frequently described as the called: "among whom you also are the called of Jesus Christ" (Rom 1:6). The call of God to Abraham exhibits this call of God to those he has chosen, a call which was later extended to all Israel when he brought them to Sinai (Gen 12:1–3; Exod 19:4). Jesus speaks of this call in a way that points to a knowledge of particular individuals: "he calls his own sheep by name and leads them out" (John 10:3); it is a call which leads to justification and glorification and is therefore distinct from the call of the gospel to all people (Rom 8:30). Hebrews describes it as a "heavenly calling" (Heb 3:1). It is a term which creates an intimate picture of a personal God calling to himself those he has known and loved before the foundation of the world; it should fill the soul with comfort, just as when a parent calls their child and embraces them. Many verses in the Epistles connect this call to its purpose, for example: holiness (1 Pet 1:15; 2 Tim 1:9); purity of life (1 Thess 4:7); peace, unity, and hope (Col 3:15; Eph 4:1, 4); fellowship with God's Son (1 Cor 1:9); and final glory (1 Pet 5:10).

(v) Conversion—Repentance and Faith

Conversion is a change of course from a wrong way to a right one. David, renewed after his repentance, determines to turn others too: "Then I will teach transgressors Your ways, And sinners shall be converted to You" (Ps 51:13). Peter, speaking to those responsible for the death of Messiah, calls upon them to "be converted, that your sins may be blotted out" (Acts 3:19); they are to change course in their attitude to Jesus. Gospel conversion therefore has two elements, repentance and faith; as Paul puts it, "testifying to Jews, and also to Greeks, repentance toward God and faith toward our Lord Jesus Christ" (Acts 20:21).

(a) Repentance

Repentance is a change of mind and in a gospel context points to a person taking a different view of their beliefs and behavior before God. Isaiah speaks of the Redeemer coming to those who "turn from transgression in Jacob" (Isa 59:20, and the Thessalonian believers "turned to God from idols" (1 Thess 1:9; see also 1 Pet 1:18). This is more than an intellectual matter as is shown by Jeremiah's description of Ephraim's repentance—"Surely, after my turning, I repented; And after I was instructed, I struck myself on the thigh; I was ashamed, yes, even humiliated" (Jer 31:19)—and by Paul's similar words in 2 Cor 7:10: "For godly sorrow produces repentance leading to salvation." There is a deep grief, sorrow, and regret at the offense. This is a work of the Spirit as he enlightens sinners through the gospel to their own evil behavior and God's requirements.

(b) Faith

There is faith in repentance because it involves believing that God exists (Heb 11:6) and believing God's word (Ps 106:12). However, *saving faith* has a particular object. Under the old covenant it was faith in God's provision of atonement by a blood sacrifice: "he shall lay his hand on the head of the sin offering . . . So the priest shall make atonement for him, and it shall be forgiven him" (Lev 4:29–31). Isaiah points to the need to believe on God's servant Messiah (Isa 53:1), who was to be a trespass offering (see Isa 53:10, where the word for "offering" is the Hebrew *asham*, pointing to the fact that he paid for all categories of sin, including those in ignorance and those in religious observance). Yeshua was that *asham*, and saving faith trusts in him and his redemptive work on the cross of bearing the sinner's penalty: "Whom God hath set forth to be a propitiation through faith in his blood" (Rom 3:25, KJV). This object of faith carries with it other things essential to be believed: Jesus' resurrection (1 Cor 15:1–4; 1 Thess 4:14), that God raised Jesus (Rom 4:24; 10:9), and that Jesus is the Messiah and Son of God (John 20:31). The object of saving faith is often expressed as Jesus himself; comprehending everything true of him (Acts 16:31; John 7:38; 11:26).

This faith is more than intellectual assent, something of which demons are capable (Jas 2:19), but requires the commitment of the whole person and life to Yeshua, expressed by the words "heart" and "confess" in Rom 10:9: "if you confess with your mouth the Lord Jesus and believe in your heart that God has raised Him from the dead, you will be saved." Conviction and trust are therefore essential elements of saving faith. Such faith sets a high personal value on Yeshua: "to you who believe, He is precious" (1 Pet 2:7).

It is important to understand that saving faith is itself a gift: "For by grace you have been saved through faith, and that not of yourselves; it is the gift of God" (Eph 2:8). In Eph 2:1–10 Paul emphasizes how the salvation of sinners utterly depends on God, including the part we play—exercising faith—as it is a gift from God at the moment of salvation. Paul summarizes: "we are His workmanship" (Eph 2:10, see Isa 26:12).

(vi) Forgiveness and Justification

(a) *Forgiveness*

Forgiveness of sin belongs to God because he is the offended party, the one whose law is broken "To the Lord our God belong mercy and forgiveness" (Dan 9:9; see also Exod 32:32; 2 Chr 6:21; Ps 25:18; 1 John 1:9). The one who sins is indebted to God and forgiveness requires he remit the debt (see Matt

6:12). This God is willing to do and has promised forgiveness to the repentant, yet in a way which is just and righteous, as John writes: "If we confess our sins, He is faithful and just to forgive us our sins" (1 John 1:9). His justice demands that the price is paid—"without shedding of blood there is no remission" (Heb 9:22)—and this was promised in the new covenant, which Yeshua inaugurated through his death: "this is My blood of the new covenant, which is shed for many for the remission of sins" (Jer 31:34; Matt 26:28). As Son of Man and Son of God, Yeshua has authority to forgive sins (Matt 9:6; John 8:34–36) and this forgiveness is central to gospel proclamation: "repentance and remission of sins should be preached in His name to all nations" (Luke 24:47, see also Acts 10:43). However, forgiveness of debt is only one side of the coin of redemption, the negative side, although a very wonderful negative; justification focuses on a person's righteousness before God, the positive side of the same coin.

Traditional Judaism's teaching on receiving forgiveness of sins contains a mixture of dependence on God's mercy and human merit as illustrated by the following quotations from the service for the Day of Atonement:

> O thou who art clothed with majesty, according to thy mercy, act mercifully by us, for thine own sake;[1]
>
> regard the merit of him [Abraham] who walked before thee, and was perfect; and for his righteousness remove the stain of our sins;[2]
>
> For the sake of the blood that hath been spilt of those who suffered death for the sake of thy name; for the love of them, I beseech thee now to forgive my sins;[3]
>
> with this may his iniquity be expiated, and his wound healed, if he repents before his light is quenched.[4]

(b) Justification

Justification is a declaration of God in which he imputes the righteousness of Messiah Jesus to the repentant, believing sinner, and regards them as just in his sight. Put simply, the sinner is accounted righteous before God. This is not an act of power but the act of a judge, as in Deut 25:1: "If there is a

---

1. *Festival Prayers*, vol. 2, 30.
2. *Festival Prayers*, vol. 2, 173.
3. *Festival Prayers*, vol. 3, 73.
4. *Festival Prayers*, vol. 3, 15.

dispute between men, and they come to court, that the judges may judge them, and they justify the righteous and condemn the wicked." It does not involve a subjective change, a bestowal of virtue, but is a new status, which can be illustrated by Balaam's words about Israel: "He has not observed iniquity in Jacob, Nor has He seen wickedness in Israel" (Num 23:21); words which, taken subjectively, were manifestly untrue, but they reflect the status God had given them as his redeemed people. The New Testament has the same teaching: in Rom 4:5 Paul, the preeminent expounder of justification in the New Testament, writes of God, "Him who justifies the ungodly."

Believers in Old Testament times knew what it was to be justified and the blessings it entailed. Of Abraham it was said, "he believed in the LORD, and He accounted it to him for righteousness" (Gen 15:6); Isaiah portrayed the imputing of righteousness as a robe: "For he has clothed me with the garments of salvation, He has covered me with the robe of righteousness" (Isa 61:10); and the psalmists wrote of it (Pss 31:1; 32:2; 71:14–16). Isaiah foresees that this righteousness is closely connected to YHWH's person: "In the LORD all the descendants of Israel Shall be justified, and shall glory" (Isa 45:25). It is not simply a declaration by God but entails receiving what is achieved by God himself. Isaiah and Jeremiah give us more detail when they prophesy of Messiah as the one who brings this righteousness: "By His knowledge My righteous Servant shall justify many, for He shall bear their iniquities" (Isa 53:11), and "I will raise to David a Branch of righteousness . . . this is His name by which He will be called: THE LORD OUR RIGHTEOUSNESS (Jer 23:5–6). Therefore the Old Testament expects YHWH himself, incarnate as Messiah, to live a righteous life and bear the penalty of sin; by this means justification is "in the LORD." The New Testament quotes Isaiah's prophecy and points to Yeshua as that person: "Then Philip opened his mouth, and beginning at this Scripture, preached Jesus to him" (Acts 8:35).

The New Testament describes this righteousness as a free gift: "those who receive abundance of grace and of the gift of righteousness will reign in life through the One, Jesus Christ" (Rom 5:17). It is a gift procured by the obedience of Yeshua through his sinless life under the law and his submission to the law's penalty for sin. It becomes ours by imputation: our sin was imputed by God to him and his righteousness is imputed to us; our death was his and his righteous life is ours (2 Cor 5:21, see also Rom 5:9; 4:25). The means by which God's gift is received is faith. The New Testament contrasts this free gift received by faith in Messiah Jesus with human efforts to achieve a righteousness by keeping the Mosaic laws: "by Him everyone who believes is justified from all things from which you could not be justified by the law of Moses" (Acts 13:39, see also Gal 2:16; 2 Cor 3:7–9; Rom 3:21–25; Phil

3:9). Yeshua forcibly portrayed this contrast in his parable of the Pharisee and the tax collector (Luke 18:9–14).

This teaching has been misunderstood, as if it allows freedom to sin to those who are justified and under grace. Paul had to confront this error: "What shall we say then? Shall we continue in sin that grace may abound? Certainly not!" (Rom 6:1–2). He goes on to present the Christian as one in a new realm where sin is abhorred and righteousness loved: "How shall we who died to sin live any longer in it?" (Rom 6:2, 12–13). However, Paul does not minimize the importance of good works as an inevitable consequence of this new status: "For we are His workmanship, created in Christ Jesus for good works, which God prepared beforehand that we should walk in them" (Eph 2:10, see also Matt 5:16; 2 Tim 3:17; Heb 10:24).

Other texts appear to conflict with Paul's emphasis on justification by faith alone, as if works are part of justification. Yeshua said, "by your words you will be justified, and by your words you will be condemned" (Matt 12:37); James wrote, "You see then that a man is justified by works, and not by faith only" (Jas 2:24); and Paul himself wrote, "the doers of the law will be justified" (Rom 2:13). In all such texts the context makes it clear that the problem of a false confidence is being addressed, whether it is trusting a correct manner of life whilst ignoring evil speaking, or having a nominal belief whilst overlooking evil behavior, or possessing God's revelation whilst not obeying it. The apparent contradiction between Paul and James is especially important to understand. Paul and James were facing different problems: James faced those who belittled works and hence he emphasizes works as an evidence of a person being justified; Paul faces those who exalted human works as an essential contribution to our salvation and hence he underlined salvation as a gift received by faith alone. Yeshua himself faced the same erroneous mentality regarding works, which is why he so often said, "Your faith has saved you."

Confusion may be caused by the use of the words "righteous" or "blameless" to describe a believer's lifestyle, such as: "The effective, fervent prayer of a righteous man avails much" (Jas 5:16), and "That you may become blameless and harmless, children of God without fault" (Phil 2:15). The use of such terms does not imply a person's behavior is the source of their justification but they are descriptive of the life of a mature and consistent believer with a good conscience before God, one not prone to frequent, open failure.

The teaching of the Roman Catholic and Orthodox churches denies justification by faith alone: "If anyone saith that justifying faith is nothing else but confidence in the divine mercy which remits sins for Christ's sake alone . . . let him be anathema,"[5] and "Justification is not a once-for-all, instantaneous pronouncement . . . neither is it merely a legal declaration that an unrighteous person is righteous."[6] Despite an appearance of change through their ecumenical dialogue with Lutherans, the Roman Catholic Church continues to oppose Scripture on justification: "in baptism the Holy Spirit unites one with Christ, justifies, and truly renews the person."[7] Here there is no mention of the faith of the person (an infant), so that everything depends on the ministry of the church through the priest. These churches confuse justification with sanctification by teaching that the believer's lifestyle and works are essential parts of being in a justified state: "justification is a living, dynamic, day to day reality for the one who follows Christ."[8] The Roman Catholic doctrine of purgatory, as a place and experience after death whereby "souls suffer for a time after death on account of their sins,"[9] underlines their error in giving an essential contribution to people; it is something extra to the work of Christ for their entry to heaven and hence their standing and justification before God.

Traditional Judaism rarely uses the term "justification" and one reason may be found in this extract referring to Messiah in the Machzor for Yom Kippur: "Our righteous anointed is departed from us: horror hath ceased us, and we have none to justify."[10]

The more recently developed "New Perspective on Paul," or *covenantal nomism*, is a more recent deviation from New Testament teaching, which asserts that Judaism in New Testament times was not, as so often negatively portrayed, a religion of works righteousness but one of remaining faithful to YHWH by keeping the law of Moses and adhering to his people. That seems a very rosy view of Judaism in New Testament times. Indeed, there were many like Zacharias and Elizabeth who kept the law as devout Israelites (Luke 1:5–6), who through faith not works attained to the law of righteousness, but Paul is clear that the majority sought it by their own works (Rom 9:31–32; 11:5–7). The Judaism which emerged after the destruction of the temple demonstrates that its parent was a religion which included works righteousness.

5. Council of Trent (Session VI, CAN.12).
6. "What Orthodox Christians Believe," 7.
7. 1999 Joint Declaration on the Doctrine of Justification, section 28.
8. "What Orthodox Christians Believe," 7.
9. Catholic Truth Society, *Catechism of Christian Doctrine*, 18.
10. *Festival Prayers*, vol. 3, 33.

(vii) Regeneration (or New Birth)

Various terms are used for this work of God in the human soul. Moshe wrote of circumcision of heart, "And the LORD your God will circumcise your heart . . . to love the LORD your God with all your heart" (Deut 30:6), a work not exclusive to New Testament times but true of the experience of all the LORD's Old Testament saints, for example David, who was described by YHWH as "a man after His own heart" (1 Sam 13:14; Acts 13:22; see also Rom 2:29). Paul's words "the carnal mind is enmity against God; for it is not subject to the law of God, nor indeed can be" (Rom 8:7) underline the impossibility of a heart after God without God working a fundamental change, a new birth. Jesus expected Nicodemus, a scholar of the Tanakh, to know about this necessity (John 3:10). The difference between the old covenant and the new in this respect was that under the old regeneration was not guaranteed to all in the covenant; in the new it was: "I will put My law in their minds, and write it on their hearts . . . they all shall know Me, from the least of them to the greatest of them" (Jer 31:33–34).

"Regeneration" is a term meaning "born over again" and is equivalent to the term "new birth" as used by Jesus in John 3:1–8 and Peter in 1 Pet 1:23. John uses the terms "born of God" and "seed" in 1 John 3:9 and Paul writes of the believer as a "new creation" or "new creature" in Gal 6:15. All these Scriptures make clear that the new birth is entirely a work of God, and that it is essential for entry into God's kingdom (John 3:3, 5). The parallel with natural birth emphasizes that people play no part; natural birth is something done to us, not by us. The new birth is not an act of the soul or a mental exercise leading to psychological change; it is something quite different to any form of natural change; it is not a process, any more than a natural birth is. It should not therefore be confused with sanctification, that gradual change in a follower of Yeshua as they increasingly know him and obey him; the new birth is instantaneous. As with natural conception and birth, there is an element of mystery about the new birth (John 3:7–8); a seed of God is planted in the human soul which renews all its faculties, hence some use the term "new principle of life." As discussed earlier some understand the word "spirit" when clearly distinguished from "soul" to refer to this new creation, this seed of God (1 Thess 5:23; Heb 4:12). Although it is a direct work of the Spirit the new birth should not be divorced from the teaching of the word of God, as 1 Pet 1:23 underlines: "having been born again, not of corruptible seed but incorruptible, through the word of God which lives and abides forever."

It should be remembered that the new birth is not the focus in coming to faith; the focus is Yeshua. The new birth is not necessarily accompanied by strong emotions because a person's emotions when they come to repentance and faith depend on many factors. Some quietly believe from the heart what they had always accepted in their minds, e.g., children of Christians; others are filled with strong emotions as they discover something totally new to them which delivers from a lifestyle which held them in bondage. What will always be the case is a changed perspective and way of life—Paul describes the new birth as a spiritual resurrection: "And you He made alive, who were dead in trespasses and sins" and "For we are His workmanship, created in Christ Jesus for good works" (Eph 2:1, 10). Changes will always take place which prove the new birth has occurred; the regenerate soul is alive to a whole new realm, a new way of seeing everything, such that there is a focus upon God and his will and new powers to love him and his people (see 1 John 3:9; 4:7; 5:1, 4, 18).

(viii) Regeneration and Saving Faith

Differences exist among true believers as to whether regeneration precedes the exercise of saving faith or vice versa. Some who place faith first do so because they have a defective conception of the effects of the fall and understand fallen people as able to exercise faith in Jesus for salvation, arguing that God would not command people to do something of which they are incapable. Others have a true conception of the effects of the fall but argue that God offers the gift of faith to all, and some exercise it and some refuse to believe. Those who argue against such views not only underline humankind's total depravity due to the fall, and their responsibility to repent and believe despite their inability to do so, but also stress their inability to want to believe, and hence the need for regeneration.

Yeshua's words, "unless one is born of water and the Spirit, he cannot enter the kingdom of God" (John 3:5), and Paul's words, "the carnal mind is enmity against God; for it is not subject to the law of God, nor indeed can be" (Rom 8:7), when taken together teach people's utter inability to willingly accept the truths of the gospel from the heart, repent and believe, unless they are regenerate. This understanding is the earlier one in the history of the church and the one taught in all the great confessions of faith of the sixteenth and seventeenth centuries. It is often expressed by the Latin term *Sola gratia*, which underlines that at every point salvation is by grace alone; fallen men and women having no faculty of the soul uncorrupted by sin, thus rendering them incapable of repentance and faith. Paul speaks of the gift of saving faith: "For by grace you have been saved through faith, and that not of yourselves; it is the gift of God, not of works, lest anyone should boast" (Eph 2:8–9), so that even the faith to believe is to be seen as God's gift. We are faced with the mysterious working of the Spirit, and cannot expect to have complete knowledge of all his workings in bringing a soul to faith, but what we must ensure is that we attribute all the power and glory to him and none to hopeless and helpless sinners.

(ix) Adoption, the Spirit's Indwelling, and Union with Christ

The person who believes in Yeshua and is born again is immediately aware that they are in a father-child relationship with God. This has two aspects, an objective one (adoption) and a subjective one (the Spirit's indwelling). The words used in English translations are "adopt," "sons," and "children."

(a) Adoption

YHWH called Israel his "son," his "firstborn," when he redeemed and called the nation out from Egypt (Exod 4:22; Hos 11:1; Rom 9:4). Similarly, God's people of the new covenant are called his "sons": "For you are all sons of God through faith in Christ Jesus" (Gal 3:26). There is no natural right to this, especially not for sinners, but it is a status granted by God through adoption; a familiar concept in the days of the New Testament, as it is today, whereby the adopted one is granted equal status with natural-born children. This is how John expresses it: "But as many as received Him, to them He gave the right [authority, power] to become children of God" (John 1:12). It is a status bestowed upon them now, not something they have yet to receive, although its full experience lies in the future (1 John 3:2).

Adoption arises from God's predestinating love, a love which leads John the apostle to marvel, bearing in mind our willful rebellion (Eph 1:5; 1 John 3:1). It is only made possible by the redeeming work of Yeshua leading to acceptance in him (Gal 4:4–5; Eph 1:5–6), so that the believer has equal family status with God's unique Son, is a joint heir with Christ, and is as beloved as he is (Eph 1:6; Rom 8:17). All this is received through faith in Yeshua (Gal 3:26; John 1:12). Hence the Christian life is a family one, a life together with the Father, especially underlined by Jesus' encouragement to pray to the Father (Matt 6:9; John 16:23–24). In God's family all have unity and equal status as John anticipated: "that He [Yeshua] would gather together in one the children of God who were scattered abroad" (John 11:52; Gal 3:26–28). It is a status which Paul contrasts with Israel's under the law: he sees believers in Yeshua as enjoying the liberty of grown sons compared to Israel's slave-like condition of childhood (Gal 4:1–7). Consequently he marvels that believers should want to regress to childhood under the law (Gal 1:6; 4:9; 5:1–6).

Adoption is a status which is not yet enjoyed in its fullness. Believers are heirs—"and if a son, then an heir of God through Christ" (Gal 4:7)—and so an inheritance awaits them in the new heavens and the new earth. There they will be perfectly transformed into the image of God's only begotten Son—"we know that when He is revealed, we shall be like Him" (1 John 3:2)—and this transformation includes their bodies which have yet to be redeemed, completing their adoption (Rom 8:23).

Moshe's words describing Israel in Deut 33:29 come to glorious fulfillment in Messiah's people: "Happy are you . . . Who is like you, a people saved by the Lord!"

(b) The Spirit's Indwelling

The converted, regenerate, and adopted person receives the gift of the Spirit, who then indwells them: "And I will pray the Father, and He will give you another Helper, that He may abide with you forever—the Spirit of Truth . . . He will be in you" (John 14:16–17; Luke 11:13; Acts 11:17), or as Yeshua puts it another way, "We will come to him and make Our home with him" (John 14:23). This indwelling occurs when saving faith is exercised: "Therefore He who supplies the Spirit to you . . . does He do it by the works of the law, or by the hearing of faith?" (Gal 3:5). This is a grand privilege of new covenant believers, not granted to those under the old covenant, who only experienced his influence but not his permanent indwelling (2 Chr 15:1; John 7:39; 14:17). There is no such thing as a believer in Yeshua who is not indwelt by the Spirit: "Now if anyone does not have the Spirit of Christ, he is not His" (Rom 8:9).

The Spirit is called the "Spirit of adoption" and his indwelling affirms God is now the believer's father, leading them to address God in an intimate manner as their a child does its father: "you received the Spirit of adoption by whom we cry out, 'Abba, Father.'" The Spirit witnesses to the souls of believers that they are children of God (Rom 8:15–16; Gal 4:6). Paul uses the image of the Spirit as a seal to express the same thought of belonging to God, being owned by him. This carries with it the certainty of an eternal future with God, such that the Spirit's indwelling is described as "the guarantee [or earnest] of our inheritance" (2 Cor 1:22; Eph 1:13–14). Because of this all believers possess a measure of assurance that they are God's children (see also 1 John 4:13), although it needs to be said that this can be diminished by sin and Satan, of which more later.

The Spirit's indwelling leads Paul to describe believers as a temple, pointing to the believer's life as one of holiness, praise, and service (1 Cor 3:16; Eph 2:21–22).

(c) Union with Christ

As described at the beginning of Part 5, every aspect of salvation is connected in Scripture to being in Christ. Here we briefly focus on the initial experience believers have of this when the Spirit unites them to Jesus. Paul describes the church as the body of Christ: "For we are members of His body, of His flesh and of His bones" (Eph 5:30; 4:12–13; 1 Cor 12:27). It is the Spirit who brings the believer into this body, this union with Messiah: "For by one Spirit we were all baptized into one body" (1 Cor 12:13). This baptism should not be confused with Messiah baptizing with the Spirit; it is the Spirit immersing the believer into union with Yeshua at the moment he indwells their soul. This union is so intimate that elsewhere Paul describes it as being "one spirit with Him" (1 Cor 6:17). The new believer is conscious of being in a whole new world, and indeed they are; they are no longer in Adam, the realm of condemnation and death, but are in Messiah, the realm of life (1 Cor 15:22). This is a spiritual resurrection that even takes them to the throne of God, for "God . . . made us sit together in the heavenly places in Christ Jesus" (Eph 2:4–6). Once the Spirit enters the heart this union is effected and the believer is in a new realm, knowing Yeshua, and has access to God through him. Salvation could have been less than this but it is difficult to imagine it could have been more: "Who is a pardoning God like thee, or who has grace so rich and free!"

> For this reason I bow my knees to the Father of our Lord Jesus Christ, from whom the whole family in heaven and earth is named, that He would grant you, according to the riches of His glory, to be strengthened with might through His Spirit in the inner man, that Christ may dwell in your hearts through faith; that you, being rooted and grounded in love, may be able to comprehend with all the saints what is the width and length and depth and height—to know the love of Christ which passes knowledge; that you may be filled with all the fullness of God." (Eph 3:14–19)

Scriptures

Election: Gen 25:23; Deut 10:15; Isa 42:1; Acts 13:17; Rom 8:33; 11:2; Eph 1:4; 1 Pet 2:4, 9; 2 Pet 1:10.

Foreknowledge: Jer 1:15; Amos 3:2; Acts 2:23; Rom 8:29, 33; 9:22–23; 11:2; 1 Pet 1:20; 2:8; Jude 4.

Prevenient grace: Job 33:29–30; Matt 16:17; Acts 16:14; 26:17–18; John 16:8.

Effectual call: Matt 20:14; John 10:3; Rom 8:30.

Repentance and faith: Ps 51:13; Isa 59:20; Jer 31:19; John 7:38; 11:26; 20:31; Acts 3:19; 16:31; 20:21; Rom 3:25; 4:24; 10:9; 1 Cor 15:1–4; 2 Cor 7:10; Eph 2:8; 1 Thess 1:9; Heb 11:6; 1 Pet 2:7.

Forgiveness and Justification: Gen 15:6; Pss 25:18; 32:2; Isa 45:25; 53:11; 61:10; Jer 31:34; Dan 9:9; Matt 26:28; 9:6; Luke 24:27; Acts 13:39; Rom 3:24–25; 4:5, 24–25; 5:17; 2 Cor 5:21; Gal 2:16; 1 John 1:9.

Regeneration: Deut 30:6; John 3:18; Gal 6:15; Eph 2:1; 1 Thess 5:23; 1 Pet 1:23; 1 John 3:9.

Adoption: Exod 4:22; Hos 1:11; John 1:12; 11:52; Rom 8:23; 9:4; Gal 3:26–28; 4:4–5, 7; Eph 1:5–6; 1 John 3:1–2.

Spirit's indwelling: Luke 11:13; John 14:16–17; Acts 11:17; Rom 8:9, 15–16; 1 Cor 3:16; 2 Cor 1:22; Gal 3:5; 4:6; Eph 1:13; 2:21–22.

Union with Christ: Rom 6:1–4; 1 Cor 6:17; 12:27; 13; 15:22; Eph 2:4–6; 4:12–13; 5:30–32.

Questions

1. Did God choose those who are saved because he knew they would believe, or was it his choice of them which ensured they believed?

2. How do you see God's prevenient grace in your own life?

3. There are a number of distinct aspects to the experience of a sinner receiving salvation; describe them, and their interrelationship.

4. Is justification by works or by faith? Refer to Jas 2:14–26 and Rom 3:21–31 in your answer.

5. Both spiritual change and new status occur when a person truly believes in Yeshua; is anything further needed to enter the new heavens and the new earth?

6. For a person to come to faith there is a human work (hearing truth, repenting, and believing) and there is a divine work (gift of faith and

regeneration); is it possible for the Christian winner of souls to get in God's way?

Further Reading

Berkouwer, G. C. *Divine Election*. Grand Rapids: Eerdmans, 1960.
Calvin, John. *Institutes of the Christian Religion*. Peabody, MA: Hendrickson, 2007. See Part 3.
Ferguson, Sinclair B. *The Holy Spirit*. Leicester: InterVarsity, 1996.
Jackman, David. *Spirit of Truth*. Tain, UK: Christian Focus, 2007.
Lloyd-Jones, D. M. *Romans: An Exposition of Chapters 3:20—4:25: Atonement and Justification*. Edinburgh: Banner of Truth, 1970.
Murray, John. *Redemption Accomplished and Applied*. Edinburgh: Banner of Truth, 1961. See Part 2.
Seifrid, Mark A. *Christ Our Righteousness*. Leicester: Apollos, 2000.
Wells, David F. *God the Evangelist*. Johnson City, TN: Send the Light, 1997.

(B) LIFE IN THE SPIRIT

As stated at the end of the last section under "Union with Christ," the life of the believer is one lived in union with the Savior by the indwelling Spirit. According to Rom 5:10 believers are saved "in His life." Most translations have "*by* his life" but the Greek is *en*, which can equally well be translated "in" and serves to emphasize Paul's point—the certainty of salvation due to spiritual union with Messiah. Paul also uses the term "in the Spirit" to describe the spiritual realm of the believer, and the New Testament uses the phrase when referring to aspects of the believer's life such as: decision-making, God's guidance, speaking God's truth, prayer, fellowship, and love. This can be summed up as being "led by the Spirit of God" (Rom 8:14), an expression which is not so much referring to guidance as to the whole experience of Christian living, one in which the Spirit is leading believers' lives to bring about God's will for them. Thus they are encouraged to "walk in the Spirit" or better "keep in step with the Spirit" (Gal 5:25, NIV). This work of the Spirit is usually imperceptible, just like the Spirit's inspiration of the writers of Scripture or his work of regeneration, but the fruits are plain. All such activity of the Spirit is pure grace; we do not deserve it, which is why we frequently see the word "grace" used in a general way in the New Testament to describe God's activity in the believer; e.g., "The grace of our Lord Jesus Christ be with you all" (Rom 16:24).

The expression "in the Spirit" is often used by way of contrast with "in the flesh," the old life before faith (Rom 8:9). Likewise "life in the Spirit" is contrasted with life under the law, a life lived under rules and regulations (Gal 5:1, 5, 18). This life of the believer has many aspects and we will consider the seven main ones and the work of the Spirt in them.

(i) Knowing God's Love through Abiding in Messiah

God's love for his people is the inspiration for everything in the believer's life and it is among the earliest subjective realizations of a new believer, if not the very first. In Eph 3:14–21 the apostle tells us of a concern he has for all believers: to know the love of Christ in its fullness, something which comes about through the strengthening work of the Spirit. Through his work, Christ dwells in the heart by faith leading to a conscious, daily walk with Yeshua, and an awareness that all that happens to the believer is to be understood and experienced in terms of Messiah's love. Yeshua expressed this in terms of "abiding in" him (John 15:4–5; see also 1 John 2:24–28). The Christian life is rooted and grounded in love as believers are conformed more and more to the image of Yeshua, the one who in love laid down his life for them (1 John 3:16). This is why Peter exhorts believers to grow in knowledge of the Lord Jesus Christ (2 Pet 3:18), a knowledge that is firstly about him, all that he did and does in love for his people. It is this which Peter understands as key to the list of qualities he exhorts believers to gain in their life, the pinnacle of which is love (2 Pet 1:5–8). The world to come will be a world of love and believers are prepared for it by growing in experience of divine love now.

(ii) Assurance

This is surely the birthright of every believer, even though some often experience uncertainty and all will experience Satan's attacks upon it. Assurance of salvation has various aspects.

(a) The Assurance of Faith

To trust Messiah Jesus necessarily involves a confidence in him, and this act of saving faith is a gift from God by the Spirit who leads to the Savior. The Spirit bears witness to the truth of the gospel as it is heard, and as it is received the believer has the witness of the Spirit within the heart (1 John 5:6,

10). Hence the exercise of faith brings with it, by the Spirit, an assurance for believers that the promise of forgiveness and eternal life is theirs. This is illustrated by the words frequently used by Yeshua after a healing: "Your faith has saved you. Go in peace" (Luke 7:50). The description in Acts 2:41–47 of the first believers illustrates this confidence: they were diligent disciples, shared their goods, met daily for worship, were glad in the good things God gave, and were filled with praise; all marks of confidence in their salvation.

(b) Cleansing and Renewal

The work of the Holy Spirit in regeneration has two aspects, cleansing from sin and a renewal of nature: "He saved us, through the washing of regeneration and renewing of the Holy Spirit" (Titus 3:5). The same two aspects are expressed by Jesus in his words to Nicodemus concerning being born of water and the Spirit (John 3:3). Hebrews expresses it as a heart sprinkled from an evil conscience and bodies washed with pure water, and encourages believers to draw near to God in full assurance on this basis (Heb 10:22). By the Spirit the believer is given a confidence they are cleansed of sin and its polluting effects on body and soul.

(c) Owned and Adopted

The believer is "sealed with the Holy Spirit of promise" (Eph 1:13); that is, they are marked as owned by God and are aware of this in their own souls as he comes to dwell within. Similar to this is their adoption into God's family; their relationship with God is as a child to its father and they cry out by the Spirit "Abba, Father" (Rom 8:15). This is true of all believers, although experience shows it is known to different degrees.

(d) Life Evidences

Scripture encourages believers to be assured of the genuineness of their faith by the new life manifested by them. James wrote, "I will show you my faith by my works" (Jas 2:18), pointing to Christian living as an evidence of having true faith. A number of evidences can be mentioned. *Abiding in the truth* of the gospel is due to the work of the Spirit—an anointing that keeps believers in the truth and hence in union with Jesus (1 John 2:19–20, 27). To believe Jesus is Messiah is evidence of being born of God (1 John 5:1), which may sound inadequate as many prove to be false, but in the next two verses John links this belief to the *love of others* who are born of God and also to *loving God and keeping his commandments*. Believers who observe such things in their lives can deduce they are of the truth and be persuaded of it in their hearts (1 John 3:19). Another evidence is that of not continuing in a sinful lifestyle (1 John 3:9) or, as John puts it elsewhere, *overcoming the world*: "For whatever is born of God overcomes the world" (1 John 5:4).

(e) The Inner Witness of the Spirit

The presence of the Spirit in the heart of believers witnesses to them of their union with Yeshua (1 John 3:24; 4:13); he is with them always, and they know they can turn to him. Similarly, as stated above, the Spirit gives the awareness of being in a child-father relationship with God.

This witness may be experienced to a high degree as indicated by Paul's language in Rom 5:5: "the love of God has been poured out in our hearts by the Holy Spirit who was given to us." This is strong language; the word translated "poured out" is the same word that Peter uses to describe what occurred on the Day of Pentecost (Shavuot). Paul is indicating that believers ought to experience their own Pentecost, or better, in the plural—their own personal Pentecosts. Here is an overwhelming awareness of God's love. Peter puts it this way: "you rejoice with joy inexpressible and full of glory" (1 Pet 1:8), pointing to times when believers may be overwhelmed to the point of speechlessness!

This leads into a consideration of the terms "baptism with the Spirit" and "filled with the Spirit," about which there is much controversy. A few points can be made.

1. The expression "filled with the Spirit" is used in two different ways, firstly to describe the sort of experience indicated in the preceding paragraph. For example, it is used to describe what happened on the Day of Pentecost (Acts 2:4) and also in Acts 4:31: "they were all filled with the Holy Spirit, and they spoke the word of God with boldness." Both events were powerful experiences, given by the Spirit. Secondly, it is used by way of a command by Paul: "be filled with the Spirit, speaking to one another in psalms and hymns and spiritual songs . . . giving thanks always . . . submitting to one another" (Eph 5:18–21). Here it is an encouragement to live under the control of the Spirit in praise and obedient Christian living. This describes believers seeking to live up to their responsibilities and knowing the Holy Spirit enabling them. This is not the same as the unique and empowering spiritual experiences granted from time to time as described in 1 Pet 1:8.

2. Some understand the expression "baptized with the Spirit" in Acts 1:5 to be identical with being *baptized by the Spirit* in 1 Cor 12:13, and hence they teach that all believers are both baptized *with* the Spirit and *by* the Spirit when they come to faith. But it should be noted that Jesus is the one who baptizes *with* the Spirit, and baptism *by* the Spirit is an action of the Spirit, not Jesus. This author therefore understands being baptized *with* the Spirit as an act of Yeshua sending his Spirit upon a believer to empower for witness, but being baptized *by* the Spirit, as in 1 Cor 12:13, as an act of the Spirit uniting the believers to Yeshua.

The points of agreement are, firstly, that all believers are indwelt by the Spirit and united to Messiah by the Spirt at conversion. Secondly, that Yeshua gives experiences of himself subsequent to conversion which fill the believer with wonder, love and praise, and empower for witness. The danger of the view that Acts 1:5 and 1 Cor 12:13 describe the same thing is that believers are not encouraged to seek empowering encounters with Messiah Jesus. A danger with distinguishing the two texts is that believers may wrongly conclude there are two levels of Christian living.

Empowering to witness is the emphasis of Acts 1:5, 8: "you shall receive power . . ." This was fulfilled for the first believers on the Day of Pentecost (Shavuot). It should be carefully noted that what they experienced is also described as being filled with the Spirit (Acts 2:4), as was the subsequent experience of Acts 4:31. It should therefore be possible to agree that while Pentecost was a unique event in redemption's history, the first giving of the Spirit, the experience of the believers at Pentecost should not be considered unique. The same disciples were filled again in Acts 4:31, and it was repeated later in the life of other believers, including the apostle Paul (Acts 8:14–17; 9:17; 19:1–6). Furthermore, the descriptions by Paul and Peter quoted earlier of overwhelming experience of the Spirit are assumed by them to be something of which all believers would be aware. It is therefore the birthright of all believers, but not something all have experienced. Such a filling of the Spirit leads to strong assurance of salvation and, when taken with the other aspects of assurance mentioned above, is often described as "full assurance."

(f) The Place of God's Word

It needs to be emphasized that no aspect of assurance can be divorced from the word of God. It is the Scriptures which teach the nature of assurance and it is by believing their revelation and obeying it that the Spirit witnesses to believers that they are God's children. Experiences which do not lead to obedience are spurious.

The Roman Catholic Church teaches against the above, viewing such assurance as presumptuous, asserting that believers cannot be absolutely sure of their salvation, but can only await the Day of Judgment for God's final verdict. Such teaching is connected to their doctrine that the works of the believer are part of their justification before God and inevitably increases anxiety and robs of joy. Believers do indeed know doubts or experience anxiety under the assaults of Satan, but as they undertake the spiritual disciplines of the word, prayer, fellowship, and the Lord's Supper the Spirit will assure their hearts afresh. John tells us he wrote his first letter so that "your joy may be full" (1 John 1:4). Believers ought to be sure of their salvation, something which leads to joy, and commends the gospel.

(iii) Hope

Life in the Spirit has a hope—resurrection from the dead, eternal life, and the experience of God's love and glory in the new heavens and the new earth. It is the Spirit who opens the understanding to grasp this hope and its riches (Eph 1:18), and his presence in the heart is a guarantee from God of a believer's interest in it (Eph 1:14). He strengthens this hope within them so that they live eagerly looking forward to it (Gal 5:5), and his filling them with a sense of God's love ensures they are not ashamed of this hope before those who mock it (Rom 5:5). Messiah's present indwelling of believers' hearts by the Spirit guarantees there is glory to come because that is where he is now (Col 1:27). Peter makes clear that this should not be an occasional interest because it is a "living hope," something which is always part of a believer's life (1 Pet 1:3). Even persecutions and the trials of life can be a source of rejoicing because they assure believers that they will share the glory which was Messiah's after he had suffered (1 Pet 4:12).

(iv) Spiritual Warfare

This fallen universe, visible and invisible, has become a battlefield. Satan has instigated rebellion against the Almighty and is determined to oppose all that stands for his truth, most especially believers in God's Son (Rev 12:17). As John puts it, "the whole world lies under the sway of the evil one" (1 John 5:19). Not that Satan is outside of YHWH's control, as Job 1–2 clearly shows, but Satan wields very real power due to human sin. The New Testament consistently presents the life of a believer as a warfare, one in which he or she is to act as a soldier; the armor being described in Eph 6:10–18. The believer's life is like a nation at war where everything is on a war footing but the intensity of battle is only occasional; as Paul puts it, believers always live in evil days ("the days are evil" Eph 5:16) but there is also an "evil day" (Eph 6:13) when the conflict is especially sharp. Paul exhorts Timothy, and thereby all believers, to "Fight the good fight of faith" (1 Tim 6:12).

Spiritual warfare has different aspects, six of which are mentioned here. In what follows the name Satan is used to stand for the devil and all his demonic hosts.

1. Satan seeks to sow error among believers and lead them astray: "some will depart from the faith, giving heed to deceiving spirits and doctrines of demons" (1 Tim 4:1). This departure is not a departure from some form of Christianity altogether, but is out of the true faith of the gospel; it is therefore especially deceptive. Paul lists some examples of these false doctrines in 1 Tim 4:25.

2. Satan stirs up the civil and religious authorities to oppose the church, as recorded in the New Testament history and portrayed in Rev 13. There is an unseen war in which principalities, powers, rulers of darkness, and spiritual hosts of wickedness scheme to destroy God's work through influencing the minds of earthly authorities (Eph 6:12; Rev 20:7–8; 16:14; Dan 10:13—11:1).

3. Satan assaults believers with strong temptations. This is the significance of Paul's expression "fiery darts of the wicked one" (Eph 6:16).

4. Satan is constantly building and rebuilding systems of erroneous belief and thought in the minds of fallen people, which it is the task of the gospel to tear down (2 Cor 10:3–5).

5. Satan is always active to prevent God's truth getting a hold on the minds of hearers (Matt 13:19).

6. Satan takes control of individuals by possessing or oppressing them, either to crush them or to use them more directly for his purpose (Luke 13:16; John 13:27; Acts 16:16–18).

It is the work of the Spirit to equip and aid believers to fight in all these aspects of the warfare and their principal weapon for defense and attack is God's word: "And take . . . the sword of the Spirit, which is the word of God" (Eph 6:17; Rev 19:11). A strong believer is one who has learnt to fight the wicked one by the word of God (see "young men" in 1 John 2:13–14). The following are some examples of the Spirit's aid in the believer's warfare. The Spirit gives insight to discern departures from the faith (1 John 2:18–27).

Against those civil and religious authorities which oppose her, the church should seek to use spiritual weapons of the word and prayer to cast down arguments and win over rulers. If they fail, believers are called to stand: "having done all, to stand" (Eph 6:13). There is nothing in the New Testament to encourage the practice of addressing the principalities and powers who influence rulers unless they are actually present, as in the case of Paul and Elymas (Acts 13:8–11). Against strong personal temptations believers have the shield of faith, and Yeshua's example of use of the word of God in faith is their guide (Eph 6:16; Luke 4:1–13).

Erroneous systems of belief are to be exposed for what they are—high things which exalt themselves against the knowledge of God—so that sinners may be saved, not crushed (2 Cor 10:5; Acts 19:18–20). The preaching of the gospel should be done in such a way as to minimize Satan's efforts to dissipate its effects. The deliverance of those oppressed or possessed of Satan may be through their believing the gospel (Luke 4:41), or it may require direct confrontation and casting out, which is a work of the Spirit (Matt 12:28). Paul's descriptions of the believer's armor and equipment for this warfare in Eph 6:1–17 and 1 Thess 5:8 are worthy of special study, never forgetting the importance of prayer (Eph 6:18–19; Jude 20).

(v) Holiness (Sanctification)

Without holiness, Hebrews reminds us, no one will see the Lord, and in theological writing the process of achieving holiness of character is termed "sanctification." There is no salvation without sanctification: "God from the beginning chose you for salvation through sanctification by the Spirit and belief of the truth" (2 Thess 2:13; see also 1 Thess 4:3); and God's purpose for believers now is a blameless life (1 Thess 5:23; Titus 2:12). This is a work of Messiah by his Spirit: "Christ also loved the church and gave Himself for her, that He might sanctify and cleanse her with the washing of water by the word" (Eph 5:25–26).

The word "sanctify" is also used in another way in Scripture, to indicate something set apart for a particular purpose: Jeremiah was set apart (sanctified) as a prophet; unbelieving spouses are sanctified by the faith of the believing spouse; all foods are acceptable when set apart by God's word and prayer; separation from sin sets apart a believer for usefulness in Messiah's service; and Messiah himself was set apart by God for his specific calling (Jer 1:5; 1 Cor 7:14; 1 Tim 4:5; 2 Tim 2:21; John 10:36). In the same way believers are set apart by God: "To those who are called, sanctified by God the Father, and preserved in Jesus Christ" (Jude 1, see also 1 Cor 1:2,

30; Heb 13:12). This is a once and for all act of God, similar to justification, by which the person whom God draws to his side is set apart once and for all for his purposes; they are no longer their own; they are bought with a price (1 Cor 6:19–20).

(a) Old and New Covenants

Both of these forms of sanctification are seen in the Old Testament. Israel was set apart to God in his purposes (Exod 13:2, 12), and Israelites were sanctified by personal obedience: "And you shall keep My statutes, and perform them: I am the LORD who sanctifies you" (Lev 20:8). These things came to fulfillment in believers under the new covenant, who are set apart in Messiah, the firstborn, and called to obedience (Col 1:18; 1 Pet 1:12). The great difference between the experiences under the covenants is the indwelling Spirit and union with Messiah under the new, leading to greater power to change, victory over sin, and certainty of salvation.

(b) The Spirit's Work in Sanctification

It is the Spirit's work to bring Messiah's people into conformity with God's will, revealed in his word, "that the righteous requirement of the law might be fulfilled in us who do not walk according to the flesh but according to the Spirit" (Rom 8:4). The fruits in the believer's life are detailed in Gal 5:22–25 and it is important to note that the first is love, which Scripture stresses as preeminent (2 Pet 1:7; 1 John 3:23; 4:7–11; 1 Cor 13:13). These fruits, or spiritual characteristics, are more than one-off acts of obedience because through them the Spirit produces lasting spiritual change in the believer's character: "But we all, with unveiled face, beholding as in a mirror the glory of the Lord, are being transformed into the same image from glory to glory, just as by the Spirit of the Lord" (2 Cor 3:18). This is not a change to their natural personality but to their spiritual character, and it is a change which cannot be lost, though it may be eclipsed for a while by unbelief. The means by which the Spirit does this is the word of God and the faith of the believer (2 Thess 2:13, see also John 17:17; Eph 5:26). It is a daily miracle of grace but it is one in which the believer must be fully cooperative such that, to paraphrase the great Jonathan Edwards, the believer does everything and God does everything.

The sanctifying work of the Spirit through the word is always related to the Lord Jesus: "He [the Spirit of Truth] will glorify Me, for He will take of what is Mine and declare it to you" (John 16:14). Believers are to model themselves on the man Christ Jesus, seeing his glory in the word and being molded into his image by the Spirit (Rom 8:29).

(c) Union with Messiah

A major way in which the New Testament presents sanctification is in terms of believers aspiring to live up to their new status through virtue of their union with Messiah Yeshua. Paul's personal testimony to this reality is expressed in Gal 2:19–20, where he declares his status as dead to the law through union with the crucified Messiah, and his daily life as one in which Christ lives in him, motivating him by the self-giving love of Calvary. Sanctification then is not a matter of keeping a list of dos and don'ts but of life in union with Yeshua by the Spirit. Paul's exhortation in Rom 6:1–14 best expresses how believers are to see themselves and to act accordingly. They are united to Messiah in his death and resurrection, and consequently should "reckon yourselves to be dead indeed to sin, but alive to God in Christ Jesus our Lord" (Rom 6:5, 11). Such reckoning is necessary because the believer's experience is different from their status. Their body is as yet unredeemed—Paul calls it the "body of sin" (Rom 6:6)—and is the seat of indwelling sin in thought, word, and deed, so the believer is caught up in a spiritual struggle, "so that you do not do the things that you wish" (Gal 5:17, see also Rom 7:14–25). The truth of union with Messiah ensures the sanctification is not simply a matter of doing better but of believers living up to who they are in Messiah.

Misunderstanding can arise due to Paul's twofold use of the expression "old man." In Rom 6:6 the believer's old man "was crucified with Him" but in Eph 4:22 and Col 3:9 the old man is something the believer puts off; this sounds contradictory. However, this twofold use expresses the same reality of a believer being what they are in Messiah. In Rom 6:6 the expression "our old man was crucified with Him" is referring to their status, the death of their relationship to Adam (something extensively discussed in Rom 5:12–21), such that the believer is out of the Adamic realm of sin and death. However, because indwelling sin remains there is a struggle to put off the behavior patterns belonging to sin and death and put on Messiah-like ways. Some translations use the expressions "new nature" or "new self" rather than "new man" but this is unhelpful insofar as those expressions fail to focus upon the reality that the believer is no longer in the first man, Adam, but is now in the second man, Yeshua (1 Cor 15:47).

(d) The Experience of Sanctification

- *Sanctification is a growth process, one of gradual spiritual change throughout life.* Believers are renewed day by day, transformed by the renewing of their minds; they add one grace to another, and are continually washed by God's word, growing from "little children" to "young men" to "fathers" as in 1 John 2:12–14 (see also 2 Cor 4:16; Rom 12:2; 2 Pet 1:5–7; Eph 5:26). They will fail but there is forgiveness and renewal (Ps 51; Hos 14:1–8; Luke 22:31–32; 2 Cor 7:10–11). Confusion is sometimes caused by a teaching which understands being filled with the Spirit as an experience which takes believers to a new level of obedience and Christian living. There is no doubt that believers may undergo crisis experiences for a variety of reasons, such as deep conviction of sin or when caused to consider a challenging form of service, or as part of a particular trial, but Scripture does not encourage believers to seek a crisis experience which puts them in a new realm of Christian living.

- *Sanctification is not little more than a defeatist struggle against sin.* It is indeed a struggle, and there will be failure, but it is one in which victory can and will be known, "For whatever is born of God overcomes the world. And this is the victory that has overcome the world—our faith" (1 John 5:4; see also Rev 15:2). Peter writes glowingly of the power and promises that enable believers to become partakers of the divine nature, and Paul gives encouragement to walk in the Spirit and so not fulfill the lusts of the flesh; Jude encourages believers to be built up in the faith walking in God's love, and Paul encourages to follow his example and press on in hope of the coming perfection (2 Pet 1:3–4; Gal 5:6–18; Jude 20–21; Phil 3:12–16). Although believers should aim at perfection (Matt 5:48) and God has made provision that they need not sin (1 Cor 10:13), there is no sense from such passages that believers can attain what is called "sinless perfection." Both 1 John 1:8 and Phil 3:12 deny such a possibility, but believers should strive for a level of maturity described as "blameless and harmless" (Phil 2:15). First Timothy 3:2 gives an idea of what these words mean. Such a believer has a clean conscience before God, a soul at peace, a mind not tossed about by every wind of doctrine, a manner marked by self-control and governed by love for God and other people. There will be failures but when they occur will be readily confessed.

- *Sanctification is a warfare.* This warfare has been dealt with extensively in the preceding section and the Spirit uses this form of the struggle to change us more into Messiah's image.
- *Sanctification occurs primarily in the context of church life.* The New Testament focus is on life together and growth together; believers are being "built together for a dwelling place of God in the Spirit" (Eph 2:22). Most of the New Testament exhortations to holy living are in terms of how believers relate to "one another"; they are to love, receive, admonish, serve, forebear, forgive, edify, and exhort one another (John 15:12; Rom 15:7,1; Gal 5:13; Col 3:13; 1 Thess 5:11; Heb 3:13). Church life is God's means to grow in love, and difficulties play their part.

(vi) Service and Witness

All believers are called to *service* in the body of Messiah, to use their natural and spiritual gifts aided by the Spirit for the benefit of all; they depend on him for guidance, wisdom, strength, and authority. The description of the men chosen to serve in Acts 6 ought to be true for any believer contemplating some form of responsible service in the church: "of good reputation, full of the Holy Spirit and wisdom." Messiah himself was prophesied to be equipped by the Spirit to heal the brokenhearted, grant liberty to captives, and make them into righteous disciples so that they in turn might work together as "servants of our God" to rebuild God's people (Isa 61:17). This is fulfilled by believers in Jesus, who have received the promised Spirit and are called to "serve in newness of the Spirit and not in the oldness of the letter" (Rom 7:6; Isa 59:21; Joel 2:28–29; Gal 3:14; Eph 4:15–16). This is the great hallmark of the new covenant (2 Cor 3:6). Service is not a drudgery, and it is more than a duty; it is a source of joy (Col 1:10–11).

The gospel *witness* of the first believers was marked by boldness. This was not due to a maturity in faith and years of experience because most were spiritual babes, only just started on the pathway of sanctification; it was because of the empowering they had received from the Spirit. Yeshua instructed the apostles not to leave Jerusalem "until you are endued with power from on high" (Luke 24:49) and this was directly connected to their task of being witnesses in Jerusalem, Judea, Samaria, and to the end of the earth (Acts 1:8; Luke 24:48). This promise was fulfilled on the Day of Pentecost and the scriptural terminology for this empowering, as discussed above in the section on assurance, is being "baptized with the Spirit" and also being "filled with the Spirit" (Acts 1:5; 2:4). Their boldness was plain to see in

Peter's first sermon and the authorities recognized it (Acts 2:36–40; 4:13). All believers are in need of such boldness from the Spirit's empowering. It may be granted at conversion but is more usually something subsequent and, as in Acts, may be repeated. It was something for which Paul frequently requested prayer (Eph 6:18–19; 2 Thess 3:1).

(vii) Perseverance

It is difficult for a believer to be bold and joyful if they are in fear of losing their salvation. Hence Satan has attacked the doctrine of perseverance—that a regenerate person cannot lose their salvation—which has led to confusion and disagreement among God's people. But Scripture is clear that once a person puts their trust in the Savior and is born again they cannot be lost; a teaching which is closely connected to other doctrines which have been discussed already. For example, God has chosen and predestined a people as his sons, to be in the image of his Son; he has purchased them through the blood of the Savior and will bring them to their promised inheritance (Eph 1:3–14). God justifies those who believe and has promised not to remember their sins (Rom 5:1, 9; Jer 31:31–34). He has brought them into an unbreakable spiritual union with his beloved son (Col 3:1–4), and his indwelling Spirit will as surely raise them from the dead as he raised Messiah Jesus (Rom 8:11). Paul brings all these things together as he exults in the certainty believers have due to God's immutable purpose, ranging from his foreknowledge of them to their final glorification (Rom 8:28–30). He follows this with a review of all the forces which might thwart this grand purpose of God and concludes they are all impotent (Rom 8:31–39). Other texts which should be considered are: Isa 59:21; Ps 23:6; John 6:37; 10:27–29; 17:11, 20–24; Phil 1:6; 1 Pet 1:5.

Difficulty is created by texts which appear to imply a saved person can lose their salvation. Because believers are still in the flesh and the sinful nature is yet with them, the New Testament is full of warnings and exhortations to faithfulness, for example: "Abide in Me, and I in you" (John 15:4) and "Do not be deceived, God is not mocked; for whatever a man sows, that he will also reap" (Gal 6:7). Such are exhortations to faithfulness; they do not teach salvation can be lost.

However, some of those exhortations are not of a general nature but addressed to those whose behavior gives cause to doubt they are truly converted: "Examine yourselves as to whether you are in the faith. Test yourselves. Do you not know yourselves, that Jesus Christ is in you?—unless indeed you are disqualified" (2 Cor 13:5; see also 1 Cor 15:34; Gal 4:10–11,

20). Again, such texts should not be taken to imply salvation can be lost, but to state that a person may be self-deceived and needs a strong warning. Jesus said there would be many such: "Many will say to Me in that day, 'Lord, Lord, have we not prophesied in Your name'... I will declare to them, 'I never knew you'" (Matt 7:22–23; see also Matt 13:18–23; John 15:6; Phil 3:18–19; 2 Pet 2).

And then there are texts which are warnings to believers who are showing signs of wavering and in need of a firm exhortation: "if indeed you continue in the faith, grounded and steadfast, and are not moved away from the hope of the gospel" (Col 1:23, see also 1 Tim 6:20–21; Heb 2:1–3). Such exhortations warn that it is not enough to have made a profession of faith but there must be a continuing in what was first believed to show that the profession is genuine. Paul sums up all these exhortations: "'The Lord knows those who are His,' and, 'Let everyone who names the name of Christ depart from iniquity'" (2 Tim 2:19; see also 2 Pet 1:10). There is no doubt in God's mind whom he has set apart to salvation but for believers to be sure that they are among the saved they must turn from evil.

However, there are some texts which appear to clearly teach loss of salvation, for example Heb 6:4–6 and 10:26–27, but they should be viewed as the strongest versions of the type of warnings indicated in the preceding paragraph. They are addressed to people who, having made a profession of faith, are on the brink of repudiating Yeshua's salvation altogether. Any who took such a step could only be viewed as those who were false believers, as per Matt 7:22–23. Such would not be wayward or backsliders but those who publicly repudiated what they once believed. Such a step is seen as irreversible by the author of Hebrews because it is much more than a thoughtless rejection of the gospel; it is a repudiation of much Spirit-given blessing under the sound of the gospel, yet blessing which fell short of regeneration.

What causes confusion is that the terminology used in these verses of Hebrews seems to describe true believers. However, closer examination shows that not to be so. The description in Heb 6:4–8 is followed by the words "But, beloved, we are confident of better things concerning you, yes, things that accompany salvation, though we speak in this manner" (Heb 6:9). That is, the description in verses 4–6 falls short of true conversion. It is a description that would fit well for someone like Judas Iscariot, who had seen and tasted much of the powers of the world to come but whose life only bore "thorns and briers" (Heb 6:8). The warnings in Heb 10:26–27 and John 15:6 are in the same category as those of Heb 6.

It is a work of the Spirit to ensure believers persevere in faith and obedience: "I will put My Spirit within you and cause you to walk in My statutes, and you will keep my judgments and do them" (Ezek 36:27). He is the

The Work of the Holy Spirit in Our Salvation   237

one who enables believers to be strong in the Lord, use the word of God to stand firm, pray effectively, and persevere (Eph 6:10, 17–18; Gal 6:8). Other texts speak of God's power to keep his people: "being confident of this very thing, that He who has begun a good work in you will complete it until the day of Jesus Christ" (Phil 1:6; see also 2 Tim 1:12; 4:18; 1 Pet 1:5; Rev 2:7).

As previously mentioned, the Spirit is rarely referred to in any form of Judaism. Likewise, liberal forms of Christianity have little to say of his activities because the whole area of the supernatural is something which liberalism downplays. In Roman Catholicism and Orthodoxy his work is honored; however it is misunderstood because it is said to commence in an individual by regeneration and union with Christ at their baptism as an infant. It is then a lifelong experience, through the ministry of the church, to grow in faith by the aid of the Spirit. Their error is to divorce the commencement of the Spirit's saving and sanctifying work from the exercise of faith.

(C) THE SPIRIT AND THE LIFE TO COME

The gift of the Spirit to all God's people is a mark of the messianic era, the inauguration of the kingdom of God: "I will pour out My Spirit on all flesh" (Joel 2:28; see also Isa 59:21; Ezek 36:24–27). It is a kingdom which was inaugurated by Messiah Yeshua and will be consummated at his return. The Spirit's indwelling is seen as a guarantee of our future building from God, our resurrection body (2 Cor 5:1–5), and it is the Spirit who raises the body of believers from the dead, completing their redemption: "But if the Spirit of Him who raised Jesus from the dead dwells in you, He who raised Christ from the dead will also give life to your mortal bodies through His Spirit who dwells in you" (Rom 8:11, 23; Eph 1:13–14; Rev 11:11–12). This resurrection body is also described as a glorious body, one like the glorified body of Yeshua, fit for the glory of the world to come (Phil 3:21; 1 Cor 15:43). Another description is a spiritual body, one which is incorruptible, powerful, and under the control of the Spirit and spiritual in nature (1 Cor 15:42–49). Yeshua's resurrection appearances give us an idea of what this will be like.

The Spirit's work within believers is also spoken of as a "firstfruits" (Rom 8:23), so that what they experience now is a foretaste of his work in them in the world to come—all that he does now he will do in greater measure then: greater holiness, love, understanding, wisdom, oneness, praise, joy, and righteousness. Similarly, Hebrews describes this firstfruits as a taste of "the powers of the age to come" (Heb 6:5). It is also a work of the Spirit to ensure that the works believers have done follow them; i.e., they receive a reward (Rev 14:13). It should be noted that the indwelling of the Spirit is not only described in individual terms but also corporately: the totality of all believers are a "dwelling place of God in the Spirit"; they are "a holy temple in the Lord" (Eph 2:21–22; 1 Pet 2:5). This is forever. It is in the context of praying for this perfect oneness that Yeshua also prays, "that they also whom You gave Me may be with Me where I am, that they may behold My glory which You have given me" (John 17:24). What is seen now is a pale reflection of what will one day be seen face to face. Finally, it is the Spirit who encourages within believers a longing for that day: "And the Spirit and the bride say, 'Come!'" (Rev 22:17). Amen!

> Blessed be the God and Father of our Lord Jesus Christ, who according to His abundant mercy has begotten us again to a living hope through the resurrection of Jesus Christ from the dead, to an inheritance incorruptible and undefiled and that does not fade away, reserved in heaven for you, who are kept by the power of God through faith for salvation ready to be revealed in the last time. (1 Pet 1:3–5)

Scriptures

Life in the Spirit

General: Rom 5:10; 8:9, 14; Gal 5:1, 5, 25.

Knowing and abiding in God's love: John 15:4–5; Eph 3:14–21; 2 Pet 1:5–8; 3:18; 1 John 2:24–28; 3:16.

Assurance: *Of faith*: Luke 7:50; Acts 2:41–47; 1 John 5:6, 10. *Cleansing and renewal*: John 3:3; Heb 10:22; Titus 3:5. *Owned and adopted*: Rom 8:15; Eph 1:13. *Life evidences*: Jas 2:18; 1 John 2:19–20, 23; 5:1–3; 3:19; 5:4. *Inner witness*: Acts 1:5, 8; 2:4, 33; 4:31; 8:14–17; 9:17; 19:1–6; Rom 5:5; Eph 5:18–19; 1 Pet 1:8; 1 John 1:4; 3:24; 4:13; 5:10. *God's word*: 1 John 2:14 "young men."

Hope: Rom 5:5; Gal 5:5; Eph 1:14, 18; Col 1:27; 1 Pet 1:3; 4:12.

Spiritual warfare: Job 1–2; Dan 10:13—11:1; Matt 12:28; 13:19; Luke 4:1–13; 13:16; John 13:27; Acts 16:16–18; 19:18–20; 2 Cor 10:3–5; Eph 6:10–19; 1 Thess 5:8; 1 Tim 6:12; 4:1–5; 1 John 2:13–14; 18–27; 5:19; Jude 20; Rev 12:17; 13; 19:11; 20:78.

Holiness: Exod 13:2, 12; Lev 20:78; Jer 1:5; John 10:36; 17:17; 16:14; Rom 8:4, 13–14, 29; 1 Cor 1:2, 30; 6:19–20; 7:14; 13:13; 2 Cor 3:18; Gal 5:22–25; Eph 5:26; Col 1:18; 2 Thess 2:13; 5:23; 1 Tim 4:5; 2 Tim 2:21; Titus 2:12; Heb 12:14; 13:12; 1 Pet 1:12; 2 Pet 1:7; Jude 1; 1 John 3:23; 4:7–11.

Union with Messiah: Rom 6:1–14; 7:14–25; 1 Cor 15:47; Gal 2:19–20; 5:17; Eph 4:22; Col 3:9.

Experience of sanctification: *Growth*: Ps 51; Hos 14:1–8; Luke 22:31–32; Rom 12:2; 2 Cor 4:16; 7:10–11; Eph 5:26; 2 Pet 1:5–7; 1 John 2:12–14. *Victory*: Matt 5:48; 1 Cor 10:13; Gal 5:6–18; Phil 2:15; 3:12–16; 1 Tim 3:2; 2 Pet 1:3–4; 1 John 1:8; 5:4; Jude 20–21; Rev 15:2. *Church life*: Eph 2:22; John 15:12; Rom 15:7, 11; Gal 5:16–26; Col 3:13; 1 Thess 5:11; Heb 3:13; Eph 4:3.

Service and witness: *Service*: Isa 61:1–7; 59:21; Joel 2:28–29; Acts 6:3; 2 Cor 3:6; Gal 3:14; Eph 4:15–16; Col 1:10–11. *Witness*: Luke 24:49; Acts 1:8, 5, 14; 2:4, 36–40; 4:13, 23, 31; 8:4; Eph 6:18–19; 2 Thess 3:1.

Perseverance: Ps 23:6; Isa 59:21; Jer 31:31–34; Ezek 36:27; Matt 7:22–23; John 6:37; 10:27–29; 15:4; 17:11, 20–24; Rom 5:1, 9; 8:11, 28–30, 31–39; 1 Cor 15:34; 2 Cor 13:5; Gal 4:10–11, 20; 6:7, 8; Eph 1:3–14; 6:10, 17–18; Phil 1:6; 3:18–19; Col 1:23; 3:1–4; 2 Tim 1:12; 2:19; 4:18; Heb 6:4–6, 9; 10:26–27; 1 Pet 1:5; Rev 2:7.

The Spirit and the Life to Come

John 17:24; 1 Cor 15:42–49; 2 Cor 5:1–5; Rom 8:11, 23; Eph 1:13–14; 2:22; Phil 3:21; Heb 6:5; 1 Pet 2:5; Rev 11:11–12; 14:13; 22:17.

QUESTIONS

1. What is life in the Spirit, and how does it compare with life under the law within the old covenant? Take special note of Paul's teaching in Rom 8 in your answer.
2. What is sanctification and how is it brought about?
3. Is the "old man" dead or alive?
4. How would you guide and encourage a believer who was uncertain of their salvation?
5. What is meant by being baptized with the Spirit?
6. Is "once saved, always saved" a teaching of Scripture? Discuss the difficulties.
7. How has the Holy Spirit led you in your service of Messiah?
8. What is the Christian hope and what is its relevance for Christian living?

Further Reading

Berkouwer, G. C. *Faith and Perseverance*. Grand Rapids: Eerdmans, 1958.
Bridges, Jerry. *The Practice of Godliness*. Colorado Springs, CO: NavPress, 2016.
Ferguson, Sinclair B. *The Christian Life*. Edinburgh: Banner of Truth, 2013.
———. *The Holy Spirit*. Leicester: InterVarsity, 1996.
———. *Maturity*. Edinburgh: Banner of Truth, 2020.
Gale, Stanley D. *What Is Spiritual Warfare?* Sanford, FL: Ligonier Ministries, 2012.
Gibbs, Eddie, and Brian Draper. *Way to Serve*. Leicester: InterVarsity, 2003.
Lloyd-Jones, D. M. *The Christian Soldier*. Edinburgh: Banner of Truth, 1977.
———. *The Christian Warfare*. Edinburgh: Banner of Truth, 1976.
———. *The Law: Its Functions and Limits*. Edinburgh: Banner of Truth, 1973.
———. *Romans: An Exposition of Chapter 5: Assurance*. Edinburgh: Banner of Truth, 1971.
———. *Romans: An Exposition of Chapter 6: The New Man*. Edinburgh: Banner of Truth, 1972.
———. *Romans: An Exposition of Chapter 8:17–39: The Final Perseverance of the Saints*. Edinburgh: Banner of Truth, 1975.
———. *The Sons of God*. Edinburgh: Banner of Truth, 1974.
Milton, Michael A. *What Is the Perseverance of the Saints?* Phillipsburg: Presbyterian and Reformed, 2019.
Ryle, J. C. *Holiness*. Apollo, PA: Ichthus, 2017.
Sproul, R. C. *The Assurance of Salvation*. Sanford, FL: Ligonier Ministries, 2018.
Stott, John R. W. *The Contemporary Christian*. Leicester: InterVarsity, 1992.

ו

PART 6

God's People

28

God's One People

ALL THOSE REDEEMED FROM sin since the fall of Adam and Eve in the Garden of Eden are one people. They are all saved by Messiah's sacrificial death (Rev 7:14–17; Rom 3:23–24; Heb 9:15), and they will make up one people in the new heavens and the new earth (John 17:23–24). Their lives on earth may look different because of the different periods and covenants in which they lived, but their unity is seen by God's work in them: bringing them to repentance and faith in the sacrifice he provides, regenerating them, creating a new nature without which they cannot obey God, leading them into a righteous life involving obedience to his commands and love for one another and their fellow humans, and bringing them into ever closer trust and fellowship with him.

The term "covenants of grace" is frequently used as an overarching term which encompasses all the promises and covenants after the fall. It is a term intended to point to the essential oneness of God's dealings under all the covenants, in that all of them find their origins in his gracious initiative and operation; as Paul wrote, "Therefore it is of faith that it might be according to grace" (Rom 4:16). All God's gracious covenants and promises are a consequence of what is sometimes called the "covenant of redemption," a term used to describe the deliberation within the Godhead before the foundation of the world by which the Father chose a people for salvation in his Son and for his Son (Eph 1:3–4; John 17:10), sending the Son to redeem them (John 10:18; 14:31; 17:2, 4, 6, 8, 18), and the Son submitted to the Father's will out of love to him (John 10:18; 14:31). A quick overview of the promises and covenants will underline their grand unity in God's gracious initiative.

After their disobedience, and despite their failure to repent, Adam and Eve received God's promise of a deliverer for all their descendants (Gen 3:15), and he graciously provided a covering for them (Gen 3:21). The flood brought both judgment and a fresh covenant promise for all the world, and it was based on grace shown to one man: "But Noah found grace in the eyes of the LORD" (Gen 6:8). God intervened in Abram's life while he was lost in the idolatry of the Chaldeans (Josh 24:22) and made abundant promises to him (Gen 12:1–3), sealed in covenants; it was all of grace. The LORD broke into Moses' life, revealing himself at the burning bush, and then using him to deliver Israel, making a covenant with them at Sinai. Moses understood this was all of grace to him and to Israel: "For how then will it be known that Your people and I have found grace in Your sight, except You go with us?" (Exod 33:16). The Mosaic law was founded on grace. Messiah's new covenant was inaugurated by the One who was "full of grace and truth" (John 1:14), and the apostle Peter sums it up as "the true grace of God in which you stand" (1 Pet 5:12).

None of this is meant to undermine the importance of the obedience of those who receive God's mercy and grace, in whatever age they lived. If there is no obedience, there is no trust and no grace. It is sad to see how traditional Judaism has lost sight of "by grace alone." It does not neglect our need of God's grace and mercy, but it gives a place to our works in salvation. For example, the story in the midrash of Abram destroying idols after discovering for himself that there was only one God is pure fiction and denies grace. Judaism does indeed teach a hope for all the world, but the main focus is on Israel and there is no emphasis on an equality for Jew and Gentile. Even the early Jewish believers in Yeshua seemed to lack this vision and struggled with Gentiles being included (Acts 11:18).

Scripture contains many images and metaphors for God's people, which we will refer to as we proceed. Those which are more appropriate to the oneness of God's people through the ages are:

- *a people* (Exod 6:7; Matt 1:21; 1 Pet 2:9–10; 2 Cor 6:16);
- *a family* (Gen 4:26—5:32; 17:7–8; Amos 3:2; Hos 11:1; Gal 4:7; John 11:52; Eph 3:14–15);
- *a kingdom* (Exod 19:6; 1 Chr 17:11–14; Eph 2:19 "citizens"; Col 1:13).

Paul's unique image of God's people as an *olive tree* (Rom 11:16-24) shows their unity across the Mosaic and new covenants, and will be explored later.

29

Israel under the Mosaic Covenant

WHAT GOD DID FOR Abraham, Isaac, and Jacob as a family he did for their descendants as a people under Moses. He delivered them from a great oppressor, gave them his law, separated them from the nations into their own land, provided a means of approach to him, and revealed to them a great future hope.

Certain images of God's people are especially appropriate to this period. The family, people, and kingdom metaphors become more concrete. Added to them is the thought of Israel being a kingdom of priests: "And you shall be to Me a kingdom of priests and a holy nation" (Exod 19:6). There was an anointed priesthood of Levi, but this expression "kingdom of priests" points to God's goal that all his people should know him and offer praise and intercession to him. Israel was likened to a vineyard (Isa 5:1–7); she was to bear fruits of holiness and righteousness to YHWH. She is also likened to a beloved, a bride (Deut 33:12; Ps 60:5; Jer 11:15; Hos 2:16, 19; Ezek 16:7–8; Song 5:1, 6:3), and a dwelling place for God (Exod 25:8–9; Ps 132:13–14; 2 Chr 5:7—6:2).

(A) NATIONAL LIFE

The law was given through Moses so that every area of life was regulated, guiding God's people into just and compassionate ways of living. It was the task of the Levites to teach the law and give judgments (Mal 2:4–7; Deut 17:8–9) and the role of prophets to call Israel back to obedience and give further revelation. No Israelite was left in ignorance. There were gatherings throughout the land which undoubtedly promoted understanding (Ps 74:8) and were especially seen in Ezra's days and subsequently (Neh 8:1–12).

God provided a place of worship where Israel could approach him in praise and intercession and this was a national event at the three festivals: Pesach, Shavuot, and Sukkot. The sacrificial system was designed to enable the sinner to approach in repentance and confession (sin offering), to dedicate themselves wholeheartedly to God (burnt offering) and enjoy a fellowship meal with God and one another (peace offering and various free will offerings). The words of the Tehillim enabled them to express in word and song a whole range of human spiritual emotion.

Israel was not exclusively Jewish; "strangers" were welcome: "The stranger who dwells among you shall be to you as one born among you, and you shall love him as yourself" (Lev 19:34). They were welcome to enter the covenant through circumcision and, for example, to celebrate Pesach (Exod 12:48). Israelites who committed gross sin were to be put to death or banished (Lev 17:10; 20:3). Israel was to be a holy people and outsiders who loved righteousness were welcome, and insiders who did not might be expelled.

(B) INDIVIDUAL LIFE

Israel's national life could never be what it was meant to be unless individuals were holy people. In the Mosaic covenant, YHWH promised the two things most basic to holiness: forgiveness of sin and a new heart. The sinner was encouraged to bring a sacrifice, confess his sins over it, and kill it, and the priest sprinkled its blood before God. God's promise was "so the priest shall make atonement for him before the Lord, and he shall be forgiven" (Lev 6:7). Many, like David, experienced this knowledge of sins forgiven: "I said 'I will confess my transgressions to the Lord,' and You forgave the iniquity of my sin . . . Be glad in the Lord and rejoice, you righteous" (Ps 32:5, 11).

YHWH indicated the need for spiritual change in the *brit*—something had to be removed to be one of his people. Moshe's call to Israel in Deut 10:16, "circumcise the foreskin of your heart, and be stiff-necked no longer," whilst it was a call to them to live up to their responsibilities, it also clearly indicated the need for an inner, spiritual change. Later, Moses revealed God's promise to do this for them: "the Lord your God will circumcise your heart" (Deut 30:6). This is not a specific promise of the new covenant, although that covenant's promise of a new heart is surely included; rather it is a general promise of spiritual blessing after they return from any chastising banishment among the nations.

Solomon's prayer at the dedication of the temple includes a petition for God to restore to their land any taken captive by Israel's enemies when they turn back to him; a prayer which is surely based on these words of Moshe in Deut 30:10 (see 1 Kgs 8:46–53). The core of this promise of God is to bring them back and give them a new heart. This was especially so after the return from Babylon and both Jeremiah and Ezekiel refer to it: "I will bring them back to this land . . . I will give them a heart to know me" (Jer 24:6–7), and "I will gather them from the peoples . . . I will give them one heart, and I will put a new spirit within them" (Ezek 11:17–19). This can especially be seen in the renewal and revival which took place under Ezra's ministry (see Neh 8). Yeshua expected Nicodemus to know of this need for a divine renewal: "Are you a teacher of Israel, and do not know these things" (John 3:10). The major difference from the new covenant is the lack of the indwelling Spirit, but his work of forgiveness, regeneration, and sanctification was the same in essence.

In the Tanakh and the NT we have accounts of the life of faith of ordinary people in Israel which demonstrate their awareness of acceptance, and of having a heart for God. For example: the story of Ruth and Boaz, the life and prayer of Hanna (1 Sam 1—2:10), the gracious wisdom of Abigail (1 Sam 25:14–34); and in the NT (but really under the Mosaic covenant) the upright and gracious Joseph, the submissive Mary (Matt 1:19, Luke 1:38), and the hope-filled Zachariah, Simeon, and Anna (Luke 1:67–79; 2:25–32, 36–38).

(C) THE FUNCTION OF THE LAW

What often causes confusion regarding the life of God's people under Moses' law is the teaching about the law in the New Testament, especially in Paul's writings. Paul appears to be predominantly negative, but that is because he was so often dealing with those who placed a wrong emphasis on law-keeping, yet his teaching is multifaceted. This perception of Paul's teaching as negative has led many Christians to a predominantly negative view of Israel under the old covenant, one characterized by legalism and failure. What were the different facets of the teaching?

(i) Law-Keeping Cannot Save

"Your faith has saved you" is a frequent phrase of Yeshua to a healed person, a phrase designed to counter the prevailing belief that people received good in this life because they were good; i.e., they kept the law (see Luke 7:3–5). Paul sought to counter a similar mentality in his preaching: "by Him everyone who believes is justified from all things from which you could not be justified by the law of Moses" (Acts 13:39). Gentile Christians who had started keeping the law were condemned: "You have become estranged from Christ, you who attempt to be justified by law" (Gal 5:4).

(ii) The Law Makes Things Worse

The law actually makes our condition worse due to sin's sinfulness: "But sin, taking opportunity by the commandment, produced in me all manner of evil desire" (Rom 7:8; see also 7:5).

(iii) The Law a Period of Childhood

Because of this power of sin, the law was seen as a period of childhood for God's people, acting as a strong restraint (Gal 4:1–5).

(iv) The Law Not a Better Way for Christians

Believers in Colosse who saw spiritual value in submitting to the regulations of the law were told, "These things indeed have an appearance of wisdom in self-imposed religion, false humility, and neglect of the body, but are of no value against the indulgence of the flesh" (Col 2:23, see also 2:16–23). Those who focused on the details of the law were rebuked by Paul (1 Tim 1:3–7; Titus 1:13–14).

(v) The Law a Privilege

Possessing God's law was a privilege for Israel according to Paul (Rom 3:1–2), adding in Rom 7:12, "the law is holy, and the commandment holy and just and good," and in Rom 7:22 he declares his own delight in it. The law was good in that it produced conviction of sin, "But the Scripture has confined all under sin . . . the law was our tutor to bring us to Christ" (Gal 3:22, 24; see also 3:19–25). Despite the law's powerlessness to save it had glory, "the ministry of death, written and engraved on stones, was glorious" (2 Cor 3:7; see also 3:7–18).

(vi) The Law Emphasized Faith

The law taught that true obedience required faith in the heart: "the righteousness of faith speaks in this way . . . 'The word is near you, in your mouth and in your heart' (that is, the word of faith which we preach)" (Rom 10:6, 8; quoting Deut 30:14).

(vii) The Law Is to Be Valued under the New Covenant

According to Paul in Rom 8:4 the law continues to have value under the new covenant, where he underlines that the aim of the gospel is "that the righteous requirement of the law might be fulfilled in us"; the righteous requirement being the spiritual principle in the law's regulations, not the legal requirement itself.

(D) WEAKNESS AND PREPARATION

The Mosaic covenant was not an end in itself but a means to an end—the coming of Messiah and the new covenant. Because it was a preparatory period it was marked by weakness and frequent failure (e.g., Judg 2:11–23; 2 Chr 36:15–21) but there were times of revival and restoration (2 Chr 14–15) and there was always a faithful remnant (Isa 1:9). Not only did many come to a living faith under the Mosaic covenant, but God's sovereign and gracious work of preparation meant that many in Israel received his Son when he came among them, and through that the world began to hear.

> Great is the LORD, and greatly to be praised;
> And His greatness is unsearchable.
> One generation shall praise Your works to another,
> And shall declare Your mighty acts. (Ps 145:3–4)

Scriptures

God's one people: Gen 3:15; Matt 25:34; John 3:3–6; 10:14–16; Rom 4:1–12; 5:18–19; Gal 5:4; Eph 1:6; 2:5; Heb 9:22; 11:16; 12:14; Rev 17:8; 20:15.

Spiritual life under the Mosaic law: *Provision*: Ps 37:25. *Fear of the* LORD: Ps 111:10. *Imputed righteousness*: Pss 24:5; 22:1–2; Isa 61:10. *Atonement and sin forgiven*: Deut 32:43; Pss 85:2; 86:5; Dan 9:19. *Prayer and communion with God*: Pss 5:2; 24:3–4; 55:17. *Confession and repentance*: Pss 32:5; 51:1–9. *Blessing of a godly life*: Ps 1:1–3. *Rejoicing*: Pss 21:1; 35:9; 108:7. *Love of God's word*: Ps 19; 97; 105; 119:18. *Trust in God*: Ps 115:9–11. *Heart religion*: Pss 10:17; 13:5; 17:3; 27:8. *Delight in God*: Ps 37:4. *Walking in God's ways*: Ps 25:4–5. *Examined by God*: Ps 139. *Integrity*: Ps 25:21. *Led and taught by God*: Ps 23:3; 86:11; Isa 30:21. *Careful speech*: Ps 141:3. *Refuge in trouble*: Ps 46.

Grace under the Mosaic law: Exod 33:19; Ps 84:11; Isa 33:2.

QUESTIONS

1. What truths help us to see the essential unity of God's believing people throughout human history?

2. What were Israel's privileges under the Mosaic covenant? Answer with reference to the general condition of the Gentile nations.

3. Imagine yourself living under the Mosaic covenant; write an account of coming to repentance and saving faith, and of living a righteous lifestyle under the law. Try to use the main elements of your own journey to faith in your account.

FURTHER READING

Barton Payne, J. *The Theology of the Older Testament*. London: Hodder & Stoughton, 1973.

Kaiser, Walter C., Jr. *Toward an Old Testament Theology*. Grand Rapids: Zondervan, 1978.

McComiskey, Thomas E. *The Covenants of Promise*. Leicester: InterVarsity, 1985.

30

Messiah's People of the New Covenant

THERE IS NO GREATER privilege than to be a part of the people of God's Son, Messiah Jesus. It is one which brings Jew and Gentile together in a way as nothing else can. It is a way of life which must be lived out corporately as believers in Messiah trust Yeshua and serve him together in this world.

Whilst the new covenant heralds a new day for God's people, it has the same basic aim for them as under all covenants—to equip them for life with God forever, to prepare them for glory. There is no greater privilege and no better covenant to live under—Messiah in the hearts of his people, the hope of glory.

(A) DEVELOPMENT IN THE NEW TESTAMENT

It needs to be remembered that the New Testament writings do not begin with a full-fledged picture of Messiah's new covenant people, the church; there is development in the pages of the New Testament. The story begins with Yeshua being born under the law and ministering to Israel under the law. The earliest days of the church after Yeshua's ascension are set in the land of Israel, a land where the law of Moses regulated much of daily life. As the gospel goes out to the nations, local assemblies of believers are formed, composed of a cross section of the societies in which they were set, including Jews in many places. To begin with, the presence of the apostles provided leadership and bound the new churches together, but later, when they had passed on, their letters provided teaching on how the churches were to function in their absence. In all this development, one great uniting factor is plain: Yeshua present among his people. The New Testament closes with a vision in Revelation of Jesus in glory, standing among seven individual candlesticks. Israel's menorah represented God's sevenfold light of truth shining forth among his people in one location—it was one candlestick; the seven candlesticks of Revelation represent the light of the world located among his people scattered throughout the world.

(B) NEW TESTAMENT TERMS FOR GOD'S PEOPLE

There are three Greek words used to refer to God's new covenant people, whether as a local group or in their entirety. By far the most frequent is *ekklesia*, translated "church." It is a word used by the Septuagint for the Hebrew word *qahal*, usually translated "congregation" or "assembly" and meaning a gathering called together, or called out (see Exod 35:1; 2 Chr 20:3–5). As God called Israel to himself from out of Egypt, so the church is called out of the world to Messiah (1 Cor 1:9). One of the first translations of the Bible into English, by William Tyndale (1524), had *ekklesia* consistently translated as "congregation," thus focusing on the people. The later English word "church" is derived from the Greek *kuriakon*, meaning "the Lord's," but with the thought of it being the Lord's house. The focus thus shifted to include the building and the hierarchy of the church (curia). This has been unhelpful because it fails to focus on the people. The simple Greek term for an assembly or gathering is *sunagoge* and it is used once of a church in Jas 2:2, and in its verbal form in Heb 10:25 (see also Acts 11:26). Both James and Hebrews use the word *ekklesia* in referring to the church (Jas 5:14, Heb 12:23), so there is no suggestion they were avoiding it. It is understandable that the terms *ekklesia* and *sunagoge* might have been used alongside each other in the early days, although we only have this one instance of it in the NT, but it is probable that *sunagoge* was dropped as the tensions between the churches and the synagogues increased. The source of that tension, belief in Jesus the Messiah, remains. The Greek word *paneguris* is used in Heb 12:23 and is translated "the general assembly" or just "assembly" and seems to refer to the entire new covenant people of God.

(C) NEW TESTAMENT IMAGES OF THE CHURCH

Almost all of the images of the church found in the New Testament are carried over from the Old Testament, underlining that the new fulfills the old—it is not a fresh start which ignores the past. Two images are new: the body of Christ and the olive tree. Each image teaches a truth about God's people under the new covenant, but no one image is the whole picture; for that they need to be viewed together.

(i) The People of God

The fundamental of all covenants is: *I am your God, you are my people* (see Exod 6:7), and is used of the church by Peter—"His own special people" (1 Pet 2:9)—and by Paul (Titus 2:14). No one can claim this status but it depends upon God's call. He called Israel to himself (Exod 19:4), Jesus called his disciples to follow him (Matt 4:19, 9:9) and his apostles called Jew and Gentile to become disciples of Messiah (Acts 2:39), so that Paul actually describes believers as the called, "those who are the called according to His purpose" (Rom 8:28).

(ii) The Kingdom of God

The word "kingdom" points to a body of people which has a head. It is not a democracy, but a theocracy. God is their king or, to be more precise, Yeshua the Messiah, who is at the right hand of God ruling God's kingdom until he hands back the kingdom to God the Father (1 Cor 15:24–25). God's people are therefore a people who expect directions and instructions from their king (John 15:17) and their place is to be his servants (Rom 1:1; 1 Pet 2:16). In one sense they are like slaves—"You were bought at a price; do not become slaves of men" (1 Cor 7:23)—so that they have an allegiance to Christ which trumps all others. Messiah's kingdom rule is wider than his rule over the church, for it extends to all things, but the church is the body which actively seeks to submit to Messiah's kingship.

(iii) The Family of God

Here the picture is more intimate. God is the Father of his people—"I will be a Father to you, And you will be my sons and daughters" (2 Cor 6:18)—and the Son is the head of the household as the mediator of the new covenant (Heb 3:6). God's people are all brothers and sisters who care for one another (Jas 2:15–16). Remarkably, the Son even calls his people brothers and sisters (Mark 3:35). Leaders are exhorted to treat church people as family members (1 Tim 5:12). Their high calling is to love one another as Yeshua loved them.

(iv) The Flock of God

Jesus portrays his relationship to his people as that of a shepherd to his sheep, his flock (John 10:1–30; especially vv. 14–16). He is the good shepherd who gives his life for his sheep, which is why Hebrews describes him as "that great Shepherd of the sheep" (Heb 13:20). This image points to the vulnerability and helplessness of his people; how he tenderly cares for them, guides them, and meets their every need.

(v) The Body of Christ

This image stresses the interrelationship and interdependence of believers, who are like members of a body which depends on each part for the proper working and growth of the whole (1 Cor 12:12–27). No Christian is to be a loner, however much his or her background prejudices them against the church. And just as a body functions under the direction of the head, so believers are governed by Messiah in their working together (Eph 4:15–16).

(vi) The Bride of Christ

As Israel was often portrayed as God's beloved bride, so his new covenant people are Messiah's bride, a delightful image of intimate and indissoluble love and affection (2 Cor 11:2; Eph 5:25–32). His love is such that he gave his life for the church, and he desires her perfection in purity and love so that love might be fully expressed and enjoyed. As a loving husband, Yeshua looks after, nourishes, and cherishes his church as if his own flesh.

(vii) The Temple-Building of God

God's dwelling with Israel was manifested by his Shekinah above the mercy seat in the temple; now he dwells in the hearts of his people by his Spirit: "you are the temple of God and the Spirit of God dwells in you" (1 Cor 3:16). Whilst this is true for each believer individually, the New Testament views the temple as the whole body of believers, which is portrayed as a building under construction: "you also, as living stones, are being built up a spiritual house" (1 Pet 2:5; see also Eph 2:21–22). Hence every local gathering of the Lord's people is to be viewed as an ever-growing dwelling place of God, a community where he is praised and worshiped. Likewise, the worldwide church is ever growing; a vast body from which worldwide praise is offered to the one, true God who is in them.

(viii) The Field and Vineyard of God

Paul tells Christians in Corinth, "you are God's field" (1 Cor 3:9), an image which points to bearing fruit for God: the fruits of the Spirit in heart and life (Gal 5:22–23), and fruitfulness in ministry and witness (Rom 1:13; Phil 4:17). To Yeshua's hearers this image was familiar in the form of a vineyard, by which Isaiah had portrayed Israel. In his vineyard parable Yeshua warns Israel that disobedience entails loss of privileges, and the warning is the same for his church today (Mark 12:1–11). To avoid this, and to ensure fruitfulness, believers are to see Yeshua as a vine and themselves as branches (John 15:18) which can only bear fruit if they abide in the vine.

(ix) A Kingdom of Priests

The apostle Peter is most pointed in the use of this image describing the church as both a holy priesthood and a royal priesthood, whose task is to offer up spiritual sacrifices and proclaim praises (1 Pet 2:5, 9). Paul presents the whole Christian life under this metaphor—"present your bodies a living sacrifice" (Rom 12:1)—and views its particular aspects as akin to an offering: "the things sent from you, a sweet-smelling aroma, an acceptable sacrifice, well pleasing to God" (Phil 4:18). The church shares in Yeshua's priestly ministry through sacrificial living in prayer, praise, and service.

(x) The Olive Tree

Paul presents God's people as an olive tree with natural branches, engrafted wild olive branches, and cut-off branches. The tree is God's people viewed as they move from the old to the new covenant, with a focus on Jew and Gentile in the church. Paul's especial purpose is to rebuke Gentile believers who were boasting over the branches which were cut off, i.e., those of Israel who did not believe. The church is now mostly composed of Gentiles, but the smallness of the number of Jewish believers does not mean God has abandoned Israel, nor that Jewish believers cease to be the natural branches; the tree remains "their own olive tree" (Rom 11:24). Gentile believers should recognize this and be humble; Jewish believers should recognize it and identify with the church.

Some refer to the "Israel of God" (Gal 6:16) as an image of the church. It is more likely that "Israel of God" refers to the body of Jewish believers in Yeshua and this will be considered in more detail later in this part of the book.

(D) THE NATURE OF THE CHURCH

The word "church" is used not only of a gathering of believers—e.g., Paul wrote to "the church of God which is at Corinth" (1 Cor 1:2, see also 2 Thess 1:4; Acts 8:11)—but also of the wider body of all believers on earth at one time—"I persecuted the church of God beyond measure and tried to destroy it" (Gal 1:13)—and also of the worldwide body of believers throughout the ages (Matt 16:18). The terms usually used are the "church local" and the "church universal."

The church can also be thought of in terms of all those who come to faith in Messiah Jesus during the new covenant period, past, present, and future. Hebrews refers to them as "the general assembly and church of the firstborn" (Heb 12:23), where the context shows they are being contrasted with the assembly of Israel (vv. 18–21).

The term "invisible church" is a theological term which refers to all who are redeemed by the Savior throughout world history: "the church of God which He purchased with His own blood" (Acts 20:28; see also Rev 5:9). The term "visible church" is another term for the universal church on earth at any one time, as mentioned above. It refers to all the visible congregations across the world.

(E) THE BASIC MARKS OF A NEW TESTAMENT CHURCH

There are many groups using the name "church" and calling themselves Christian and yet, due to the sort of church decline which the New Testament describes (Rev 2:5; 3:16; Gal 4:11, 19–20) it has to be asked: are they all really churches? What makes a New Testament church?

Is a group of people gathering in a home, discussing the Scriptures, and praying a church? Jesus has certainly promised to be present (Matt 18:20) but certain basics are lacking. The New Testament has a great stress on teaching by those set apart to that ministry (Matt 28:19–20; Acts 2:42; 6:2; 20:25; 2 Tim 4:1–5; 1 Tim 5:17). There must be baptism so that it is clear who has professed faith and is recognized as a disciple (Matt 28:19;

Acts 2:41). The early believers knew who was one of them: "altogether the number of names was about a hundred and twenty" (Acts 1:15; note: most versions omit the word "names" but it is in the original). The Lord's Supper must be rightly administered because it was both a command of Yeshua and early church practice (1 Cor 11:23–26; Acts 2:42; 20:7). It is a test of those who are continuing to follow the Savior; they continue to proclaim the Lord's death (1 Cor 11:26). Those who are openly failing to do so should be barred (Matt 18:17; see also 1 Cor 5:1–5). The leaders of the Reformation saw these as the marks of a true church, a functioning body of believers under the authority of God's word and with some form of control as to who was to be considered a disciple and who was not.

The Roman Catholic Church has taken a uniquely different view, which they term "the power of the keys." Their claim is that Jesus delegated special power and authority to Peter (Matt 16:18) and through him to all succeeding bishops in Rome. They claim there is an unbroken succession of laying on of hands in their church, so that only they can teach the word and administer sacraments. Undoubtedly, Peter held a special leadership position but Jesus did not indicate he would have successors in this role. It is the call and anointing of God, recognized by those in ministry, which is the true succession of apostolic ministry (Acts 16:1–2; 1 Tim 4:13–14).

There is no doubt that many who use the term "church," or its equivalent, have to be viewed as false churches. For example, the Jehovah's Witnesses and the Mormons deny major Christian doctrines essential to salvation. "Liberalism" is a term used to describe a form of Christianity (Protestant or Catholic) which rejects the orthodox view of the Christian faith in Scripture and the historic creeds. Such churches cannot be viewed as true churches. Not all church situations which are in decline are so clear, and it is difficult to discern if they have crossed a red line. In Revelation the risen Savior warns some such churches that they are perilously close (Rev 2:5; 3:3, 16).

If these marks of a true church had been more firmly held to and practiced as the church grew and expanded into the world, then the numbers of churches, church leaders, and church people with negative attitudes to the Jewish people would have been greatly reduced. The Jewish people would then have more easily understood that a Christian cannot be anti-Jewish.

(F) CHARACTERISTICS OF THE CHURCH

(i) Unity and Purity

The goal of God for his people is a oneness which comes from sharing the life of God, as Yeshua prayed, "that they all may be one, as you, Father, are in Me, and I in You" (John 17:21). Purity is also the goal: "But there shall by no means enter it anything that defiles" (Rev 21:27). But God's people on earth have not attained such unity and purity yet, although they must strive for it.

This inevitably means that local churches will be a mixture of believers at different levels of maturity: children, young men, and fathers, as John terms them (1 John 2:12–14). A local church will also be a mix of true believers and those whose faith is not genuine. It is not always possible to distinguish the two and some will not be aware of their falsity until the Day of Judgment (Matt 7:21–23; Jude 12–19). But this does not mean the church is to tolerate falsity in its midst when it is open and continuing. Those whose teaching opposes fundamentals of the faith are to be confronted and if they refuse to change are to be removed from the church and ministry (e.g., Hymenaeus and Alexander, 2 Tim 2:17–18; 1 Tim 1:19–20). Teachers in error, but on doctrines of less significance, are to be helped to see their error (e.g., Apollos, Acts 18:24–28). We have an example which concerns Peter and Paul where Paul corrects Peter (Gal 2:11–14), but it is important to note that Peter was not teaching error; rather his practice was inconsistent with his own teaching and belief (Acts 15:5–11). The behavior of God's people frequently fails to manifest unity and purity and Yeshua gives one example of how failure is to be addressed (Matt 18:15–18). The aim is restoration but an unrepentant person is put out of the church. Some quote the parable of the wheat and the tares to teach such things must be left to God at the end (Matt 13:24–30), but in the parable the sphere of action is not the church but the world (see v. 38).

But what of a situation where the church fails to address seriously wrong teaching or behavior in its midst? Such was the situation in Thyatira (Rev 2:20). Yeshua promised he would intervene although we are not told how. But if that is not heeded a believer has a responsibility to become part of a faithful church (2 Cor 6:14–18).

Unity and *uniformity* are different things. Uniformity indicates an organizational unity, and many Christians see value in seeking to express gospel unity by some form of organizational structure by which churches stand together and help each other. In their day the apostles provided a measure of uniformity, but it was not a rigid ecclesiastical structure which dictated a common form of worship and administration. Through the apostles they were aware of each other's needs and helped each other (see Rom 15:25–28; 1 Cor 16:1–4; Acts 11:27–30; Rom 16:1–2; Acts 18:27–28, 16:1–2).

Attempts to create rigid structures and impose them on others have led to the stifling of life, compromise with error, and stressful divisions. This can be seen in the history of the Roman Catholic Church, which claims its uniformity, by contrast to Protestantism's fragmentation, is an evidence of it being the true church. But Roman Catholicism was itself the result of a division from the Orthodox Church in 1054. It has not held to the pure gospel and its hierarchy has frequently been exposed as corrupt.

No church is immune from such failure but history shows that the more rigid the structure the greater the difficulty in responding to challenges to return to Scripture. Protestant denominations were created out of a desire for a unity based not only on fundamental doctrine but also on common church practices, such as baptism, Communion, and leadership, enabling a working together. Beyond such church structures alliances have been formed, usually on a national basis, by which churches from one group can express their unity with those of another, or none, and work together for the gospel; this has also been done on a regional basis. The support of churches for organizations doing mission, church planting, gospel apologetics, Christian compassion, etc. is seen by many as an expression of unity, without overarching uniformity.

Churches need to beware of a unity that is cultural as well as spiritual. Of course, if a church is set in a one culture area then the cultural feel of the church will be monocultural. However, many churches will be made up of those from different cultures and they need to find ways to maintain both unity and diversity, and not ask newcomers to convert to another culture as well as to Christ. Such churches can be a significant witness to the unity Yeshua brings.

(ii) Holiness

The word "holy" is often used interchangeably with "pure" but they are not exact equivalents. God's holiness is his utter Godness, his being separate and different. Obviously this separateness encompasses moral purity but it includes far more—"My thoughts are not your thoughts, Nor are your ways My ways" (Isa 55:8). His people are a holy people because they are set apart to him; they are not their own, they are bought with a price. The word "sanctity" is equivalent to "holiness" and is used to describe God's people as set apart to him in a once-and-for-all manner at conversion, when a believer is taken out of Satan's kingdom and placed in Messiah's forever (Col

1:13). Paul describes this setting apart as one of several things to happen at conversion: "But you were washed, but you were sanctified, but you were justified in the name of the Lord Jesus and by the Spirit of our God" (1 Cor 6:11). But this setting apart is only the beginning of God's work of making his people progressively more like himself, the work of sanctification: "For this is the will of God, your sanctification: that you should abstain from sexual immorality" (1 Thess 4:3), and indeed from all behavior contrary to God's law and the gospel.

A church is a group of people determined to follow God's ways and Peter calls them a holy people (1 Pet 2:9). A brief reading of the New Testament letters reveals the failures of the churches to be holy, even in those remarkable days of gospel power, so we are not to expect perfection, but rather a gathering of people pressing on towards it. Leaders are to set a high standard (1 Tim 4:12).

(iii) Openness

This is often expressed by the word "catholicity." The church of Messiah Jesus is open to all who express repentance and faith in him, regardless of social background, color, ethnic background, sex, intellect or previous moral lifestyle. Yeshua's command was "make disciples of all the nations" and only a cursory reading of Acts shows the church was made up of every type in society. Churches today need to beware of creating additional requirements for membership, such as adherence to their own doctrinal distinctives, particular cultural practices or even dress codes.

This openness marked a change from the old covenant arrangement, which, although the stranger (non-Jew) was welcome, was largely confined to Israel, such that to be born an Israelite conferred automatic entry to the covenant people. The catholicity of NT churches meant they also stood out from the cults and secret societies with their restricted membership.

As the church expanded into the world and heresies crept in, the word "catholic" came to be used to describe those churches which adhered to orthodox doctrine as defined in the established creeds of the church. The Roman Church used the term as part of its claim to be the sole expression on earth of Christ's universal church, and because of this the word "catholic" is little used outside the Roman Catholic Church, being often replaced by terms like "open to all."

(iv) Apostolicity

God's people of the new covenant are founded upon the teaching of the apostles. Yeshua himself wrote nothing but committed the communication of his gospel to twelve men whom he specially appointed and were eyewitnesses of his resurrection (Luke 6:12; Acts 1:21–22; 1 Cor 9:1; 15:8–9). They are therefore described as the foundation of the church: "having been built on the foundation of the apostles and prophets, Jesus Christ Himself being the chief cornerstone" (Eph 2:20). "Prophets" here is a reference to New Testament ones, like Agabus, who, like the twelve apostles, were given both revelation and inspiration to teach infallibly (see Eph 3:5; Acts 11:27–28; 21:10–11). These two offices do not continue in the church; the foundation does not need to be laid again and again. They taught the first believers (Acts 2:42; 28:30–31) and continue to teach the church in all ages through their writings in the New Testament.

Some churches assert the need for an unbroken succession of ministers from the apostles as a sign of their apostolic authority. This is an error; it has not been possible for any church to prove historically, and those who claim it have signally failed to preserve the apostolic gospel. The Church of Rome is a primary example of this. The New Testament does not point to a historical succession of ministers but the continuance of the truth among God's people: "the church of the living God, the pillar and ground of the truth" (1 Tim 3:15). Our Lord's mention of building his church upon Peter in Matt 16:16–19 makes no reference to a succession of ministers from him; what is vital for apostolicity is the upholding of Peter's confession of Yeshua as Messiah and Son of God.

The New Testament describes as apostles men other than the twelve Yeshua specifically appointed: "the apostles Barnabas and Paul" (Acts 14:14, see also Rom 16:7). The word means "sent one," and is therefore used of those sent by the churches: "if our brethren are inquired about, they are messengers [literally, apostles] of the churches" (2 Cor 8:23). The New Testament clearly distinguishes those sent by Yeshua from apostles of the churches: "remember the words which were spoken before by the apostles of our Lord Jesus Christ" (Jude 17). Is it wise to use the title "apostle" today? In the past it has been avoided and terms like "evangelist" and "missionary" have been used. This was to avoid any impression that a preacher today has an authority equivalent to the twelve apostles who founded the church. The use of "apostle" today runs the risk of creating that impression and is best avoided. If a person has a teaching ministry which is wider than one church then the New Testament has a title like "teacher" (1 Cor 12:28); if he is evangelizing and church planting it has the title "evangelist" (Acts 21:8; Eph

4:11). The New Testament records the use of the title "apostle" by deceivers who desired to boost their ministry (Rev 2:2; 2 Cor 11:12–15) and therefore believers need to be on their guard.

(v) Authority

The authority of the church is limited to the teaching and application of God's word in the life of God's people. Leaders have no authority to add to what Scripture demands for salvation and a walk with God, but they do have authority to insist on those things, to correct the unscriptural behavior of individuals (Titus 2:15), and to exercise church discipline on those who persist in waywardness (Matt 18:17). The church is not a democracy, whereby beliefs and actions can only be pursued by the vote of the majority; leaders are to lead, and by persuasion to bring those under them to be followers through the teaching of God's word. No church or its leadership is infallible, and mistakes will be made, calling for humility, patience, and love. The Roman Catholic Church asserts its teachings are infallible but that is a relatively recent claim; the church at Rome and its bishop never had any preeminence in early church councils.

(vi) Missional

God's preparation of Israel for Messiah's coming contained a vision for the world brought back to God (Gen 12:3). His servant Messiah is for the world as well as Israel (Isa 49:6).

As Messiah Yeshua finished his earthly ministry he commanded his apostles to make disciples of all nations, beginning at Jerusalem, then Judea, Samaria, and to the end of the earth (Matt 28:19; Acts 1:8), and the book of Acts tells that story from Jerusalem to Rome. The world continues until all the nations have heard (Matt 24:13). It is sometimes said that Old Testament Israel failed in this task but that is inaccurate. Moses encouraged obedience so that the nations would say, "Surely this great nation is a wise and understanding people" (Deut 4:6), and Isaiah described Israel as God's witnesses (Isa 43:10), but Israel under the old covenant was never given a command to go out into the world and proclaim God's truth. However, she was under the new covenant; and she did as those first disciples, who were all Jews: she went to the Gentiles preaching the gospel. That witness of Israel to the nations continues through the Scriptures, all written by Israelites. Israel is always fulfilling her commission to be a light to the nations.

The Acts of the Apostles does not enter into great detail as to methods, leaving the church to adapt to new situations, but the preaching of God's word in the power of the Spirit is paramount (Acts 4:29; 1 Cor 2:4; 1 Thess 1:5), coupled with the ongoing witness of the churches which are established (1 Thess 1:8). There is no emphasis on large numbers, although three thousand Jewish people saved through one sermon is no small thing, but the emphasis is on God's power at work through his word (Acts 19:20). Some are called and set apart to the specific role of taking the gospel to the lost; Paul calls them "evangelists" (Eph 4:11), and Philip is an example of such a ministry, speaking one to one and to crowds (Acts 8:5–13; 26–40). Pastors and teachers are also to be gospel preachers (2 Tim 4:5) but their focus is more towards the believers, to teach the word and thereby equip God's people for ministry, such as gospel witness (2 Tim 4:2; Eph 4:12).

Throughout Acts there is an emphasis on taking the gospel first to the Jewish people. This was geographically so when the apostles began in Jerusalem and Judea, but even as Paul moved into the Gentile world an effort was always made to go first to the Jews (Acts 13:5,14; 14:1; 17:1–2,10,17; 18:4; 19:8), so that it is described as Paul's custom (Acts 17:2). This practice was continued to the end of Paul's recorded ministry (Acts 27:17). Here is a pattern for mission for the church today because Paul establishes Jewish priority as a fundamental part of the gospel in Rom 1:16–17, for the simple reason that it is a fulfillment of promise (Acts 13:32–33). This means that the churches continue on where Paul left off, always reaching out to all and always making a special effort to reach the Jewish people, either by their own witness or by giving support to the witness of others.

What place in the witness of the church is there for the provision of education, medical aid, and sociopolitical involvement? Some argue that our witness is to do everything that Jesus came to do for the world, and that includes the general improvement of human experience that comes through believers being salt and light in the world. Such improvement is no doubt important but it comes about primarily through the lives of believers; it is not the verbal proclamation of the truth which Yeshua commanded in Matt 28:19–20. The story of gospel proclamation in Acts makes no reference to such things as a form of gospel proclamation. Such things will be part of mission from time to time, either because there is no other option or because human needs are so pressing, but there is always the need to be aware of their slowly but surely crowding out the essential place of verbal testimony and proclamation.

It should be a cause for grief and repentance that many churches have lost sight of their missional role. After two thousand years all the world still has not heard and the fullness of Israel has yet to be brought in (Rom 11:12,

26). Yet the Lord Jesus has been gathering in his elect despite the weakness of his people, as he promised: "I will build My church, and the gates of Hades shall not prevail against it" (Matt 16:18). May God revive his people worldwide to finish the task.

(G) THE INDIVIDUAL AND THE CHURCH

The New Testament norm is that believers in Yeshua are part of a local church. That is how things began in Jerusalem as the apostles gathered the believers together (Acts 2:42) and it is how Paul operated (Acts 14:21–23) so that the letters of the apostles are mostly written to particular churches or church leaders, and when that is not the case (Hebrews, James, 1 and 2 Peter, 1–3 John, Jude) then the recipients are expected to be in churches (e.g., Heb 13:7; Jas 5:14). Of course the crucial thing for a believer is their union with the Savior, and for those whose circumstances mean isolation from other believers by, for example, imprisonment, a controlling family, or a difficult marriage, then the Lord will give special help to grow and endure. The antagonism of family and friends and the tension between church and synagogue over many centuries has made it difficult for new Jewish believers to start to attend a church and feel comfortable. Some have encountered anti-Jewish sentiment or misunderstanding. Jewish believers need to persevere, and be encouraged by the significant contribution to church life and mission which has been made by those Jewish believers who have taken their place in Messiah's new covenant congregations.

(H) THE CHURCH AND CIVIL GOVERNMENT

This subject is rarely examined in books such as this but its impact on the Jewish community means it should be considered in this volume, even if only briefly.

(i) Definitions

The *church* is a people called out by the gospel to be God's people. *Civil government* is the authority established by a people and their leaders to order their life together, a life which initially emerges from their ethnic self-awareness, common language, culture, and geography. The people may be a tribe, a nation-state, or an empire extending over many peoples. A *Christian* is an individual member of God's people who is also a citizen of a people group.

(ii) Some Biblical Principles

It should be noted that the church in our NT accounts is within an empire (Rome) and was initially viewed as a Jewish sect (Acts 28:22), but one which was beginning to spread its wings and take on a more universal character. It did not experience the favor it later received from civil authorities in some parts of the world and hence the NT record of interaction with the civil authorities does not cover all the models we will consider below. However, God's word supplies us with principles.

   a. Christians are subjects of a kingdom which is not of this world, whose Lord is Messiah Jesus, God's Son, and this may lead them into conflict with the civil authorities they live under (John 18:36; Col 1:13; Acts 4:18–20; 5:28–29).

   b. Christians are urged to submit to the civil government as the ordinance of God. They are to give to Caesar what is Caesar's: honor, good behavior, and financial support (Rom 13:1–7; Matt 22:17–22). These principles are underlined by OT examples (Jer 29:7; Dan 6:1–3).

   c. Civil rulers are accountable to God for their decisions and actions, and authorized to punish evil behavior, collect taxes, and rule so as to encourage good behavior, honoring those who excel (Rom 13:1–7; 1 Pet 2:13–14).

   d. Some believe the OT theocracy should be seen as a model for the link between church and state. But it ought to be noted that the OT theocracy is fulfilled by the church under Messiah, not by the church and the state as a conjoined body under Messiah.

   e. In the NT the support of the civil authorities is never enlisted for the spread of the gospel, although their failure to uphold their own laws or moral principles were sometimes challenged (2 Cor 2:17; 5:11; Acts 16:35–40; 24:10–21; 28:17–20).

   f. There is no example of church authorities engaging in the political structures of their day and the apostles never encouraged such. However, individual believers are to be salt and light in a fallen world and have a responsibility to improve the lot of their neighbors and fellow citizens as their circumstances and gifts allow (Gal 6:10; Rom 16:23).

   g. The civil authorities sometimes see the church as a threat to the status quo (Acts 17:6–9), and some church teaching could be seen as an undermining influence, e.g., on slavery and the status of women. Peter encourages good behavior as a counter to this fear (1 Pet 2:13–17).

Paul's experience of trial, imprisonment, and release by the civil authorities was a vindication of the Christian faith as a good influence in society, not a challenge to civil government.

h. Opposition and persecution by civil authorities, national or local, is to be expected from time to time because the gospel proclaims Yeshua as supreme over all human government (Acts 17:7–9) and therefore appears subversive despite the teaching of Rom 13:1–7.

i. The leadership model in the church is different from the usual practice of civil government. Christian leaders are servants who are to lead sacrificial lives for those whom they lead (Luke 22:24–27; 1 Pet 5:2) but civil leaders all too often lord it over the people and vie for honor and position. History shows that when church leaders become enmeshed in politics there is a strong tendency for them to become more like the world.

(iii) Models for the Church-State Relationship

Here I acknowledge my debt to Os Guinness, quoted in *The Subversive Puritan* by Mostyn Roberts, for the terms used for the three models below.

a. The *Sacred Public Square* Model

This model gives a preferred and usually constitutional place to one religion in society's public life. Examples are the Church of England in England, the Lutheran Church in a number of European nations, and Islam in Muslim nations like Iran.

b. The *Naked Public Square* Model

Here religion is excluded from a public life which is avowedly secular, and all religious expression is confined to the private sphere. A strong example is China and a weaker one is France.

c. The *Civil Public Square* Model

All are free to engage in public life, and those with religious convictions are free to enter with those convictions guiding their moral arguments. Examples would be the many Western-style liberal democracies where either Christianity dominates or sits alongside a number of other faiths; an example is the USA.

There are Christians who advocate none of these models and teach believers to withdraw from activity in the civil sphere because the church is viewed as a spiritual diaspora awaiting deliverance from this present, evil world.

In models b and c the church as an institution has either no voice in civil government or is limited to encouraging its members to play their part as they are able as one voice among many. It is when the church grows strong because there are many believers in a society, and the civil authorities recognize the value of the church, that there comes an opportunity to seek a preferred place in society's life. This has pros and cons. One major pro is the opportunity to influence government to pass laws that are just, fair, and compassionate. Two cons are: the danger of becoming enmeshed in the machinery of government, so becoming like the world; and the danger of using their influence to encourage the state to act against those of other faiths or none, thus encouraging outward conformity to the Christian faith and belittling freedom of conscience. Whether the church is weak or strong, it should always be ready to insist that the civil government protects the freedom of the marketplace of ideas for all.

Jewish people have often suffered due to being a minority faith in the *sacred public square*, whether Christian or Muslim. In what might be called "Christian Europe," after the Roman Empire, the church and the state were always seen as two spheres which were to work in harmony for the betterment of society and the promotion of Christianity. Isaiah's image of kings as foster fathers and queens as nursing mothers (Isa 49:23) was invoked to charge civil authorities with a responsibility to protect and promote the church (although it seems to this author that the text is referring to kings and queens caring for Israel returning from Babylon, which certainly occurred). Could things have been different?

Constantine's edict of toleration in 313 AD ended the outbreaks of persecution of the churches by Roman emperors, giving Christianity an equal place alongside other religions and, for example, allowing influence within the Roman court. As a professing Christian, Constantine began to have a personal influence upon church affairs, chairing church councils and influencing appointments to the most important church positions. Could his well-motivated incursion into church affairs have been curbed? One imagines that Roman emperors were not easily opposed. After Constantine, Christianity's influence grew such that during the reign of Theodosius I (379–395 AD) it became the state religion, and laws were enacted by Rome to suppress paganism (laws which did not cover Judaism, which was still a protected faith). Was it possible to have prevented this process of state endorsement? There were no doubt some church leaders who saw the dangers but there were others who welcomed the power and influence and used it to their advantage. History shows there is a downside: firstly that church leaders started to act in worldly ways, and secondly that nominalism increased as the gospel was spread in association with worldly power. The downside for the Jewish community was that as paganism disappeared it became the odd man out in a Christian society; sometimes viewed as malign and hence opposed, sometimes seen as beneficial and hence protected, but always the odd man out.

It seems to me that it could have been different if the church leaders had prevented any civil government influence in their affairs and had not sought the aid of the Roman civil power in dealing with opponents and internal problems. If they had then maybe something similar to a *civil public square* model could have developed in those early days. But that is the wisdom of hindsight in someone who has little experience of a world of people groups and empires where state and religion were always intertwined. The best record for the treatment of Jewish citizens is held by those nations which have developed the *civil public square* as their relationship between church and state, nations like the USA, where church leaders are not allowed any formal role in politics and Christian believers are free to engage in government processes at all levels.

> Walk about Zion,
> And go all around her.
> Count her towers;
> Mark well her bulwarks;
> Consider her palaces;
> That you may tell it to the generation following.
> For this is God,
> Our God forever and ever;
> He will be our guide
> Even to death. (Ps 48:12–14)

SCRIPTURES

Images of the Church

People: Acts 15:14; Rom 9:24–26; 2 Cor 6:16; 1 Pet 2:9–10; Rev 21:3.
Kingdom: Matt 16:18–19; Acts 14:21–22; Rom 14:17; Col 1:13.
Family: Mark 3:35; 1 Cor 1:3; 8:13; Eph 3:15; Gal 3:26.
Flock: Luke 12:32; John 10:14–15; Acts 20:28; 1 Pet 5:2.
Body: Rom 12:5; 1 Cor 12:27; Eph 1:22–23; 5:30.

Bride: John 3:29; 2 Cor 11:2; Eph 5:31–32; Rev 21:2.

Temple: 1 Cor 3:16; 6:19; 2 Cor 6:16; Eph 2:21.

Field/vineyard: Matt 21:33–43; John 15:1–2; 1 Cor 3:9.

Kingdom of priests: Rom 12:1; Phil 4:18; Heb 13:15–16; 1 Pet 2:5, 9; Rev 1:6; 5:10; 20:6.

Olive tree: Rom 11:16–24.

Nature of the Church

Local: Matt 18:17; Acts 9:31; 13:1; 14:23; 20:17; Rom 16:4; 1 Cor 1:2.

All the church, all time/invisible: Eph 3:21; 5:25, 27.

Visible on earth: 1 Cor 10:32; 12:28; 15:9.

All new covenant people: Matt 16:18; Acts 2:47; Eph 1:22; 3:10; Col 1:18; 1 Tim 3:15; Heb 12:23.

Basic marks of the church: Matt 18:17; 28:19–20; Acts 2:41–42; 14:23; Rom 6:3; 1 Cor 11:23–26; Col 2:12; 1 Tim 5:17; 2 Tim 4:1–2; Titus 1:5–9.

Characteristics of the Church

Unity: John 10:16; 11:52; 17:11, 21–23; Rom 12:4–5; 15:5–6; 1 Cor 10:17; 12:13; Gal 3:28; Eph 2:14–18; 4:3, 13; Phil 1:27.

Purity: Matt 18:17; Acts 5:1–11; Rom 16:17–20; 1 Cor 5:1–5, 11–12; Gal 4:29–30; 2 Thess 3:14–15; 1 Tim 1:20; 3:9; 5:22, 24; 2 Tim 3:5; 2:24–26; Titus 3:10–11; 2 Pet 2:1–22; 3 John 9–10.

Holiness: 1 Cor 3:17; Eph 2:21; 5:27; Col 1:22; 2 Tim 1:9; 1 Pet 1:15–16; 2:5, 9.

Openness: Acts 8:26–39; 10:44–48; 15:4–11; 28:30–31; Rom 10:11–13; Gal 3:28; Eph 2:14; Col 3:11.

Apostolicity: Matt 10:2; Luke 6:13; Acts 2:42; 15:2, 6; 16:4; Rom 1:1; 11:13; 1 Cor 12:28; 2 Cor 12:12; Eph 2:20; 3:5; 4:11; 1 Pet 1:1; Jude 17; Rev 21:14.

Authority: Matt 28:19–20; Rom 14:1–13; 1 Cor 10:23–33; 2 Cor 4:1–2; 10:8, 12–18; 2 Tim 4:1–5; Titus 2:15; Phlm 8–10.

Missional: Matt 28:19–20; Acts 1:8; 5:14–16; 8:5; 9:32–43; 10:34–48; 13:2–3; 16:9–10; 23:11; 28:17–31; 2 Cor 2:14–15; 1 Thess 1:8; 2 Tim 4:5; 3 John 5–8.

Questions

1. Ten images of the church are mentioned above. What does each teach about God, his relationship to us, and our relationship to him? Which ones are unique to the new covenant and why?
2. Consider each of the six characteristics of the church mentioned above. Demonstrate they are biblical and discuss how true they are of the church you attend.
3. What is the unity of the church and how should it be manifested?
4. What differences of form and spirit are there between the synagogue worship you were brought up with (or are aware of) and the churches with which you are familiar?
5. Distinguish the different groups described by the word "church" (*ekklesia*) in the New Testament. Discuss the usefulness of these distinctions.
6. Was it an error for the Christian church in a country to become a state religion established by law? Discuss the pros and cons, for all and for the Jewish people.

Further Reading

Allen, Roland. *Missionary Methods: St Paul's or Ours?* Grand Rapids: Eerdmans, 1962.
Berkouwer, G. C. *The Church*. Grand Rapids: Eerdmans, 1976.
Carson, D. A. *Christ and Culture Revisited*. Grand Rapids: Eerdmans, 2008. See chapter 5.
Carson, Herbert M. *Roman Catholicism Today*. Leicester: InterVarsity, 1964.
Clowney, Edmund. *The Church*. Leicester: InterVarsity, 1995.
Griffiths, Michael. *A Task Unfinished*. Oxford: Monarch, 1996.
Keller, Tim. *Generous Justice: How God Makes Us Just*. London: Hodder & Stoughton, 2012.
Lloyd-Jones, D. M. *The Basis of Christian Unity*. Leicester: InterVarsity, 1962.
Pakula, Martin. *First to the Jew*. Melbourne: Bible College of Victoria, 2007.
Piper, John. *Let the Nations be Glad*. Leicester: InterVarsity, 1993.
Roberts, Mostyn. *The Subversive Puritan*. Darlington: Evangelical, 2019.
Stibbs, Alan M. *God's Church*. Leicester: InterVarsity, 1959.

(I) THE PURPOSE AND LIFE OF THE CHURCH

Everything considered so far has practical implications and this section addresses them—what is the church meant to be doing as she waits for the return of her Lord and Savior? All that she does prepares her for her glorious future with God in his eternal kingdom; she will worship and serve forever just as she begins to do that now. Believers are to grow spiritually so as to be more like their Savior, and they are to use all the means he has provided to that end: reading his word, listening to it taught, prayer, fellowship together, and observing Messiah's two ordinances, baptism and the Lord's Supper. And the church is an ever-growing body as she tells the world and makes disciples. These themes will be dealt with only briefly as readers of this book will probably have considered them in some detail already.

(i) Worship

The word in English is the equivalent of "worthship," that is, ascribing worth to God. In the Old Testament this is strongly associated with bowing down, the literal meaning of the word *shachah*, and usually indicates a bowing of the head: "So the people believed . . . then they bowed their heads and worshiped" (Exod 4:31). In the New Testament the most familiar word is *proskuneo*, which sometimes is associated with bowing down (see Matt 2:11; Rev 5:14), but is more often a general word for homage: "God is Spirit, and those who worship Him must worship in spirit and truth" (John 4:24). Another word is *latreuo*, which has the root meaning of "service" in NT Greek and is always connected to service towards God, pointing to worship as a service to God. It is sometimes translated "service" and sometimes "worship." It is used by the New Testament of the divine worship of the Old Testament: "the first covenant had ordinances of divine service" (Heb 9:1). However, it is also used of a life of service to God—"For God is my witness, whom I serve with my spirit in the gospel" (Rom 1:9)—so that for a believer all of life can be seen as worship: "present your bodies a living sacrifice, holy, acceptable to God, which is your reasonable service" (Rom 12:1). The life of the believer is to be seen as one of ascribing worth to God, whether in a gathering for praise or the living out of daily obedience. There is a danger of stressing one of these two aspects to the exclusion of the other but in the New Testament it is not either/or but both/and. The emphasis in this section is on the service of worship in the gatherings of the churches.

Much of the content and form of the worship of God's people of the new covenant was carried over from the worship familiar to the first Jewish believers, so it is worth noting here what they had grown up with. The temple worship was marked by words of prayer, praise, and thanksgiving, many examples of which are in the book Tehillim. There was music as the Levites led in song and playing of instruments. The law was read every seven years and much of its truth was reinforced by annual festivals such as Pesach, Shavuot, and Sukkot. Sacrifices, both prescribed and voluntary, were offered as a means of confession and atonement for sin, for expressing devotion to God, and for fellowship with him. Gifts were given for the support of the temple and priesthood. This was all led by the priests and Levites and the people were to enter into it all and affirm with a united amen (Neh 8:6).

Much of the content would have had a set form and wording but extempore prayer and praise was not unknown; for example, both Solomon and Jehoshaphat led Israel in extempore prayer (2 Chr 6; 20:1–13). Certainly extempore prayer and praise was part of the personal lives of true believers, of which the Old Testament has many examples (e.g., Judg 13:8), and can also be seen in early New Testament times in a woman like Anna (Luke 2:36–37). In the synagogue of those times there was praise, prayer, and instruction, which involved readings from the Scriptures and an exposition (see Luke 4:21; Acts 13:15). Although little is recorded about singing, we know that Jesus and his disciples sang at the seder (Matt 26:30). Something akin to a synagogue had early origins in Israel (see Ps 74:8) but it was Ezra's influence that led to its firm establishment.

The worship of a modern synagogue contains all these traditional elements, and some of the prayers are probably very ancient and uplifting, but what is lacking today is a careful exposition of Scripture and extempore prayer.

The worship of the early churches contains all these elements and more. We do not have a detailed description of a gathering, and no doubt that was deliberate, to avoid giving the impression that gatherings for worship should be the same everywhere and for all time. However, we can discern the principle elements. That they gathered together is plain (Acts 5:12–13; 1 Cor 14:26). These gatherings were marked by: prayer and praise (Matt 18:19–20; Acts 2:42; 4:24–31; 1 Tim 2:1–8), which included a corporate amen (1 Cor 14:16; 2 Cor 1:20); singing (1 Cor 14:26; see also Col 3:16; Eph 5:19); reading of the Scriptures (1 Tim 4:13; see also Col 4:16); exposition of the Scriptures and teaching (1 Tim 4:13; Acts 2:42; 2 Tim 4:2; Heb 13:7); collection of gifts for gospel work (1 Cor 16:2); the Lord's Supper (Acts 2:42; 20:7; 1 Cor 11:20–26); and the short creedal-type statements we read in Paul's letters may indicate such words were well known in the churches through reciting them in their gatherings for worship (see 1 Tim 3:16; 2 Tim 2:11–13).

When did the churches meet? As in all times of spiritual blessing there was a tendency to meet as often as possible (Acts 2:46, "daily"), and Paul's words "Whenever you come together" (1 Cor 14:26) point to a freedom as to time and frequency. However, it is clear that the first day of the week emerged as a special day for gathering, marking the Lord's resurrection (John 20:19; Acts 20:7; 1 Cor 16:2), a day which became known as "the Lord's Day" (Rev 1:10). That is not to say it was a rest day like the Jewish Sabbath or Sunday in the nations of Christendom, but a gathering took place at some time in the day, with a focus on the resurrection, and to celebrate the Lord's Supper.

The New Testament churches gathered in the name of Jesus, their Lord and Messiah, who had promised to be in their midst when they met. They approached the one God through the Son by the enabling of the Holy Spirit (Matt 18:20; 1 Cor 5:34; Acts 4:23–31). A more theological expression of that same worship is recorded by Paul in Eph 1:3–14, where the apostle perfectly expresses worship, adoration, praise, and dependence on God the Father, God the Son, and God the Spirit. The Holy Spirit is vital to the aspects of worship mentioned in the preceding paragraph: worship in general (Phil 3:3), prayer and praise (Acts 2:4; Rom 8:26), singing (Eph 5:18–19), exposition and instruction (John 15:26–27; Acts 20:28; 1 Cor 2:4,10–13), leading in God's will (Acts 13:2–3; 15:28), gifts for edification (1 Cor 12:1–11), and collecting offerings (Acts 6:3–5).

Throughout church history God's people have adopted different styles of worship due to the twin influences of their culture and the examples they have discerned in Scripture. Cultural influences will be considered later on in this Part 6. If we consider both the Old and New Testaments then we see the following. The simple worship of the patriarchs, with its focus on sacrifice and calling on the name of the Lord (Gen 12:8; 13:4); there is something similar to this in a New Testament gathering where the main focus is the Lord's Supper (1 Cor 11:23–26; Acts 20:7). The temple worship was liturgical in style, where all was according to a set pattern, the main elements being praise, prayer, and sacrifice (1 Chr 25:1–7; 2 Chr 5:6, 11–14; 7:1–6; Ezra 3:10–11), with opportunity for worshiper response (2 Chr 7:3; Ezra 3:11; Ps 136). There does not appear to be any New Testament equivalent to this use of liturgy, although it is possible to discern forms of words such as the Lord's Prayer which might be incorporated into a service of worship (see also Phil 2:5–11; Col 1:15–20; 1 Tim 3:16). The worship which developed after the return from Babylon had a much stronger focus on the reading and teaching of God's word, an emphasis brought by Ezra (Ezra 7:10; Neh 8–9). The teaching of God's law was not absent from Israel's life prior to that but it does not seem to have been a part of the regular temple worship (e.g., the tribe of Levi was scattered throughout Israel to teach the law; see especially 2 Chr 17:7–9; see also 2 Kgs 4:38). This development is maintained in New Testament worship which is focused on the preaching of God's word (Acts 5:20; 6:2; 11:26; 20:27; 2 Tim 4:1–2). The exercise of spiritual gifts in the gatherings for worship at Corinth (1 Cor 12, 14) indicates that members of the congregation not in recognized leadership positions could lead the worship at a particular point, and this freedom was not confined to the exercise of spiritual gifts but included other contributions (1 Cor 14:26). Throughout church history, churches have worshiped God somewhere on this spectrum, from liturgy only to congregational contributions only. Healthy New Testament churches will be those led by men of spiritual maturity and have the preaching of God's word central, with an appropriate place for all the other elements of worship, such as reading, prayer and praise, song, exhortation, the Lord's Supper, and offerings.

(ii) Fellowship

Fellowship is a fundamental experience of the believer in Messiah Jesus; it is one of the four marks of the life of the early church in Acts 2:42. The Greek word is *koinonia*, which means "sharing" or "communion" in something. One of the great purposes of salvation is to draw believers into a unity like that of God's triunity: "that they all may be one, as You, Father, are in Me, and I in You; that they also may be one in Us" (John 17:21). Fellowship is the living out of this unity, which is made possible by the Spirit, "the communion of the Holy Spirit be with you all" (2 Cor 13:14). Its preeminent characteristic is love for one another: "A new commandment I give to you, that you love one another; as I have loved you" (John 13:34). It is a preparation for our everlasting togetherness in the new heavens and the new earth, a world of love, and it grows out of our fellowship with the Father and his Son Jesus Christ (1 John 1:3). Of course, spiritual fellowship existed among believers before Messiah's coming: "As for the saints who are on the earth, They are the excellent ones, in whom is all My delight" (Ps 16:3; see also Esth 9:22; Zech 7:9; Mal 3:16); however it is immeasurably deepened by the truths of the gospel and the indwelling of the Spirit. The word "fellowship" (*koinonia*) is used in a number of contexts which demonstrate its main aspects: an understanding of the gospel (Gal 2:9), walking in the light (1 John 1:6–7), suffering for Messiah (2 Tim 3:12), financial support of other believers in need and of missionary work (Phil 4:10–20; 1 Cor 9:14; 3 John 5–7).

Spiritual fellowship between believers is a multifaceted experience, especially understood by the use of the phrase "one another" in the New

Testament: "Have salt in yourselves, and have peace with one another" (Mark 9:50). There is to be love; the honoring of others; mutual acceptance, instruction, and exhortation of each other; comfort; service towards each other; forgiveness; submission; encouragement; and hospitality. And all this cannot but be seen by others and is to be a means of showing the truth of the gospel, and therefore of drawing unbelievers to Yeshua: "that they also may be one in Us, that the world may believe that You sent Me" (John 17:21).

(iii) Ministry

"The Son of Man did not come to be served, but to serve" (Matt 20:28; Mark 10:45); with these words Yeshua established a pattern for the lives of his people—service to God, to one another, and towards all whom they met. A believer who fails to enter into this will end up an impoverished soul.

(a) Gifts for Service

All people have natural gifts and go through experiences in life which equip them to help others, even when those experiences have been harmful. When a person becomes a Christian, the indwelling Spirit will sanctify those gifts and experiences to be a blessing to others in the church. For example, Peter was a born leader but not one without faults. However, his Spirit-enabled willingness to receive correction led to him emerging as the leader among the apostles.

All believers are given a gift by God and these gifts are many and varied: "As each one has received a gift, minister it to one another as good stewards of the manifold grace of God" (1 Pet 4:10). More details of the gifts and the ministries they enable are in five passages of the New Testament: 1 Cor 12 8–10, 28; Eph 4:11; Rom 12:6–8; 1 Cor 7:7. Such lists are not comprehensive in detail but certainly cover gifts and ministries in a general way. Peter divides them into two main areas: speaking God's truth and serving one another's needs. When the expression "gifts of the Spirit" is used it usually points to the gifts listed in 1 Cor 12:8–10, but it ought to be recognized that, as Peter puts it, God's gifts are manifold and not to be confined to the list in 1 Cor 12. Some gifts lead to a recognized ministry, such as deacons and elders, which will be considered in the next section. All gifts are to be exercised in love so that the body of Messiah grows by what each contributes, all to the glory of God.

The gifts of the Spirit listed in 1 Cor 12:8–10 have been a cause of controversy in evangelical churches for over a century because some teach they are to be sought and exercised today and others assert they have ceased. The issues should be carefully considered through the Further Reading recommended at the end of this section but a few points can be made here. Those who believe the gifts of 1 Cor 12:8-10 have ceased (cessationists) hold that the revelatory teaching gifts were needed before the New Testament was complete, as were the miraculous gifts which attested the truth, but when God's written revelation was complete such things were no longer needed and the gifts ceased. Those who argue for their continuance assert there is no clear Scripture teaching regarding their cessation, and point to the spiritual decline of the churches as a reason for their withdrawal. The main concern of cessationists is that the exercise of the revelatory gifts (word of wisdom, word of knowledge, prophesy, interpretation of tongues) is liable to be viewed as equal to, if not above, Scripture, and they point to examples of this among practitioners of the gifts. Those who defend the use of such gifts recognize that there are abuses but maintain that such gifts are not revelatory and inspired in the way Scripture is because they are to be tested by the hearers (1 Cor 14:29; 1 Thess 5:19-21), which is never suggested of the written Scriptures or the teaching of the apostles. A teaching has emerged known as "Sovereign Spirit," which recognizes the force of the argument that such gifts are less necessary since Scripture was completed but that they have not been totally withdrawn and may be sovereignly given and manifested among believers as the Spirit wills. This author takes that view, and believes it is difficult to argue for the redundancy of these gifts when an apostle himself so values one particular gift that he writes, "I thank my God I speak with tongues more than you all," and encourages believers to "earnestly desire the best gifts" (1 Cor 14:18; 12:31).

(b) Set-Apart Ministries

In this section we will consider ministries in the church which for their proper functioning require the church to recognize and set apart those gifted for such ministries. In doing so the church must be aware that while its action gives authority to a ministry, the primary authority is Messiah himself. It is he who gives ministries to his people, as a gift from him as the ascended Lord (Eph 4:1-12).

There is a certain development of ministries in the New Testament such that the church today should seek to conform to the pattern which emerged by the close of the New Testament revelation. To begin with, during Yeshua's earthly ministry we read of twelve men set apart by him to have a teaching ministry which included healing and miracles (Matt 10:1-8), and a further seventy set apart by him to prepare the way before him and to heal the sick. After Yeshua's resurrection the church in Jerusalem was led by the twelve apostles (Acts 2:42; 5:12) but a further seven men were appointed to oversee a practical ministry of distribution to meet daily needs (Acts 6:1–7). Alongside the apostles we read of prophets whose ministry was one of teaching (Acts 15:32), and also involved foretelling (Acts 11:27), a ministry which appears to have been patterned on the Old Testament prophets. They were people who received revelation concerning the new order of things under the new covenant (Eph 3:5), and were inspired by the Spirit in teaching and prophecy (Acts 21:10). In some senses they were on a level with the twelve apostles in the founding of the church and worked alongside them (Eph 2:20; Acts 15:32–40). Their ministry is to be distinguished from those described as prophets in 1 Cor 14:29 because such were to have their utterances weighed by the church, indicating their precise words were not under the direct inspiration of the Spirit. At some point elders were appointed to assist the apostles in a teaching and ruling ministry but in settled locations (Acts 15:6); this development drew on a synagogue and temple leadership structure which had existed among God's people for centuries.

As churches were established among the Gentiles, Paul continued this pattern, establishing a plurality of elders to lead churches in his absence (Acts 14:23). Such men were to rule and have the ability to instruct (1 Tim 3:5; Heb 13:7; Titus 1:9), and it would seem that among them there would be those who had a public teaching ministry (1 Tim 5:17). Such men led the gatherings of the church and exercised discipline when necessary. They were not to lord it over God's people, especially not legislating things which were not commanded in God's word or based on a principle within it (1 Pet 5:3).

The office of deacon developed in this period and it appears to be based on the ministry of the seven in Jerusalem. The word "deacon" comes from *diakonos*, meaning "servant," and the role was one of ordering the practical affairs of the church so that the elders were free to lead and teach (Acts 6:2). It was a significant ministry alongside the elders, to be exercised by spiritually mature men (Phil 1:1; Acts 6:3; 1 Tim 3:8–13).

During this period we also read of the ministry of an evangelist. Acts 8:5–40 describes Philip preaching Messiah to an Ethiopian official and then to crowds in Samaria, many of whom came to faith. By the end of Acts Philip has the title of evangelist (Acts 21:8), indicating a set-apart ministry of gospel preaching for which Acts 8:5–40 is a pattern; there were probably many people like Philip who took the gospel both to reached and unreached regions.

The writings of the apostles give clear indications as to which of these offices would continue. Their own ministry and that of prophets are seen as foundational and not intended to be an ongoing order (Eph 2:20). Paul's instructions to Titus to appoint "elders" (Gk. *presbuteros*) or "overseers" (Gk. *episkopos*) indicates this ministry continues (Titus 1:5; see also 1 Pet 5:12), as does that of deacons (1 Tim 3:8–10, 12–13). All Protestant churches consider Paul's instructions to Timothy and Titus as a model for the role of minister or pastor in a church, a person who is responsible for the leadership of a local church, its teaching ministry, the appointment of other officers, and for church discipline. Some see elements in the ministry of Timothy and Titus which justify considering an overseer, or bishop, as a role above local church elders, having authority over a group of churches in a region, as was the case for Titus on Crete (Titus 1:5). Others would argue that the words "overseer" and "elder" are referring to the same local church office, and that Titus's role over many churches on Crete was only possible due to his being specially authorized by an apostle. For further study of this important subject see the books recommended in the Further Reading section. There is no indication that the ministry of evangelist ceased, and its precedence in the list of Eph 4:11 is not necessarily one of authority over pastors and teachers but one of priority of operation—evangelists founded churches and others subsequently led them. Some use the term today and others prefer to use the term "missionary"; there is an equivalence when the role of the missionary is one of the word, to bring others to salvation and in some cases to establish the churches.

The question arises, who appoints to these ministries now? The answer will depend on the system of church government that a church or churches understand to be in Scripture, and this will be briefly examined later. But all will answer "Christ," in that he gives the gifts, calling, empowering, and fruitfulness that is necessary to authenticate a ministry. However, there must be recognition by God's people, something required even by the apostles (Acts 6:3; 16:13). This process will end with a solemn setting apart for ministry by the laying on of hands by those already in authority (Acts 6:6; 13:3; 1 Tim 4:14), at which point specific gifts may be imparted by God (1 Tim 4:14).

(c) Male and Female Roles in Ministry

Yeshua's attitude to the woman of Samaria surprised his disciples (John 4:27), and he did not discourage those women who followed him as diligently as did the twelve apostles, contributing to his needs and those of the apostolic group. Women were among the first to see the risen Jesus. On the Day of Pentecost Peter quotes from Joel to the effect that women would receive the Spirit's enabling to prophesy as men would, and we know this occurred in Corinth (1 Cor 11:5) and probably did on the Day of Pentecost. Some engaged in practical ministries authorized by a church, such as Phoebe (Rom 16:1); others, like Priscilla, were enabled to privately instruct men of immature understanding (Acts 18:26); and some worked alongside Paul in his gospel ministry (Phil 4:3). It is quite clear in Scripture that men and women are equal with regard to salvation in Messiah (Gal 3:27). The key question is whether women may exercise authority over men in the public life and gatherings of the church, either by preaching God's word or in a leadership role. Paul wrote, "I do not permit a woman to teach or to have authority over a man, but to be in silence. For Adam was formed first, then Eve" (1 Tim 2:12–13). He clearly forbids a woman to exercise authority over men and bases this not on some passing cultural norm, but on God's order in creation. It should also be noted that all Yeshua's apostles were men and there is no evidence for women preachers, elders, or deacons in the apostolic churches (see 1 Tim 3:1, 12; Titus 1:6).

This does not mean women were not set apart by churches to specific ministries. First Timothy 3:11 refers to a qualification for women to serve in the church (the Greek for "wives" and "women" is the same word) and would seem to refer to women with a recognized pastoral or practical ministry towards other women. Regarding the issue of women prophesying, this role was not one which involved public preaching and teaching of God's word but was one of edification, exhortation, and comfort (1 Cor 14:3), which was subject to the judgment of others. In Corinth its exercise was one contribution among many and not a leadership teaching role (1 Cor 14:26–30). Recommendations for Further Reading follow on this subject, which today it is highly contentious.

(d) Ministering God's Word

This ministry of the word takes place in three contexts: private bible study, one-another contexts, and the public teaching of God's word by those in leadership.

PRIVATE BIBLE STUDY

Daily, prayerful reading of God's word and meditation upon it should be the aim of every believer in Jesus; it was the delight of faithful Israelites of old (Pss 1:2; 119:97). Some parts of God's word are straightforward but not all, and public teaching by experienced men will guide individuals in their private study into how to understand the truth in its different literary forms, and to know how to apply it.

One-Another Bible Study

Iron sharpens iron, and it is good for believers to meet together to study and discuss God's word. This group bible study is best done with trained leaders so as to avoid sinking into a pooling of ignorance.

Teaching and Preaching by Church-Ordained Leaders

God has always raised up and prepared people to teach his truth. From Enoch, Noah, and Abraham to Moses and the priesthood, to the judges and prophets and teachers like Ezra, his people were never left in ignorance, having no one to explain the truth of God revealed. The Lord has set the same provision in place for his new covenant people. First of all, and uniquely, Messiah himself. Then in Eph 4:11 Paul lists those ministries whose focus is the teaching of God's people, stressing the crucial importance of the public preaching and teaching of God's word. God wants his people to be taught and exhorted by those he has gifted with insight into his word, who have been trained to rightly divide the word of truth (2 Tim 2:15), and who have matured in wisdom and grace by walking with him (1 Tim 3:6). Jesus trained the apostles, the effectiveness of which led others to marvel (Acts 4:13); the apostles then trained others as recorded in Acts and Paul's letters to Timothy and Titus. Preaching is a face-to-face encounter in which both speaker and hearer are sensitive to each other and to God. No modern forms of electronic communication can replace it.

This primacy of teaching must affect any practice of ritual in church life. Two are ordained—baptism and the Lord's Supper—and they should not be performed without teaching from God's word, to avoid any impression that observing them or performing them carries some power to bless apart from an understanding of the ritual's significance. The same applies to other festival celebrations or rituals brought into a church's life. Such things must never be mere theater, moving the senses but bypassing the understanding.

Different cultures have different attitudes to a person standing up and declaring something clearly and boldly, and the church must take account of such trends as it reaches out to a fallen world but never jettison or diminish the centrality of the public preaching of God's word.

(e) Characteristics of New Testament Preaching and Teaching

I have used the phrase "preaching and teaching" a few times. Some readers may wonder if there is a distinction intended between the two. All Bible preaching should contain teaching, and all Bible teaching is more than mere communicating of facts. Yet there is a difference between an occasion when the aim is the careful teaching of truth, especially new truths or hard truths, requiring a less declaratory style—teaching—and an occasion when truth is being taught in a more declaratory style with more forceful application—preaching.

The public preaching recorded in the New Testament was always drawn from a text or texts of Scripture. For Messiah himself the words "it is written" were an end to debate. The Sermon on the Mount is Jesus expounding the law; Peter's sermon at Pentecost is an exhortation based on the prophets (Acts 2:14–39); and Paul's sermon in Antioch was based on Israel's history and prophets (Acts 13:15–41). Their use of Scripture was always exegetical; that is they took note of the author, his context, the meaning of his words in that context, and that the author's message was part of the overall theme of Scripture—the revelation of God's salvation in the person of his Son; as Yeshua said of the Scriptures: "these are they which testify of Me" (John 5:39). The teaching always came with authority, due to the speaker's conviction of being sent by God and an enduement of the Spirit's power at the moment of preaching (Matt 7:28–29; Acts 4:13; 6:10; Eph 6:19–20; 1 Pet 4:11; 1 Cor 2:4).

Readers who have attended a synagogue will have noticed the difference between a rabbi and a preacher of the gospel. The rabbi may be a fine man but his teaching position is more akin to a lawyer who brings the weight of ancient opinions to bear on a current situation. He may do so with eloquence and conviction but there will not be a sense of "thus says the Lord" about the delivery. The Christian preacher will bring that sense, and the Spirit will underline it as the preacher witnesses to God's truth (John 15:26–27).

In the NT we have a few examples of sermons preached to the unconverted but nothing of sermons preached to believers, which surely indicates a freedom of style according to time, place, culture, and hearers. If the Epistles are seen as being like a sermon then good preaching emulates the writing of the apostles to believers and churches—doctrinal, practical, situational, and with exhortation and application, all to be understood and felt by the speaker.

(f) Dangers and Other Emphases

1. The New Testament knows nothing of church leaders being in any sense mediators between the believer and God, e.g., like a priest offering a sacrifice, as in the mass of the Roman Catholic and Orthodox churches. No minister is called "priest" in the New Testament, and all believers are seen as a priesthood to offer spiritual sacrifices (Heb 13:15; Rom 12:1; 1 Pet 2:5). There will be more on this subject under "Ordinances." Nor does the New Testament know anything of leaders charging believers to obey teachings and commands which are not clearly taught in Scripture, except to condemn such approaches (3 John 9–10).

2. Ministers are not a clerical order of a higher class in Christ than "ordinary" believers. When such an idea begins to gain ground the abuses in the paragraph above will develop. The authority of church leaders does not go beyond God's word.

3. Ministers do not derive their authority from what is called "apostolic succession," as examined earlier. Ordination to office by those who are ordained themselves is important, and brings with it authority under Christ, but its authority is based on holding to the doctrine of the apostles (2 Tim 2:2).

(iv) Corporate Prayer

It has always been important for God's people and their leaders to pray together. When under threat from Moab and Ammon, Jehosaphat gathered all Israel together to pray (2 Chr 20:4, 13), and when Amalek attacked Israel in the wilderness Moses interceded with Aaron and Hur (Exod 17:8–16). This becomes a more obvious and frequent activity in the pages of the New Testament. Yeshua taught the apostles to pray (Luke 11:1–13) and encouraged them to ask, "Until now you have asked nothing in My name. Ask, and you will receive, that your joy may be full" (John 16:23–24), and he specifically taught the value of prayer together (Matt 18:19). Corporate prayer marked the early days of the church in Jerusalem (Acts 1:13–14; 2:42; 4:23–31) and was a feature of church life (Acts 12:12; 1 Thess 5:25; Acts 13:2–3; 20:36). The first giving of the Spirit was an answer to corporate prayer (Acts 1:8,

12–14) and subsequent outpourings of the Spirit have usually been preceded by much corporate prayer.

> But you are a chosen generation, a royal priesthood, a holy nation, His own special people, that you may proclaim the praises of Him who called you out of darkness into His marvelous light; who once were not a people but are now the people of God, who had not obtained mercy but now have obtained mercy. (1 Pet 2:9–10)

Scriptures

Purpose and Life of the Church:

Worship: Exod 4:31; Neh 9:1–3; Ps 122; Matt 2:11; 18:20; Mark 14:22–26; John 4:24; Acts 2:42; 4:24–31; 13:2–3; 20:7; Rom 1:9; 8:26; 12:1; 1 Cor 11:20–26; 14:26; 16:2; Eph 1:3–14; 5:19; Phil 3:3; Col 3:16; 4:16; 1 Tim 2:1–8; 4:13; 2 Tim 4:2; Heb 10:19–25; 13:7, 15; Rev 5:14.

Fellowship: Ps 16:3; Mal 3:16; John 13:34; 17:21; Acts 2:42; Rom 12:10; 15:7, 25–26; 1 Cor 10:16; 12:25–26; 16:1; 2 Cor 13:14; Gal 2:9; 5:13; Eph 4:32; 5:21; Phil 4:14–16; 1 Thess 5:11; 2 Thess 1:3; 2 Tim 3:12; Heb 3:13; 1 Pet 4:9; 1 John 1:6–7; 3 John 5–7.

Ministry: Mark 4:10–12; 10:45; 9:35; Acts 6:3–6; 8:5–40; 13:3; 14:23; 18:26; 20:28; Rom 12:6–8; 16:1; 1 Cor 2:4; 7:7; 11:5; 12:8–10, 28; 12:31; 14:1; Eph 4:11–12; Phil 4:3; 1 Thess 5:19–21; 1 Tim 2:12–13; 3:5, 8–13; 4:14; 5:17; 2 Tim 2:2, 15; 4:2; Titus 1:9; 2:15; Heb 13:7; 1 Pet 4:10–11; 5:1–2; 21:8.

Prayer: Exod 17:8–16; 2 Chr 20:4, 13; Matt 18:19; Acts 1:13–14; 2:42; 4:23–31; 12:5; 13:2–3; 20:36; Rom 12:12; Eph 6:18; 1 Thess 5:17, 25; 1 Tim 2:1; Jas 5:14–15.

Questions

1. Discuss the similarities and differences of gatherings for worship under the Mosaic covenant, in the synagogue, and under the new covenant.
2. What guidance does Scripture offer regarding freedom and form in new covenant gatherings for worship?
3. What is the basis for Christian fellowship and how is it to be expressed?

4. Gifts are for service; what are the gifts mentioned in the New Testament and what type of service might they lead to? What natural and spiritual gifts do you believe you have?

5. Do you believe the gifts of the Spirit listed in 1 Cor 12:7–11 are given today? If so, how are they to function in the life and gatherings of the church? If not, what lessons can be drawn from 1 Cor 12–14?

6. Which set-apart ministries exist in the church today? What are the New Testament requirements for appointment to them and who appoints them? Is there such a thing as "apostolic succession"?

7. In what ways did women play a prominent role in church life in the New Testament times? Should women be appointed to teaching or ruling positions which lead to exercising authority over men?

8. The preaching and teaching of God's word is central to church life. How should this affect the form of church gatherings? Give examples of what may develop when preaching and teaching are not central.

9. What are the characteristics of preaching in the New Testament?

10. Corporate prayer is more important than private prayer; discuss.

Further Reading

Ashton, Mark. *Christ and His People*. Epsom, UK: Good Book, 2016.

Carson, Herbert M. *Hallelujah!: Christian Worship*. Darlington, UK: Evangelical, 2000.

———. *Roman Catholicism Today*. Leicester: InterVarsity, 1964.

Dever, Mark. *The Deliberate Church*. Wheaton, IL: Crossway, 2005.

Grudem, Wayne. *Bible Doctrine*. Leicester: InterVarsity, 1999. See "Gifts of the Holy Spirit," pp. 396–424.

Kostenberger, Andreas J., and Thomas R. Shreiner, eds. *Women in the Church*. 2nd ed. Grand Rapids: Baker Academic, 2005.

Lloyd-Jones, D. M. *Preaching and Preachers*. London: Hodder, 1971.

Martin, Ralph P. *Worship in the Early Church*. Grand Rapids: Eerdmans, 1975.

Motyer, Alec. *Roots: Let the Old Testament Speak*. Tain, UK: Christian Focus, 2009.

Smith, Claire. *God's Good Design*. 2nd ed. Kingsford, Australia: Matthias Media, 2019.

(v) Ordinances (or Sacraments)

Yeshua ordained two visible signs for his people to observe: baptism and the Lord's Supper (or Communion). They signify entry into and continuance within the covenant community, and they have both an edifying and a protecting function. They edify because they are a means of receiving God's gracious blessing when they are observed in faith. They protect, firstly because they declare core gospel truths—salvation through the death of Yeshua and union with him—and secondly because they are a means of defining a church's membership and therefore to maintain its purity.

It is important to see the Mosaic covenant background of these two ordinances. For Jewish believers, the words "baptism" and "Lord's Supper" can have many negative connotations due to those experiences of Jewish people in Christendom which have been negative. Forced baptisms, and the persecutions which often arose at Easter, especially associated with the Lord's Supper, have given the terms "baptism" and "Lord's Supper" a strong negativity. Help to overcome this can be found through understanding their Mosaic ancestry and in realizing they speak so eloquently of Messiah's love for his people.[1]

The ritual washings of the Mosaic law are one precursor of new covenant baptism, in which the use of water portrays cleansing from sin (Acts 22:16). Both priests and people needed to observe many such cleansings by water so as to be ritually pure for covenant life and especially temple worship (Lev 14:18; Num 19; Exod 29:4). Furthermore, entry into the Mosaic covenant was marked by circumcision for males and its fulfillment in the new covenant by circumcision of the heart is another of the things symbolized in baptism: "In Him you were also circumcised with the circumcision made without hands, by putting off the body of the sins of the flesh, by the circumcision of Christ, buried with Him in baptism, in which you also were raised with Him" (Col 2:11–12). In the early pages of the Gospels we read of John the Baptist preparing people for Messiah's coming by a call to repentance, to be confirmed by submitting to an immersion in water, symbolizing cleansing (Mark 1:4–5; John 3:23), and later we read of Yeshua's disciples following this practice for those who became committed followers (John 3:22; 4:1). Now immersion was not required by the law but it is difficult to imagine John or Jesus practicing something totally foreign to their hearers, so it would seem that a ritual of immersion in water did develop in the

---

1. Some might argue it is best to use a different term altogether, such as "Mikveh," but this is misleading as the Mikveh is the receptacle in which the person is immersed. "Tevilah" is a better alternative term as it focuses on the act of immersion and therefore connects better with the thought of dying and rising again (as well as cleansing).

Second Temple Period, similar to today's Mikveh (or Mikva). S. McKnight draws this conclusion in the *Dictionary of New Testament Background*: "It is reasonable then to argue that baptism, as an initiation rite, was a symbolic rite in progress in Judaism when John, probably Jesus and certainly early Christians like Paul began to use the rite as the prevailing entry rite into the newfound movement."[2] After the Bar Kokhba Revolt of 135 AD there is clear evidence of immersion as a feature of Judaism and it would seem that all the immersion rituals associated with today's Mikveh have developed from that. Part of the initiation for a convert to Judaism today is to ritually immerse in water, signifying cleansing and new life.

The Lord's Supper was instituted by Yeshua within a seder shared with his disciples (Matt 26:17–30) and celebrates his fulfillment of the Passover deliverance by his death as the lamb of God (1 Cor 5:7; Luke 22:15–16; John 1:35–36). The lack of a lengthy celebration with a meal might initially disappoint some Jewish believers but there is no evidence that was a requirement of Jesus and the apostles. When Paul reminds the Corinthian church of what he had taught them of the Lord's Supper, he only emphasizes eating the bread and drinking the cup as essentials, even though he does make it plain it was originally given in the context of a supper (1 Cor 11:23–26). It does seem that the Corinthian church combined celebrating the Lord's Supper with a meal together but this is not commanded as an essential, although churches are free to do it and some do on an occasional basis.

There are differences between churches on the understanding and practice of these two ordinances, and I will endeavor to present them fairly whilst expressing my own Baptist convictions. The reasons for the differences are varied. Some of them are over minor details of practice with agreement on essentials. Some agree on the essentials but have a significant difference over the question of infant baptism. Other differences are major and have led to serious controversies because they expose differences over such fundamental questions as how a person becomes a Christian and how they remain on the Christian pathway.

(a) Terminology

Well-known terms have been used in the above writing but they need comment. Our word "baptism" is from the Greek *baptizo*, which means "to dip or immerse." The term "Lord's Supper" is used by Paul in 1 Cor 11:20 and one alternative term, "Communion," is derived from 1 Cor 10:16, "The cup of blessing which we bless, is it not the communion of the blood of

---

2. Evans and Porter, *Dictionary of New Testament Background*.

Christ?"—a text which expresses an essential of the remembrance: communion together with our Savior. For that reason some churches use the term "Holy Communion" to distinguish it from all other forms of communal activity. Another term is "breaking of bread" (see 1 Cor 10:16). There is also the term "Eucharist," which is derived from the Greek for "thanksgiving."

Some use the term "sacraments" and some "ordinances" to refer to these two visible signs, both of which can be defined as "the outward and visible sign of an inward and spiritual grace." The older term is "sacrament" and derives from the Latin *sacramentum*, pointing to an act with mystical significance. The misunderstanding of the nature of the two sacraments in the medieval church prompted others to adopt an English term more closely associated with the thought of Messiah ordaining the two signs, and hence the term "ordinance." Protestant churches affirm two ordinances, baptism and the Lord's Supper, but the Roman Catholic and Orthodox churches add five more—confirmation, penance, holy orders, matrimony, and extreme unction (and also healing for the sick in the Orthodox Church)—but none of these were ordained by Yeshua or his apostles as outward signs of spiritual realities.

(b) Efficacy

How does the observance of the ordinances communicate God's blessing? There is no inherent power in them or the person who administers them so that the observance automatically confers the blessing of God on the soul. The biblical emphasis is on worthy reception—"But let a man examine himself, and so let him eat of the bread and drink of the cup" (1 Cor 11:28)—and this involves an act of faith by which the Lord's body and blood are remembered and discerned (1 Cor 11:24–25, 29). This is more than a mere remembrance on people's part; it also involves communion and fellowship with the Lord himself (1 Cor 10:16–21).

This does not mean these two observances bring some special form of God's blessing, inherently different to the blessing he gives by all the other ways he works in us. If they did we would expect the New Testament to give them a position above all other activities, but they are one of a number of activities in worship which get equal mention (see Acts 2:42, and note Paul himself wrote he was too busy preaching to baptize, 1 Cor 1:14–17). Both the Roman Catholic and Orthodox churches deviate from this biblical perspective by asserting the blessing of God is communicated *ex opere operato*, i.e., by the act performed, so that as long as a sacrament is performed properly by an ordained priest the blessing of God follows. Because of this the Lord's Supper in particular has become the central focus of their worship.

(c) Baptism

The act of baptism in the New Testament is a public confession of repentance of sin and faith in Yeshua for salvation: "Then Peter said to them, 'Repent, and let every one of you be baptized in the name of Jesus Christ for the remission of sins'" (Acts 2:38). It expresses a determination to follow Yeshua in a new life—"For as many of you as were baptized into Christ have put on Christ" (Gal 3:27)—and has the certain hope of life with Messiah in the world to come (1 Pet 3:21–22). The symbolism in the act of water baptism is firstly the washing away of sin, something very familiar to the first Jewish believers (Acts 22:16). Secondly, it portrays union with Messiah in his death and resurrection—"buried with Him in baptism, in which you also were raised with Him through faith in the working of God, who raised Him from the dead" (Col 2:12)—thus assuring believers their sins are dealt with as certainly as death has no more hold over Jesus, and encouraging them to live a new life as Jesus lives to God (Rom 6:3–11).

The mode of baptism is indicated by three things. Firstly the meaning of *baptizo*, the verb "to baptize," which means "to dip or immerse."[3] Secondly, the New Testament practice, which, while there is little by way of description of the act, yet when there is the presence of much water is often mentioned, implying immersion (John 3:23). Thirdly, the symbolism of burial (Rom 6:4) is best expressed by being immersed and then rising out of the water. Those who argue for an effusion of water onto the person point to the Old Testament washings as not being by immersion, and to a baptism of suffering or of the Spirit as an outpouring upon. They also point to situations where it is unlikely there was sufficient water for immersion, like the baptism of the Philippian jailer and his household (Acts 16:32–33). It would seem to this writer that immersion is the ideal but where the subject is in poor health or there is insufficient water then effusion may be used without invalidating the baptism.

The subjects of baptism are those who have repented of sin and expressed trust in Jesus for salvation, i.e., those of sufficient understanding to make a credible profession of repentance and faith. The New Testament accounts point to this requirement because it is only believers who are baptized: "Then those who gladly received his word were baptized" (Acts 2:41;

---

3. See Greek-English lexicons, e.g., Bauer, *Greek-English Lexicon of the New Testament*.

Acts 18:8). Furthermore, this act requires "the answer of a good conscience toward God" (1 Pet 3:21) and "calling on the name of the Lord" (Acts 22:16), which must involve a good understanding.

The *baptism of infants* is practiced in many churches and this needs to be considered. A distinction ought to be made between those who hold that infants are regenerated at baptism and those who deny it. The former include the Roman Catholic and Orthodox Churches, the latter include Episcopalian (e.g., Anglican), Presbyterian, and Congregational churches. Under the heading "Efficacy" above, the teaching of *ex opere operato* was discussed and it is this understanding that leads Roman Catholicism and Orthodoxy to teach that the exercise of faith by the one baptized is not essential; the action of the ordained priest can confer the spiritual reality symbolized by baptism, that is: regeneration, removal of original sin, and union with Christ. Use is made of John 3:5 where "born of water" is said to refer to baptism. However, it is clear by comparing that verse with Titus 3:5 that new birth by the Spirit has two aspects—cleansing from sin and renewal of the soul. Baptism is nowhere in view in those two crucial texts but only the work of the Spirit in the soul. As Jewish people know only too well, the consequences of teaching baptismal regeneration have been disastrous. It has led multitudes of Gentiles to believe they are Christians, hopeful of forgiveness and eternal life, when their lives show no evidence of faith and holiness. This brings the gospel into disrepute. Among these unrighteous people have been those who have reviled and persecuted Jewish people in the name of Jesus, and hardened many Jewish hearts against the gospel.

Those who deny baptismal regeneration but yet baptize infants do so on other grounds. They are usually referred to as "pedobaptists." Many who do this are fine Christians who live sacrificial lives for their Savior, and therefore great care needs to be taken in expressing differences. The main justification is provided by drawing a parallel between circumcision under the Mosaic covenant and baptism in the new. Because children were covenant members in the Mosaic it is taught that they must be so in the new and hence, as baptism is the rite for entry to the new covenant, infants should be baptized. Churches like the Presbyterian and Congregational only consider children of church members as eligible. National Episcopalian churches like the Anglican Church have a similar qualification but because in their national history there was a time when everyone was baptized, and subsequently all their children were baptized, the number of those baptized in infancy in their churches has tended to be much greater. In both cases the great danger is that those baptized in infancy grow up assuming they are Christians; they hold to a nominal faith and want their children baptized and thus such Christian communities have more and more unconverted members, even though the leadership may be faithful to the doctrines of Scripture.

In addition to the circumcision/baptism justification, two New Testament examples are quoted. Firstly, Peter's words in Acts 2:39 are cited—"For the promise is to you and to your children"—but this overlooks the fact that Peter was speaking to Israelites, to whom such a promise was made (Gen 17:7); no such promise was made to other nations (although the prophets certainly indicated God's intention to bless them through Israel's Messiah). Secondly, Acts records households being baptized such as those of Lydia, Stephanas, and the Philippian jailer (Acts 16:15; 1 Cor 1:16; Acts 16:33). In the cases of Stephanas and the jailer it is clear that all believed, but that is not so for Lydia's household. However, there is no evidence there were any infants in that household so it becomes an argument from silence, which is always inconclusive.

Regarding the argument based on the circumcision/baptism equivalence, it needs to be considered that the membership of the two covenant communities is defined differently. Entry into the covenant community in the patriarchal and Mosaic period was by birth and the exercise of faith was urged later, but for the new covenant community the exercise of faith was a necessary condition from the start. Covenant pedobaptists do not argue that the baptized infant is regenerate but that their baptism symbolizes "probable future regeneration." Some pedobaptist churches define such baptized infants who reach adulthood without exercising saving faith as adherents but not as members. Hence, it seems to me that such pedobaptists are operating with one foot firmly in Old Testament practice. Whilst their motivation may be good, such practice falls short of the New Testament requirements for baptism.

It should also be noted that the New Testament knows only of a community of believers, not one of believers plus their children plus their servants, as in the Old Testament. This change in entry requirement is paralleled by other differences, such as the physical temple is fulfilled by a spiritual temple. However, it needs to be asked whether Baptists fail to sufficiently consider this continuity between the testaments. Two considerations would argue against such a charge. They emphasize cleansing from sin in baptism, and they stress the importance of believers' infants being brought before the church for prayer, aware that the Lord desires the salvation of households (Acts 16:31).

The *effects of baptism* are a blessing to the soul, which is why it is spoken of as a means of grace. God grants spiritual enrichment to those who obey him by this act of confession of his Son. There is assurance as believers are caused to focus in faith on all God has done in uniting them to Yeshua in his death and resurrection (Col 2:12). There is joy given to the obedient, as in the example of the Ethiopian baptized by Philip who went on his way rejoicing (Acts 8:39).

The *necessity of baptism*: baptism is not essential for salvation; otherwise Jesus could not have said to the thief on the cross, "today you will be with Me in Paradise" (Luke 23:43). However, it is a commanded obedience (Acts 2:38) and those who are unhindered from being baptized, and who fail to obey, are living in disobedience to Christ.

On the minimum *age for baptism*, nothing is said in the New Testament as this will obviously vary. What is necessary is a credible profession of faith in Yeshua and that requires sufficient maturity of heart and mind for the person to express that faith to others.

Baptism and church membership: the New Testament knows nothing of a baptized believer who is not part of a local church. The baptized believers at Pentecost were described as "added," meaning to those already counted as part of the church, which was about 120 known by name (Acts 1:15). All are then described as participating in church activities (Acts 2:42). The knowledge of who is part of a church is important for spiritual care and discipline; hence it is important for believers to commit themselves to a church and its leadership: "Obey those who rule over you, and be submissive, for they watch out for your souls" (Heb 13:17; see also Heb 13:7; Acts 20:28).

Water baptism and Spirit baptism: union with Messiah is brought about by the Holy Spirit, who spiritually unites the believer to Messiah: "he who is joined to the Lord is one spirit with Him" (1 Cor 6:17). This is elsewhere described as being baptized *by* the Spirit into Christ: "For by one Spirit we were all baptized into one body" (1 Cor 12:13). By this spiritual union we are united with Messiah in his death and resurrection. It is this work of the Spirit which is symbolized in water baptism; it is something which happens at the moment of conversion and water baptism is a testimony to it. This is why some texts which speak of baptism seem to be using the one word "baptism" to speak of both the act of water baptism and its spiritual reality: "For as many of you as were baptized into Christ have put on Christ" (Gal 3:27). Misunderstanding of the usage of the word "baptism" in such texts has led some to teach the act of baptism actually regenerates. Note: baptism by the Spirit into Christ ought to be distinguished from the work of Christ as the baptizer with the Spirit—"He will baptize you with the Holy Spirit" (Matt 3:11, see also Acts 1:5)—which is an empowering for service (Acts 1:8); see pgs 226–227; 234–235.

(d) The Lord's Supper

It was no coincidence that the Lord's Supper was instituted at Pesach, during the seder. By doing so Yeshua revealed himself as the One who fulfilled all that the exodus and Passover had foreshadowed—deliverance from the power of sin and Satan by his death as a substitute, God's lamb. By inaugurating a new covenant at the seder, confirmed by the shedding of his own blood, symbolized in the cup which he offered to them, he announced the messianic era had come. It was a momentous event. He commands his disciples to eat bread and drink from the cup which represented his body broken on the cross and his blood shed, the evidence of a life laid down in death.

Both Luke and Paul tell us that the cup was "the cup after supper," the one which traditionally represents the Passover lamb, thus underlining Messiah Jesus as the fulfillment of the Passover lamb. Yeshua commanded the eating of bread and drinking from a cup to be repeated by his disciples as a remembrance of him. The focus is on his death but Yeshua pointedly says "in remembrance of *me*"; we are never to lose sight of the person involved, his love which took him to Golgotha and the personal suffering he endured for us. As water baptism signifies entrance into the covenant community, so participating in the Lord's Supper signifies a renewal of covenant commitment by the believer.

In the New Testament the Lord's Supper is always presented as a communal event, not an individual one, and hence it also expresses believers' fellowship with one another, in Messiah: "For we, though many, are one bread and one body; for we all partake of that one bread" (1 Cor 10:17). The Lord's Supper also has a future perspective as it looks to its consummation in the new heavens and the new earth, as Paul wrote, "till He comes" (1 Cor 11:26). It is this aspect which helps believers to maintain their focus on the Lord's return. On all these points there is agreement among evangelicals.

The precise *form of the Lord's Supper* is not stipulated in Scripture, save the breaking and eating of bread and the drinking from a cup. The emphasis on a cup is significant; Paul calls it "the cup of blessing" (1 Cor 10:16), and this seems to be drawn from the Old Testament emphasis on a full cup as a sign of God's blessing, but this cup is a blessing more than any other. Ideally then, it would seem that the use of one loaf (we, though many, are one bread) and one cup (only one is mentioned) best symbolizes all the truths involved. However, there may be good reasons for doing things differently and as long as the broken body and shed blood are clearly in view there can be no objection. We need to bear in mind that in some places neither bread nor wine are available.

The *participants in the Lord's Supper* are believers in Yeshua, and in the New Testament such are always baptized believers. Every care should be taken by church leaders that all who participate are believers as this enhances the sense of oneness as believers partake together, and hinders unbelievers from drinking judgment on themselves by not discerning the Lord's body (1 Cor 11:29). The primary responsibility for ensuring worthy participation lies with the individual believer—"let a man examine himself" (1 Cor 11:28)—but leaders have a responsibility when those who are obviously not baptized believers seek to participate.

The *benefit of participation in the Lord's Supper*: there are three different views among Protestants on this question, which stem from differences at the time of the Reformation. The Zwinglian view is that it is a simple act of remembrance, akin to the remembrance of a significant national event, so that the believer benefits by a renewed focus on Messiah and his death, but Messiah is not present in any way other than his normal indwelling of believers. In practice, this seems to be the approach of many of today's evangelicals. The Lutheran view is that the Lord is really present in or under the elements of bread and wine, yet with no change in the nature of these two elements. The believer partakes of the glorified body of Jesus at the same time as eating the bread and drinking from the cup. The Reformed view, argued by Calvin and others, was of a spiritual communion with Messiah as the elements are taken in faith, so that there is a special communion with him by the work of the Spirit. In 1 Cor 10:16–21 Paul parallels Communion with attending idol feasts, which he condemns because it creates fellowship with demons, hence his parallel points to a special fellowship with the Lord in taking of the bread and the wine.

Serious error concerning the Lord's Supper: the three views expressed above were the different ways the Reformers responded from Scripture to the understanding prevailing in the two main churches of their day, the Roman Catholic Church and the Orthodox Church. The Roman Catholic understanding involves three errors. Firstly, the cup is withheld from the people and it is asserted that Christ, whole and entire, is received via the bread; but at the first Lord's Supper all drank of the cup (Matt 26:27). Secondly, it is asserted that the bread and wine are changed into the literal body and blood of Jesus, though they retain the appearance and taste of bread and wine. The purpose of the second teaching is to provide justification for the third error, which is that the Lord's Supper is a sacrifice, a reoffering of Messiah as a sacrifice for sin: "The Holy Mass is one and the same Sacrifice with that of the Cross, inasmuch as Christ, who offered himself, a bleeding victim, on the cross to his heavenly Father, continues to offer himself in an unbloody manner on the altar, through the ministry of his priests."[4] This teaching was the touchstone of orthodoxy before the Reformation and was the key to this church's power over the people; those who denied it became martyrs. It is a blasphemous teaching because it denies the once-for-all work of propitiation by Messiah on the cross (Heb 9:27–28; John 19:30). Furthermore, there is no mention of Christ's ministers as priests in the New Testament. The understanding of the Orthodox churches is similar, teaching that the bread and wine become the very body and blood of the Lord. However, they do not speak of a repetition of the sacrifice of Messiah but of the events of Christ's sacrifice being made present: "The same divine act, both takes place at a specific moment in history, and is offered always in the sacrament."[5] The participation of the faithful is said to obtain pardon for sin; it is a sacrifice. This too is blasphemy.

It is tempting for Jewish believers to overlook these serious errors of the Roman Catholic and Orthodox Churches. The relatively small numbers of Jewish believers and the sense of isolation which some experience may lead them to value contact with any fellow Jews who confess Jesus as Messiah. It is a temptation to be resisted. Paul pronounces anathemas on those who preach another gospel (Gal 1:8–9) and these errors are definitely another gospel, for they deny both the sufficiency of Messiah's once and for all sacrifice and justification by faith alone.

(vi) Spiritual Growth

Believers are to grow more like their Savior so as to be fit for the coming glory: "But we all, with unveiled face, beholding as in a mirror the glory of the Lord, are being transformed into the same image from glory to glory, just as by the Spirit of the Lord" (2 Cor 3:18). The New Testament expects this growth to take place in the context of spiritual interaction with each other (Eph 4:15–16). As believers take part in church life—its worship, fellowship, prayer, ministry of the word, participation in the ordinances, witness to the world, and suffering for Messiah—the Spirit of God will change them to "grow in the grace and knowledge of our Lord and Savior Jesus Christ" (2 Pet 3:18).

---

4. Catholic Truth Society, *Catechism of Christian Doctrine*, 47, q. 278.
5. Evdokimov, quoted in Ware, *Orthodox Church*, 287.

(vii) Witness

The missional role of the church has been considered. Here the emphasis will be on the individual believer communicating the salvation message. Believers are not only to witness by their lives but are to be telling others of the Savior and giving a reason for the hope that is in them (Acts 8:4, Gk. "tell good news"; 1 Pet 3:15). Witness is both a divine and a human activity. Yeshua said to his disciples, "But when the Helper comes . . . the Spirit of truth . . . He will testify of Me. And you also will bear witness, because you have been with Me from the beginning" (John 15:26–27). Our message is primarily one of God's truth, not our own testimony, though that is valuable. We are to tell people of the one, true God who created and sustains each of us, of our sin against him, how he sent his Son to save us by bearing the punishment we deserve, and his requirement that we repent and trust his Son for salvation (Acts 17:24–31; John 3:16). To Jewish people that same message is presented as a promise fulfilled (Acts 3:24–26). And our presentation is not to be merely academic, a bare recounting of facts, but it is an exhortation, truth we ourselves have felt being communicated with feeling (Acts 2:40; 1 Cor 2:1–5). As we do this we have the promise that the Spirit will bear witness in our hearer's heart and mind that what we say is truth. And we know that unless he does that, and unless he enlightens them and regenerates them and gives them faith, all our words will be in vain (2 Cor 4:6; John 3:5; Eph 2:8). We need to beware of applying the sort of psychological pressure which fails to trust the Spirit to do his work.

The parable of the sower teaches that there will be different responses to bearing witness by God's word. There will be indifference and there will be short-lived enthusiasm; there will be commitment which slowly dies and there will be love of God's truth which leads to a faithful, persevering life for God (Matt 13:3–9, 18–23); there will also be hostility because sinners hate the light (John 3:19–20), and they will oppose it, seeking to snuff it out (1 Pet 4:12–14; see also 2 Tim 3:12; Rom 8:17).

(J) IS IT JEWISH? CONTINUITY AND CHANGE

Christians often encourage a Jewish friend to consider Jesus by telling them Christianity is Jewish, but to the Jewish friend it doesn't look that way; maybe it didn't to you. The usual church buildings look different to a synagogue, both inside and out; the services and rituals are different; any food provided will be rarely be "Jewish" and the mixing and mingling will feel Gentile. So, why did one particular rabbi who came to faith in Yeshua think the church he entered was Jewish? Because the Old Testament was read, psalms were sung, and the sermon was from Isaiah; and that gets us to the spiritual heart of Jewishness.

Much has been written in this sixth part of the book ("God's People") which connects God's people of the new covenant with those in earlier eras, especially the Mosaic. So much so that perhaps the heading of this section should be: "What Is Not Jewish?" Here is a brief reminder of the similarities:

- Repentance and faith in the sacrifice God provides, followed by a righteous life, has always been expected;
- The God of the new covenant has always been a covenant-making God;
- The metaphors for God's people under Moses, such as people, family, kingdom, and bride, all reappear in the New Testament;
- Israel's national life centered on worship, teaching, sacrifice, and a hope of the Messiah are realities which are part and parcel of the life of believers in Jesus;
- The law was central to Israel's life and it is not abandoned under the new covenant;
- Faith has always been crucial to justification and sanctification; and
- The two main ordinances of the church are closely connected to circumcision and Passover under Moshe.

Most, though not all, of these beliefs and practices are familiar to a Jewish person who has some synagogue background.

Change, however, is to be expected, or the new covenant would not be new. The biggest change is that the expectation has become a reality; Messiah has come, and God's Spirit is given to all who believe, to indwell them. More is given and more is expected of those who live under the new covenant. A door is opened for the nations to come in on an equal basis, and the dwelling place of God is no longer a localized temple but a people spread across all the earth. Under the new covenant it is the righteousness of the law which is to be lived, not the letter of the law through all its commands and regulations. It is not surprising that these religious realities appear different—churches are not "Mosaically" Jewish or culturally Jewish but spiritually Jewish. A metamorphosis has taken place, just as a caterpillar becomes a butterfly; there is a change of form but not of substance.

[K] THE CHURCH'S FUTURE

The life of believers now should be characterized by a longing for Yeshua's return and a desire for the joy of greater communion with God in a perfect world: "For our citizenship is in heaven, from which we also eagerly wait for the Savior, the Lord Jesus Christ," and "Nevertheless we, according to His promise, look for new heavens and a new earth in which righteousness dwells" (Phil 3:20; 2 Pet 3:13). More on this subject will be considered in Part 7.

> Then those who feared the LORD spoke to one another.
> And the LORD listened and heard them;
> So a book of remembrance was written before Him
> For those who fear the LORD
> And who meditate on His name.
> "They shall be Mine," says the LORD of hosts,
> "On the day that I make them My jewels." (Mal 3:16–17)

SCRIPTURES

Purpose and Life of the Church

Ordinances: Pre-New Testament church: Gen 17:9–11; Exod 12; 19:14; 29:4; Lev 14:1–18; Num 19; Jer 31:31–34; Matt 3:1–17; 26:17–30; 20:22; Mark 1:4–5; John 1:35–36; 3:22–23; 1 Cor 5:78; 10:2.

Baptism: Matt 20:22; 28:19; John 3:23; Acts 1:5; 2:38, 39, 41; 8:16, 36, 39; 9:18; 10:47; 16:15; 22:16; Rom 6:3–11; 1 Cor 1:13–17; 12:12; Gal 3:27; Col 2:12; 1 Pet 3:21.

The Lord's Supper: Matt 26:26–30; Mark 14:22–26; Luke 22:14–20; John 19:30; Acts 20:7; 1 Cor 10:16–17; 11:20, 23–31; Heb 9:27–28.

Spiritual growth and witness: Pss 26:7; 48:12; Isa 43:10; Matt 13:3–9, 18–23; 28:19–20; John 3:5, 16; 15:26–27; Acts 1:8; 2:40; 3:24–26; 4:20; 8:4; 17:24–31; Rom 8:17; 1 Cor 2:1–5; 2 Cor 4:6; Eph 2:8; 4:15–16; 2 Tim 3:12; 1 Pet 2:2; 3:15; 4:12–14; 2 Pet 3:18.

Is it Jewish? Continuity and change: Gen 9:8–17; 15:6; Exod 19:6; 35:10–33; Lev 4:27–31; Num 14:11; Deut 18:15; Josh 1:8; 1 Sam 1:3; 3:21—4:1; Neh 8:7; Isa 42:1–4; 44:22; Joel 2:28–29; Mal 3:1; Matt 5:17–18; 9:29; 26:28; John 1:45; 2:19–21; 7:39; 20:21–22; Acts 2:38; 11:4–26; 12:1–3; 16:31; 18:5; Rom 3:22; 8:2, 4; 11:17–24; 15:17–21; 1 Cor 5:7; 14:25; Gal 2:11–14; Eph 2:11–22; 1 Pet 2:9.

Questions

1. How many ordinances are there according to the New Testament? Justify your answer and describe their place in church life.
2. In what ways do baptism and the Lord's Supper fulfill Old Testament events and practices?
3. Who should and who should not be baptized?
4. What truths are signified in the Lord's Supper, and what should participants expect to receive by partaking?
5. What are the differences and what are the similarities in witness to Jews and Gentiles?
6. How would you explain the Jewishness of the church to a Jewish friend you have invited to a church event?

Further Reading

Beasley-Murray, George R. *Baptism in the New Testament*. Milton Keynes: Paternoster, 1972.
Carson, Herbert M. *Roman Catholicism Today*. Leicester: InterVarsity, 1964.
Dever, Mark. *The Gospel and Personal Evangelism*. Wheaton, IL: Crossway, 2017.
Kevan, Ernest. *The Lord's Supper*. Darlington: Evangelical, 1966.
Newman, Randy. *Engaging with Jewish People*. Epsom: Good Book, 2016.

31

The New Testament Church in History

THE AIM OF THIS section is to provide a very brief overview of the main epochs, from New Testament times to the present day, with a particular focus on the differences of church order that emerged plus brief comments on Jewish experience in those epochs, followed by some observations on more recent global developments.

After the apostolic period the churches developed organizational structures to aid interchurch cooperation and especially to combat heresy, and this led to a three-tier leadership composed of bishops over the churches of a region, local church leaders, and local church deacons. Today this three-tier structure is known as "Episcopalianism" and is found in the Anglican, Lutheran, and Methodist churches of Protestantism, and in the Roman Catholic and Eastern Orthodox Churches. There were protests against this creation of a supralocal church authority but it was justified as a replacement for the role of the apostles and men like Timothy and Titus. The division of the church into Western and Eastern in this early period was partly due to the division of the Roman Empire into West and East, but more significantly to differences over the nature of Christ and the procession of the Holy Spirit. This period saw the heightening of the tensions between the church and synagogue which began in apostolic times. The rise of the church to acceptance and influence within the Roman Empire led some church leaders and individual Christians to repay the oppression they had endured at the hands of Jewish leaders by acting oppressively towards their Jewish neighbors. It was not easy to be Jewish and Christian.

During the Middle Ages in Europe (west and east) the church was the dominant force in society. The split between the Western and Eastern churches hardened due to the Roman (Western) claims to preeminence over all churches and their chief bishop's claim to infallibility (later termed "papal infallibility"). The claim that the Roman Church was to be identified with the kingdom of God on earth meant it influenced every area of life and every level of authority, even asserting its authority extended over kings and princes. By this time both the Western and Eastern church taught that their ministers were priests and Holy Communion was a sacrifice for sin. It was an all-encompassing religious structure and theological system which held all citizens in its grip. There were protest movements, e.g., the Lollards led by John Wycliffe, but they were ruthlessly suppressed. During this period life became ever more difficult for the Jewish communities living within Christendom. At worst they were viewed as a fifth column undermining Christianity from within, at best as second-class citizens within societies which outwardly acknowledged Jesus as Lord; they suffered both petty restrictions and serious outbreaks of persecution.

The Reformation began as a protest movement led by Martin Luther in the early sixteenth century, initially within the Western church and then beyond it. By the grace of Christ and the power of his word it was successful in breaking Rome's grip, and Protestantism emerged. The Reformers like Luther, Calvin, Zwingli, and Bucer held to all of the traditional doctrines of the Western and Eastern churches, for example those expressed in the great creeds of the church, like the Apostolic, Nicene, and Athanasian; however their careful study of Scripture led them to a different understanding to the Western and Eastern churches of their day on truths, such as how God justifies sinners, how salvation is received, the spiritual life, the church, and Christian ministry. Differences on church order emerged among Protestants. Luther taught an Episcopalian system but Calvin taught what has become known as "Presbyterianism." This is a two-tier system of elders and deacons in each local church, but providing a structure for interchurch fellowship and discipline through the elders of all the individual churches in a region meeting regularly in a synod, and all synods meeting once a year in a general assembly, making decisions which were binding on all their churches. Members of a local church had a say in the appointment of their ministers. The Anabaptists of this period were, except for a few fanatics, those who believed in the independence of the local church from any external church authority, with a membership composed of those baptized as believers.

The Reformation was a time of spiritual and theological ferment and some Reformers lost their lives in the struggle. In the midst of all this there was little time or pressure to consider what later generations have termed "the Jewish question." Europe at that time was viewed as Christian, and rulers and magistrates had a responsibility to protect the faith and uphold it. The Jewish community was seen as a polluting influence, and at times a threat when individual Jews opposed New Testament teaching. Luther, Calvin, and others hoped for Jews to be saved, and believed in a great future blessing for Israel, but the difficult and practical question to be answered was: What to do with the large number of unbelieving Jews among them? Their theological answers differed little from those of their oppressive predecessors, and it was left to their princes and political leaders to show, for purely pragmatic reasons, a more tolerant attitude to their Jewish subjects.

The Reformation was a great spiritual revival and spawned much new theological thinking. The Puritan period in England and America which followed stirred deeper thought on the spiritual life and church order, and also a renewed interest in the Jewish people and their place in God's future purposes, including speculation on a return to the land; all of which led to calls for their readmission to nations from which they had been expelled. The first political constitution granting full religious liberty to the Jewish community was that of the American colony on Rhode Island in 1657; credit for such toleration is often given to Enlightenment thinking and the French Revolution but that came one hundred years later. The Rhode Island community was led by Roger Williams, one of many Puritans who had themselves experienced persecution for their faith from other professing Christians, leading them to work out a theology of toleration.

The developments regarding church order led to Congregationalism and independency, which though similar are not identical. Congregationalism was similar to Presbyterianism but it rejected the binding authority of decisions made by local synods and a general assembly, giving them only an advisory role. Independency allowed for no organizational structure outside of and over a local church. The Protestant denominations which emerged in the eighteenth and nineteenth centuries, such as Congregational, Baptist, and Pentecostal, were essentially congregational in order, although the new churches which emerged from revivals, such as the Methodists, tended to adopt a church order similar to the body from which the revival leaders emerged. Generally speaking all these churches adopted the positive attitude to the Jewish people stimulated by Puritan thinking.

Protestant churches initiated missionary movements, whether through their denominational mission or by supporting interdenominational missions; and missions to the Jewish people were among them. The first phase of such mission work in unevangelized regions was often hard going and painfully slow but it eventually bore fruit in the many and vibrant churches in what is often termed the "Global South": Sub-Saharan Africa, Latin America, the Pacific Islands, and Eastern nations such as India, China, and Korea. Migration patterns have led to ethnic churches being established beyond their countries of origin and stimulating older church groupings. Fruitfulness among Jewish people led to the formation in 1922 of the International Hebrew Christian Alliance (IHCA) to foster fellowship and mutual support among Jewish believers. The rise of the messianic movement in the 1970s, encouraging and equipping Jewish believers to be more culturally Jewish in expressing their faith, led to the IHCA changing its name to the Messianic Jewish Alliance. The worldwide charismatic renewal movement of the mid-twentieth century not only brought new life to many established churches but also spawned new church denominations, many of which are similar to Episcopalianism in their structure, having "apostles" who have a leadership role over all their churches.

The disparate nature of Protestantism, with its many denominations and a tendency to decline, led to efforts in the nineteenth and twentieth centuries to find ways of expressing their essential evangelical unity, leading to the founding of organizations like the Evangelical Alliance in 1846. Similar efforts were made through what later became known as the "ecumenical movement," leading to the formation of the World Council of Churches. The concern was for a show of unity with dialogue and joint action, but the basis of unity was too broad, and there was insufficient clarity on the nature of the gospel; it has now become a spent force. Whether it will metamorphose into something like a world council of faiths remains to be seen. The Lausanne Consultation for World Evangelization was formed in 1974 to strengthen the missionary focus and cooperation of evangelical churches and missions through conferences and subgroups called "consultations." The Lausanne Consultation for Jewish Evangelism is a vibrant grouping among them.

The new challenges which face the evangelical churches of the twenty-first century are numerous; seven key ones are:

- the rise of secularism;
- the reviving of jihad in Islam;
- global migration;
- multicultural churches;
- new movements in the Roman Catholic Church without significant doctrinal change;
- encountering poverty in mission work; and
- the worldwide rise of anti-Semitism.

In facing these challenges the churches must hold to the old truths of the gospel and apply them to the new situations which constantly emerge; remembering that such are not fundamentally new, and hence Scripture is always a sufficient guide.

32

Israel in the New Covenant Period

THE NEW TESTAMENT HAS much to say about the situation of Israel during the new covenant period and that is our focus in what follows.

(A) GOD'S PEOPLE

In Rom 11:1 Paul describes the Jewish people as "His people," underlining that Israel remains a covenant people despite the unbelief which has been Paul's concern in Rom 9–11. God's promise to Abraham remains intact, as expressed by Jeremiah—"I will be your God, and you shall be My people" (Jer 7:23)—and by Paul: "but concerning the election they are beloved for the sake of the fathers" (Rom 11:28, see also Rom 11:1). In the light of such teaching it is impossible to argue, as some do, that Israel's unbelief has led to the annulling of God's covenant with them.

Paul teaches that both the gospel and judgment are "for the Jew first and also for the Greek [Gentile]" (Rom 1:16; 2:9-10); a priority which has nothing to do with Israel being better or worse than anyone else but arises from their privileged position as recipients of God's promises of salvation. The gospel is a message of a promise fulfilled and hence as long as the gospel is in the world the people who received the promises will remain the people of promise. What this status means for Israel in the new covenant period will be considered in the following sections.

What awareness is there in the Jewish community of being God's people? Among those who take their Judaism seriously there is no doubt they are God's people; they believe the Scriptures and the history. For those who are secular, atheist, or agnostic their sense of God underlined by the Bible story and Jewish history is not easily erased from their Jewish consciousness; however it is often suppressed. It is a history which has the unmistakable mark of divine deliverance, providence, and judgment upon it, witnessing to them that they are God's people. To coin a phrase, we might call it the *Am Adonai Daath* consciousness ("people of the Lord knowledge").

(B) ISRAEL'S PRIVILEGES

In the early verses of Rom 9 Paul expresses his deep concern at Israel's loss due to unbelief. He underlines this by listing the privileges which God has showered upon them under previous covenants. As a people they are named after a great man of faith, Israel, and could look back to the example of their fathers and to the promises God made to them. They were adopted as God's people, unique among all the nations of the earth. God manifested his presence among them and added covenants to cement his plan and purpose through them, along with all the promises of grace and blessing those covenants enshrined. They had God's perfect law given by Moses and interpreted by the prophets, and a means of access to YHWH through the sacrifices and priesthood he instituted. Above all, God himself had been incarnate among them in the Messiah. The influence of these things is not lost, even if some are not a present experience, such as the temple, sacrifices, priesthood, the Shekinah, and God's Son incarnate and on earth. However, some continue to have a direct influence on their present experience: their status, the promises, and the law, along with the hope of Messiah. Despite many forms of unbelief in the Jewish community, the influence of these privileges creates a strong susceptibility to return to the religious undergirding of their peoplehood, especially in times of crisis.

(C) REMNANT

Paul's first response to the suggestion God has abandoned Israel is to point to the remnant, those throughout Israel's history who have believed. The word "remnant" is used not to imply there were only ever a very small number of believers but to assure readers that, even at those times when things appeared to be reducing to zero, some could always be found (see Isa 1:9; 10:20; Joel 2:32). Paul saw himself as one such at the time he wrote Romans, a time when already so much hardening to the gospel had taken place in Jewish communities of the Roman world.

The remnant are also termed the "elect" (Rom 11:7). This points to the reason why some believed and some did not; the believers were chosen for salvation (see Eph 1:4), underlining that there was nothing better about them but they owed their believing entirely to God's grace, "the election of grace" as Paul puts it in Rom 11:5.

The remnant are "regrafted ones." Paul's metaphor of the olive tree in Rom 11:16–24, representing God's people as they transitioned from old to new covenant, portrays believing Jews as natural branches who are grafted back into their own olive tree when they believe (Rom 11:23–24). To be precise, there was one generation of believers like Simeon, Anna, Miriam, Joseph, and the first disciples who had a true faith and were never cut off through unbelief, but they were a unique generation. Since those days, and through all the centuries since, Jewish people have been brought up in unbelief. Whatever faith in God they may possess, it is, as Paul puts it, "not according to knowledge" (Rom 10:2), being ignorant of, or rejecting outright, God's righteousness received only through faith in Yeshua. But not only is God able to graft them in again but there is a sense in which that is a more natural step for them than for Gentiles, as they are rejoining something which is theirs, not a foreign faith (Rom 11:24).

(D) CUT OFF

Paul's metaphor of an olive tree is hopeful but it is also a somber one for the Jewish people, because it uses terms like "broken off" and "cut off" to describe those who did not believe in Yeshua. Cut off from what? Romans 11:17 mentions the root and fatness of the olive tree, which must be referring to God's presence among his people and all the blessings which that brings. Under the Mosaic covenant the Jewish people and proselytes could draw near to God through the means of grace: the priesthood and the law, with the words of the prophets. Under the new covenant the same blessing was made available through God's word and Spirit manifested among those who gather in Yeshua's name. But to reject Yeshua was to cut oneself off from the channel through which God's blessing flowed. There was what is known as a period of transition when the temple and the new covenant assemblies existed side by side, but once the temple was destroyed, as Yeshua said it would be (Matt 24:12), there was but one channel for grace, the assemblies of Yeshua's people. All the privileges mentioned in the previous section did indeed continue to exert a beneficial effect on Jewish people, but unless they turned to the Lord through Yeshua there could be no eternal, saving benefit (2 Cor 3:15–16).

Cutting off is an action of God, a judgment upon rejection of his Son. Paul describes it as being blinded, being given a spirit of stupor by God (Rom 11:7–8), a veil upon the heart (2 Cor 3:14–15), and Yeshua describes it as a hardening of the heart by God (John 12:39–40). It is a fearful thing to contemplate, and has had dire consequences not only for individuals but for Israel as a people.

Loss of the Kingdom

Yeshua warned the leaders of Israel that they were in danger of losing God's kingdom by their rejection of him (Matt 21:43); that as an ethnic nation they would no longer be the exclusive possessors of access to God via his temple, living in a holy land, set apart for living lives of service to him. This happened in 70 AD when the Romans invaded Judea, conquered Jerusalem, and destroyed the temple. It was this traumatic loss of the kingdom which lodged such great grief in Paul's heart (Rom 9:1–5).

This loss of the kingdom did not deny Jewish people access to God's means of grace because through faith in Yeshua a greater access could be received by joining what Yeshua described as "a nation bearing the fruits of it" (Matt 21:43). The word used for "nation" is *ethnos* and it needs to be distinguished from *laos*, usually translated "people." These two terms contain overlapping ideas but emphasize distinct concepts as can be seen by their both being used in John's full-orbed description of the whole human race: "Out of every tribe and tongue and people [*laos*] and nation [*ethnos*]" (Rev 5:9). *Ethnos* is applicable to national entities bound together by ties of blood, geography, history, culture, etc. *Laos* is best translated "people" and is more general, and can be used to describe a group gathered for some purpose or defined by a common experience. It might have been expected Yeshua would use *laos*—his kingdom would be transferred to a group of true believers—but he used *ethnos*, which must have been traumatic for his hearers because it sounded like another national group would receive the kingdom (e.g., the Persians or Greeks). We know that was not so, but the use of *ethnos* underlines the drastic change that would come about. Here was to be a community distinct from Israel and distinct from the Gentile nations around; it was to be defined by "righteousness and peace and joy in the Holy Spirit" (Rom 14:17). It is neither a Jewish national entity nor a Gentile national entity, which is why a new term was coined to describe it—Christian (Acts 13:26), a community of Jews and Gentiles who followed the Christ (Messiah). The promise to Abraham that in him all the nations would be blessed was being fulfilled.

It is taught by some that there is a distinction made between the expression "kingdom of heaven" (used only in Matthew's Gospel) and "kingdom of God" (used in Matthew, Mark, Luke, John, Acts, and some Epistles). The thought is that the kingdom of God concerns God's rule over all things, especially the church of Jew and Gentile, but the kingdom of heaven was something announced for Israel only, but due to Yeshua's rejection by Israel was postponed until his return in glory, when he will reign from Jerusalem, on David's throne. According to this teaching the kingdom (of heaven) will return to Israel.

A few points need to be made. Firstly, it is not unusual for authors to abbreviate biblical expressions; e.g., "the ark of the covenant of the LORD" is often reduced to "the ark of the covenant" or "the ark of the LORD." Similarly Daniel's mention in 2:44 of the God of heaven, and of his kingdom being established, may have prompted different expressions like "the kingdom of the God of heaven" or "the kingdom of heaven" or "the kingdom of God." It is not surprising that Matthew, whose Gospel presents Yeshua in a Jewish context, should make more use of "kingdom of heaven."

Secondly, there are examples where the two expressions refer to the same thing: "Assuredly, I say to you it is hard for a rich man to enter the kingdom of heaven. And again I say to you it is easier for a camel to go through the eye of a needle than for a rich man to enter the kingdom of God" (Matt 19:23–24). Similarly, the kingdom in the parables of the sower, the mustard seed, and the leaven appears in Matt 13 as "the kingdom of heaven" but in Mark and Luke as "the kingdom of God."

Thirdly, if the apostles understood this distinction, then why did they not use the expression "kingdom of heaven" when they asked Yeshua, "Lord, will you at this time restore the kingdom to Israel" (Acts. 1:6)? The implication is that they only knew of one kingdom. Furthermore, the book of Hebrews underlines the obsolescence of the temple, priests, and sacrifices (Heb 8:13) and will be considered in more detail in the next section.

We need to briefly consider the term "replacement theology" at this point. It is a confusing term because it is used in different ways, but it is mainly used by those who hold to the above distinction between the terms "kingdom of God" and "kingdom of heaven," holding the twin beliefs that the kingdom will be restored to Israel when Messiah returns and that the NT church is an interlude in the purposes of God of which the OT prophets were ignorant. They use the term negatively to describe the theology of those Christians who do not believe those twin beliefs are in Scripture. It is often assumed that Christians who disagree with them have little interest in the Jews. It has to be acknowledged that there are Christians who have little interest because they deny a covenant remains so that Israel is no longer the people of promise, and such thinking is to be deeply regretted, especially when it masks anti-Jewish feelings. However, there are many Christians who, whilst they do not hold those twin beliefs, recognize Israel as in covenant with YHWH and pray and work for the salvation of the Jewish people, both remnant and fullness. Such thinking is gloriously positive towards the Jewish people, understanding salvation in Yeshua for Jew and Gentile as the fulfillment of God's promises revealed to Israel; theirs is a "fulfillment theology." If it is of value to stress the historical continuity between Israel and the NT church, then "engrafting theology" is a useful term, as per Paul's imagery in Rom 11:17–24.

(E) FULLNESS OR ALL ISRAEL SAVED

Paul's words in Rom 11:7 sum up what we have considered so far: "What then? Israel has not obtained what it seeks; but the elect have obtained it and the rest were blinded." The question arises: Will there only ever be a remnant? To which Paul answers that there will be a fullness, implying something much more (Rom 11:11–15). This will be examined further in the final part of the book but it is necessary to give it some consideration here, in particular the interrelationship of Jew and Gentile salvation.

Paul's whole approach to the Jewish question in Rom 9–11 is an apologetic for why all Israel, that is, the majority of the nation then living, did not believe when Messiah came. That was surely Israel's expectation, which was not surprising in the light of prophecies like "they shall all know me" (Jer 32:34). Paul answers in terms of election and human responsibility, and then assures of a remnant; however, that is not the end of the story: there will be a fullness (Rom 11:12). He argues that all Israel will indeed be saved as had been expected, but *after* the Gentiles had come in: "blindness in part has happened to Israel until the fullness of the Gentiles has come in. And so [And in this manner] all Israel will be saved" (Rom 11:24–25). "In this manner" points to God's method; that is, not at the start of the messianic age but at the end. Paul says this is a mystery (Rom 11:24), which means it was not clear from the prophets; however his quotation from Isaiah shows it is scriptural. Paul's praise of God's *ways* in Rom 11:33—that they are past finding out—underlines this understanding. The truth to marvel at in this verse is not so much that he has saved Jews and Gentiles and has brought in the fullness of each, but the *manner* in which he has done it. It was unexpected. At some point yet future God will save a fullness of the Jewish nation, not necessarily every individual but the vast majority (all Israel does not have to mean every Israelite; see 1 Sam 14:40); but it will be *after* the nations have heard.[1]

This interrelationship of the salvation of Jew and Gentile is also seen in the way in which both come to faith. To begin with, some Jewish people come to faith and through their preaching to Gentiles many are saved. Subsequently Jews are provoked to jealousy by seeing Gentiles believing, and some believe (Rom 11:11, 14), and Gentiles enjoy salvation by partaking of the root and fatness of what was promised to Israel (Rom 11:17). Then at some point in history, when the Gentiles have heard, Israel is blessed through Gentile testimony and many Jewish people are saved. The outcome surely intended is, "that no flesh should glory in His presence" (1 Cor 1:29). It is not just that Jew and Gentile cannot glory because salvation is all of grace, but they cannot boast over each other because God has made them depend on one other in the way the gospel has spread. God is glorified in the mystery of his ways and judgments (Rom 11:33).

(F) BLESSINGS AND JUDGMENTS

Israel's story in the new covenant period is often told by epochs of trouble and suffering; however Israel is still here, so it is also a story of God's goodness and faithfulness.

(i) Blessings

In terms of salvation there will always be a remnant and one day a fullness; this is God's faithfulness to his promises and his abundant grace. The nation which has been marked by hostility to his Son will one day be marked by love for him.

There is also the blessing of God's providence, which is essential for his purposes of salvation. God made promises to Abraham that a great nation would come from him, and Jeremiah prophesied the nation would always continue (Jer 31:35–36). This providential care in Messiah's days of a persecuted and scattered nation is portrayed in Rev 12:1–6, 13–17. Israel is the woman who brings the Messiah into the world, but her subsequent experience is a wilderness one, yet it is one in which God cares for her. Satan attempts to destroy her using human means (flood), but he fails through

---

1. Some argue that "Israel" in Rom 11:25 means all Jews and Gentiles who have believed, but this is strange exegesis. In the preceding verse 24 and the following verse 28 Israel refers to ethnic Israel (described as blind and enemies); how then, without a word of explanation or qualification, does "Israel" in verse 25 take on a different meaning?

God's use of human means (earth). This has been the Jewish story for two thousand years. Anti-Jewishness or anti-Semitism is essentially a satanically inspired phenomenon, because Satan is dedicated to the destruction of all God's works, especially his people—Israel and the church. God has certainly allowed him some success but, as with Job, no more than God has determined, so that the nation has always survived. And indeed more than survived, for the Jewish people have not sunk into degradation and stupidity like many other nations who had a great past in history, but continue to be full of energy and ingenuity, through God's providential grace.

(ii) Judgments

This is a difficult subject, which has already been considered in Part 4 in chapter 16, "God the Provider and Ruler," and in chapter 19 under "The Fall of Humankind," but here we will focus on the unique Jewish situation. Scripture is crystal clear that humans are responsible for their actions and God judges them accordingly. His judgment does not usually occur immediately, and there is forgiveness for those who repent and trust his Son. Judgment is his "strange work" and he takes no pleasure in the death of the wicked (Isa 28:21; Ezek 33:11). Indeed, when Yeshua pronounced the judgment that would come upon Jerusalem for Israel's rejection of him we read, "He saw the city and wept over it" (Luke 19:41). And there can be no doubt that Israel's continuing rejection of him is a source of grief, for he is "the same yesterday, today, and forever" (Heb 13:8); a spirit of grief which was deeply manifested in Paul (Rom 9:1–3). The judgment he wept over came—in 70 AD at the hand of the Romans—and it has been a continuing story with Israel scattered among the nations.

Yet it has not been trouble at all times. There have been long periods of relative peace and prosperity, as in Spain from 700 AD to 1100 AD (although enduring Islam's dhimmitude status), and as in the USA throughout its existence. So, why troubles in one place and not another? Paul gives us insight into this in 1 Thess 2:14–16, a very sobering passage, where he describes the unique sins of the Judeans who rejected Yeshua, and the subsequent consequences: "to fill up the measure of their sins" and "wrath has come upon them to the uttermost." The principles here apply to all God's judgments, upon both Gentile and Jew, but the context here is the Jewish one. The initial focus is the sin of the "Judeans," a word which does not here stand for all Jews but for that class which Paul describes as having "a zeal for God, but not according to knowledge" (Rom 10:2); the ones who had taken the lead in opposing Yeshua, plotting his death, and delivering him to the Romans, and who subsequently persecuted the apostles. Judgment came upon that generation but Paul also has subsequent history in view by using the word "always" in "always to fill up the measure of their sins" (1 Thess 2:16).

The lamentable fact is that the Jewish people, and especially their religious leaders, have continued to reject Yeshua, denying the prophets spoke of him, and have continued to oppose gospel preaching. There is no neutral position, as Yeshua said, "He who is not with Me is against Me" (Luke 11:23). The concept of filling up sin is mentioned in Gen 15:16 regarding the sin of the Amorites, and also in Matt 23:32 regarding the opposition to Yeshua of the Jewish leaders: "Fill up, then, the measure of your fathers' guilt." What this indicates is that there is a point in a people's rebellion and wicked behavior which God fixes as the point he will act against them in judgment. We cannot know beforehand when God will so act; they are "The secret things" which "belong to the LORD our God" (Deut 29:29). But reflection afterwards may lead us to see God's hand of judgment on peoples, Gentile and Jew, who have turned their backs on him.

What is "wrath to the uttermost"? Paul says it has already come on the Judeans at the time he wrote, so it does not refer to the destruction of the temple or something more recent, such as the Holocaust. What had happened to Israel prior to 70 AD which merits such an awesome description? It can only refer to the kingdom being taken away. Nothing was more disastrous than for a covenant people to lose God's special presence among them and all the means of grace, leaving them as Ichabod ("the glory has departed"). YHWH is not to be trifled with; he is long-suffering but when the time for judgment comes he is a consuming fire (Heb 12:28–29).

Jewish thinking both agrees and disagrees with such an understanding of these significant times of troubles in Jewish history. Some are atheists and just see man's inhumanity to man as the human race tries to evolve to a better state. Many are God-fearing but uncertain, asserting God's ways can never be understood. Some turn to Torah and see troubles as God punishing his people for present disobedience as per Deut 28. The more thoughtful religious thinkers trace the dispersion and its troubles to sin in the land, and view all subsequent troubles as a consequence of failing to deal with the ancient sin; this was the view of former Chief Rabbi of the UK and Commonwealth Immanuel Jakobovits. Some religious leaders opposed the creation of a day for Holocaust remembrance because they saw that terrible event, when viewed theologically, as of the same kind as other periods in Jewish history of trouble, suffering, and death, and to be remembered on Tisha b'Av when the destruction of the first and second temples is mourned. The Hebrew expression *hester panim* is used by the Orthodox to create a vivid image of God's displeasure. It refers to YHWH turning his face away, the opposite of "make his face shine upon you" in the priestly blessing. It implies being left to themselves in the hand of enemies, something King David greatly feared (2 Sam 24:14). A fuller discussion of this difficult subject can be found in my book *Jewish Themes in the New Testament*.

(G) RETURN TO THE LAND

This subject cannot be ignored in our consideration of Israel in the new covenant period; however it overlaps with what will be discussed in the next part of the book, which will cover the last things, Messiah's return, and the new creation. In that next part we will consider the promise of the land, the Old Testament prophecies of a return, and Israel's relationship to what is termed the "millennium." At this point we will confine ourselves to what the new covenant writings have to say about the return in recent times and the establishment of the state of Israel.

The surprising fact is that the New Testament has very little to say about a return of the Jewish people to their ancient homeland. There are early passages in the Gospels where the hope of living righteously under God's anointed king, unmolested by enemies, is expressed in very national terms, for example the words of Zacharias in Luke 1:67–79, and also there is the question of the apostles in Acts 1:6. These texts do not specifically mention the land but obviously assume that the hope expressed will take place there; but such texts are not considering a *return* to the land after a period of banishment, rather a there-and-then establishment of Messiah's kingdom in the land. Yet that hope gradually evaporated as Israel's rejection of Yeshua grew and hardened; Yeshua's warnings of judgment were beginning to be fulfilled. What is significant is that all thoughts of a return to the land are absent from apostolic teaching. The place we might expect to find it is in Rom 9–11, where Paul specifically addresses God's dealings with Israel in unbelief and considers their future hope. Remarkably, he makes no mention of a return to the land as a future hope, but he does reveal a return to Messiah. Clearly, the apostles did not see a return to the land as a center-stage development of God's eschatalogical purpose.

The apostles' question to Jesus in Acts 1:6, "will You at this time restore the kingdom to Israel?" receives an ambivalent answer. Some assert that there will indeed be a restoration of the kingdom and hence a return to the land, because Jesus does not correct their hope. However, that is an argument from silence, and Yeshua's silence can just as well be interpreted as his refraining from entering a discussion of hard truths which they were not yet ready to bear (e.g., see John 16:12–13, and note the Spirit had not yet been given when they asked this question). The dialogue shows us their hope, and his unwillingness to confirm that hope.

In Luke 21:20–24 Yeshua predicts the destruction of Jerusalem, and the capture and captivity of many of Israel. Similar words are found in Mark and Matthew but Luke has one further thought: "And Jerusalem will be trampled by Gentiles until the times of the Gentiles are fulfilled" (Luke 21:24). An end to Gentile trampling of Jerusalem points to the hope of a return—a return to Jewish rule. Some doubt this because Yeshua says nothing of what happens next, and so it is assumed this Gentile rule over Jerusalem continues until Yeshua returns. But if that is so why did Jesus not use a phrase like "until the end" or "until the Son of Man comes"? His silence on future developments can best be understood as a reluctance to focus on such a hope in a discourse which was one of warning and judgment. Another thing to note is that Jesus does not quote an Old Testament text, which would underline this return as a grand eschatological hope; more on this in the final part of the book. What we have here is an undramatic, rather quiet statement to the effect that the dispersion is not forever; there will be a return to Jewish control of Jerusalem and hence a return to the land. This has surely been fulfilled in recent times and especially the events of 1967, when Jerusalem was returned to Jewish control.

So, on what basis has God brought Jewish people back to the land? How are we to interpret God's providential actions? It is not connected to a significant turning back to himself as there is no widespread acceptance of Yeshua. Clearly Israel's covenant-keeping God is being gracious. In his providence he has brought his people back in unbelief; he is acting in *covenant faithfulness*, choosing to fulfill again his promise to Abraham, despite their disobedience. To such graciousness Israel needs to respond by covenant obedience—a national receiving of Yeshua as Messiah. If we link this with the hope of the salvation of all Israel in Rom 11:26 we may surely hope that this return to the land is a means to that end.

All this raises the question: How should Israeli Jews live in the land, and especially towards its non-Jewish inhabitants? The potential for end-time excitement among Israeli Jewish believers may lead some to think and act as if they already have one foot in the conditions of the earthly messianic kingdom, with its attendant danger of belittling the rights on non-Jews in the land. Does Scripture provide guidance? The return has not been like that under Joshua with a divine mandate, one which led to subjecting, displacing, or destroying the existing inhabitants; nor like that under Zerubbabel, when subject to Persian power and still in the time of the Mosaic covenant. So, how to rule?

Helpful principles may be derived from the behavior of the patriarchs as they first settled in the land among the existing inhabitants. They had God's promise of the land but did not act high-handedly or unjustly. They shared the benefits of the land with others (Gen 34:10); they bought land (Gen 33:18–20), made compromises in tense situations (Gen 26:16–32), argued what was right to change a situation (Gen 21:25–31), and made agreements for mutual defense and peaceful coexistence (Gen 14:13; 21:22–24; 26:28–30). They also acted to defend themselves (Gen 14: 13–16). Here are good principles for Jews, Palestinians, and Arabs to live peaceably in the land. Jewish people may be back in the land of promise by God's providence but they are to live there as exhorted by the prophet Micah: "to do justly, to love mercy, and to walk humbly with your God" (Mic 6:8). For those who believe Messiah will one day establish his rule there, with a significant role for messianic Jews, the conclusion must be: wait for him; there is no command for you to prepare the way; his priority in the land and the whole world at this stage of history is clear—preach the gospel.

This hope of a return has always been strongly embedded in the thinking of Orthodox Jews. For them it is a hope connected to the coming of the Messiah, and hence many of them initially oppose the establishment of a secular state. However, once it was established most among the Orthodox ceased their opposition and understood it as a stepping-stone to a Torah-observant society which would prepare the way for Messiah's coming. As part of that preparation some among the Orthodox see it as important to occupy all the biblical land of Israel, but most believe peace and righteousness are more important at this stage, trusting the Messiah will resolve the land question when he comes to reign. A tiny minority among the Orthodox still oppose the secular state. For non-Orthodox and secular Jews the return was seen as a way to escape Gentile animosity and to create a place for Jews to live in a Jewish way; somewhere they could manage their own affairs and be free to defend themselves. Their right to return was asserted on the basis of their history, on a continuous presence in the land, and on a right, like that of all peoples, to live in a place of safety and self-government. For some the obligation to continue the Jewish story in the land of their forebears was highly significant. This came to prominence in the Six-Day War of 1967, when something like an awakening of religious consciousness took place among Jews around the world; Israel's survival was under threat and Jewish people's thoughts instinctively turned to God.

33

Jewish Believers in the Church and Israel (the People)

JEWISH BELIEVERS IN YESHUA have two spiritual identities, one in the church and one in Israel. In the church, made up of people from all peoples and nations, they are one among many, all of whom have the identity of saints, set-apart ones. They go by terms like "Hebrew Christian," "Jewish Christian," and "Jewish believer," the noun identifying them as Christian in faith and the adjective as Jewish in ethnicity. Within the people of Israel they are the remnant, those who believe Messiah has come, and at this point in history a minority. The same terms may be used to identify them as the remnant but the term "Messianic Jew" more clearly emphasizes their membership of Israel, having "Jew" as the noun.

(A) THE ISRAEL OF GOD

This is a collective term used by Paul in Gal 6:16 for the believing remnant. However, over the centuries many Christians have understood it to refer to the church; an understandable error because the church is described in terms that come from Israel's religious experience, such as "temple of the living God" (2 Cor 6:16, see also John 2:19–22, Eph 2:21). This connection has led Gentile Christians to devise terms like "new Israel" or "spiritual Israel" to express their link with all that has gone before in redemption history. This is a laudable aim but an unwise solution. It should be noted that the word "Israel" is never used to describe the church in the NT because that word describes the Jewish people, and to call the church "Israel," or even "spiritual Israel," is to rob Israel of their identity; an error which has led to the belittling of the Jewish people in Christendom. A suitable and preferable alternative term would be "children of Abraham," as used by Paul for the Galatians.

The text of Gal 6:16 itself is not conclusive. Paul desires that those who walk according to the rule of verse 15—circumcision has no significance in salvation—will have peace and mercy, but who are those so described? All believers or a subgroup within them? It is true that "and" (Gk. *kai*) in the phrase "*and* upon the Israel of God" can be translated "even," which points to "the Israel of God" being a term for all who walk by the rule that circumcision avails nothing in salvation, i.e., the church, but it is equally valid for *kai* to be translated "and," which points to the Israel of God being a separate entity within those who walk by the rule. Most English versions use "and."

The immediate and wider context must therefore be taken into account to enable a decision to be made. Concerning the *immediate context*, it is argued that Paul's whole concern in Galatians is encapsulated in the preceding verse; that is, circumcision has no salvific value, so it is asked: Why would he confuse matters by mentioning a distinct, circumcised group within all believers? A fair point, but it fails to take account of Paul's use of the word "Israel" in Galatians, a word Paul has not used at all in this letter. In Galatians his arguments have consistently gone back to Abraham. What about the wider context? First of all, we need to ask why the Galatian (Gentile) Christians would think the word "Israel" referred to them. Christians today may be used to such terminology, but what about the Galatian believers? Their only close contact with Israel was through Jews like Paul and Barnabas preaching Christ to them, and also with false brethren, called by Paul "the circumcision," who were stressing the importance of circumcision for Gentile believers (Gal 2:4; 2:12; 5:3; 4:17; 5:7–8, 12). They may have had some contact with Jewish traders or residents but such would have been seen as quite distinct from themselves. To the Galatians, Israel was a far-off people, some of whom were now coming to them to tell them of the living God; there was no reason for them to think that Paul's use of "Israel" was referring to them. The wider context was Paul's ongoing conflict with a group of Jewish followers of Yeshua, "the circumcision," who were the cause of the difficulties in Galatia. Paul refers to them in the Epistle to the Galatians in 4:17 and 5:7–8, 12; elsewhere Paul is more specific about these false teachers who frequently dogged his steps (see Phil 3:2; 2 Cor 11:12–15, 22; Titus 1:10–16). The Galatians had first heard the truth from Paul and believed what he preached, then this other group of Jewish teachers came from Jerusalem teaching circumcision and disparaging Paul as a late addition to the apostles, not a representative of Jerusalem orthodoxy, and therefore suspect. Hence it should not surprise us that in the final words of his letter to the Galatian Christians he emphatically dismisses the false teachers by announcing that only Jews who walked by the rule were of God—they alone were the Israel of God, God's chosen within Israel.

Being the Israel of God brings unique privileges and responsibilities for Jewish believers as a Jewish witness to Messiah among their own people, and as a witness in the church to the Jewish roots of the Christian faith. Therefore maintaining Jewishness is important. Not that Jewishness can be lost, especially as Messiah and the Scriptures are Jewish, but mixing with many Gentiles in church life can blunt its edge. Ways need to be found to strengthen Jewishness—mixing with family and Jewish associations, support for Israel, meeting with other Jewish believers, keeping a kosher home if that is appropriate, etc., all summed up as keeping in touch, keeping involved.

(B) ONE NEW MAN FROM THE TWO

Under the Mosaic covenant "strangers" were welcome to enter the covenant and worship YHWH, but only if they became as an Israelite, i.e., circumcision and keeping of the law of Moses. Then they were equal in all respects but one: they had no land inheritance; that was something reserved spiritually for Messiah's days as Ezekiel revealed: "And it shall be that in whatever tribe the stranger dwells, there you shall give him his inheritance" (Ezek 47:21–23). When the gospel was first preached to Gentiles the change came; Gentiles received equal status with Jews such that the way the righteous life was to be lived was new for both. As Paul wrote of Messiah's people, "so as to create in Himself one new man from the two" (Eph 2:15), the two being Jewish and Gentile believers. There is a oneness and newness for both. Atonement is through Messiah's one sacrifice, in his one body; and access to the Father is by the one Spirit (Eph 2:16–18). The one way of life is not for Gentiles to be under Moses' law, as in the past, because there is now a newness. The law of commandments contained in ordinances was abolished; all were to live in the Spirit by the "righteousness of the law," not by observing its legal commands (see Rom 8:4; Eph 2:14–15). By this Yeshua does what humans could not do: unite Jew and Gentile in one body. To express this Jews and Gentiles who believe should be together in local churches, living and witnessing for their one Messiah. In the New Testament the churches among the Gentiles, many of which included both Jews and Gentiles (Acts 11:19–26; 14:1), were distinguished by location (Corinth, Ephesus, etc.), not by ethnicity, gender, or social status, all of which were treated as irrelevant for inclusion and fellowship (Gal 3:28). This is demanding and requires accommodating each other, and the New Testament provides us with examples (see Acts 15:19–29; Rom 14:1–23; 1 Cor 10:23–33).

Messianic Congregations and Synagogues

Throughout the world Christians have established ethnic churches in multicultural populations, which are usually justified as necessary due to the language difficulties of new immigrants. However, that is not the justification given for Jewish ethnic churches in the diaspora, usually called "messianic congregations" or "messianic synagogues." They are justified in the diaspora by some or all of the five following reasons, all of which are very understandable:

- anti-Jewishness in churches;
- a desire to follow Messiah in a culturally Jewish way;
- a desire to evangelize fellow Jews sensitively;
- fulfilling Israel's commission to be a light to the Gentiles; and
- a desire to be accepted as Kol Yisrael by expressing faith in Yeshua as a Judaism (i.e., Messianic Judaism).

This author believes these concerns and desires can be addressed by other means, and books listed in Further Reading go into more detail. However, expressing faith in Yeshua as a Judaism needs some examination here.

The problem is that the term "Judaism" as generally used does not refer to Old Testament religion but to the religion of the Jewish people as it developed after the destruction of the second temple. The New Testament presents that religion, at its core, as opposed to the gospel. Paul describes it as hostile to the church and zealous for the traditions of the fathers (Gal 1:13–14), and as opposed to Yeshua and Israel's prophets (1 Thess 2:15). It was a religion that eventually excluded Jewish believers in Yeshua from the Jewish community. Judaism has many good moral and religious qualities but it fails to save. In the light of these considerations, can believers in Yeshua call their faith a Judaism? In effect Messianic Judaism creates two new men: a new man for Jews who worship Yeshua and keep many of the practices of Judaism, and a new man for Gentiles who turn from unbelief to faith in Jesus, keeping only new covenant traditions. Other problems are: the practice of a Judaism will always have a significant place for traditions in congregational life, but Paul considers this as spiritually unhealthy, (see Col 2:17–23); Gentiles who attend are being asked to incorporate the traditions of the OT and Judaism into their religious life; and Messianic Judaism is an attempt to remain within Israel's religious camp as a branch of Judaism, but Hebrews encourages Jewish believers to go outside the camp, to be religiously separate from the Messiah-rejecting majority of the Jewish community (Heb 13:13).

Jewish believers have much to contribute to local church life in the diaspora, encouraging an interest in the Old Testament and the Jewish roots of Christian faith, a sensitivity to unsaved Jews, and as "outsiders" helping Christians of the majority culture to discern what is biblical and what is simply cultural in their church life. They may also help preachers to be careful with the language they use when referring to Jews in the accounts of the Scriptures.

Congregations in Israel also face the challenge of being one new man from the two. The population of Israel is not exclusively Jewish; there are Arab citizens, and many visitors from abroad who come for long periods to study, do business, participate in Israel's cultural life, etc. The obvious difference is that the surrounding culture in Israel is Jewish, though with many variations. A congregation of believers is culturally Jewish simply by virtue of the majority being Jewish. Sensitive evangelism can be easily conducted through the national festivals and holidays which are inspired by biblical realities. The issue of asking non-Jews to do Jewish things takes on a different character as Jewish things dominate national life, but sensitivity to non-Jews, especially those who are Israeli citizens, is vital; they must not feel as though they are second-class members. The temptation to be accepted as a Judaism (Messianic Judaism) is greater in Israel but the same problem exists: Judaism opposes faith in Yeshua, and its claim to be the faith of the state of Israel means believers are still outside the camp; it includes a stress on externals that is spiritually unhealthy; and Messianic Judaism creates two new men, not one.

(C) CULTURALLY JEWISH

Every people group develops a unique culture, manifested in their agriculture, arts, and artifacts, ways of communication, social institutions to order family and community life, historical experience, and religion to express metaphysical realities. Israelite culture was unique among cultures because at its core it was God's national culture in God's land. Jewish culture today is no longer the theocracy of old Israelite culture but it contains many remnants of it, and has also gathered many additional elements as Jewish people have been dispersed among other cultures. Hence it is now a culture like any

Jewish Believers in the Church and Israel (the People)

other, with healthy and unhealthy elements, according to how it has held on to God's righteous ways or set them aside. Paul acknowledged the existence of a distinctive Jewish culture when he wrote, "to the Jews I became as a Jew, that I might win Jews; to those who are under the law, as under the law, that I might win those who are under the law" (1 Cor 9:20). There were Jews who devoutly kept the law, but there were also those who did not but who still had a Jewish culture; they were not Gentiles, and Paul adapted himself to that when evangelizing them. Jewish culture is more than the law and rabbinic traditions. It is therefore understandable that Jewish believers want to express that culture and meet together to do so, and many have found ways to do that without starting separate churches.

The practice of Jewish religious traditions by Jewish believers was not viewed negatively in the times of the apostles, although Paul warned against a wrong emphasis (see Acts 12:12; 10:14; 21:20; Phil 3:4–7; Col 2:16–23). However, as time went on an emphasis on Jewishness and Jewish religious practice was viewed as an unhealthy legalism. Today that has changed and churches increasingly recognize the freedom of Jewish believers to live as Jews, including the use of some practices of Judaism in their personal lifestyles. Particular New Testament examples which give principles for today's Jewish believers are:

- Paul's vow as an aid to devotion, modeled on the Nazarite vow (Acts 18:18);
- Paul's circumcision of Timothy to make a smooth path for the gospel (Acts 16:1–3);
- Paul's performance of a temple ritual to promote harmony between believers (Acts 21:20–26); and
- Ananias' law-observant lifestyle, commending faith in Yeshua by placing no stumbling blocks before those of a similar lifestyle (Acts 22:12).

(D) PROVOKING TO JEALOUSY

In Rom 11:13–14 Paul speaks of magnifying his ministry. That is, he made much of being the apostle to the Gentiles, with the aim of provoking his fellow Jews to jealousy. He wanted them to be aroused by the fact that many, many Gentiles were coming to know and worship Israel's God, and love righteousness. Being aware of the hostility to Gentiles among his own (see Acts 22:21–22), it would have been tempting for Paul to downplay this, but he did not; and Jewish believers in Yeshua should not either. No doubt the substandard behavior of many who are called "Christians" is an inhibiting factor but there was plenty wrong with Gentile Christians in Paul's day (read 1 Corinthians), yet Paul was not inhibited.

(E) WARNINGS FROM HEBREWS

All Christians saved from other religions face pressures to return, but Jewish believers face unique pressures because Judaism can claim a link to the revelation of God. This was a strong pressure in New Testament times because the Mosaic economy was still in place, beckoning them back to something emphatically of God. Furthermore those early believers faced disappointed hopes—all Israel had not believed and Yeshua was not reigning in Jerusalem—and on top of that they were suffering for their faith. Heb 10:23 makes clear the impact of these pressures: "Let us hold fast the confession of our hope without wavering, for He who promised is faithful." Those pressures still exist today, although in a modified form; and there are additional ones: the fraught relationship over many centuries with churches within Christendom, the strong intellectual pressures from an educated community with many centuries of experience of rebutting the claims of Messiah Yeshua, and the emotional pressure of the loss of the familiar—the church is not the synagogue and is not culturally Jewish. It is all too easy to hanker for the familiar when trials and disappointments press believers down. The response in Hebrews aims to teach, encourage, and warn, and is relevant for Jewish believers under pressure today. Its teaching may be considered under four headings: "Doctrinal," "Spiritual Perspective," "Exhortation," and "Remembering the Past."

(i) Doctrinal

The truths expounded in Hebrews all aim to establish the superiority of the new covenant revelation over all that preceded, particularly the Mosaic. The following is a summary of those truths.

- All that preceded was preparatory; God has now spoken by his Son (Heb 1:1–2, 4).
- His lowly condition while upon earth should not be misunderstood, for it was essential for our salvation that he might become a merciful and faithful high priest (2:17–18).

- Moses was great as God's servant over the house of Israel, but Yeshua is greater as God's Son over his own house, the people of the new covenant (3:5–6).
- Although important in God's unfolding purpose, the land of Israel was not the goal of the rest promise; that is fulfilled in the new heavens and the new earth: "But now they desire a better, that is, a heavenly country" (11:16; see also 4:11).
- Believers take the first step to enter God's rest by ceasing from their own works for salvation (4:10).
- There is a need to realize that, important as it was, the old covenant in and of itself achieved nothing in the securing of salvation: "the law made nothing perfect; on the other hand, there is the bringing in of a better hope, through which we draw near to God" (7:19).
- Those who were saved before the coming of Yeshua were only saved on the basis of his sacrifice (9:15); the sacrifices of the law did not take away sins (10:14).
- The priesthood of the law was weak due to the sinfulness and mortality of its members, but Messiah's priesthood is enduring due to his sinless perfection and endless life (7:25–28).
- His priesthood is of a line that is superior to and existed before that of the law—that of Melchizedek—and replaces the Levitical (7:11–16).
- Those who trust in Messiah have a priest in heaven, with access to the Most High, not one on earth prevented by a veil (9:24; 10:19–22; 9:7–8).
- Messiah inaugurated a new covenant, indicating the ineffectiveness of the Mosaic: "For if that first covenant had been faultless, then no place would have been sought for a second," and "In that He says, 'A new covenant,' He has made the first obsolete" (8:7, 13).

Judaism today claims to be the continuation of all God provided under Moses, although adapted for the loss of the temple. It claims a superior revelation and leader (Moses). It claims a hope of peace and everlasting life through a law which is God's last word. It ignores the significance of Melchizedek and the messianic import of the prophecy of Ps 110:4, and rejects the need for the shedding of blood for the propitiation of God and the removal of the sinner's guilt. The new covenant is variously interpreted by the rabbis: some view it as a time of spiritual renewal under the Mosaic; others as pointing to a more spiritual order of things in Messiah's days; others ignore it altogether. Judaism's power to bring in perfection is inevitably less than the Mosaic which it imitates, of which it is said, "the law made nothing perfect" (Heb 7:19).

(ii) Spiritual Perspective

Spiritual life under the old covenant and under Judaism has a significant focus on the seen—the temple, priesthood, rituals, and the land. Hebrews calls Jewish believers to follow their forebears and focus on the unseen, and not be shaken by those who glory in the externals of their faith (Heb 11:13–16; 13:9–15; 12:2).

(iii) Exhortations and Warnings

These appear throughout the letter rather than in a section at the end. Most have the nature of a general warning: "let us lay aside every weight, and the sin which so easily ensnares us, and let us run with endurance the race that is set before us" (Heb 12:1; see also 2:1; 6:1; 4:16). Other warnings are very serious, envisaging the danger of rejection by God because of rejecting the only sacrifice for sin he accepts: "For if we sin willfully after we have received the knowledge of the truth, there no longer remains a sacrifice for sins, but a certain fearful expectation of judgment, and fiery indignation" (Heb 10:26–27; see also 3:14; 6:4–8).

(iv) Remember Previous Faithfulness

Believers who have faltered are encouraged to repent and press on, to "imitate those who through faith and patience inherit the promises" (Heb 6:12). The list of those they are to imitate is not one of perfect individuals who never failed but faulty men and women who pressed on (see Heb 11). Those who fail can be sure God does not forget their past faithfulness (Heb 6:10).

> A light to bring revelation to the Gentiles,
> And the glory of Your people Israel." (Luke 2:32)

SCRIPTURES

God's people: Luke 1:54–55, 68; 2:32; 7:16; 13:16; Acts 3:25; Rom 11:1, 28.

Israel's privileges: Rom 9:1–5; 3:1–2; Luke 1:67–79; 2:32; Acts 3:26; 13:26; Rom 1:16.

Remnant and fullness: Matt 23:37–39; Luke 13:34–35; John 6:66–67; Rom 11:5–7, 12, 15, 23, 25–26; 2 Cor 3:15–16.

Cut off: Matt 21:33–43; 24:1–2, 15; Luke 21:20–24; Rom 11:7–10, 12, 15; 1 Thess 2:16.

Blessings and judgments: Matt 23:13–39; Luke 11:23; 19:41–44; Rom 9:4–5; 11:5, 12; 1 Thess 2:14–16; Rev 12:1–6, 13–17.

Return to the land: Zech 14:1–5; Luke 21:20–24; Acts 1:6.

Jewish believers in Israel: Rom 11:5; Gal 6:16; Heb 13:10–13; Jas 1:1; Rev 7:4–8.

Jewish believers in the church: Acts 11:19–26; 14:1; 15:19–29; Rom 14:1–23; 1 Cor 10:23–33; Gal 1:13–14; 2:11–14; 3:28; Eph 2:14–18; Col 2:17–23.

Culturally Jewish: Acts 10:14; 12:12; 16:1–3; 18:18; 21:20–26; 1 Cor 9:20; Phil 3:4–7.

Provoking to jealousy: Acts 22:21–22; Rom 11:13–14.

Warnings from Hebrews: Heb 2:1–3; 3:12–19; 4:1, 11; 5:12; 6:4–8; 10:23–29, 35–39; 12:1–2, 12–15.

Change in Hebrews: Heb 1:1–2; 3:3; 4:9; 7:11–12, 19; 8:6; 9:11–12; 10:1.

Questions

The Church in History

1. Discuss from Scripture and practice the merits and demerits of Episcopalianism, Presbyterianism, Congregationalism, and Independency as structures for church government. Which is your preference?

2. What are the challenges you envisage the worldwide church to be facing in the twenty-first century? How do they affect your church?

Israel in the New Covenant Period and Jewish Believers in the Church and Israel

1. What does it mean to you to be Jewish?

2. How is the kingdom of God manifested in the new covenant period? Do you expect a return of the kingdom to national Israel? Justify your answers.

3. What does Scripture have to say about the sufferings of the Jewish people since Yeshua's days? Discuss the Holocaust in your answer.

4. Paul uses two terms to describe the saved in Israel, "remnant" and "all Israel" (Rom 11:5, 26); how do you understand them and their relationship to the church?

5. Should Jewish believers join ethnically diverse churches or ethnically Jewish ones? Justify your answer from Scripture. Discuss your experience of one or the other or both.

6. What significance do you give to the return to the land in recent times?

7. How do you give cultural expression to your Jewishness?

8. Have you, or Jewish believers you know, been tempted to return to Judaism? What were the pressures and how were they overcome?

Further Reading

The New Testament Church in History

Catherwood, Christopher. *Church History*. Wheaton, IL: Crossway, 2007.
Needham, Nick. *2000 Years of Christ's Power*. Fearn: Christian Focus, 2017.

Israel in the New Covenant Period, Jewish Believers in the Church and Israel

Bell, John. *How to Be Like the Messiah*. Orangeburg, NY: Chosen People, 1987.
Fruchtenbaum, Arnold. *Hebrew Christianity*. San Antonio: Ariel Ministries, 1983.
Goldberg, Louis, ed. *How Jewish Is Christianity?* Grand Rapids: Zondervan, 2003.
Holwerda, David E. *Jesus and Israel: One Covenant or Two?* Grand Rapids: Eerdmans, 1995.
Jocz, Jacob. *The Jewish People and Jesus Christ*. London: SPCK, 1962.
Keith, Graham. *Hated without a Cause*. Carlisle: Paternoster, 1997.

Kjaer-Hansen, Kai, ed. *Jewish Identity and Faith in Jesus*. Jerusalem: Caspari, 1996.

Morris, Paul. *Jewish Themes in the New Testament*. Milton Keynes: Paternoster, 2013.

Robinson, Rich. *The Messianic Movement: A Field Guide for Evangelical Christians*. San Francisco: Jews for Jesus, 2005.

Telchin, Stan. *Messianic Judaism Is Not Christianity*. Grand Rapids: Chosen Books, 2004.

Torrance, David. *Israel God's Servant*. Milton Keynes: Paternoster, 2007.

PART 7

God's New Creation

THE FINAL PART OF our study should strengthen our eagerness for the day our Messiah will appear in glory, and we shall be with him forever. This is a strong NT hope: the faith of the young Thessalonian church was marked by "waiting for His Son from heaven" (1 Thess 1:10; see also Heb 9:28; Titus 2:13). The danger that accompanies such a good anticipation is the desire to know exactly when it will happen, and to have in our minds an exact order of events leading up to his coming. Scripture disappoints us in this regard because, as we shall see, it does not give us a detailed order of events but a number of isolated texts, like the pieces of a puzzle, such that we are left to compare Scripture with Scripture and draw conclusions, one of which will be that God has deliberately left things such that the pieces of the puzzle will only come together when the events occur. Was this not so with Messiah's first coming? To us, as we read the Hebrew Scriptures in the light of the New Testament, all appears so clear, but if we read the efforts of faithful Jews in the intertestamental period, who had all of the Old Testament revelation before them, we see their struggles to produce a coherent picture of Messiah, and none foresaw his atoning death or divine nature. Yet it was all there in the writings of Moshe and the prophets.

We are in the same position regarding the return of Messiah; it is all there in the pages of the New Testament but God has revealed it in such a way that we will not connect it all into a coherent picture until Messiah comes. This is obviously deliberate on God's part and has important lessons.

Firstly, God desires to keep us humble; he alone knows all things. Secondly, God requires us to live by faith not sight; we are to wait in faith for his purposes to unfold. Thirdly, it warns us against developing a detailed picture of end-time events, their order, and timing. This note of warning especially needs to be sounded in this book because it is addressed to Jewish believers, who have every reason to be excited about the events in the Middle East, the return of Jerusalem to Jewish control, and the growth of the number of Jewish believers worldwide. It appears the stage is being set for a significant development in the Lord's purposes in which Israel and the Jewish people are taking center stage again. Intoxicating stuff, but readers should beware of drinking too deeply. It is good to remember that the return of the Savior will be to save, not to congratulate; "The Lamb is all the glory of Immanuel's land."

34

Messiah's Return

THE RETURN OF YESHUA in glory will bring an end to the order of things as we know them and usher in a new order; it will be the most decisive event of all human experience. It will be the climax of the kingdom of God.

(A) SCRIPTURE'S TERMINOLOGY

The Hebrew Scriptures do not have a distinct teaching of a return of Messiah, and have no specific terms to describe it; but those places which speak of Messiah's coming in power and judgment are indications of a coming which is of a different order to that of entering Jerusalem on a donkey's colt (see Dan 7:21–27; Isa 63:1–6; Zeph 3:14–17; Zech 14:3–7). The Greek Scriptures of the NT have three words which are used to describe the return of the Lord to the earth. *Parousia* literally means "presence" or "arrival" (2 Thess 2:1, 8) and refers to him being personally present as surely as he was in the days of his earthly ministry; bodily he will come from where he is now to this earth. *Apokalypsis* means "revelation" (2 Thess 1:7) and points to his return being an event at which all humanity will understand who he is. *Epiphaneia* means "appearing" (2 Tim 4:8), having the idea of drawing back a veil; i.e., he is present in the sense that he fills all things but this event reveals him to our sight.

(B) A SCRIPTURE TEACHING

A few texts will be quoted here to illustrate that the return of Yeshua is a fundamental teaching of the Scriptures. As stated in the paragraph above, there are Old Testament texts which point to a time when Messiah's presence will be of a different order, pointing to a new situation. There are other Old Testament texts which were only partially fulfilled at Yeshua's first coming (e.g., 2 Sam 7:16; Ps 72; Isa 2:1–5) but they are not specific about a second coming. They speak of a great expansion of Messiah's kingdom, which Christians have understood in different ways, and will be considered later.

Regarding the New Testament texts, there are more than 250 which teach unambiguously a glorious return of Yeshua to this earth. The following references show the teaching is spread across the books of the New Testament: Matt 24:29–31; 25:31–46; Mark 13:24–37; Luke 21:27–28; John 14:3; Acts 1:11; 3:21; Rom 14:9–12; 1 Cor 15:22–24; 1 Thess 4:13—5:3; 2 Thess 1:7–10; Phil 3:20–21; 1 Tim 6:14–15; 2 Tim 4:1; Titus 2:13; Heb 9:28; Jas 5:7; 1 Pet 1:7; 2 Pet 3:4–13; 1 John 3:2; Rev 1:7; 22:20. It is a teaching which does not rely on interpreting symbols and visions but is clearly stated in familiar, descriptive prose and is therefore a cardinal doctrine of God's word.

(C) THE NATURE OF YESHUA'S RETURN

Yeshua referred to himself during his earthly ministry as the "Son of Man," and he uses that title to describe himself at his return: "and they will see the Son of Man coming on the clouds of heaven with power and great glory" (Matt 24:30). His return is therefore personal; it is he himself. As John puts it, "we shall see Him as He is" (1 John 3:2). But there is something quite different here to his earthly ministry, it is with power and glory, and in the clouds of heaven, indicating his divinity. No one will miss this event: "Behold, He is coming with clouds, and every eye will see Him" (Rev 1:7). It will be overwhelming for all who have ever lived and there will be a sense within many of foreboding: "all the tribes of the earth will mourn" (Matt 20:30). But among the justified it is a moment of hope: "look up and lift up your heads, for your redemption draws near" (Luke 21:28). Although there are a number of events connected to the return, its beginning is sudden and is compared to the suddenness of the flood of Noah's days (Matt 24:44).

There are attendant manifestations which draw the attention of all to what is about to take place, just like a theatre manager quieting the audience before the curtain is raised. There will be the sign of the Son of Man (Matt 24:30); a trumpet will be heard (Matt 24:31); the voice of an angel will sound, and there will be a shout from the Lord himself it would seem (Matt 24:31; 1 Thess 4:16); and the elect will be taken out of the earth (Matt 24:31). Whilst all is sudden and dramatic, Yeshua does not suddenly appear in a magical way; he comes into the world from the heavens, he descends (Acts 1:9–11; 1 Thess 4:16).

(D) THE PURPOSE OF YESHUA'S RETURN

Yeshua's return in glory has a number of purposes, some of which will only be stated briefly here and enlarged upon in subsequent sections.

(i) His Return Is His Vindication

It is the *apokalypsis*, the revelation of who he is, what he achieved by his death and resurrection, and the rightness of his people's trust and hope in him: "when the Lord Jesus is revealed from heaven . . . taking vengeance on those who do not know God . . . to be glorified in His saints and to be admired among all those who believe" (2 Thess 1:3–12, especially vv. 8–10; 1 Pet 1:3–7, 13; 1 Pet 4:12–13; 1 Cor 1:7; see also Mark 14:62; Rev 12:10). All who have ever lived will know.

(ii) He Returns for His Complete and Spotless Bride

All his chosen ones through all ages will be raised, glorified, and gathered to him: "And He will send His angels with a great sound of a trumpet, and they will gather together His elect from the four winds, from one end of heaven to the other" (Matt 24:31; 24:40–42; 1 Thess 4:14–17; Rom 8:19, 23; 2 Thess 2:1).

Under both the Mosaic and the new covenants the relationship of the Lord to his people is portrayed as equivalent to that most intimate and loving of human relations: husband and wife (Hos 2:16, 19–20; Song of Songs; Mark 2:19–20; John 3:29; Eph 5:22–32).The full experience of redemption, its completion, is when Messiah returns for his bride, an occasion which is, as in human marriage, marked by a marriage supper: "the marriage of the Lamb has come, and His wife has made herself ready . . . Blessed are those who are called to the marriage supper of the Lamb!" (Rev 19:7, 9, see also Eph 1:13–14). For the first time ever all the redeemed will be gathered together for their Redeemer; for the first time he will see no sin in them, for they will be robed in his righteousness and their righteous acts (Isa 61:10;

Rev 19:8). Surely then will be fully fulfilled the words of Isaiah and Zephaniah: "He shall see the labor of His soul, and be satisfied"; "The LORD your God in your midst . . . will rejoice over you with singing" (Isa 53:11; Zeph 3:17); an occasion beyond human description.

(iii) His Return Overcomes Evil

He will bring an end to the destructive behavior of the powers of evil in creation. The Old Testament anticipates this overthrow in texts like Isa 27:1; 66:22–24; and Mal 4:1, 3. The New Testament explicitly connects this overthrow to the time of Messiah's return. In 1 Cor 15:23–26 we read, "He puts an end to all rule and all authority and power . . . The last enemy that will be destroyed is death." In 2 Thess 2:3–10 the destruction at Yeshua's return of Satan's man of sin is especially taught.

(iv) There Will Be a General Resurrection of the Dead

This is clearly taught in both the Old and New Testaments. All who have ever lived from Adam onwards will have their bodies raised from the dead: "the hour is coming in which all who are in the graves will hear His voice and come forth—those who have done good, to the resurrection of life, and those who have done evil, to the resurrection of condemnation" (John 5:28–29; see also Dan 12:12; Acts 24:15; 1 Cor 15:12–58). At that moment the whole human family will be gathered together as one for the first and last time; all will be there. There will always be those who have doubts, as Hymenaeus and Philetus (2 Tim 2:17–18), but "Is anything too hard for the LORD?" (Gen 18:14).

(v) The Present Earth Will Be Removed at Yeshua's Return

The new earth and heavens and their relation to the existing order will be discussed further on but it is clear that this present order will be removed out of sight at his coming and at the final judgment: "Then I saw a great white throne and Him who sat on it, from whose face the earth and the heaven fled away" (Rev 20:11; see also 2 Pet 3:10; Isa 51:6).

(vi) Yeshua Returns to Judge

All who have ever lived will stand before him, "the living and the dead" (2 Tim 4:1). He judges as the Son of Man: "When the Son of Man comes in His glory, and all the holy angels with Him, then He will sit on the throne of His glory. All the nations will be gathered before Him" (Matt 25:31–32). This is clearly taught in the Old Testament and elsewhere in the New Testament (Isa 63:1–7; see also Isa 34 and Jer 50:39–40; 51:25–26, where Edom and Babylon are a type of unrepentant sinners; Matt 16:27; 2 Cor 5:10; Rev 20:11–15). For believers this is an assessment of stewardship with the granting of rewards (1 Cor 3:12–15); for unbelievers it marks the commencement of eternal separation from God with a punishment commensurate with the light they received and their response (Luke 12:47–48). The whole human race gathered with only one focal point—the great white throne! We are given no details as to the how, only that we will be there.

(vii) The Completion of the Messianic, Mediatorial Kingdom

After a complex of events surrounding his return, Yeshua hands back his mediatorial kingdom to the Father: "Then comes the end, when He delivers the kingdom to God the Father, when He puts an end to all rule and all authority and power . . . when all things are made subject to Him, then the Son Himself will also be subject to Him who put all things under Him, that God may be all in all" (1 Cor 15:24, 28). The prophets spoke of God's anointed one who would rule and save on his behalf (Ps 2:6; Isa 53:6), and Yeshua spoke of his exercise of a delegated authority as the Son of Man to be God's unique channel of blessing to humanity, to forgive sins, to give eternal life, to raise the dead, and to judge sinners (John 1:51; Matt 9:6; John 5:25–27; 6:27).

The terms used to describe the kingdom in its final state in the new creation are seldom any different to those used for Messiah's mediatorial kingdom, terms such as "kingdom of God" and "kingdom of heaven." In two places we read of the "kingdom of Christ and of God" and "kingdom of the Son of his love" (Eph 5:5; Col 1:13), terms which refer particularly to the mediatorial kingdom of Messiah; the Ephesians reference underlining the equivalence of the kingdom of Messiah and the kingdom of God prior to the handing back of the kingdom to the Father. There will come a moment when the Son's messianic, mediatorial role will be complete, when all God's enemies are defeated and judged, and when he hands back his universal rule and authority as the Son of Man to God the Father, who delegated it to him. See Matt 13:43 for the unique phrase "kingdom of their Father," a term describing the final form of God's kingdom.

(E) THE TIME OF YESHUA'S RETURN

When considering this subject two thoughts must always be kept in mind: firstly that Yeshua said, "It is not for you to know times or seasons which the Father has put in His own authority" (Acts 1:7); and secondly, "for that Day will not come unless the falling away comes first" (2 Thess 2:3). That is, some things are revealed which point to the time of his coming and some do not, so caution is necessary. Furthermore, readiness for his coming is never encouraged in Scripture in terms of knowing the time, but through walking in the light and having a heart filled with hope and anticipation.

(i) Events Throughout the Last Days

Yeshua spoke of events the dramatic nature of which might lead his people to think the time is near, but they would be wrong (Luke 21:9). Such things as: false prophets and messiahs (Matt 24:11; Luke 21:8), wars and revolutions (Luke 21:9), natural disasters (Matt 24:7), heavenly disturbances (Luke 21:11), persecution (Matt 24:9), and a significant falling away from faith (Matt 24:10). However, towards the end there will be an intensification and increasing frequency of these things (Luke 21:25–26), especially indicated by Yeshua's metaphor of birth pains (Matt 24:8, "sorrows" but literally "birth pains").

(ii) Clearly Predicted Indicators

Certain definite events will precede Yeshua's return but they are revealed so that believers may be stirred to a faithful response; they do not help to precisely fix the time.

(a) The Falling Away

"That Day will not come unless the falling away comes first" (2 Thess 2:3), where the use of the definite article indicates something more than a few here and there, but a significant departure from the faith by many. Paul elaborates on this in 1 Tim 4:1–3, where he mentions erroneous doctrines, hypocrisy, and forbidding marriage and certain foods, and in 2 Tim 3:1–5, where he warns of hard-hearted and worldly believers. No doubt such things have to some extent already occurred but there is worse to come.

(b) The Man of Sin

Scripture speaks of the rise of an individual who will oppose and exalt himself against all that is called "God" (2 Thess 2:3–8); he is also called the son of perdition" (2 Thess 2:3) and "the Antichrist" (1 John 2:18). Such terminology points to his arising from within the professing church and as being very deceptive (Matt 24:24; 2 Thess 2:10)—Satan's counterfeit messiah to rule the world on his behalf. He is prefigured by a similar personage revealed in Dan 8:9–14 as the persecutor of God's old covenant people, and is probably the little horn referred to in Dan 7:8, 19–27. The fact that he is finally destroyed by Yeshua's personal return (2 Thess 2:8) means that his arising will indicate that the return is near, but even so the day and hour will not be known. In the light of this Yeshua's return should be seen as a very much needed deliverance of those of his people who will be living at that time.

(c) Worldwide Witness

"And the gospel must first be preached to all the nations" (Mark 13:10); words of Jesus which indicate all people groups will hear the gospel before he returns. It is probable that Paul's phrase "fullness of the Gentiles" in Rom 11:25 is referring to this. There is mystery here, for Peter speaks of "hastening the coming of the day of God" (2 Pet 3:12), indicating our diligent obedience to Yeshua's commission to go to all the world will bring his return sooner. This awareness that the world will hear first is a spur for action.

(d) The Salvation of "All Israel"

This will be considered more fully below, including the differing views. My understanding is that in Rom 11 Paul indicates that Israel's condition of unbelief will change at some future point. With respect to faith in Yeshua, Israel will then be marked by a fullness as opposed to a remnant (Rom 11:5, 12). Yeshua indicated this when he spoke of a time when the house of Israel would view him as YHWH's Messiah (Matt 23:37–39). Paul sets a time for this—after "the fullness of the Gentiles has come in" (Rom 11:25)—which indicates a time towards the end of history.

(e) The Return of Jerusalem to Jewish Control

Yeshua's words "And Jerusalem will be trampled by Gentiles until the times of the Gentiles are fulfilled" (Luke 21:24) indicate that the destruction of Jerusalem by the Romans is not the end of the story for his people in the land, but there will be a return. It ought to be recognized that his language is very low key, presumably because the main import of the passage is to warn of judgment. It should also be noted that there is no Old Testament quotation as in the case of the destruction (Matt 24:15). The return should therefore not be seen as an end in itself, but a means to an end, the salvation of all Israel. The return of Jerusalem to Jewish control has taken place, even if it is often under threat. This is a spur to gospel ministry in the land.

(iii) Some Cautionary Words

(a) Scripture speaks both positively and negatively of the signs of the times. Yeshua warned Israel's religious leaders that they were failing to recognize certain signs, ones which pointed to him as Messiah (Matt 16:2–3), and the author of Hebrews writes, "but exhorting one another, and so much the more as you see the Day approaching" (Heb 10:25), clearly implying there are signs that indicate the time is drawing near and believers should be alert to them.

(b) In looking for the fulfillment of clearly revealed signs as in (ii) above, it is tempting when a likely person appears or a possible situation begins to develop to speak of it as the fulfillment, even before things have fully unfolded, but in Scripture fulfillment is only definitely known after the event. For example, the end of the seventy years' captivity in Babylon was not known in advance as the starting point was unclear, but only when the Medes and Persians conquered Babylon (Dan 9:1–2). Similarly, Messiah's death for sins only became clear after the event when Yeshua gave the explanation (Luke 24:25–27). This underlines our need for a humble attitude when considering the signs of the times; we are highly likely to judge wrongly if we try to speak with certainty before events have fully unfolded.

A danger related to this is taking action to forward what we believe is God's plan. Of course, where Scripture charges us with such action, like taking the gospel to all the world, then we should act. However, when the action is not commanded, and it is predicated on something which is far from certain, then we should beware, especially if it distracts us from higher priorities. A prophecy of Daniel rebukes such behavior in connection with the events he predicted (see Dan 11:14).

(c) The Lord's return will not be expected; that is, the exact time will be known to no one, even believers (Matt 24:44). Even our Lord in his earthly ministry did not know the time, which is a great mystery (Matt 24:36). In Acts 1:6–7 the disciples ask for the time of a hoped-for event and he replies, "It is not for you to know times or seasons." Scripture may tell us of events to come but not the time of them.

(d) God's timetable is more extended than we tend to expect. Second Peter 3:8–9 gives us two reasons for this. Firstly, it is God's desire that all should come to repentance; that is, sinners should have ample opportunity to repent. Secondly, God's experience of time is different to ours—"with the Lord one day is as a thousand years, and a thousand years as one day"—so we should beware of a hasty spirit.

(e) The term "last days" is frequently used in both Old and New Testaments to refer to the period which begins with Messiah's first appearing and covers the whole messianic age, not simply to a period close to Messiah's second coming (see Isa 2:2; Acts 2:17; Heb 1:2). Hence it should not be assumed that wherever the term "last days" or "latter days" appears it refers to a time near the very end of history. The same may be said of the expression "last times" in the New Testament.

(f) During church history godly and highly valued leaders have ventured to think the time is near and have been proved wrong. Luther believed the weakening of the Church of Rome through the Reformation was the defeat of Antichrist and hence the Lord's return was imminent. He was wrong. This may also explain his ungodly and shameful advice on the treatment of Jews, which, despite all appearances to the contrary, was aimed at their conversion, something he believed had to occur before Jesus returned. A renowned missionary to the Jews in the UK, John Wilkinson (1824–1907), not a man given to speculation, believed the focus of his ministry should change because the Jews of London would soon return to Israel; he was wrong. There is a need for caution.

(g) Preparing for the Lord's return is firstly by an eager anticipation of his return (Phil 3:20; 2 Tim 4:8). Secondly, it is by diligence and faithfulness in Messiah's service inspired by an awareness of his coming return (Matt 24:45 to 25:46), examples of which are: enduring trials (1 Pet 1:7), self-denial (Matt 16:24–27), not revenging (Rom 12:19), avoiding judgmental attitudes (Rom 14:1, 10), gospel witness (2 Cor 5:11), cultivating purity and holiness (Eph 5:26–27; 1 John 3:23), humble service (Matt 10:42), and love of the brethren (1 Pet 1:22).

We should therefore beware of constructing detailed plans and timetables; however, we should not treat lightly or ignore what is revealed of the signs of the times. We should keep focused on Yeshua's literal return in glory, and that there is a heaven to be gained and a hell to be shunned.

(F) THE PLACE OF YESHUA'S RETURN

This might appear a redundant consideration as Peter speaks of the heavens passing away and the earth being burned up on the Day of the Lord. However, that day involves a complex of events the order and connection of which are not clear to us. Zechariah 14:3–4 speaks of Israel's deliverance in a final conflict against her in the land, and the deliverer is the LORD himself, of whom we read, "in that day His feet will stand on the Mount of Olives, Which faces Jerusalem on the east." If this conflict is to be taken literally, and not as a portrayal using Old Testament language of the final conflict of all God's people with the Antichrist, then Yeshua's return will involve a physical coming to a believing Israel to deliver them (see also Matt 23:39). This would occur at the same time as he comes to deliver all his people worldwide. Some would point to Luke 24:50–51 and Acts 1:9–11 as a confirmation of this but those verses point to the manner of his return, not the place.

(G) FURTHER CONSIDERATIONS: ANTICHRIST, ISRAEL, MILLENNIUM

(i) Antichrist

Further to what is written above, it must be remembered that John points us to a spirit of Antichrist, which was already in the world in his own day, long before a particular individual whose coming lay in the future: "and as you have heard that the Antichrist is coming, even now many antichrists have come" (1 John 2:18). This spirit of Antichrist is marked by an opposition to Christ and all he is and taught. In particular John describes this spirit as untrue, denying the Father and the Son, and denying that Yeshua was truly man (1 John 2:22; 4:3; 2 John 7). If we add to John's testimony that of Daniel, Paul, and our Lord, this spirit is one of great self-importance; it opposes and persecutes God's people (Israel and the church), functions without regard to law (lawlessness), succeeds by deception, and may at times be given credibility through the miraculous (Dan 7:19-27; 2 Thess 2:3-10; Matt 24:24). This spirit has had many manifestations in history, among which would be the religious leaders of Israel who oppose Yeshua, church leaders and sects that have denied God's triunity and Jesus' divinity, gnostics who have denied his true humanity, other religions which deny Yeshua is God's Son and the only Savior, and state-sponsored atheism which opposes all that stands for God, especially Israel and the church. Such error within the churches must be steadfastly opposed and rooted out by the faithful, and opposition from the outside world must be both argued against and, when necessary, endured (2 Cor 10:5; John 15:18-21; 1 Pet 4:1).

Scripture is clear that a particular individual will arise who encapsulates all these characteristics and is the culmination of humanity's rebellion against its Creator, someone who opposes all that is called "God" and thinks he is God (2 Thess 2:4). We know that he appears toward the end of history because Yeshua's return brings about his final destruction. When a suitable candidate has arisen, attempts have been made to prove this is the one; but it would seem that, despite his deceptiveness, one who claims to be God and opposes and exalts himself above all that is called God, and therefore has worldwide influence and impact, will not be easy for true believers to miss. It should be noted that the Reformers and many of the great traditional confessions of faith of the churches (e.g., the Westminster Confession of Faith) identify the Church of Rome as a spirit of antichrist and the pope as the Antichrist. Those who follow the modern tendency to think of the Antichrist as connected to secularism and atheism may perceive such a traditional view as outmoded but it is not easily dismissed. Scripture's view of Antichrist has a strong religious element, and his fall is seen as a process with a climax: "whom the Lord will consume with the breath of His mouth and destroy with the brightness of His coming" (2 Thess 2:8).

(ii) Israel

Believers have held differing views of the status of the Jewish people, their future place in God's purposes of redemption, and the hope of a return to their ancient homeland. Such differences are not crucial to an individual's salvation and so the issues have often been viewed as secondary. Today, the return of many to the land in recent times, and the establishment of the state of Israel as a vibrant society surviving against the odds, has focused many believers' minds on the issue, leading to differences being strongly held and increased tension among believers when the subject is raised. Hence it is a subject which needs careful and humble consideration. Gentile believers need to take note of Paul's warning that they should avoid a spirit of boasting over the Jews which dismisses the whole subject (Rom 11:18, 20), and Jewish believers need to be careful not to make agreement with their own understanding a condition of fellowship. The central focus of all must always be the salvation of Jewish people through the presentation of the gospel.

(a) The Status of Israel

The New Testament describes the Jewish people in unbelief as God's people: "I say then, has God cast away His people? Certainly not!" (Rom 11:1). Hence their covenant status remains through the promises made to Abraham and his offspring via Isaac and Jacob (Gen 12:1–3; 21:12; 28:13–14). Paul confirms this in Rom 9:1–5 by listing the blessings and promises given to his people and he does not speak of them as of past significance only. Jewish people who believe the promises of God to them in Messiah Jesus are the saved remnant (Rom 11:5); those who do not are blinded (Rom 11:7–10), but even such judicial blinding indicates that the promises are indeed theirs and that they are responsible to believe them. There are Christians who disagree, who in the light of Rom 9:6–7 understand that only those Jews who believe are Israelites, and that the nation is cast off. This is a failure to hold in tension the truth that the nation is in covenant but that the covenant blessings only take effect for those who are elect, who come to faith. Two reasons stand out as to why some Christians fail to do this. Firstly, some overreact to those who exaggerate the place of Israel and understate the place of the church. Secondly, some feel the need to please those who by history and culture are strongly opposed to the state of Israel and even to the Jewish people as a people.

(b) The Salvation of Israel

Scripture is clear that there is only one way of salvation for Jewish people and that is through faith in Messiah Jesus (Acts 4:12). However, some theologians from within both Judaism and Christianity have built on Israel's covenant status to teach the *two-covenant theory*, which states that the Mosaic covenant is the means of grace and salvation for Jews and the new covenant is the means of grace and salvation for Gentiles. Hence Judaism is not thought of as unbelief but rather a fulfilling of their covenant obligations. We have already examined the New Testament teaching on the covenants and in the light of Heb 8:7–13 this theory is clearly unbiblical. The vanishing away of the Mosaic covenant finally occurred when the second temple was destroyed, rendering obedience to the first covenant impossible.

Christians who have no doubts about the unique status of the Jewish people nevertheless differ on the meaning of Paul's words "all Israel will be saved" in Rom 11:26. There are three main interpretations: firstly that "all Israel" refers to the sum total of Jews believing in Yeshua; secondly that "all Israel" points to all believers (Jew and Gentile) throughout the ages; and thirdly that "all Israel" indicates a large proportion of the Jewish people at a time towards the end of history. The first two make "Israel" to mean something other than ethnic Israel. However, it is doubtful Paul ever does that without some accompanying words to indicate his intention; for example, "they are not all Israel who are of Israel" (Rom 9:6) and "the Israel of God" (Gal 6:16). Another difficulty for the first two is that they require a change in the meaning of "Israel" in verse 26 from its use in the preceding verse 25 without any indication in the text, and similarly a different use to verse 28, in which "Israel" are referred to as enemies. It should be noted that some who understand "all Israel" in verse 26 to be all the redeemed, Jew and Gentile, are not necessarily rejecting a great ingathering of Jewish people in the future; Calvin was one such, who understood the term "fullness" in verse 15 to indicate future gospel blessing for the Jewish nation.

My own view is the third one and I repeat briefly here what was written in "Israel in the New Covenant Period" (chapter 32). What must be noticed is that in Rom 11 Paul is still responding to the initial difficulty he raised in Rom 9:1–7, that so few of Israel have believed in Messiah. Clearly it was a common expectation that all of Israel, i.e., most of the nation, would believe when Messiah came. His mention of "all Israel" in 11:25–27 indicates this issue is still in his mind. His further response to the difficulty involves revealing a mystery: "blindness in part has happened to Israel until the fullness of the Gentiles has come in. And so [i.e., 'in this manner'] all Israel will be saved" (11:25–26). The words "in this manner" underline that the expectation that most of Israel would turn to Messiah was correct, but it will happen only *after* the Gentiles have come in, not before. That was the mystery. "All Israel" points to a very large part of the people coming to faith at some future point when the nations have heard. With Paul we can only marvel at God's wisdom and mercy.

(c) The Return to the Land

This subject has been examined in part; what remains to be considered is the promise of the land, the Old Testament prophecies of a return, and the eschatological relevance of the return.

THE PROMISE OF THE LAND

YHWH promised a land to Abraham and his descendants "from the river of Egypt to the great river, the River Euphrates" (Gen 15:18). In a time of no maps this was no doubt a general description, which Scripture reveals was fulfilled in Solomon's days: "So Solomon reigned over all kingdoms from the River [Euphrates] to the land of the Philistines, as far as the border of Egypt" (1 Kgs 4:21). It would seem therefore that there is no justification for saying God has yet to keep his promise of Israel possessing the land from the Euphrates to the border of Egypt.

THE RETURN TO THE LAND AND OLD TESTAMENT PROPHECY

Is the return to the land in recent times a fulfillment of prophecy? This is a difficult question and one which has exercised the minds of many godly, able leaders of God's people. Here we can only make a few brief points and refer the reader to the Further Reading list. (Note: these points should be kept in mind for the next section on the millennium.)

What of the prophecies in the Tanakh that point to a return to the land? Can they be applied to today? As already stated, the New Testament has almost nothing to say on a return of the Jewish people to the land of promise, even in Rom 11; therefore there is a need for caution. The New Testament never quotes an Old Testament text to this effect. The Old Testament texts taken to refer to the present return fall into three broad categories:

- those uttered before the Babylonian captivity and promising a return from Babylon;
- those uttered before the Babylonian captivity in which the promise of a return is described in terms which seem to exceed what happened; and
- those which were uttered after the return from Babylon and refer to events in the land but which do not appear to have taken place prior to the expulsion in 70 AD.

In the *first category of texts* is Jer 24:5-7: "I will bring them back to this land; I will build them and not pull them down, and I will plant them and not pluck them up." There are many such texts, e.g., Isa 14:1-2; Jer 31:1-26; Ezek 36:1-15; Amos 9:13-15; Mic 7:11-12; Zeph 3:18-20. The only way such texts can be used to teach a return other than the Babylonian one is to speak of a *further fulfillment*; i.e., they provide a principle of the Lord's grace and point to what he may do again, after any subsequent dispersion. That is what Paul does in Rom 11:26-27 when he quotes Isa 59:20-21 to point to a future gospel blessing for Israel. It is not obvious in the Isaiah text because it clearly refers to events in Messiah's earthly ministry and the subsequent gift of the Spirit, hence any further meaning is hidden, a "mystery" as Paul terms it. The question is: Do we have authority to do the same thing with texts which refer to a return to the land but are clearly in their context limited to the return from Babylon? We do if there is a New Testament example of such but the author is not aware of any.

In the *second category of texts* is Amos 9:13-15: "'Behold, the days are coming,' says the LORD, 'When the plowman shall overtake the reaper . . . I will bring back the captives of My people Israel; They shall build the waste cities and inhabit them.'" Other similar texts are: Jer 31:23-28; 33:1-13; Ezek 36:11, 33-35; Zech 8:1-23. Phrases like "the plowman shall overtake the reaper" and "This land that was desolate has become like the Garden of Eden" seem to go beyond Israel's experience after Babylon. How are they to be understood? Some spiritualize them to refer to the rich spiritual blessings promised for God's new covenant people when Messiah comes. Others view them as a literal description of an earthly millennium. And some believe they do indeed reflect Israel's experience in the 450 years after the close of the Old Testament because Israel did not remain under the conditions described in the days of Ezra and Nehemiah, but rather the Gospel accounts indicate a prosperous society in Galilee and Judea, so that such texts aimed to encourage Israel during her long wait for Messiah. This author is of the opinion that the first view is correct for some of this type of text and the third view for others of this type.

In the *third category of texts* in Zech 14:2-4: "For I will gather all the nations to battle against Jerusalem . . . Then the LORD will go forth And fight against those nations . . . And in that day His feet will stand on the Mount of Olives." Other similar texts are few but Zech 10:9-10 is an example. How are such texts, which are post the return from Babylon, to be understood? This is akin to asking how Zech 12-14 is to be interpreted. There are different views:

1. Some understand these chapters as a summary, an overview, of what Zechariah has already written about Israel's return in his own day, ending with deliverance by the Lord into a state of eternal peace through the gospel.

2. There are those who understand the whole passage as a focus on Israel's experience in the land at some future time, pointing to Israel's return, their security, their national conversion, their persecution, and their deliverance at Messiah's return followed by his earthly millennial reign.

3. There are those who see in the passage principles regarding God's dealings with his new covenant people.

There are various permutations and combinations of these approaches. No one finds these chapters of Zechariah easy because there are obvious references to events yet future, but embedded within the chapters are events which the New Testament sees as fulfilled in New Testament days (see John 19:34, 37 and Matt 26:31). There is much spiritual encouragement and warning here for God's people in all ages, and the unfolding of events alone can provide certainty as to what is to be taken literally.

The Eschatological Relevance of the Return to the Land

There are many things which can be described as a hope in connection with events preceding the return of Messiah Jesus in glory, and the salvation of all Israel is one of them. However, whereas Israel's return to YHWH is an eschatological hope in the New Testament, it is difficult to argue the New Testament presents the return to the land in that light. There will be further examination on the differing views on this in the next section on the millennium.

(iii) The Millennium

On this subject there are significant differences of understanding that connect to how Old Testament prophecy is interpreted, which was explored in the preceding section, and should be referred to in what is considered here.

It is worth stopping to consider why there are such significant differences.

1. As stated before, God has not revealed to us in one place in Scripture the detailed order of the steps in his plan for the world; hence dogmatism is out of place.
2. The "millennium," the term for the one thousand years mentioned by John in Rev 20:16, is only referred to in a book which is full of symbols like beasts, bowls, and seals; this suggests the need for caution in interpretation.
3. No other New Testament author makes any clear reference to a one-thousand-year period and what it entails, such that some have asserted it was only revealed to John, which seems very unlikely.
4. Our present circumstances, hopes, and desires of our hearts may well affect our interpretation.

For Jewish believers there is an understandable tendency to prefer a view which restores Israel to blessing and a position of prominence. The sad corollary is that there are some Gentile believers whose negative attitude towards Jews leads them to adopt a view that does not restore all Israel to faith or to a position of prominence. All must strive to have their head rule their hearts and hold to what the Scriptures teach—no more and no less.

What are the main teachings of Rev 20:1–10? There will be a period described as lasting one thousand years and during this time Satan's power to deceive the nations will be restrained, but at the end of the period he will be released to deceive them again, leading to a final conflict in which the nations will join together against God's people but be defeated by a divine intervention. There is a resurrection of those described as beheaded for their witness to Jesus and they live and reign with Christ for the one thousand years; this is termed the "first resurrection" and ensures deliverance from eternal punishment. What follows are the main views of the millennium.

(a) Amillennialism

According to this view the millennium is not a literal one thousand years but symbolizes the whole gospel period in which Messiah reigns at the right hand of God. The fact that the millennium is mentioned towards the end of the book of Revelation does not mean it occurs at the end of history. The martyrs mentioned as ruling with Messiah represent all believers who have died, making the point that even those most abused are not defeated but reign over their enemies. They are not in the body and hence portray something of the activity of those who are with Yeshua in glory before his return; in some manner they take an active part in his rule. The first resurrection is understood as regeneration. The binding of Satan is connected to the redeeming work of Yeshua whereby the repentant are released from his grip. The mention of nations being deceived indicates that although many individuals may continue to be deceived by Satan yet whole nations will not because many among them will believe; however at the end an international, confederate rebellion of nations will be permitted. Some amillennialists hold to the salvation of all Israel and their return to the land, and some do not.

Criticisms are:

- Amillennialism overspiritualizes this passage in Revelation, meaning that Messiah's mediatorial kingdom rule is never a visible rule over the present world order, or an invisible one clearly demonstrated by a worldwide period of great numbers turning to him.
- The promises to Israel are ignored by those amillennialists who do not believe there is a national salvation or a return to the land.

(b) Postmillennialism

The millennium is taken literally as a very long period of time towards the close of the gospel period during which the gospel is universally believed and Christianity is the religion of all nations. Thus Messiah is understood to be the ruler of all rulers so that there is an earthly aspect to his universal rule. The martyrs who rule with him are representative of a church which is victorious; the first resurrection is regeneration. Satan is bound during this long period so that his deceptions do not turn people and nations from the gospel, but towards the end he is permitted to deceive again and instigate a worldwide rebellion of the nations. The second coming is viewed as one event that takes place after this period of great gospel blessing, hence the term "postmillennial."

Postmillennialism definitely expects a national conversion of Israel, as per Rom 11, which will be the catalyst for the long period of gospel triumph (Rom 11:12, 15). Postmillennialists understand this long period of gospel blessing to be the fulfillment of Old Testament prophecies like "For the earth shall be full of the knowledge of the LORD as the waters cover the sea" (Isa 11:9, see also Pss 2; 72; Mic 4:3; Zech 9:10). Some would expect a return to the land as a part of this hope.

Criticisms are:

- Yeshua and the apostles present the church as always in a position of conflict (Luke 9:23; 2 Tim 3:12), looking to his return for their deliverance.
- Nowhere else in the New Testament are believers taught to expect this very long period of blessing.
- A worldwide rebellion of the nations inspired by Satan is difficult to envisage after such a long period of blessing, and tends to diminish the triumph of Messiah's rule through the gospel which it is said to manifest.

(c) Classic Premillennialism

Because premillennialism presents a much more detailed understanding of the millennium and its surrounding events, there are significant differences on the details among premillennialists, but the following is generally accepted. The millennium is a literal one-thousand-year reign of Messiah on earth. Messiah's return will defeat Antichrist and remove Satan and his evil forces from the earth. He will resurrect believers who have died and those who are alive at his return will be transformed; this is the rapture. All Israel will be saved, either just before or at his appearing. Then follows his one-thousand-year reign from Jerusalem, ruling over perfected and glorified believers in resurrection bodies, a converted Israel (not resurrected or perfected), and those unsaved who have survived the great tribulation, many of whom will have been converted. Sin and death are still present. Old Testament passages such as Isa 65:20 are used to justify this mixed state of affairs. Temple worship is restored and the natural world transformed. Towards the end of the millennium, Satan is freed to lead a final rebellion but is defeated by a divine interposition.

Criticisms are:

- The literalism demanded by premillennialism is not applied consistently in Rev 20 because those who reign with Messiah are described as souls and beheaded martyrs.
- Similarly it is a literalism which fails to take account of typology in the Scriptures, e.g., the temple prefigures God's new covenant people (Eph 2:19–22).
- The oneness in Messiah established in his new covenant community is reversed in the millennium when Jewish believers are at the center in the land of Israel.

- Events which premillennialism places either side of the one thousand years are taught in the New Testament as concurrent, e.g., John 5:28–29, where the resurrection of just and unjust are at the same hour.
- Finally, texts like Heb 9:26 speak of this present gospel age as "the end of the ages," leaving no room for a millennium.

(d) Dispensational Premillennialism (Usually Known as "Dispensationalism")

As its name suggests, dispensational premillennialism has in common with classic premillennialism the belief in a literal reign on earth by Yeshua for one thousand years after his return. Dispensationalism has two main differences from classic premillennialism. Firstly, a clear distinction is made between Israel and the church, and secondly, as indicated by the word "dispensational," God's requirements of humanity differ in different dispensations—the dispensations being periods of time usually marked out by the various covenants made by God.

There are significant variations among dispensationalists on the details due to the changes dispensationalism has gone through from its earliest days (1830s onward), to revisions in the 1950s, to the "progressive dispensationalism" of the 1980s onwards. It is the revised forms which predominate today with progressive dispensationalism gaining increasing influence. For example, there are differences over who is resurrected when, and who rules with Messiah on earth, resulting in a distinction between those Jews and Gentiles who believe. Progressive dispensationalism differs in that it rejects as a backward step the separation of Jewish believers and Gentile believers and expects all who have believed to be raised and to inhabit the earth in the millennial period. Hence it is more akin to covenant theology in that it does not rigidly separate the dispensations but understands each one as a progression from the previous, such that the present rule of Yeshua and the existence of the New Testament church are understood to be the inauguration of the kingdom, the fullness of which arrives with the millennial rule.

The criticisms mentioned above regarding classical premillennialism apply to all forms of dispensationalism. Other criticisms are:

- Premillennialism, with its focus on Israel, has an ancient pedigree in the church, but dispensationalism was never taught until the 1830s, begging the question as to whether so many spiritually minded and able teachers over 1,800 years could be so seriously wrong.

- The significant differences among dispensationalists and the revisions since its early days all point to a theory with weaknesses.
- Yeshua spoke of the kingdom being taken from Israel (Matt 21:43).
- The differences between the dispensations means, for example, that regeneration never occurred until the Spirit was given at Pentecost, so that all Old Testament saints were unregenerate, suggesting an improbable conclusion that all the psalms were written by people whose minds were carnal and at enmity with God (Rom 8:7).
- The assertion that the Old Testament makes no mention of the New Testament church of Jew and Gentile, but rather it is a mysterious parenthesis in God's purpose, is not supported by the New Testament because not only does the New Testament describe the church as the fulfillment of the Old Testament hope (Acts 24:14; Acts 15:13–18), it also describes the revealed mystery of Eph 3:3–7 as the greater clarity the New Testament has on the oneness of Jew and Gentile in Messiah compared to the Old Testament revelation (see Eph 3:5 and note the word "as" is used and not the word "but").

(iv) Approaches to the Book of Revelation

The different approaches to the book impinge on different views on the millennium and are worth further study via the Further Reading suggestions. It may help to mention by name the four categories of approach to the book.

- The *futurist or eschatological view* asserts that the bulk of the book, chapters 4–21, all refer to future events close to the end.
- The *historicist view* asserts that the book is an unfolding of history from John's day until the end of time.
- The *preterist or contemporary-historical view* asserts that all the book's prophecies were fulfilled in the early years, either by the fall of Jerusalem in 70 AD or the fall of Rome around 476 AD.
- The *idealist or timeless-symbolic view* asserts that the book contains no reference to specific historical events but uses symbolic language to describe the spiritual realities operating in every age.

(H) HISTORICAL SURVEY

I believe it is helpful to realize how the church has leaned towards different views on the millennium at different times in history, so what follows is a brief overview, including views on the special position of the Jewish people as God's people and hopes for the restoration of Israel to faith in Yeshua.

(i) The Early Centuries

There is little evidence of disputes around the meaning of the millennium; the challenges to Christian doctrine of those times centered on God's tri-unity, the person of Messiah, and the consequences of the fall. The focus of the creeds of that period is upon Messiah's return in glory to judge the world. Premillennial views were held by some leaders, like Tertullian and Justyn Martyr; it was Augustine who most clearly articulated the amillennial view, and his influence led to the eclipse of premillennialism. Those early premillennialists had positive attitudes to the Jewish people as can be seen in Justyn Martyr's *Dialogue with Trypho*, and whilst Augustine opposed an earthly millennial kingdom he spoke strongly against persecution of the Jews.

(ii) The Medieval Period

As the gospel spread, which in some cases led to whole kingdoms adopting Christianity, God's kingdom became increasingly tied into the kingdoms of this world. The Roman Catholic Church in particular claimed it was the kingdom of God on earth. Focus on a spiritual kingdom and a kingdom yet to come faded from view. However, there were pietistic groups which formed on the fringes and they were known to give serious consideration to end-time issues. Among theologians of the period Augustine's view predominated.

(iii) The Reformation

The Reformers risked their lives, and some died horribly, to stand for the vital truths of salvation which had been obscured by Rome. They understood the Roman papacy to be the Antichrist and saw themselves in a last-times spiritual battle prior to Messiah's return. It seems they had little leisure to write books on end-time eschatology; rather their focus was on the spiritual attitudes and behavior Jesus' return should stimulate within believers; some were premillennial but most were amillennial. Many in this period, such as Bullinger and Peter Martyr, shared the view that Rom 11 pointed to a future salvation of Israel. In the case of the two best-known names, Luther and Calvin, both were amillennial but expected that Israel would turn to the Lord prior to Messiah's return: "the Jews who expelled Christ to the Gentiles, where he now reigns, will come to him in the end" (Luther); "When the Gentiles have come in, the Jews also shall return from their defection to the obedience of faith" (Calvin). I mention this because they and other Reformers like them are often understood to have considered the Jewish nation as cast away. The Anabaptists had a similar expectation regarding the turning of the Jewish nation to Messiah but were more premillennial in their outlook.

(iv) The Seventeenth Century

The security of Protestantism in much of Europe and North America during this period meant more attention could be given to other areas of truth, including eschatology and the place of the Jewish people. Some of the greatest confessions of the Christian church were written at this time. Concerning the Lord's return, all held to the basics but there was a moving away from traditional amillennialism, with more writers espousing a premillennial scheme, men such as Alsted (1625), Gouge (1621), and Goodwin (1642) in Europe, and Increase Mather in the Americas (1669). Scottish theologians resisted premillennial schemes and began to develop what we now call "postmillennialism." All were prone to date-setting, especially from Daniel. The salvation of Israel as per Rom 11 was a significant interest for many. A minority firmly expected a return of Jewish people to the land, notably the Dutch theologian W. Brakel (1635–1711).

(v) The Eighteenth Century

The great gospel revivals in Europe, Britain, and the Americas led to the strengthening of postmillennialism; it was a day of hope for gospel advance. Missions were formed, including ones to the Jewish people. There were still strong advocates of premillennialism, such as Bengel, and there were many leaders who expected a conversion of the Jewish nation, such as Whitefield and the Wesley brothers, although some like Cotton Mather moved from a premillennial position to an amillennial one and did not anticipate a large-scale conversion of Israel.

(vi) The Nineteenth Century

The growth of the churches through revival and mission continued; however the rise of nationalism, liberal Christianity, and the theory of evolution encouraged a man-centeredness which blunted the hopes of postmillennialism. Jewish mission continued on with fruitfulness but no mass turning to Yeshua. Premillennialism was strengthened by evangelicals reacting to the liberal approach of spiritualizing even fundamentals such as the virgin birth, so that being as literal as possible was seen among evangelicals as being more faithful to Scripture. It was in this atmosphere that dispensationalism, the most literal of all the schemes, emerged through the Brethren movement and the influence of J. N. Darby. Outbreaks of persecution against Jewish communities in Europe stimulated more thought on a long-term solution, raising the issue of a return to the land as a place of safety and self-government; something which many premillennial evangelicals saw predicted in the OT and part of God's plan for their national salvation.

(vii) The Twentieth Century and Today

No major new developments took place in Christian thinking on end-time issues but the differing positions were more carefully developed with better interaction between their advocates. Amillennialism gained more adherents due to an increased interest in Calvinistic/Reformed theology, which stressed the essential oneness and continuity of the covenants in opposition to the dispensational approach. However, Reformed theologians such as Wayne Grudem and D. A. Carson upheld a classic premillennial understanding. The expression "optimistic amillennialism" arose to describe that established strain of amillennialism that believed in a national salvation of Israel. The Lausanne Consultation on Jewish Evangelism, established in 1980, among whose members there is the whole range of millennial views, demonstrated that such differences need not hinder cooperation in missionary work.

The seminal event was the establishment of the state of Israel, raising questions like: Was it a fulfillment of prophecy? Was it a sign of the nearness of Jesus' return? Would all Israel soon be saved? A new term emerged, "Christian Zionist," which came to describe those who not only understood it as a fulfillment of prophecy but also saw it as a Christian duty to support the fledgling state. Others were critical of what sometimes appeared to be unthinking support, with little obvious care for those non-Jews who suffered in the ensuing wars and ongoing conflict. Those Christians who engaged with the Arab world in compassion and mission were less prone to see the state as a fulfillment of prophecy but rather a state like any other. Others, sympathetic to the state and prophecy being fulfilled, were critical of a lack of mission-mindedness among many Christian Zionists. There is a need for Christians to be sensitive to moral responsibilities in the conflict, and to maintain focus on Yeshua's command to preach the good news.

The grievous history of anti-Semitism within Christendom can lead all too easily to the conclusion that it is only in recent days, and especially since the establishment of the state of Israel, that the churches have paid attention to the Jewish people. The human tendency to focus on the negative and neglect the positive encourages such an erroneous view. Note should be taken of these words of Increase Mather (1639–1723), minister of the North Church (Congregational) in Boston, president of Harvard College, and author of *The Mystery of Israel's Salvation* (1669): "That there shall be a general conversion of the tribes of Israel is a truth which in some measure has been known and believed in all ages of the church of God, since the Apostles' days."

(I) RABBINIC VIEWS ON THE MESSIANIC AGE AND THE WORLD TO COME

Most readers will probably be well aware of this subject but I trust something here will be useful. It is necessary to cover rabbinic views on the messianic age together with their views on the world to come because they so often overlap, as this quotation underlines: "there is a good deal of confusion in the rabbinic literature about the World to Come. The phrase may refer to the days of the Messiah and to a purified earth . . . But this age is not to last forever: it is to be succeeded by the real End: the resurrection of the dead and the last Judgment. Then begins the true world to come."[1] This means that much of what follows in this subsection (I) is equally relevant to chapters 35 and 36 on "Human Destiny" and "Final Human Destinies."

The traditional expectation of Messiah's reign is for the coming of an anointed one of the house of David who will restore Israel to their land, rebuild the temple, and turn Israel to love God and obey his Torah. The earth will be restored to its original perfection, with Israel in their land and the nations serving YHWH in theirs. The rabbis stress the importance of individuals turning from their sin so that the righteous Messiah reigns over a righteous world, as per Isa 11:3–9. These fundamentals are expressed at the close of the daily services in the Aleinu prayer, with words such as:

---

1. Montefiore and Loewe, eds., *Rabbinic Anthology*, 581.

"therefore we [Israel] put our hope in You, Adonai our God, to soon see the glory of Your strength . . . for all living flesh to call upon Your Name . . . to You every knee must bend and every tongue must swear loyalty." There is much speculation on matters such as: the signs preceding his coming, the time of his coming, the coming of Elijah, the war with God and Magog, and the nature of the renovation of the world; some have sought to fix the date but were invariably wrong. The attitude encouraged by traditional Judaism is to long and wait for divine intervention.

Mystical forms of Judaism aim to speed the arrival of the messianic era by closer communion with the divine and obedience to Torah. They see their devotion as repairing (Tikkun) the world by returning the divine holy sparks to their source, vessels which harness God's creative energy, ready for the messianic era. Modern forms of Judaism, such as Reform, have made a distinction between the messianic age and the Messiah, preferring to focus on an age which dawns through gradual improvement, in which Judaism plays its part: "We recognize in the modern era of universal culture of heart and intellect the approach of the realization of Israel's great messianic hope for the establishment of the kingdom of truth, justice and peace among all men."[2]

Hence Judaism experiences the familiar tension between the sovereignty of God and human responsibility. Some believe we can only patiently wait for God to intervene by sending Messiah; others stress our responsibility to hasten his coming.

Zionism emerged from the sufferings of the Jews in Central and Eastern Europe and was initially a secular movement but it drew upon the age-long hope of a return to the land, as expressed by Ben Gurion in July 1957: "the suffering of the Jewish people has been a powerful factor, but it was only the Messianic vision which made that factor fruitful." Initially the rabbis of traditional Judaism opposed Zionism because only Messiah regathers the exiles, but others, religious Zionists, saw this movement for return as the beginning of the end of the exile, a first step to Messiah's coming, a vital step in a return to God and Torah. Once the state was established the vast majority of the traditionalists accepted the fait accompli as of God and aimed to work with it to develop a Torah-observant nation.

Rabbinic Judaism has always seen the messianic era as a preparation: "the Kingdom of God in its messianic setting and earthly fulfillment is but preparatory to the consummation of the Kingdom in the suprahistorical and supernatural world to come."[3]

---

2. "Pittsburg Platform," 1885, a Reform Statement.
3. Epstein, *Judaism*.

Before that new world is entered into there is the resurrection of the dead and the Day of Judgment. Those who have a share in the world to come are the righteous of the nations and all Israel, except those who deny the resurrection of the dead and the divine authorship of the law, and who mock rabbinic learning.[4] There are significant rabbinic differences on some details: some hold that after death you sleep until the general resurrection and the last judgment; others hold that when the righteous die they immediately enjoy the life of the world to come, but sinners go straight to hell; most believe that only a few remain in hell because after purging the majority go to the world to come, although a few rabbis hold even the most wicked do not remain in hell but are annihilated. Hence most rabbis are universalists. In the new, perfect, and eternal world the righteous will have perfect bodies, will know each other, will receive rewards, and will not rebel.

The maintenance of these two hopes in rabbinic Judaism—the messianic era and the world to come—is a testimony to the gracious influence of YHWH to keep Israel aware of these truths and hopeful of their realization. He has not abandoned Israel but has held his promises before them, purposing always to save some, and one day many, when they believe in Yeshua as the key to the receiving of his promises.

> Behold, I am coming quickly, and My reward is with Me, to give everyone according to his work . . . And the Spirit and the bride say, 'Come!' And let him who hears say, 'Come!' And let him who thirsts come. Whoever desires, let him take the water of life freely." (Rev 22:12, 17)

Scriptures

Messiah's return: Isa 63:1–6; Dan 7:21–27; Zeph 3:14–17; Zech 14:3–7; Mal 4:1; Matt 24:29–31; 25:31–32; John 5:25–27; 14:3; Acts 1:11; Rom 14:9–12; 1 Cor 15:24–28; 2 Cor 5:10; Phil 3:20–21; 1 Thess 4:13—5:3; 2 Thess 1:7; 2:1–8; 1 Tim 6:14–15; 2 Tim 4:1, 8; Titus 2:13; Heb 9:28; Jas 5:7; 1 Pet 1:7; 2 Pet 3:4–13; 1 John 3:2; Rev 1:7; 19:7–9; 22:20.

Waiting for Messiah's return: Matt 24:45—25:46; Acts 1:7; 1 Cor 1:7; Phil 1:23; Titus 2:13; Heb 9:28; 1 Thess 1:9–10; 2 Pet 3:8–9.

The Antichrist: Ezek 38–39; Dan 7:19–27; Matt 24:24; 2 Thess 2:3–11; 1 John 2:18–22; 4:3; 2 John 7.

---

4. *b. Sanh.* XI, 1, 2.

Israel, status and salvation: Gen 12:1–3; 21:12; 28:13–14; Deut 30:1–10; Ezra 6:16–22; Jer 31:37; Matt 23:37–39; Rom 9:1–7; 11; Gal 6:16; Heb 8:7–13.
Israel, land: Gen 15:18; Luke 21:24; Rom 9:4.
The millennium: Pss 2; 72; Isa 11:9; Mic 4:2–5; Rom 11:12, 15; Rev 20:1–10.

Questions

1. What are the key Scripture texts which teach the personal return of Messiah Jesus? What do they teach about the nature and purposes of his return?

2. What events does Scripture predict must occur before Yeshua's return? Have any of them happened yet?

3. What does Scripture teach about the time of Yeshua's return? How are believers to be ready?

4. What effects does the New Testament expect this truth of Messiah's return to have on believers?

5. What expectation do you have for the Jewish people in God's end-time purposes? Justify your answer from Scripture.

6. State briefly the different views on the millennium. Justify your preference from Scripture. How does it affect your life as a believer now?

7. What do you understand to be the most significant agreements and differences between rabbinic Judaism's teaching on the messianic era and the world to come and that of the Scriptures?

Further Reading

Allis, Oswald T. *Prophecy and the Church*. Phillipsburg, NJ: Presbyterian and Reformed, 1974.

Berkouwer, G. C. *The Return of Christ*. Grand Rapids: Eerdmans, 1972.

Blaising, Craig A., and Darrell L. Bock. *Progressive Dispensationalism*. Grand Rapids: Baker, 2000. (Dispensationalism)

Bock, Darrell, ed. *Three Views of the Millennium and Beyond*. Grand Rapids: Zondervan, 1999.

Burge, Gary M. *Whose Land? Whose Promise?* Milton Keynes: Paternoster, 2003.

Cohn-Sherbok, Dan. *The Jewish Faith*. London: SPCK, 1993. See pp. 107–16.

Fairbairn, Patrick. *The Interpretation of Prophecy*. Edinburgh: Banner of Truth, 1964.
Grier, W. J. *The Momentous Event*. Edinburgh: Banner of Truth, 1970. (Amillenialism)
Johnston, Philip, and Peter Walker, eds. *The Land of Promise*. Leicester: Apollos, 2000.
Ladd, George Eldon. *The Blessed Hope*. Grand Rapids: Eerdmans, 1956. (Premillenialism)
Morris, Paul. *Jewish Themes in the New Testament*. Milton Keynes: Paternoster, 2013. See chapter 20.
Murray, Iain. *The Puritan Hope*. Edinburgh: Banner of Truth, 1991. (Postmillenialism)

35

Human Destiny

Here we will consider the teaching of Scripture which concerns the destiny of every human individual.

(A) DEATH

Scripture always links death to sin; it is God's judgment upon sin, not an essential consequence of our natural existence—"the wages of sin is death" (Rom 6:24; see Gen 2:17). In general the word "death" refers to the death of the body but it is also used to refer to spiritual death, a condition in which communion with God is broken as such a person chooses unrighteousness and rebellion (Eph 2:1–3; compare Gen 3:24 and 2:17). The second death (Rev 20:14) refers to a fixed state of spiritual death in the body after the resurrection and Day of Judgment. There is nothing in Scripture which connects death to annihilation, a cessation of being.

God's plan for humans is an embodied existence; the separation of body and soul which occurs at physical death is not the human ideal but is described by Paul as being unclothed and also as being naked (2 Cor 5:3–4). Such language makes it clear that the soul has a separate existence when the body dies (see section below). Philosophy speaks of the immortality of the soul but Scripture does not use such terms. God alone is immortal (1 Tim 6:16), but it is his design that humans should live forever, such that the word "immortal" is used to describe believers with their resurrected bodies (1 Cor 15:53–54), a state which is also described as "incorruptible." Unbelievers also live forever but it is not life in the true sense of the word and the word "immortality" is not used to describe their condition. Although the penalty of sin was paid at the cross, it is still God's will that believers experience the effects and consequences of sin as they live on in this life, and that they experience physical death. It should be viewed as a discipline which encourages us to grow in faith, holiness, and hope (1 Cor 15:57–58; 2 Cor 5:1–8; Phil 3:10–11; 1 Pet 4:6).

(B) THE INTERMEDIATE STATE

Many Scriptures point to a conscious existence for the soul after death. The parable of the rich man and Lazarus points to a conscious state for Old Testament believers through the mention of Abraham (Luke 16:19–31). The dying thief was assured of being with Jesus in paradise (Luke 23:43); Paul spoke of having "a desire to depart and be with Christ, which is far better" (Phil 1:23); and Revelation portrays departed saints as worshiping God (Rev 7:9–10, 14–17). Likewise for unbelievers a conscious state is indicated by the same parable of the rich man and Lazarus, and also by Jesus preaching to the spirits of Noah's generation at the time of his death and resurrection (1 Pet 3:19–20); but see Rev 20:5a.

It seems unlikely that those who have died will experience time as they do on earth but it is probably incorrect to assert, as some do, that the dead are aware of no gap between their death and Messiah's return in glory. Scripture speaks of the disembodied state as being "with Christ, which is far better" (Phil 1:23); the departed saints are portrayed as with others who are actively serving God (Heb 12:22–23, see also Rev 20:4), and the martyrs are portrayed as waiting (Rev 6:9–11). The use of the term "sleep" to describe believers who have died has led some to assert there is no conscious existence for believers after death, but it seems best to understand the term as assuring those who grieve the loss of loved ones that their separation is temporary, just like a person being asleep breaks communication for a while. It expresses the relationship to the departed of those left behind, not the experience of the departed believer (Matt 9:24; John 11:11; 1 Cor 15:20; 1 Thess 4:13–18). Conscious existence points to development, and although Scripture makes no reference to this there must be some form of development in adapting to a new state of existence and fuller opportunity to worship and serve. As for the location of departed spirits, Heb 12:22–23 speaks of believers in the presence of Messiah, which in Paul's terminology would be "the third heaven" (2 Cor 12:2–4), but for unbelievers Paul's reference to those "under the earth" may indicate a location (Phil 2:10; see also Rev 5:3, 13).

Both the Orthodox and Roman Catholic Churches teach a doctrine of further purification between death and entering God's presence. For some this may not be necessary due to having already attained a purity of heart but for most it is necessary. Roman Catholicism teaches "Purgatory is a place where souls suffer for a time after death on account of their sins."[1] This is justified from 1 Cor 3:15 but Paul is referring there to rewards for service and the loss to those whose service is unworthy; there is no suggestion of the person suffering for sin; rather it is their work that is being destroyed. The Orthodox Church accepts that many will be kept in "a condition of waiting" after death prior to entering Christ's presence but they reject the idea that it is a place of punishment; rather it is an experience of spiritual refining. Both of these churches accept the living may pray for the dead who are going through such experiences. Traditional Judaism teaches Gehenna as a place of punishment after death but only a few, the very wicked, remain there. Others who have not gone immediately to Gan Eden at death experience a period of purification, said to be twelve months, prior to admittance to Gan Eden. All such teachings are inconsistent with justification by faith alone as taught in both the Tanakh (Gen 15:6; Isa 61:10) and the New Testament (Acts 13:38–39): those who are clothed with the perfect righteousness of Messiah and whose sin is forgiven and forgotten are thereby fit to enter God's presence at death.

Is there a further opportunity to repent after death? Hebrews 9:27 answers in the negative: "And as it is appointed for men to die once, but after this the judgment." Peter's account of Yeshua's preaching to those who died in the flood due to their disobedience is not teaching hope for them but vindication for Noah, who was a type of messiah, standing alone against all the world.

The ideas of karma and reincarnation are nowhere taught in the Scriptures, which emphasize that we are responsible individuals created by God, having one earthly life to live as God requires, with the hope through Messiah of continuing on in a new world as the same individual person. Mystical Judaism based on the Kabbalah has a doctrine of *gilgul*—reincarnation, or as it is sometimes termed the "transmigration of souls." Behind it is the same notion of purification, but also righting injustice and unusual suffering. Those who taught this doctrine did not expect all to have to experience it, and for those who did there was usually a maximum of three times. It indicates the influence of Indian and Eastern ideas which Isaiah spoke of in his day (Isa 2:6). Traditional Judaism and Jewish philosophy reject the notion of *gilgul*.

---

1. Catholic Truth Society, *Catechism of Christian Doctrine*, 18.

(C) RESURRECTION

The bodily resurrection of all who have lived is a fundamental doctrine of Scripture, taught in both the Tanakh and the New Testament. Yeshua was clear: "the hour is coming in which all who are in the graves will hear His voice and come forth" (John 5:28–29). For the patriarchs this hope was expressed by phrases like "you shall go to your fathers in peace" (Gen 15:15), but made much more explicit by Job's words, "And after my skin is destroyed, this I know, That in my flesh I shall see God" (Job 19:26), and Isaiah's words, "Your dead shall live; Together with my dead body they shall arise" (Isa 26:19). Yeshua's rebuke of the Sadducees in Luke 20:38, asserting God as the God of the living, and that all live to him, underlines that life after death inevitably involves the resurrection of the body. The New Testament teaches the resurrection of the dead in many places, especially in 1 Cor 15; for example, verse 52, "For the trumpet will sound, and the dead will be raised incorruptible, and we shall be changed." This is assured on the basis of Jesus' resurrection, who is "the firstborn from the dead" (Col 1:18). In Acts 26:6, 8 Paul refers to it as a hope of the faithful in all ages: "And now I stand and am judged for the hope of the promise made by God to our fathers . . . Why should it be thought incredible by you that God raises the dead?"

As to what the resurrection body will be like, the New Testament indicates both differences and similarities. The most explicit point is that it is incorruptible. We shall be changed; the flesh and blood with which we are now familiar will not inherit the kingdom (1 Cor 15:50). We are to be like Jesus, for we shall bear the image of the heavenly man (1 Cor 15:49), and his resurrection body was not governed by time and space as ours now are (Luke 24:31–43); it was a spiritual body and believers' bodies will be also. Paul compares it to the difference between a seed sown and the plant or tree which grows from it. But there is a continuity with the body now, even though it dies. Yeshua spoke of raising that which is in the grave (John 5:28–29) and Rev 20:13 describes the sea giving up the dead in it. Such a thought staggers us with the immense power and knowledge required, but "Is anything too hard for the LORD?" And Yeshua warns those prone to skepticism, "You are mistaken, not knowing the Scriptures nor the power of God" (Matt 22:29). Paul's words of comfort to grieving believers whose loved ones have died assure us of a recognizable similarity between the body now and the body to come: "God will bring with Him those who sleep in Jesus . . . Therefore comfort one another with these words" (1 Thess 4:14, 18). There is no such comfort for the ungodly whose bodies are raised from the dead. There is no promise of an end to corruption; rather Paul writes of "everlasting destruction from the presence of the Lord" (2 Thess 1:9), a fate almost impossible to imagine and too fearful to contemplate.

(D) JUDGMENT

YHWH is a God who "loves justice" (Ps 37:28) and is therefore steadfast in his opposition to evil, promising to punish it (Mal 4:1), but delighting in righteousness, promising to reward the righteous (Ps 58:11). This does not always appear so but YHWH has promised a day when all actions of men and women will be judged righteously and justly. In the Old Testament there is anticipation of this day in Isa 63:1–6, where Messiah is portrayed as punishing sin at the time he finally redeems his people. The New Testament is explicit that it will be at the time of Jesus' return in glory (Matt 25:31–46). All who have ever lived will be judged, both the godly and ungodly (2 Cor 5:10–11; 2 Tim 4:1). Though awesome to contemplate, because every mouth will be stopped and all the world will become guilty before God (Rom 3:19), there is also a sense of satisfaction and even of joy because justice will be done (Ps 96:11–13).

The godly need not fear the judgment for their guilt is removed and there is no condemnation of those who are in Christ Jesus, but they will be judged in relation to their life and stewardship. Paul writes, "each one's work will become clear; for the Day will declare it" (1 Cor 3:13), and he goes on to promise rewards for faithfulness and to warn of loss—not of salvation but of reward (1 Cor 3:14–15; see also Rom 14:12). Believers are thus warned against accommodating sin and laziness in service. Yeshua's two parables which describe gifts given to servants are interesting to compare. In Luke 19:11–27 the servants are given the same but those who do more with what they have are rewarded proportionally. In Matt 25:14–30 the servants are given differing amounts but appear to receive no extra reward for making more than those who started with less. The lesson to be drawn is that all believers start equal with the gift of salvation and some will build more upon it than others; but there are differences of gifting and in that respect to those to whom much is given much is expected.

The judgment of the ungodly is a fearful thing but there must be no doubting God's justness (Gen 18:25; Ps 89:14); a justness which was most perfectly exhibited at Golgotha, when YHWH did not spare his own Son for our sakes so that justice might be done and be seen to be done. God's judgment of the ungodly will be according to their response to the revelation they have received, a truth which Jesus emphasized when he warned that those who rejected him would be punished more severely than those who have lived in sin yet had not heard of him (Matt 11:24). All who have lived have received revelation of God through his created world and their moral consciousness, and Paul refers to the punishment of those who have failed to respond to this by repentance: "For as many as have sinned without law will also perish without law" (Rom 2:12, see also Rom 1:18–21; 2:1–3). Israel, and those who knew of God's revelation through them, enjoyed the revelation of Moses' law, and for them there will be judgment according to their response to it (Rom 2:12). For those who have heard the gospel of Messiah Jesus and rejected it, they will not see life but must endure God's wrath (John 3:36; Heb 10:26–31).

36

Final Human Destinies

(A) HELL

THOSE WHO ARE RAISED from the dead and condemned at the judgment seat of Christ will be destined for hell, an English word inspired by the name in Hebrew and Greek of a valley near Jerusalem where rubbish was burned and where, in times of idolatry, children had been sacrificed by fire. Hell is described in Scripture as a place where God's wrath is experienced forever (Matt 5:29–30; Rev 14:11). Isaiah uses language like the worm that dies not and the fire which is unquenched, language which Yeshua adopts (Isa 66:24; Mark 9:48). Whether we are to take it literally is uncertain but we are to take it very seriously as expressing the horror of such an experience. The language certainly points to unending remorse and suffering. Other expressions which describe the experience of hell are "everlasting destruction," pointing to an unending diminishing of being, and "the blackness of darkness," pointing to a place away from all happiness and hope. It is a place where both humans and demons are punished.

Such teaching has not gone unchallenged by some within the professing church. Universalism holds that all will be saved, quoting texts such as "we trust in the living God, who is the Savior of all men, especially of those who believe" (1 Tim 4:10), and usually combining such quotes with the sentiment that it is inconceivable that a God of love would send anyone to everlasting punishment. The use of the word "all" in such texts needs to be understood in the particular context, so that "all" may refer to available to all, or it may refer to all who have trusted as opposed to those who have not, or it may refer to all submitting to Jesus whether they are willing or not (Phil 2:10–11). If all are to be saved, why are there severe warnings like, "fear Him who is able to destroy both soul and body in hell" (Matt 10:28)? We are prone to take sin too lightly but God opposes it as rebellion against his rule and requirements, and there can be no place in his presence forever for those who have refused to repent.

Another challenge comes from questioning the immortality of the unrepentant, some asserting that due to unbelief they lose the immortality which all humans have by nature, others asserting they fail to receive immortality because it is connected to the eternal life which only believers receive. Such thinking founders on texts which allot the same duration to the future of believers and unbelievers (see Isa 66:22–24; Matt 25:41, 46; 2 Thess 1:7–9; Rev 21:3–8). Against such texts some argue that the use of terms like "destruction" and "perishing" imply the termination of existence (see Matt 7:13; John 10:28; 2 Cor 2:15; 1 Thess 5:3). It is better to understand such texts as expressing the corrupting effects of punishment in hell.

To contemplate Scripture's clear teaching on everlasting punishment is to be overwhelmed and awed, and should lead us to fear him with whom we have to do, and thank him for the One who endured hell's punishment for us.

(B) NEW HEAVENS AND A NEW EARTH

The destiny of the godly is to live with YHWH forever in new heavens and a new earth, an expression found in both Old and New Testaments (Isa 65:17; 2 Pet 3:13; Rev 21:1). Some understand that which is new to be the conversion or liberation of what now exists (Rom 8:21; Matt 19:28), akin to the resurrection of the body, and others understand it as a completely new creation (see Rev 21:1; 2 Pet 3:10–13). Whichever is correct, in both there is a breaking of all links with the old, corrupt, and cursed world, and a creation of a new, perfect, and eternal world.

Certain things about this new world and our experience in it are unknown to us. We do not yet know the exact nature of our new bodies but there should be no doubting it is an embodied existence. We do not know the nature of our service but we are to be actively engaged in whatever work God has ordained for us (Isa 56:6–8; Matt 25:21; Rev 22:3). We know little of other intelligent beings (angels, etc.) that we shall be with and relate to, but we shall worship and serve together (Rev 5:8–14; 22:8–9). We find it difficult to imagine life which is eternal, without the passing of days and years which we presently experience, but the eternal life we now possess will be experienced in fullness.

However, there are things which are clearly revealed to us, even though their full experience is mysterious. We shall *see Yeshua the Lord as he is* and we shall be like him (1 John 3:2). It is Yeshua, described in Revelation as "the Lamb," whom we shall see in this new world, revealing to us the glory of God in all its fullness (Rev 21:22; 22:3). Through him God shall be all and in all (1 Cor 15:28). This new world will be *God centered*, a world in which he is worshiped (Isa 66:22–23; Rev 5:8–10; 7:9–10), *fellowship with God* is enjoyed (Isa 65:17–19; Rev 7:17; 21:3), and he is served (Rev 22:3). Service implies it is a world in which God's people have *responsibilities to fulfill* and the words "reign with Him" are also used (Dan 7:18, 27; 2 Tim 2:12; Rev 22:5), implying we shall rule over others, but whom are ruled is not clear. It will be a *perfect* world in every respect, beautiful and with no decay of any sort, with no possibility of sin as believers have the divine nature due to their new birth (2 Pet 1:4; Rev 22:4). There will be a *perfect understanding* and acceptance of all God's ways, many of which are at present hidden from us (1 Cor 13:12). There will be a full awareness and empowering for all things which are required of us, and all our needs will be met (Rev 21:4; 22:1–3).

Above all it will be a world marked by *love*—love for YHWH and one another. Multitudes will be there and our *spiritual communion and social life* together will all spring from love, the same love which marks the Father, Son, and Holy Spirit in their relations to each other. This will make it a world of *joy*. This implies it will be a world of *development*, developing ever deeper relationships with God and one another. The Holy Spirit indwells all God's people and will continue to guide, inform, and enable us in all God requires, so that Paul's prayer will find ever-increasing fulfillment in us, that we shall be "filled with all the fullness of God" (Eph 3:19). This life is *endless*. No wonder Bernard of Cluny (mid-twelfth century) wrote in his poem "Jerusalem the Golden," "beneath thy contemplation sink heart and voice oppressed." Indeed, such thoughts overwhelm us!

It is my prayer that through the study of these truths of God's holy word you will be increasingly set free from the darkness of mind and sinfulness of behavior which afflicts us all to become pure in heart and so "see God," looking forward to that day when you will see our great God and Savior, Yeshua HaMashiach, and be with him and all his people forever. Amen.

> Blessing and honor and glory and power
> Be to Him who sits on the throne,
> And to the Lamb, forever and ever!" (Rev 5:13)

Scriptures

Death: Gen 2:17; Eccl 3:2; Jer 31:30; Ezek 18:4; Rom 6:24; 8:13; 1 Cor 15:22, 56; Eph 2:1–3; Heb 9:27; 1 Pet 4:6; Rev 20:14.

Intermediate state: Ps 9:17; Luke 16:19–31; 23:43; John 11:11; 1 Cor 15:20; Phil 1:8, 23; 2:10; 1 Thess 4:13–18; Heb 12:22–23; 1 Pet 3:19–20; Rev 5:3, 13; 6:9–11; 7:9–10, 14–17; 20:4.

Resurrection: Gen 15:15; Job 19:26; Isa 26:19; Dan 12:2; Matt 22:29; Luke 20:38; 24:31–43; John 5:28–29; Acts 26:6, 8; 1 Cor 15; Col 1:18; 1 Thess 4:14, 18.

Judgment: Gen 18:25; Pss 37:28; 58:11; 89:14; 96:11–13; Dan 12:2–3; Mal 4:1; Matt 3:7; 13:41–43; 25:31–46; Rom 3:19; 14:10; 2 Cor 5:10–11; 1 Thess 1:10; 2 Tim 4:1; Heb 12:23; 2 Pet 2:4, 9; Rev 20:11–15 *According to light received*: Matt 11:24; Rom 1:18–21; 2:1–3, 12 *Of the godly*: Matt 25:14–30; Luke 19:11–27; Rom 14:12; 1 Cor 3:12–15.

Hell: Isa 66:22–24; Matt 5:29–30; 10:28; 25:41, 46; Mark 9:48; 2 Cor 2:15; 1 Thess 5:3; 2 Thess 1:7–9; Rev 14:11; 21:3–8.

New heavens and new earth forever: Pss 16:8–11; 23:6; Isa 65:17–19; 56:6–8; Dan 7:18, 27; Zeph 3:17; Matt 6:19–21; 25:21, 34; Rom 8:19–25; 1 Cor 6:2; 13:12; 2 Tim 2:12; 2 Pet 3:13; 1 John 3:2; Rev 5:8–10; 7:9–10; 19:7; 21–22.

Questions

1. What is the fate of the ungodly after death and after the Day of Judgment? How would you justify this to a person who believes a God of love would never act in such a way? Is annihilation justifiable from Scripture?

2. What does traditional Judaism's burial service tell you about hope within Judaism?

3. What do we know of the experience of believers in the intermediate state? Do you believe in purgatory?

4. What does Scripture teach about the resurrection of the body?

5. On what basis does God judge sinners? Is there a difference for Jews and Gentiles?

6. What awaits the godly at the judgment seat of Messiah Jesus? Is this justification by works?

7. What is your expectation of the life which will be experienced in the new heavens and the new earth? How does it affect you now?

FURTHER READING

Baxter, Richard. *The Saints' Everlasting Rest*. London: Epworth, 1961.
Berkouwer, G. C. *The Return of Christ*. Grand Rapids: Eerdmans, 1972.
Blanchard, John. *Whatever Happened to Hell?* Darlington: Evangelical, 2014.
Cotterell, Peter. *What the Bible Says about Death*. Eastbourne: Kingsway, 1979.
Milne, Bruce. *The Message of Heaven and Hell*. Leicester: InterVarsity, 2002.
Morris, Leon. *The Biblical Doctrine of Judgment*. Carol Stream, IL: Tyndale, 1960.

Bibliography

Alexander, T. D., and B. S. Rosner, eds. *New Dictionary of Biblical Theology*. Leicester: InterVarsity, 2000.
Allen, Rowland. *Missionary Methods: St Paul's or Ours*. Grand Rapids: Eerdmans, 1962.
Allis, Oswald T. *Prophecy and the Church*. Philadelphia: Presbyterian and Reformed, 1974.
Ashton, Mark. *Christ and His People*. Epsom: Good Book, 2016.
Barton Payne, J. *The Theology of the Older Testament*. London: Hodder & Stoughton, 1973.
Bauckham, Richard J. *God Crucified*. Milton Keynes: Paternoster, 2002.
Bauer, Walter, ed. *A Greek-English Lexicon of the New Testament and Other Early Christian Literature*. Chicago: University of Chicago Press, 1979.
Baxter, Richard. *The Saints' Everlasting Rest*. London: Epworth, 1961.
Beasley-Murray, G. R. *Baptism in the New Testament*. Milton Keynes: Paternoster, 1972.
Bell, John. *How to Be Like the Messiah*. Orangeburg, NY: Chosen People, 1987.
Berkof, Louis. *A History of Christian Doctrines*. Edinburgh: Banner of Truth, 1969.
Berkouwer, G. C. *The Church*. Grand Rapids: Eerdmans, 1976.
———. *Divine Election*. Grand Rapids: Eerdmans, 1960.
———. *Faith and Perseverance*. Grand Rapids: Eerdmans, 1958.
———. *The Providence of God*. Grand Rapids: Eerdmans, 1952.
———. *The Return of Christ*. Grand Rapids: Eerdmans, 1972.
Blaising, Craig A., and Darrell L. Bock. *Progressive Dispensationalism*. Grand Rapids: Baker, 2000.
Blanchard, John. *Whatever Happened to Hell?* Darlington: Evangelical, 2014.
Blocher, Henry. *Evil and the Cross*. Leicester: Apollos, 1994.
———. *In the Beginning*. Leicester: InterVarsity, 1984.
———. *Original Sin*. Leicester: Apollos, 1997.
Bock, Darrell, ed. *Three Views of the Millennium and Beyond*. Grand Rapids: Zondervan, 1999.
Boice, James Montgomery. *Foundations of the Christian Faith*. Leicester: InterVarsity, 1986.
Brawer, Naftali. *Judaism: Theology, History and Practice*. London: Robinson, 2008.
Bridges, Jerry. *The Practice of Godliness*. Colorado Springs, CO: NavPress, 2016.
Brown, Michael. *Answering Jewish Objections to Jesus*. Vol. 1, General and Historical. Grand Rapids: Baker, 2000.

———. *Answering Jewish Objections to Jesus*. Vol. 2, Theological. Grand Rapids: Baker, 2000.
———. *Answering Jewish Objections to Jesus*. Vol. 3, Messianic Prophecy. Grand Rapids: Baker, 2003.
———. *Answering Jewish Objections to Jesus*. Vol. 4, New Testament. Grand Rapids: Baker, 2007.
———. *The Real Kosher Jesus*. Lake Mary, FL: Charisma, 2012.
Bruce, F. F. *The Books and the Parchments*. Glasgow: Pickering & Inglis, 1971.
———. *The New Testament Documents*. Leicester: InterVarsity, 1971.
Burge, Gary M. *Whose Land? Whose Promise?* Milton Keynes: Paternoster, 2003.
Calvin, John. *Institutes of the Christian Religion*. Peabody, MA: Hendrickson, 2007.
Carson, D. A. *Christ and Culture Revisited*. Grand Rapids: Eerdmans, 2008.
———. *How Long, O Lord?* Leicester: InterVarsity, 2006.
Carson, Herbert M. *Hallelujah! Christian Worship*. Darlington: Evangelical, 2000.
———. *Roman Catholicism Today*. Leicester: InterVarsity, 1964.
Catherwood, Christopher. *Church History*. Wheaton, IL: Crossway, 2007.
Catholic Inquiry Centre. *Life of Faith*. London: Catholic Inquiry Centre, 1967.
Catholic Truth Society. *A Catechism of Christian Doctrine*. London: Catholic Truth Society, 1971.
Clowney, Edmund. *The Church*. Leicester: InterVarsity, 1995.
Cohn-Sherbok, Dan. *The Jewish Faith*. London: SPCK, 1993.
Cotterell, Peter. *What the Bible Says about Death*. Eastbourne: Kingsway, 1979.
Denney, James. *The Biblical Doctrine of Reconciliation*. Eugene, OR: Wipf & Stock, 2018.
———. *The Death of Christ*. Carol Stream, IL: Tyndale, 1951.
Dever, Mark. *The Deliberate Church*. Wheaton, IL: Crossway, 2005.
———. *The Gospel and Personal Evangelism*. Wheaton, IL: Crossway, 2017.
Edersheim, Alfred. *The Life and Times of Jesus the Messiah*. Peabody, MA: Hendrickson, 1988.
Edwards, Brian. *Nothing but the Truth*. Darlington: Evangelical, 1978.
Epstein, Isidore. *Judaism*. Hammondsworth: Penguin, 1979.
Evans, Craig A., and Stanley E. Porter, eds. *Dictionary of New Testament Background*. Electronic text, version 2.4. Downers Grovel IL: InterVarsity, 2000.
Fairbairn, Patrick. *The Interpretation of Prophecy*. Edinburgh: Banner of Truth, 1964.
———. *The Typology of Scripture*. Los Angeles: Hardpress, 2019.
Ferguson, Sinclair B. *The Christian Life*. Edinburgh: Banner of Truth, 2013.
———. *The Holy Spirit*. Leicester: InterVarsity, 1996.
———. *Maturity*. Edinburgh: Banner of Truth, 2020.
Festival Prayers, Service for the Day of Atonement. London: A. Abrahams, 1890.
Fruchtenbaum, Arnold. *Hebrew Christianity*. San Antonio: Ariel Ministries, 1983.
Gale, Stanley D. *What Is Spiritual Warfare?* Sanford: Ligonier Ministries, 2012.
Garner, Paul. *The New Creationism*. Darlington: Evangelical, 2009.
Gibbs, Eddie, and Brian Draper. *Way to Serve*. Leicester: InterVarsity, 2003.
Girdlestone, Robert B. *Synonyms of the Old Testament*. Peabody, MA: Hendrickson, 2000.
Goldberg, Louis, ed. *How Jewish Is Christianity?* Grand Rapids: Zondervan, 2003.
Goldin, Judah. *The Living Talmud*. New York: Mentor, 1957.
Goldsworthy, Graeme. *The Goldsworthy Trilogy*. Milton Keynes: Paternoster, 2001.
Goodwin, Thomas. *The Work of the Holy Spirit*. Edinburgh: Banner of Truth, 1979.

Grier, W. J. *The Momentous Event*. Edinburgh: Banner of Truth, 1970.
Griffiths, Michael. *A Task Unfinished*. Oxford: Monarch, 1996.
Grudem, Wayne. *Bible Doctrine*. Leicester: InterVarsity, 1999.
Guinness, Os. *The Dust of Death*. Leicester: InterVarsity, 1973.
Habershon, Ada R. *Study of the Types*. Grand Rapids: Kregel, 1974.
Hallesby, O. *Conscience*. Leicester: InterVarsity, 1950.
Hammond, T. C. *In Understanding Be Men*. Leicester: InterVarsity, 2009.
Harvey, Richard. *Mapping Messianic Jewish Theology*. Milton Keynes: Paternoster, 2009.
Helm, Paul. *The Providence of God*. Leicester: InterVarsity, 1993.
Hitchens, Peter. *The Rage against God*. Grand Rapids: Zondervan, 2010.
Holwerda, David E. *Jesus and Israel: One Covenant or Two?* Grand Rapids: Eerdmans, 1995.
Jackman, David. *Spirit of Truth*. Tain, UK: Christian Focus, 2007.
Jacobs, Louis. *Jewish Biblical Exegesis*. Springfield, MA: Behrman House, 1973.
———. *A Jewish Theology*. Springfield, MA: Behrman House, 1973.
Jensen, Peter F. *The Revelation of God*. Leicester: InterVarsity, 2002.
Jocz, Jacob. *The Jewish People and Jesus Christ*. London: SPCK, 1962.
Johnston, Philip, and Peter Walker, eds. *The Land of Promise*. Leicester: Apollos, 2000.
Jones, Mark. *Knowing Christ*. Edinburgh: Banner of Truth, 2017.
Jukes, Andrew. *Types in Genesis*. Grand Rapids: Kregel, 1976.
Kaiser, Walter C. Jnr. *Toward an Old Testament Theology*. Grand Rapids: Zondervan, 1978.
Keith, Graham. *Hated without a Cause*. Carlisle: Paternoster, 1997.
Keller, Tim. *Generous Justice: How God Makes Us Just*. London: Hodder & Stoughton, 2012.
———. *The Reason for God*. London: Hodder & Stoughton, 2009.
Kelly, J. N. D. *Early Christian Creeds*. Abingdon: Routledge, 1982.
———. *Early Christian Doctrines*. London: Continuum, 2000.
Kevan, Ernest. *The Lord's Supper*. Darlington: Evangelical, 1966.
Kjaer-Hansen, Kai, ed. *Jewish Identity and Faith in Jesus*. Jerusalem: Caspari, 1996.
Kostenberger, Andreas J., and Thomas R. Shreiner, eds. *Women in the Church*. 2nd ed. Grand Rapids: Baker Academic, 2005.
Ladd, George Eldon. *The Blessed Hope*. Grand Rapids: Eerdmans, 1956.
Lennox, John. *God's Undertaker: Has Science Buried God?* Kidderminster: Lion, 2009.
Letham, Robert. *The Message of the Person of Christ*. Leicester: InterVarsity, 2013.
———. *The Work of Christ*. Leicester: InterVarsity, 1993.
Lewis, C. S. *Miracles*. Glasgow: Collins, 2012.
Lewis, Peter. *The Glory of Christ*. Milton Keynes: Paternoster, 1992.
Lloyd-Jones, D. M. *Authority*. Edinburgh: Banner of Truth, 1984.
———. *The Basis of Christian Unity*. Leicester: InterVarsity, 1962.
———. *The Christian Soldier*. Edinburgh: Banner of Truth, 1977.
———. *The Christian Warfare*. Edinburgh: Banner of Truth, 1976.
———. *Ephesians: God's Ultimate Purpose*. Edinburgh: Banner of Truth, 1978.
———. *The Law: Its Functions and Limits*. Edinburgh: Banner of Truth, 1973.
———. *Preaching and Preachers*. London: Hodder, 1971.
———. *Romans 3:20—4:25: Atonement and Justification*. Edinburgh: Banner of Truth, 1970.
———. *Romans 5: Assurance*. Edinburgh: Banner of Truth, 1971.

———. *Romans 6: The New Man*. Edinburgh: Banner of Truth, 1972.
———. *Romans 8:17–39: Final Perseverance of the Saints*. Edinburgh: Banner of Truth, 1975.
———. *Romans: Atonement and Justification*. Edinburgh: Banner of Truth, 1998.
———. *The Sons of God*. Edinburgh: Banner of Truth, 1974.
Longman, Tremper, III, and Raymond B. Dillard. *An Introduction to the Old Testament*. Grand Rapids: Zondervan, 2006.
Luther, Martin. *The Bondage of the Will*. Translated by J. I. Packer and O. R. Johnston. Cambridge: James Clark, 1957.
Machen, J. G. *The Christian View of Man*. Edinburgh: Banner of Truth, 1965.
———. *The New Testament: An Introduction to Its Literature and History*. Edinburgh: Banner of Truth, 1976.
Macleod, Donald. *Behold Your God*. Fearn: Christian Focus, 1995.
———. *The Person of Christ*. Leicester: InterVarsity, 1998.
Martin, Ralph P. *Worship in the Early Church*. Grand Rapids: Eerdmans, 1975.
McCartney, Dan, and Charles Clayton. *Let the Reader Understand*. Phillipsburg: Presbyterian and Reformed, 2002.
McComiskey, Thomas E. *The Covenants of Promise*. Leicester: InterVarsity, 1985.
McGowan, Andrew T. B. *The Person and Work of Christ*. Milton Keynes: Paternoster, 2012.
Milne, Bruce. *The Message of Heaven and Hell*. Leicester: InterVarsity, 2002.
———. *Know the Truth*. Leicester: InterVarsity, 2009.
Milton, Michael A. *What Is the Perseverance of the Saints?* Phillipsburg, NJ: Presbyterian and Reformed, 2019.
Montefiore, C. G., and H. M. J. Loewe, eds. *A Rabbinic Anthology*. New York: Shocken, 1974.
Morris, Leon. *The Biblical Doctrine of Judgment*. Carol Stream, IL: Tyndale, 1960.
———. *The Cross in the New Testament*. Milton Keynes: Paternoster, 1965.
———. *Spirit of the Living God*. Leicester: InterVarsity, 1960.
Morris, Paul. *Jewish Themes in the New Testament*. Milton Keynes: Paternoster, 2013.
Motyer, Alec. *Roots: Let the Old Testament Speak*. Tain, UK: Christian Focus, 2009.
Murray, Iain. *The Puritan Hope*. Edinburgh: Banner of Truth, 1991.
Murray, John. *The Imputation of Adam's Sin*. Grand Rapids: Eerdmans, 1959.
———. *Redemption Accomplished and Applied*. Grand Rapids: Eerdmans, 2015.
———. *Redemption Accomplished and Applied*. Part 2. Edinburgh: Banner of Truth, 1961.
Needham, Nick. *2000 Years of Christ's Power*. Fearn: Christian Focus, 2017.
Newman, Randy. *Engaging with Jewish People*. Epsom: Good Book, 2016.
Ott, Ludwig. *Fundamentals of Catholic Dogma*. 2nd ed. Cork: Mercier, 1962.
Packer, J. I. *Concise Theology*. Carol Stream, IL: Tyndale, 1993.
———. *God Has Spoken*. London: Hodder & Stoughton, 1979.
———. *God's Words*. Leicester: InterVarsity, 1981.
———. *Knowing God*. London: Hodder & Stoughton, 2005.
Packer, J. I., and Mark Dever. *In My Place Condemned He Stood*. Wheaton, IL: Crossway, 2007.
Packer, J. I., and David F. Wright, eds. *New Dictionary of Theology*. Leicester: InterVarsity, 1988.
Pakula, Martin. *First to the Jew*. Melbourne: Bible College of Victoria, 2007.

Piper, John. *Let the Nations Be Glad*. Leicester: InterVarsity, 1993.
Ramm, Bernard. *Protestant Biblical Interpretation*. Grand Rapids: Baker, 1985.
Reeves, Michael. *Christ Our Life*. Milton Keynes: Paternoster, 2014.
———. *The Good God*. Milton Keynes: Paternoster, 2012.
Roberts, Mostyn. *The Subversive Puritan*. Darlington: Evangelical, 2019.
Roberts, Vaughan. *God's Big Picture*. Leicester: InterVarsity, 2002.
Robinson, Donald. *Selected Works*. Vol. 1, part 1. Sydney: Moore College, 2008.
Robinson, Rich. *The Messianic Movement: A Field Guide for Evangelical Christians*. San Francisco: Jews for Jesus, 2005.
Ryle, J. C. *Holiness*. Apollo: Ichthus, 2017.
Santala, Risto. *Messiah in the New Testament in the Light of the Rabbinical Writings*. Jerusalem: Keren Ahvah Meshihit, 1992.
Scholem, Gershom. *Kabbalah*. New York: Quadrangle/NY Times, 1974.
Seifrid, Mark A. *Christ Our Righteousness*. Leicester: Apollos, 2000.
Smeaton, George. *The Doctrine of the Holy Spirit*. Edinburgh: Banner of Truth, 1959.
Smith, Claire. *God's Good Design*. Sydney: Matthias, 2012.
———. *God's Good Design*. 2nd ed. Kingsford: Matthias, 2019.
Sproul, R. C. *The Assurance of Salvation*. Sanford: Ligonier, 2018.
Stibbs, Alan M. *God's Church*. Leicester: InterVarsity, 1959.
Stott, John R. W. *The Contemporary Christian*. Leicester: InterVarsity, 1992.
———. *The Cross of Christ*. Leicester: InterVarsity, 1986.
Strachan, Owen, and Gavin Peacock. *The Grand Design*. Fearn: Christian Focus, 2016.
Strobel, Lee. *The Case for a Creator*. Grand Rapids: Zondervan, 2014.
Telchin, Stan. *Messianic Judaism Is Not Christianity*. Grand Rapids: Chosen Books, 2004.
Torrance, David. *Israel God's Servant*. Milton Keynes: Paternoster, 2007.
Van Groningen, Gerard. *Messianic Revelation in the Old Testament*. Grand Rapids: Baker, 1990.
Venning, Ralph. *The Plague of Plagues*. Edinburgh: Banner of Truth, 1965.
Vos, Geerhardus. *Biblical Theology*. Edinburgh: Banner of Truth, 1975.
Ware, Bruce A. *The Man Christ Jesus*. Wheaton, IL: Crossway, 2012.
Ware, Timothy. *The Orthodox Church*. London: Penguin, 1997.
Warfield, Benjamin B. *Biblical and Theological Studies*. Phillipsburg, NJ: Presbyterian and Reformed, 1968.
———. *The Person and Work of Christ*. Phillipsburg, NJ: Presbyterian and Reformed, 1989.
———. *The Plan of Salvation*. Apollo: Ichthus, 2015.
Wells, David F. *God the Evangelist*. Johnson City, TN: Send the Light, 1997.
"What Orthodox Christians Believe." Ben Lomond, CA: Conciliar, 1988.
Wilkinson, David. *The Message of Creation*. Leicester: InterVarsity, 2006.
Wiseman, Donald, ed. *New Bible Dictionary*. 3rd ed. Leicester: InterVarsity, 1996.
Young, Edward J. *Thy Word Is Truth*. Edinburgh: Banner of Truth, 1972.
Zacharias, Ravi. *The End of Reason: A Response to the New Atheists*. Grand Rapids: Zondervan, 2008.
Zalman, Schneur. *Liqqutei Amarim*. New York: Kehot, 1965.

www.ingramcontent.com/pod-product-compliance
Lightning Source LLC
Chambersburg PA
CBHW050610300426
44112CB00012B/1446